Intolerance:
Political Animals and Their Prey

Edited by Bruce Chilton and Robert E. Tully

SUBEDITED BY NAOMI LACHANCE

DIALOGUES ON SOCIAL ISSUES:
BARD COLLEGE AND WEST POINT

Hamilton Books

Lanham • Boulder • New York • Toronto • Plymouth, UK

Copyright © 2017 by Hamilton Books
4501 Forbes Boulevard, Suite 200, Lanham, Maryland 20706
Hamilton Books Acquisitions Department (301) 459-3366

Unit A, Whitacre Mews, 26-34 Stannary Street,
London SE11 4AB, United Kingdom

Library of Congress Control Number: 2017936863
ISBN: 978-0-7618-6917-7 (cloth : alk. paper)—ISBN: 978-0-7618-6915-3 (pbk : alk. paper)—ISBN: 978-0-7618-6916-0 (electronic)

∞™ The paper used in this publication meets the minimum requirements of American National Standard for Information Sciences Permanence of Paper for Printed Library Materials, ANSI/NISO Z39.48-1992.

Contents

Introduction

Bruce Chilton

Bard College and the United States Military Academy at West Point pursued a collaborative project, consisting of an academic conference as well courses running in tandem, which has already resulted in the publication of *Just War in Religion and Politics* by the University Press of America (2013). In institutional, intellectual, and educational terms, we were pleased with the result, and after consultation we set up another project, "Intolerance: Political Animals and Their Prey," which has yielded the present volume.

The conference was hosted at Bard College under the auspices of the Institute of Advanced Theology and the Center for Civic Engagement. Additional funding was provided by the Mellon Foundation for Civilian-Military Educational Cooperation, which is administered by Dickinson College, as well as by several offices at Bard and West Point. The College and the Academy have also joined in the subvention of this volume. I thank all our patrons on behalf of Professor Tully and myself; we also appreciate the professional engagement of Naomi LaChance, our composition editor and a student of the course, and Hamilton Books.

Human experience vindicates Aristotle's characterization of people as imitative and therefore as political animals. He wrote that "to imitate is inherent in people from childhood, and in this they differ from other animals" (*Poetics* 4).[1] The comparison is fateful. People naturally cluster into groups as a result of various factors, and for every such group there have been outsiders: for Athenians there were Spartans and, much worse, barbarians; for Republican Romans there were demagogues and the masses; for Jews there have been their captors and persecutors; for Christians, Jews and Muslims; for denominational Christians, other denominations; for workers, capitalists; for pacifists, militarists. Reciprocal antagonisms include Sunni and Shia; reformers and traditionalists; libertarians and socialists; rationalists and traditionalists; in the realm of philosophy, monists and dualists. Individuals acquire layers of group identity pegged to race, gender, geography, and language.

The phenomenon transcends the existence of mere opposition and difference. Differences can be accepted, compromise can reconcile opposed views, but intolerance can emerge as pernicious and pervasive. The inevitability of divisions, leavened by the reinforcement of identity by means of difference in respect of others, runs so deep that holding up a mirror to ourselves yields a conflicted image: the people we want to see and the people we are happy not to be.

The purpose of the papers gathered here is to understand the sources of this dynamic, and to explore ways in which contemporary culture might deal with its influences. The authors deal with the conditions of warfare as an occasion of intolerance (Part I), with internal divisions within societies (Part II), with religious intolerance (Part III), and with political and philosophical considerations (Part IV). An epilogue by Robert Tully reflects on the whole.

An undertaking of this kind both presupposes and encourages an interdisciplinary investigation that is not routinely put into practice. The editors are grateful to their departments (of Religion at Bard and of English and Philosophy at West Point) for providing the spine of discourse. In addition, colleagues from satellite institutions of the College (in St. Petersburg and Jerusalem) as well as from other centers of learning provided additional insight. The list of contributors provides an indication of the range and depth of expertise assembled within our discussion.

"Barbarians at the Gates: the Complexities, Contradictions and Concerns about Modern Asymmetrical Warfare," by David Wallace and Cynthia Marshall, focuses on a contemporary feature of war, but against the background of a broad consideration of what leads to the condition. As a result, they comfortably relate their discussion to the strictures of David Hume, and develop a cogent focus on the war against international terrorism. That struggle has seen the consideration defended that it is outmoded to follow rules of engagement when the developed world knows they will not be followed by the terrorists whom it combats. The authors argue against any such suggestion in moral and practical terms.

Graham Parsons engages the complex issue of when wars of intervention may be fought. The legitimacy of states that do not pursue the values of the United States might be held to argue against intervention in most cases, as in the analysis of Michael Walzer. Walzer's combination of a theory of war with a theory of pluralized political legitimacy makes Parsons' focus particularly helpful, and yields Parsons's title, "Walzer *Contra* Walzer: Uncovering the Pluralist Roots of Walzer's Just War Theory." Parsons shows that massive violations of human rights may justify intervention. Although Walzer's critics have argued that pluralism is incompatible with the universal values of justice any theory of just war demands, Parsons proposes to reformulate Walzer's entire approach along *more* pluralist lines. Even when Walzer deals with war, Parsons insists, the reasoning puts the rights of communities in terms that do not derive from the rights of individuals. Membership in community becomes such a dominant concern that one community does not possess an inherent right to intervene within another. Parsons' argues that Walzer's own attempt to assert both pluralism and universalism is not viable. Instead, Parsons argues for consistent pluralism, which sees war as defensible only to preserve the rights of communities, and the people whose rights emerge within them.

As Scott A. Silverstone shows in "The Hegemon's Dilemma: Power Intolerance from Ancient Athens to the United States of America," historical content provides perspective for understanding the asymmetry of which David Wallace and Cynthia Marshall speak and the tension between universalism and pluralism that Graham Parsons details. The Peace of Westphalia in 1648 offered sovereignty as an answer to the problem of religious intolerance. The "dilemma" Silverstone identifies is that the right to self-defense, which is inherent within a sovereign state, might by its exercise produce a spiral of competition with other states. Intolerance of power can emerge as a vector of action, and Silverstone takes China's military modernization as a case in point. The lens of analysis is the conflict between Athens and Sparta. Within that confrontation, Silverstone especially concentrates on Athens' recourse to brutal tactics in order to force smaller powers to accept its empire. This "Offensive Realism" insists that security derives from hegemony, so that tolerance is a luxury states cannot afford. By contrast, "Defensive Realism" would allow other states access to power, so that potential rivals feel no need to go to war. Tolerance of concerns of security would then be more productive than attempts to dominate all other states. China and America become, in Silerstone's analysis, analogs to Sparta and Athens. And this suggests the inevitable question, whether attempting to thwart Chinese military development is realistic, or an invitation to disaster.

In "Means and Methods of Warfare: Towards an Objective Assessment for Selecting Military Targets – Beyond 'Enemy Thinking'?" Mirjam de Bruin raises the issue of the legitimacy of targets, an especially prominent question since the time mechanized warfare made factories and cities into objectives for military destruction. To that extent, the Lieber Code of 1863 finds a natural home during the American Civil War. With the emergence of digitized combat and the delivery of explosives by means of drones, civilian areas have become targets and collateral deaths a reality within the ordinary use of tactics. For that reason, civilians will be harmed inevitably, even if they are not directly attacked; the Geneva Conventions of 1949 did not answer the situation that had clearly been repeated often during and after the Second World War. Mirjam de Bruin argues that an appropriate awareness of international humanitarian law will help military commanders to counteract their own tendency toward "enemy thinking," and therefore develop better strategies to avoid or alleviate the suffering of non-combatants.

The considerations offered in "Part I: Warfare" focus on issues of morality, strategy, tactics, and civilian casualties. "Part II: Internal divisions" addresses the discovery of intolerance within the same military designed to protect a society and its values. Ty Seidule's "From Slavery to Black Power: Racial Intolerance at West Point, 1778-2015" sets out the legal terms in which it was possible for slaveholding at the United States Military Academy at West Point to continue until 1861, even after the abolition of slavery in New York State. Account books document what amounts to a color code of "servants," as well as the Federal subsidy for officers who availed themselves of slaves. The resistance of cadet culture to Abraham Lincoln's candidacy emerged as a natural result, as did moves in an increasingly radical Senate after his election to stop appropriations to West Point. After the Civil War, black Congressional nominees at the Academy were subjected to abuse by cadets and faculty alike. Seidule's documentation of the institutionalized racism, and segregation of the Academy, is remarkable and compelling, as is his account of "white terrorism" at West Point through the period of the Second World War.

President Truman's Executive Order of 1948, requiring "equality of treatment in the armed service," therefore emerges as a watershed. But the water flowed slowly at West Point, which continued to segregate barracks until after 1954, with the decision of the Supreme Court in *Brown v. Board of Education*. But an equal admission program only saw the light of day in 1968. When President Nixon ordered a monument to West Point's Confederate dead on their campus, an eruption of protest forced him to back down. Other advances continued, but after 1980 the national pattern, of the eclipse of racial progress with gender concerns, repeated itself at West Point. Nonetheless, women's rights at West Point were not less problematic, and Seidule is not sparing in his account.

Maritza Ryan contextualizes the lingering impact of misogyny in "All *Men* Are Created Equal: Misogyny under Law," which discusses wage gaps between women and men, sexual assault, and limitations of access to services of reproductive health. In particular, her lens is that of the legal system in the United States, with its exclusion from the assignment of full rights to women, slaves, and Native Americans from the outset. The assumption of a woman's rights by her husband under the common law conception of *coverture* is the particular focus. As Ryan documents by means of official and cultural resources, the incorporation of legal autonomy within the rule of the husband became a principle of female dependence upon males. The reversal of that principle, especially in the wake of the effort toward the Equal Rights

Amendment to the Constitution, has resulted in a series of legal challenges to *coverture* and its corollaries across a broad judicial front.

The admission of women into the public sphere has been an undeniable and dramatic result, although evidence of prejudice remains incontrovertible. That brings Ryan to a detailed investigation of the gender wage gap, which she enhances with treatment of the issue of maternity leave. Her sober analysis of figures related to violence against women, however, is perhaps the most affective moment in the paper. In the case of reproductive rights, Justice Sandra Day O'Connor, writing for the majority in *Planned Parenthood of Pennsylvania v. Casey*, signaled the end of *coverture.* Yet state regulation, putatively for the protection of women (one of the historic defenses of *coverture*) have palpably reduced women's access to reproductive services.

Along differing lines of approach "Part III: Religious intolerance" deals with the role of religion in the development of potential and actual violence. Nelly Lahoud identifies a persistent problem of efforts to produce tolerance that can actually result in the reverse. Entitled "On Religious (in)Tolerance," she shows that the effort to identify commonalities among religious encourages inattention to fundamental differences. Disagreements should be highlighted, rather sidelined. This approach has been basic to teaching and research at Bard College, emerging from the collaboration of Jacob Neusner with Bruce Chilton in several publications.[2] The trope within Christian theology that characterizes Christ as superseding Israel finds its counterpart in Muslim attitudes towards both Judaism and Christianity. As Lahoud demonstrates, this should long ago have cautioned scholars against any easy assertion of commonality. Indeed, she goes on to show that the traditions of Judaism, Christianity, and Islam have long recognized the vitality of difference. For reason, the essay concludes with an endorsement of John Locke's perspective, in which tolerance is to be a policy of the state in relation to religion, rather than an expectation of how one religion will relate to another.

A perennial problem posed by recent acts of terrorism has been the role of theological commitment. Ellen Charry provides examples from a range of traditions in "Theological Complicity in Religious Violence," demonstrating, as she puts it, that "theology matters," even when political or personal motives are often more prominent. The result is that some of the most extreme forms of violence encountered today have been with us for centuries, representing several commitments of faith. The roots of these behaviors, at least the theological roots, lie in the kinds of differences described by Nellie Lahoud in her essay, but the awareness of differences can and often does lead to contempt. In view of that dynamic, a common but largely unaddressed dimension of inter-faith relations, Ellen Charry calls for *intra-faith* reflection. Each religion needs to address its own sources, but religions can also learn mutually, so as to be more effective in their reforming themselves and identifying what is to be reformed. The model in which this might become is one of friendship at a collective level, a model that is explained and illustrated in the close of the essay.

Stephen F. Barker's essay, "'And who is my neighbor?' American Liberators in Transnational Content," focuses on the particular case "of Germans (mostly Jewish Germans) who emigrated to the United States before World War II, joined the U.S. Army, were sent back to fight in Europe, and then encountered some manifestation of the Holocaust." In an evocative account, he uses their experiences to trace the distinction between a bystander and a witness, and to frame this distinction in terms of Jesus' teaching regarding the Good Samaritan. In the midst of his analysis, he problematizes the category of "liberator," a dimension already introduced from the experiences of those involved. They reported both a loss of identity as combatants when they entered camps, and an impetus to inflict revenge. Stephen Barker sees in such reports a shift into the role of the witness, in which optimally "Their exposure to the inhuman made them reevaluate their own humanness."

The Abrahamic religions share a common source in the experience of the patriarch himself, and yet are locked in combat with another in many parts of the world. Bruce Chilton's essay, "Poisoned Virtue: Child Sacrifice in Abrahamic Scriptures and Interpretation," traces religious violence back to Abraham and Isaac, in the story of an obedient father and an innocent child ascending Mount Moriah. That scene, from Genesis 22, ripples through our culture as powerfully as the archetypal biblical narratives of the Creation, Fall, Flood, Exodus, and Crucifixion. Known by Jewish commentators since the second century as the Aqedah, literally the "binding" of Isaac, it has been written about exhaustively and beautifully. But the ways in which it has shaped our culture – and particularly how it is playing itself out today – have yet to be fully appreciated or understood. The Aqedah has typically been understood as marking the end of human sacrifice, but the reverse is more like the case. All three Abrahamic religions developed enormously influential interpretations of the Aqedah that state—with dreadful certainty—that no angel interrupted Abraham. Rather, he obeyed God's initial command and shed the blood of his son. Yet in the biblical story, Abraham did *not* sacrifice his son. He recognized a prohibition that was greater than his desire to prove himself. He sacrificed his ambition on Mt. Moriah, the dream of being totally acceptable to God. That line separating divine vision from the human world proved a lifeline, delineating the margin of survival for all of Abraham's family.

"Part IV: Political and philosophical considerations" brings us into the realm in which tolerance becomes a practical aim. The justice of the effort to accomplish that aim does not make it more feasible. "Plagues and Politics: Epidemics and 'Re-Framing' in Modern American History," by Andrew Forney, offers stunning cases in point. When epidemics emerge, a well-established approach traces how a given society frames the disease in cultural terms. That process results in a shared sense of the definition of the condition and the appropriate individual and social response. Andrew Forney extends that analysis into "reverse-framing," in which focus shifts to the victims of the disease themselves. Overwhelmingly, epidemics have exacerbated social lines of cleavage, and resulted in a greater attempt to isolate minorities. From the Peloponnesian War to the crisis of AIDS, victims have been claimed, and leaders have seemed unaware that moralizing illness plays into the hands of disease. Andrew Forney's strictures are especially pertinent in light of the probability that globalization in its various forms will increase contact with sources of disease.

A robust assertion of the claims of tolerance is offered by Robert Goldstein in "Residue of Intolerance: Polluting Civil Rights." Basing his argument on Civil Rights movements, he argues that environmental injustice needs to be identified as a threat to racial equality. The disposal of coal ash in the South is a particular concern, since the impact on human health has become evident, as has the disproportionate damage inflicted on poor families, often of Afro-American descent. But Robert Goldstein also documents how New York City, by means of inequality of access to political pressure, pushes the consequences of pollution down the economic ladder. After he sketches the Constitutional bases on which discrimination can be addressed, Goldstein this makes his case for the argument that environmental injustice is *de facto* discrimination. He details the ways in which particular cases of the disposal of waste have injured human health in ways that negate equal justice under law.

The grounds on which policy might be framed are analyzed by Dustin Atlas in "Cynicism and Perennial Intolerance: Mendelssohn Against the Decisionists." Appeals for tolerance often appear either naïve or cynical; naïve, when real threats or ignored, and cynical, when the policy is designed to preserve or extend entrenched power. Of the two, Dustin Atlas sees cynicism as the greater danger, because intolerance has come to be accepted as a political reality, and even defended as necessary, "serving as an ideology for those who are no longer capable of ideals." A pattern emerges in which "ethics applies in a state, and this state is created and protected by unethical behaviour." This is the "decisionism" that Atlas revises in light of Moses Mendelssohn's thought. In particular, Atlas uses Mendelssohn's analysis of contractual obligations as a way of seeing people as always in relation; the state is part of the process of relationship rather than the condition of any possible relationship. The cultivation of that process, rather like Ellen Charry's model of friendship, takes us beyond an arid paradox.

Gennady Shkliarevsky identifies modernity's defective model of rationality as a key component in the promotion of intolerance in "Overcoming Modernity and Violence." The Enlightenment has so triumphed in political and economic terms, if it is true that reason will resolve human problems, violence should be on the wane. The recent phase of confrontation with terrorism in various forms has only emphasized how cruelly disappointed that expectation has been. Shkliarevsky maintains that both the realist and the anti-realist views of reason pose "a gap between the subject and the object." This dualism is not supported by the evidence of how consciousness is formed, a "process of construction that constitutes true ontological reality." This insistence upon a relational model is reminiscent of Dustin Atlas's account of Moses Mendelssohn, and Shkliarevsky pursues the model of consciousness operating from both assimilation and adaptation, a process of construction that in his view must be accounted for in order to avoid a "flawed interpretation of reality." Chief among these flaws is the resort to violence by those whose one-sided rationality is disappointed by experience.

Reason is also the topic of Robert Tully's "Contrariety in Philosophy." Although philosophers often argue in the way of lawyers, they seem not to reach resolution in many cases, but to devolve into warring sides. Robert Tully is interested in why those who appeal to reason often wind up exemplifying its contrary. At times, this opposition runs both deep and broad. In evolutionary terms, defending one's territory might be compared to fighting for one's philosophical school and its reputation. Yet even Hobbes conceived of rational compromise as possible in society; might philosophers become similarly civil? One might think so, and even hope that "In the theater of civil society they ought to occupy the box seats," given their commitment to reason. What disappoints this expectation is that each term within philosophy is subject to investigation, and therefore to disagreement. Robert Tully provides an entertaining set of examples of philosophical viciousness in the name of reason. Some of his best instances involve the issues of consciousness and dualism in a way that cautions against taking Shkliarevsky's assertions as assured. At the same time, the discussion of consciousness closes with a cautious assertion of an "endocentric" understanding, in which parts and operations of the brain are not a sufficient explanation. To this extent, science would not be an adequate philosophical foundation; rather a metaphysical of science is required.

Darya Pushkina and Philippe Ch.-A. Guillot with Susanna An offer a practical final essay. Their concern in "Who Takes Whom to Tango: UN Neoliberal Peacebuilding in Sierra Leone" is with the evaluation of peacebuilding efforts as well as with the development of suggestions for change. The background of their focus on Sierra Leone is that while the end of the Cold War has seen a decline in inter-state warfare, intra-state conflicts have demanded far more complex responses. Darya Pushkina and her colleagues criticize the neoliberal assumption that democracy and a recognized market economy together represent the necessary solution for any crisis. In particular, they believe the universalism of the approach derives from the West's colonial heritage. When privatization was introduced in Sierra Leone, for example, the result was to promote clientism and a shielding of wealth from taxation, while reducing social spending for unemployment. Violence was a predictable outcome. Nonetheless, the authors acknowledge that in Sierra Leone the United Nations learned from failure, to engage more than local élites in their efforts by means of robust military and political management. Yet the promotional of truly national dialogue and the disproportionate usage of benefits by local élites remain nagging problems.

Although an interdisciplinary encounter such as represented by our courses and our conference cannot be expected to produce a univocal response to a topic as entrenched and vast as intolerance, the lines of convergences among our contributions remains striking. With Part I, warfare itself was addressed, the most public face of intolerance. Yet even here, the serious discussion of how to engage asymmetry (Wallace and Marshall), to set limits on intervention (Parsons), to encourage lesser powers (Silverstone), and to protect civilians (de Bruin) articulates the desire to discover controlling influences on the deployment of violent means. Even as that sensibility is enhanced, it coheres with a desire that comes to voice in Part II to improve the military's commitment to values of tolerance, particularly racial (Seidule) and gendered (Ryan). Religion has often been scapegoated in discussion of the origins of violence, but a more critical way forward is suggested in Part III. An honest confrontation of differences among religions (Lahoud), mutual projects of reform (Charry), awareness of how our actions manifest religious values (Barker), and a diagnosis of how violence emerges in religious terms (Chilton) sets out a perspective in which religion is a field in which brutality may occur, rather than simply be its perennial cause. Finally, Part IV argues that reason itself must become reflective in terms of policy and discourse for violence to be avoided. Attention to how victims become confused with their illnesses (Forney), to the way that Civil Rights has been abridged by pollution (Goldstein), to how contractual thinking might replace arbitrary assertions of civilizing force (Atlas), to the univeralist arrogance of both modernity (Shkliarevsky) and philosophical sects (Tully), and to the ways in which a concern for development must allow for variation in cultural norms (Pushkina et al.) all amount to a fresh consideration of how we see reason and its application. These threads of discussion do not amount to a single position, but they do set out coherent perspectives on how humanity might come to terms with its persistent enemy within.

NOTES

1. See D. W. Lukas, *Aristotle: Poetics. Introduction, Commentary and Appendixes* (Oxford: Clardendon, 1968). In the *Politics* (1:1253a) the thought is extended to life in society.

2. See their early work, *Jewish-Christian Debates. God, Kingdom, Messiah* (Minneapolis: Fortress, 1998).

I

Warfare

Barbarians at the Gates

The Complexities, Contradictions and Concerns about Modern Asymmetrical Warfare

David Wallace and Cynthia Marshall[1]

"Were a civilized nation engaged with barbarians who observe no rules even of war, the former must also suspend their observation of them, where they no longer serve to any purpose."[2] —David Hume

INTRODUCTION

It is believed that warfare came to the world at least 5,000 years ago.[3] Since then, it has been estimated that there have been 14,600 wars.[4] Although a seeming cliché, it is fair to say that the one permanent characteristic of warfare is that it is constantly evolving. Of course, at the most fundamental level, the nature of war never changes. It is immutable and eternal. Boiled down to its essence, at the heart of any war is the necessity to overcome an enemy's will to fight. This may be accomplished by destroying or otherwise neutralizing an enemy's fighting capabilities or exceeding its cost tolerance for engaging in a particular armed conflict.[5]

Warfare is a profoundly distressing and complex enterprise. Deeply embedded dynamics and forces dictate, describe, and define the relationship and interactions between the belligerent nations, groups, or tribes. As presciently noted by author Mark Osiel, "although war is obviously an 'antisocial' activity, the relations between belligerents displays aspects that could only be described as social in nature, as intensely social to their core."[6] As a form of collective intentionality,[7] the relationships and interactions between warring parties often raise deep paradoxes. At one level any notion of toleration, restraint, and humanity in war between belligerent groups bristles with contradictions and provokes skepticism.[8] That is, the fundamental attributes of war—violence, death, and destruction—would naturally and intuitively seem to breed intolerance, human divisiveness, and reciprocal antagonism between the parties to a conflict, regardless of whether the conflict is between nations or groups internal to a country. War, in the words of Augustine, is that human endeavor which "brings the most sorrow to our minds and makes us confess that we are indeed miserable creatures."[9]

The paradoxical and contradictory nature of war, however, is that it is, on one hand, the manifestation of intense levels of emotional frenzy or ideological driven passions to kill, injure, capture, or destroy an enemy. Speaking of war, Mark Twain commented:

> Man is the only animal that deals in that atrocity of atrocities, War. He is the only one that gathers his brethren about him and goes forth in cold blood and calm pulse to exterminate his kind. He is the only animal that for sordid wages will march out... and help to slaughter strangers of his own species who have done him no harm and with whom he has no quarrel . . . And in the intervals between campaigns he washes the blood off his hands and works for "the universal brotherhood of man"—with his mouth.[10]

On the other hand, an ethic of restraint, tolerance, and humanity has rarely ever been wholly absent from warfare.[11] Put in a slightly different manner, the pernicious and pervasive impulses of intolerance, which naturally reflect and infect the relationship and interactions of warring parties, are mitigated by humanitarian considerations, memorialized in the laws and customs regulating warfare[12] that serve to lessen, to a degree, the brutality and horrors of war. That is, a linchpin of restraint, toleration, and humanity in warfare, imperfect as it may be, is a shared commitment by all parties to the conflict to some common standards and conduct that strive to strike a delicate balance between military necessity and humanitarian aims.

History, to varying degrees, has demonstrated that mankind has sought to lessen the corrosive impacts of warfare and has "come to regard war not as a state of anarchy justifying unlimited suffering, but as an unfortunate reality that must be governed by some rule of law."[13] The regulation of warfare has been of enduring interest to scholars, statesmen, and soldiers for thousands of years.[14] In the present day, there is a much better understanding and appreciation for the fact that war and law are inextricably linked even though there are those who believe that the customs and law regulating warfare hold together better on paper than in practice.[15] Of course it would be disingenuous to suggest that the internationally agreed upon norms that attempt to regulate killed or be killed fighting between various groups of political animals works well all or even most of the time. But even in the most unpromising circumstances of war, restraint, tolerance, and humanity, does break through.[16]

Given the above dynamics and characteristics of warfare as a backdrop, this paper addresses one of the most significant contemporary challenges in modern armed conflicts: asymmetrical warfare. The characterization of some types of warfare as "asymmetrical" has in recent years become increasingly part of the lexicon of military and security forces in the developed world.[17] The concept of asymmetrical warfare will be defined and explored in greater detail below, but at its simplest, it can be described as "violent action undertaken by the 'have-nots' against the 'haves' where the 'have-not', be they state or sub-state actors, seek to generate profound effects—at all levels of warfare . . . by employing their only specific relative advantages against the vulnerabilities of much stronger opponents."[18] As highlighted by the quote from David Hume above, one of the most significant challenges in modern asymmetrical warfare is when the have-nots—the barbarians if you will—fight wars using means and methods of warfare that violate universally accepted and shared customs and laws of war commonly referred to as *jus in bello* or the law in waging war. The body of international law that regulates *jus in bello* is commonly referred to as international humanitarian law, the law of armed conflict or the law of war.

This paper will unpack the notion of modern asymmetrical armed conflict within the broader context of the different practices of the respective warring groups fighting in some of today's armed conflicts. The phenomenon of asymmetrical warfare today not only reveals profound imbalances of military capabilities between the parties to conflicts, but also significant differences in how warring nations, tribes, or groups—depending on whether they are militarily have's or have-nots—perceive the fundamental and universal norms regulating warfare. Put differently, this paper asks the question *is modern asymmetrical warfare being fought by the have-nots tearing at the very fabric of the laws and customs of war making the regulation of hostilities and the protection of the victims of armed conflicts increasingly tenuous? And, if this is the case, should this be tolerated or not?* In so many ways these questions raise profound ethical, historical, political, religious, and anthropological issues. This inquiry will be mainly, but not exclusively, through the lens of the law. Part I of the paper introduced the topic. Part II of the paper will define and explore the concept of asymmetrical warfare. Part III will provide an in-depth analysis and argumentation.

ASYMMETRICAL WARFARE

As a starting point, it is important to define and explain what is meant by asymmetrical warfare beyond the brief description above. In doing so it may be helpful to juxtapose what is symmetrical or traditional warfare. Generally speaking, symmetrical warfare means wars or armed conflicts between States of roughly equal military strength or capabilities, [19] as there is no such thing as perfect symmetry between parties to a conflict. The concepts of symmetry and asymmetry in warfare are not absolute terms but rather a matter of degree and relativity. Thought of as a continuum, in symmetrical warfare, the parties are closer together in terms of their capabilities on the continuum. As the parties move further apart, there is greater asymmetry.

Many of the large-scale wars that occurred in the eighteenth and nineteenth centuries are classic examples of symmetrical type warfare. When one reflects on wars during that time period, the Napoleonic wars, the Crimean war, and the American Civil war come to mind. Those symmetrical wars were characterized by evenly—or somewhat evenly—matched government armies clashing in violent military actions against each other using the same or similar means and methods of warfare. [20] Of course this is not meant to suggest that all wars during that timeframe fit this category. Moreover, some of the symmetrical type wars may have had an asymmetrical component to them, as when the British faced an asymmetrical enemy from early American forces during the Revolutionary War. [21]

In the twentieth century, warfare became even more complex and more unequal than warfare of the previous two centuries. [22] There were wars like World Wars I and II, when two or more State armed forces arrayed against each other with similar military powers and resources, using the same or similar tactics and weapons differing only in specific details and execution. Commenting on symmetrical wars, author Toni Pfanner notes:

> Symmetrical wars between States are risky, as it is impossible to anticipate which party will be victorious and the costs usually outweigh the anticipated benefits. Conflicts closely approximating this model, such as the war between Argentina and Great Britain over the Falklands/Malvinas Islands, the war between Iraq and Iran in the eighties or the conflict between Eritrea and Ethiopia just before the turn of the century have become rare. [23]

In terms of rights and responsibilities in symmetrical wars, broadly speaking, combatants [24] on both sides of a conflict have the same rights and are subject to the same responsibilities. [25] Under the laws governing warfare, combatants are persons who have a right to participate directly in hostilities. Moreover, combatants enjoy immunity upon capture from criminal liability for lawful acts of warfare. [26] Another important attribute of symmetrical wars is the parties to the conflict place greater trust and reliance on the laws and customs regulating hostilities like the 1949 Geneva Conventions. [27]

So by contrast, asymmetrical warfare has been defined, in general terms, as warfare in which opposing groups or nations have unequal military resources and use unconventional weapons and tactics, such as terrorism, to exploit the vulnerabilities of the enemy. [28] That is "weaker" nations or groups—militarily, logistically, or numerically—seek to achieve their political aims by leveraging their own advantages while seeking to exploit the vulnerabilities of the "stronger" adversaries.[29] Of course depending on one's perspective, resort to asymmetrical warfare may be viewed as righteous or treacherous.[30] Imbalances in military capacity between warring parties have become a prominent feature of various contemporary armed conflicts.[31] Such asymmetries are now very much structural characteristic of modern warfare.[32] Conceived more broadly, asymmetrical warfare has been defined as follows:

> In the realm of military affairs and national security, asymmetry is acting, organizing, and thinking differently than opponents in order to maximize one's own advantages, exploit an opponent's weaknesses, attain the initiative, or gain greater freedom of action. It can be political-strategic, military strategic, or a combination of these. It can entail different methods, technologies, values, organizations, time perspectives, or some combination of these. It can be short-term or long-term. It can be deliberate or by default. It can be discrete or pursued in combination with symmetric approaches. It can have both psychological and physical dimensions.[33]

Whether one uses a narrow or broad definition, it is important to note that the concept of asymmetrical warfare has been around for centuries[34] —a reinvention of concepts developed through the history of warfare.[35] That is to say, what is often mistaken as novelty in warfare is the rediscovery of well-worn concepts, modified by the application of hi-tech advances, supporting the means and methods of warfare.[36] As noted by Professor Michael Schmitt, "[y]et, asymmetry hardly represents a radically new operational model, for it is in the very nature of warfare to seek strategies, tactics, and weapons that either leverage one's own strengths (positive asymmetry) or exploit the enemy's weaknesses (negative asymmetry), or both."[37] Schmitt, one of the world's leading experts on the laws regulating warfare, classified asymmetry into various forms including: technological, doctrinal, normative, participatory, and legal or moral standing.[38] Of particular note, technological asymmetry involves not only the mobility, weapons, and munitions (range, precision, and lethality) of the have's, but also in their ability to rapidly gather, process and react to information about an adversary, while hindering an enemy's ability to do the same.[39] In terms of doctrinal asymmetry, the have's think in terms of effects based operations focused on the particular effects generated by an adversary. In contrast, the have-nots adopt low-tech approaches like guerrilla warfare or terrorism.[40]

Tales of asymmetrical warfare can even be found in the Old Testament of the Bible. More specifically, a classic example is the tale of the young shepherd David using his sling and a smooth stone to battle the Philistine giant, Goliath. After knocking Goliath to the ground, David ran over to him, lopped off Goliath's head with the giant's own sword, creating panic and fear in the Philistine ranks.[41] Two and a half millennia ago, Sun Tzu, the great Chinese

military general, strategist, and philosopher, highlighted asymmetrical warfare in his teachings in terms of exploiting an enemy's strengths while attacking his weakness.[42] In his classic work *Art of War,* Sun Tzu observed that "an
army may be likened to water, for just as flowing water avoids the heights
and hastens to the lowlands, so an army avoids strengths and strikes weaknesses."[43] Speaking about asymmetry in the so-called war on terrorism, Osama bin Laden stated:

> The difference between us and our adversaries in terms of military strength,
> manpower, and equipment is very huge. But, for the grace of God, the differ-
> ence is also very huge in terms of psychological resources, faith, certainty, and
> reliance on the Almighty God. This difference between us and them is very,
> very huge and great.[44]

Some theorists have argued that there are essentially four different kinds
of asymmetrical conflicts: 1) guerrilla wars and insurgencies, 2) wars of
intervention, 3) proxy guerrilla wars, and 4) the war on international terror.[45]
Guerrilla wars and insurgencies are the classic asymmetric conflict and often
include nationalists groups fighting against their own governments. In these
instances, it is common place to observe small guerilla armies fighting
against large, well-armed, and technologically superior forces.[46] One specific
type of these conflicts is self-determination or national liberation wars. These
types of guerrilla wars and insurgencies became an established kind of internal armed conflict that gradually came to be considered as being governed by
the laws of war applicable in international armed conflict.[47]

The second kind of asymmetrical conflict involves wars of intervention.
In these types of conflicts, States intervene in the affairs of other sovereign
states "to address threats to international peace and stability and to rescue
embattled civilians from threat of genocide, war crimes or crimes against
humanity."[48] A classic example was the international community's intervention in the Balkans conflict. Several NATO countries sent military forces to
the former Yugoslav republics of Bosnia and Herzegovina and Croatia from
1992-95 in an effort to protect civilians from intense ethnic fighting.[49] Similarly in March 1999, NATO forces were sent to protect ethnic Albanian
civilians in Kosovo.[50]

The third category is asymmetric proxy wars.[51] A state may find it to their
advantage to let others do their fighting and thereby support local conflicts
that, in some way, may weaken their adversaries. In some cases, these types
of conflicts are asymmetric. A notable example of such a course of conduct is
the Second Lebanon War between Israel and Hezbollah.[52]

The fourth and final kind of asymmetrical conflict is the fight against
international terrorism.[53] In many respects, it is this kind of asymmetrical
conflict that has made this trend in contemporary warfare so problematic and

goes to the heart of the question of whether *modern* asymmetrical warfare is tearing at the very fabric of the laws and customs of war, making the regulation of hostilities and the protection of the victims of armed conflicts increasingly tenuous. Terrorism is a much-debated concept. A powerful illustration of this notion is captured in the passage below:

> The fateful events of 11 September 2001 epitomized a situation that confronts the ICRC [International Committee of the Red Cross] in its work in many conflict zones all over the world, namely asymmetrical warfare. A handful of men armed with box-cutters humiliated the sole great power with all its highly sophisticated weaponry in front of live cameras, killed thousands of people in next to no time and graphically demonstrated the vulnerability of the United States and the entire western world.
>
> The series of terrorist strikes in Russia in the second half of 2004 were as great a traumatic experience for the Russians as the 9-11 attacks were for the Americans. The hostage-taking and ensuing massacre in the North Ossetian town of Beslan by Chechen suicide attackers demonstrated that militarily weaker opponents want to influence confrontations, this time with a diabolic target choice in a marginal war zone, potentially drawing other areas into a spiral of violence. [54]

The two most traditional and frequently adopted typologies of terrorism are that of international/domestic terrorism and typology by motivation. [55] Although there are many definitions of terrorism, it can be broadly defined as "a purposeful human activity directed toward the creation of a general climate of fear designed to influence in ways desired by the protagonist, other human beings, and through them some course of events." [56] In general terms, international terrorism can be seen as terrorist activities conducted on the territory of more than one state or involving citizens of more than one state as victims or perpetrators. [57] International terrorism, when rising to the level of an armed conflict, is often viewed as the epitome of asymmetrical warfare. [58] The difference in the military capabilities between the armed forces of nation-states and non-state terror groups could not be more profound, yet such groups like al Qaeda are becoming increasingly more lethal and ubiquitous.

Such groups deliberately rejected traditional military and legally accepted means and methods of warfare, instead opting for perfidious attacks against civilians and civilian objects. [59] Additionally, "the probable future aim of this strategy will be to cause even greater loss of human life and to inflict non-military and above all economic damage, possibly through the use of prohibited devices, in other words biological and chemical weapons." [60] Moreover, such transnational groups are becoming more and more decentralized as a global movement. For example, with al Qaeda, the central operation may be in Afghanistan or Pakistan. Its power and focus are devolving and shifting to affiliates in Iraq, Yemen, Somalia, North Africa, and other locations. [61] Structurally, al Qaeda is organized in the form of a decentralized and distributed grid network connected by multiple paths rather than a traditional military organization with a rigid top down chain of command.[62] Moreover, groups like ISIS and al Qaeda and its affiliates are able to communicate and coordinate efforts using the Internet, social media forums, and other modern instruments of global communications. In doing so, they will not only be able to distribute propaganda and recruit individuals, but also be able to coordinate attacks.[63]

ANALYSIS AND ARGUMENTATION

At one level, the challenges of regulating the conduct of warring parties to an asymmetrical armed conflict are quite obvious. Even though warfare is in no way comparable to athletics, it may be helpful to think about the frictions and frustrations of regulating asymmetrical warfare by using a sports analogy. Consider for a moment your typical college or professional football game in the United States—how would it be possible to play such a game where one team follows the established rules governing the play of the game and the other team does not? To complete the analogy, the non-compliant team not only does not abide by the rules, but also deliberately and treacherously violates the rules to undermine the compliant team. In warfare, like sports, there are rules that apply to each party that govern the conduct of hostilities (like the play of the game) and the parties are competing to win.

Intuitively, the rules regulating warfare (like in sports) necessitate reciprocity between the participants. To a certain degree, reciprocity helps explain the above paradox as to why warring parties attempt to preserve and exercise some humanity, even *in extremis* by operating pursuant to codes of custom and laws mutually recognized by the respective parties.[64] Superficially, the concept appears to be rather straightforward. That is, "any favors, benefits, or penalties one party grants to another party should be returned in kind."[65] This principle of reciprocity can be a powerful tool for motivating, creating, sustaining, and regulating behavior of individuals and groups. In the most general terms, legal systems confer the substantial benefits of the "rule of law" on individuals, groups, or entities because of the vast majority of actors regulated by the system give its rules voluntary compliance. Even in circumstances where an individual, group, or entity desires the benefits that would flow from breaking the law by departing from established norms, that individual, group, or entity will forgo those benefits and accept the burden of self-restraint in order to keep the system functioning. If the actors in the system felt that they were free to violate established norms with impunity, the system would crumble and ultimately collapse.[66]

Reciprocity is a legal, political, and sociological construct embedded, in varying degrees, in most legal regimes.[67] Reciprocity, in the context of international law and relations generally, and the laws and customs of war specifically, reflects the belief or perception that states will agree to be bound by a norm because they also will obtain some type of benefit.[68] By way of illustration, if Army A wants its soldiers treated humanely upon capture by its enemy, Army B, it almost goes without saying that it is incumbent upon Army A to treat soldiers from Army B under its control humanely as well. Likewise, if Army A wants Army B to surrender rather than fight to the bitter end, such surrender can be incentivized by the humane treatment of the captured soldiers of Army B.[69] By way of example, during World War II, "[a]fter an early series of false surrenders and prisoner atrocities, Pacific island combat was marked by an unwillingness of either side to surrender, and a savagery of the worst kind by both sides resulted. On Iwo Jima, of 21,000 – 23,000 Japanese combatants, 20,703 were killed. When the island was declared secure only 212 Japanese surrendered—less than 2 percent—because Marines and soldiers fearing that they would be murdered or mistreated if they surrendered simply put surrender out of mind and fought on, thereby increasing casualties on both sides."[70] By contrast, in the 1991 Persian Gulf armed conflict, the United States and other coalition partners afforded Third Geneva Convention protections to more than 86,000 Iraqi prisoners of war held in custody. Arguably, these Iraqi combatants would not have been so inclined to surrender but for the fact that they believed they would be treated humanely upon capture. Quite obviously, the law of armed conflict is a body of law that must be applied equally to all sides of a conflict.[71] "Few would consider practicable a legal regime that requires one side to 'fight with one hand tied behind its back' while its enemy exercised free reign."[72] That is, no state could, in theory or practice, accept such inequality.[73]

Accordingly, in today's asymmetrical armed conflicts, the have-not groups, in many cases, are flagrantly violating the laws governing armed conflict such that there is not even an illusion of reciprocity between the parties. This is particularly so with respect to terroristic activities. Think of the recently produced videos released by radicals from the Islamic State in Iraq and Syria (ISIS) also known as the Islamic State in Iraq and the Levant (ISIL). These bloodcurdlingly gruesome videos flashed over and over again across cable and network news and the social media. A Western looking captive dressed in an orange prison-style jumpsuit, purportedly intended to imitate the dress of detainees at Guantanamo Bay, is seen kneeling in the desert, silhouetted against a bright blue sky. The helpless captive stares impassively straight ahead waiting for his fate. The jihadist executioner, dressed in black, with his face almost entirely covered, holding a medium size knife in his left hand. The taunting voice of the knife wielding radical has an unmistakably British accent. Before the masked butcher takes the life of his innocent prey, he taunts the leader of his victim's country.[74]

Given the above dynamics, there are some who contend that since there is no benefit of reciprocity, the have's do not have to tolerate the barbarians actions by fighting with only one hand. Instead, it would be reasonable for the have's, like the United States, to adjust how it wages war against the have-nots fighting asymmetrically, for in the age of terror, the laws regulating warfare are "out of step with reality, perhaps even 'quaint'" as characterized by then White House Counsel Alberto R. Gonzales in 2002.[75] If when fighting the barbarians, the United States decided to not follow the laws regulating warfare, it is possible the United States could shorten the duration of a conflict and possibly deter future conflicts all together. In this new paradigm of fighting, it would be made clear that "the perpetrators of violent, misogynic policies will face a response so ferocious it will leave their nation physically and psychologically unrecognizable."[76] This would serve to "dampen the urges of even the most recalcitrant of peoples."[77] In this new paradigm, the United States would use force so staggering and unrestrained on the have-nots that it would "produce fundamental change" because it would be "massive, relentless, and profoundly shattering" and cause widespread destruction of property that would serve to remake "a society that needs remaking," because if that is what is needed, "then international and ethical norms must yield to allow it."[78] Although such an approach may seem viscerally appealing, it arguably loses sight of some very important considerations.

There are at least three compelling reasons why—even without reciprocity—the have's should abide by the laws regulating warfare. The first is that laws of war, as a general proposition, are still binding on a party to a conflict even if the other party does not comply. An illustration of this point can be found in the 1949 Geneva Conventions, perhaps the quintessential international agreements regulating conduct in warfare. Common[79] Article 1 to the Conventions, which applies to declared wars, international armed conflicts and total or partial occupations, provides that "[t]he High Contracting Parties undertake to respect and to ensure respect for the present Convention *in all circumstances*"[80] (emphasis added). In the commentary to Article I, it provides, in part, as follows:

> It is not an engagement concluded on a basis of reciprocity, binding each party to the contract only in so far as the other party observes its obligations. It is rather a series of unilateral engagements solemnly contracted before the world as represented by the other Contracting Parties. Each State contracts obligations 'vis-à-vis' itself and at the same time 'vis-à-vis' the others. The motive of the Convention is such a lofty one, so universally recognized as an imperative call of civilization, that one feels the need for its assertion, as much because of the respect one has for it oneself as because of the respect for it which one expects from one's opponent, and perhaps even more for the former reason than for the latter.[81]

A similar concept, i.e., *in all circumstances*, can be found in Common Article 3[82] of the 1949 Geneva Conventions extending the idea to non-international armed conflicts as well.

Second, if the have's deviate from acceptable norms of conduct during an armed conflict, they run the risk of losing both domestic and international support for the effort. What the last 13 years has taught the United States is that fighting in accordance with national values is key to maintaining public support for a war effort, both domestically and abroad. Without public support of its actions, a military's violence lacks legitimacy, and legitimacy is critical for a successful war effort. The need of public support is why if a U.S. soldier beheaded a have-not and put his head on a stake as a deterrence to others, that soldier's actions would work against a military victory because "[a]n act of violence one can disclose and be proud of is ultimately stronger, more *legitimate*."[83] The American public will not trust and support a military whose violence is employed in barbaric ways. The Abu Ghraib prisoner abuse scandal serves as an example of how law of war violations by U.S. soldiers delegitimized the entire American military campaign.[84] The abuse of Iraqi prisoners by U.S. soldiers was contrary to national values, delegitimized America's fighting in Iraq, and decreased domestic and international support of the United States' presence. Likewise when pictures emerged of U.S. Marines violating the law of war by urinating on Taliban corpses, there was outrage domestically and internationally.[85] As the "prohibition against desecrating the battlefield dead is almost as old as war itself," no matter if the act is to "send a message or exact a revenge,"[86] the U.S. public will not trust their professional fighting force if its actions on the battlefield do not reflect national values. And while one soldier testified how in Iraq he had urinated on the skull of a dead Iraqi after being overcome by grief after a roadside bomb killed a member of his unit,[87] the laws regulating warfare must always be obeyed "because we cannot allow ourselves to become what we are fighting and because we cannot be heard to say that we fight the right while we are seen to commit wrongs."[88]

Then there is the scandal of the enhanced interrogation techniques used on detainees during the three years following the September 11 attacks, when U.S. armed forces and intelligence agencies stripped detainees naked, subjected them to extremes of heat, cold, and noise, and deprived them of sleep for long periods.[89] These actions have served to undermine America's moral authority and fuel anti-American sentiment around the world.[90] "As President-elect Obama said during his campaign, 'we need to restore our values, because as the counter-insurgency manual reminds us, torture sets back our mission to keep the people on our side.'"[91]

The third, and related reason, is a question of morality and values. Recently the United States Senate released their hotly debated report on the CIA's use of brutal interrogation techniques against detainees in the years

following the attacks of 9-11. Drawing on millions of internal CIA documents, the "long-delayed report delivered a withering judgment" in exhaustive details that provides a macabre accounting of some of the grisliest tactics, techniques, and procedures used by the CIA to torture and imprison
terror suspects.[92] Senator John McCain, himself of victim of torture and ill-
treatment during his years of captivity as a prisoner of war in North Vietnam,
commented, in part, on the morality and propriety of such conduct.

> But in the end, torture's failure to serve its intended purpose isn't the main
> reason to oppose its use. I have often said, and will always maintain, that *this
> question isn't about our enemies; it's about us. It's about who we were, who
> we are and who we aspire to be.* It's about how we represent ourselves to the
> world.
>   We have made our way in this often dangerous and cruel world, not by just
> strictly pursuing our geopolitical interests, but by exemplifying our political
> values, and influencing other nations to embrace them. When we fight to
> defend our security *we fight also for an idea, not for a tribe or a twisted
> interpretation of an ancient religion or for a king, but for an idea that all men
> are endowed by the Creator with inalienable rights.* How much safer the world
> would be if all nations believed the same. How much more dangerous it can
> become when we forget it ourselves even momentarily. *Our enemies act with-
> out conscience. We must not.* This executive summary of the Committee's
> report makes clear that acting without conscience isn't necessary, it isn't even
> helpful, in winning this strange and long war we're fighting. We should be
> grateful to have that truth affirmed. [93] (emphasis added)

When commanders and other leaders in the armed forces are asked by
their soldiers, "why should we follow the rules, when our barbaric enemies
are beheading innocent victims and attacking helpless civilians," perhaps its
Senator McCain's answer that is most appropriate and fitting. It is ultimately
not about our enemies, but about us.

CONCLUSION

So what to make of David Hume's argument that the have's, or in his words
"civilized nations," should suspend their observance of the laws regulating
warfare when the have nots, the "barbarians" deviate from them? At one
level, such a position seems intuitive. If portrayed as a simple sports analogy,
it does not make any sense why one team should play by the rules while the
other team flaunts them. Of course, war is something far more complicated
and nuanced than a sports contest. Keeping the people, all people, on "our
side" is critical to restoring peace, and restoring peace is one of the humanitarian purposes of the law of armed conflict.[94] War must be conducted in the
interest of peace.[95] As General Washington would remind his officers during

the Revolutionary War, humane treatment of civilians would secure the affections of the population, and secure to their side "the attachment of all good men" and maybe "'open the eyes' of the British to the merits of the American cause."[96] Winning the hearts and minds during a war is as critical to keeping the peace now as it was then.

No matter if the have's are facing a foe who fights asymmetrically without any hope of reciprocity, when it comes to the laws regulating warfare, the have's must abide by the rules. Doing so is the only way for any Goliath's actions to be legitimate in the eyes of all the public. As Secretary State John Kerry said at the first ministerial-level meeting of the anti-ISIL coalition, "[o]ur coalition does not summon hate, but rather the courage to build a future that is based on shared interest, shared values, and a shared faith in one another. That contrast in goals marks the dividing line between barbarism and civilization, and it explains why we dare not fail and why we will succeed."[97] Always abiding by the laws regulating warfare will be critical to that success.

NOTES

1. The authors are currently serving on active duty in the United States Army on the faculty of the United States Military Academy at West Point. The opinions expressed in this paper are those of the authors and are not intended to represent the official positions of the United States Military Academy or the United States Army.

2. David Hume, *An Enquiry Concerning the Principles of Morals*, sec. 3, pt. 1 (1777). See Mark Osiel, *The End of Reciprocity: Terror, Torture, and the Law of War*, Cambridge University Press (2009) p. 33.

3. Gary D. Solis, *The Law of Armed Conflict – International Humanitarian Law in War*, Cambridge University Press (2010) p. 4.

4. Ibid.

5. Ibid. at 6.

6. Mark Osiel, *The End of Reciprocity: Terror, Torture, and the Law of War*, Cambridge University Press (2009) p. 45.

7. Ibid.

8. Geoffrey Best, *Humanity in Warfare*, Columbia University Press (1980) p. 2.

9. Gregory M. Reichbert, Henrik Syse, Endre Begby, *The Ethics of War: Classic and Contemporary Readings*, Blackwell Publishing (2006) p. vii.

10. Mark Twain quotes, available at http://www.goodreads.com/quotes/156338-man-is-the-only-animal-that-deals-in-that-atrocity

11. Solis, at 3 -4.

12. As will be discussed later in the paper, the body of law regulating the conduct of hostilities and the protections of the victims of war is commonly referred to as the law of armed conflict, international humanitarian law or the law of war.

13. Brian J. Bill, ed., *Law of War Workshop Deskbook*, William S. Hein & Co. Inc. Publishing (2004) p. 2.

14. Adam Roberts and Richard Guelff, *Documents on the Laws of War* (Third Edition), Oxford University Press (2000) p. 3.

15. Geoffrey Best, *War & Law Since 1945*, p. 5, Oxford University Press (2002).

16. Geoffrey Best, *Humanity in Warfare*, Columbia University Press (1980) p. 2.

17. Rod Thornton, *Asymmetric Warfare*, Polity Press (2008) p. 1.

18. Ibid.

19. Toni Pfanner, *Asymmetrical warfare from the perspective of humanitarian law and humanitarian action*, International Review of the Red Cross, Volume 87 Number 857 March 2005, p. 152.

20. Pfanner, at 152.

21. Osiel, at 42.

22. Pfanner, at 152.

23. Pfanner, at 152.

24. All members of the armed forces of a party to the conflict are combatants, except medical and religious personnel. Individuals who participate in hostilities or are a member of an organized armed group that do not meet the qualifications of lawful combatancy are often referred to as unlawful combatants or unprivileged belligerents. They do not have combatant immunity. Moreover, they do not have prisoner of war status upon capture. In a non-international armed conflict, there are no combatants. Belligerents are often referred to as fighters.

25. David Rodin and Henry Shue, Introduction, *Just and Unjust Warriors: The Moral and Legal Status of Soldiers*, ed. David Rodin and Henry Shue, Oxford University Press (2008) p.1.

26. Jelena Pejic, "Unlawful/Enemy Combatants: Interpretation and Consequences," in *International Law and Armed Conflict: Exploring the Faultlines: Essays in Honour of Yoram Dinstein*, ed. Michael Schmitt and Jelena Pejic, Martinus Nijhoff Publishers (2007) p. 336. Although oversimplified, lawful combatancy and the benefits incident to it flow from declared wars, international armed conflicts and occupations.

27. David L. Buffaloe, *Defining Asymmetric Warfare*, The Land Warfare Papers, No. 58, September 2006, P. 2.

28. Dictionary.com, available at http://dictionary.reference.com/browse/asymmetric+warfare (accessed 12 December 2014).

29. Domini D. McAlea, "Post-Westphalian Crime," in *New Wars, New Laws? Applying the Laws of War in 21st Century Conflicts*, ed. David Wippman and Matthew Evangelista, Transnational Publishers (2005) p. 112 -113.

30. McAlea, at 113.

31. Robin Geiß, *Asymmetric conflict structures*, International Review of the Red Cross, Volume 88, Number 864, December 2006, p. 757.

32. Ibid.

33. Douglas V. Johnson II and Steven Metz, *Asymmetry and U.S. Military Strategy: Definition, Background, and Strategic Concepts*, DIANE Publishing (2001); Michael N. Schmitt, *Asymmetrical Warfare and International Humanitarian Law*, (2008). 2 Air Force Law Review, Vol. 62, No. 1, 2007, p. 3-4, available at SSRN: http://ssrn.com/abstract=1600629 (accessed 12 December 2014).

34. Buffaloe, at 3.

35. Adam B. Lowther, *Americans and Asymmetric Conflict: Lebanon, Somalia and Afghanistan*, Praeger Security International (2007), p. 14.

36. Ibid.

37. Michael N. Schmitt, *Asymmetrical Warfare and International Humanitarian Law*, (2008). 2 Air Force Law Review, Vol. 62, No. 1, 2007, p. 1, available at SSRN: http://ssrn.com/abstract=1600629 (accessed 12 December 2014).

38. Schmitt, at 7.

39. Ibid. at 11.

40. Ibid. at 6.

41. Toni Pfanner, *Asymmetrical warfare from the perspective of humanitarian law and humanitarian action*, International Review of the Red Cross, Volume 87 Number 857 March 2005, p. 150 citing Old Testament, The story of David and Goliath, 1 Samuel, Chapters 16–18.

42. Buffaloe, at 3.

43. Sun Tzu, *The Art of War 101* (Samuel B. Griffith trans., 1971); see also Schmitt, at 2.

44. Schmitt, at 2.

45. Michael L. Gross, *Moral Dilemmas of Modern Warfare: Torture, Assassination, and Blackmail in an Age of Asymmetric Conflict*, Cambridge University Press (2010) p. 14-15.

46. Ibid. at 15.

47. Eve La Haye, *War Crimes in Internal Armed Conflicts*, Cambridge University Press (2008) p. 14. Examples of these conflicts include: South Rhodesia, Angola, Mozambique, South Africa and Nambia. Article 1.4 of Additional Protocol I to the 1949 Geneva Conventions expands the definition of what constitutes an international armed conflict by stating, in part, that "[t]he situations referred to in the preceding paragraph" – international armed conflicts" – include armed conflicts in which peoples are fighting against colonial domination and alien occupation and against racist regimes in the exercise of their right of self-determination. . ." *See* Solis, at pp. 123-125.

48. Michael L. Gross, *Moral Dilemmas of Modern Warfare: Torture, Assassination, and Blackmail in an Age of Asymmetric Conflict*, Cambridge University Press (2010) p. 1-17.

49. John A. Gentry, *How Wars are Won and Lost: Vulnerability and Military Power*, Praeger Security International (2012) p. 111.

50. Ibid. at 110.

51. Michael L. Gross, *Moral Dilemmas of Modern Warfare: Torture, Assassination, and Blackmail in an Age of Asymmetric Conflict*, Cambridge University Press (2010) p. 19.

52. Ibid. at 19.

53. Ibid. at 18.

54. Toni Pfanner, *Asymmetrical warfare from the perspective of humanitarian law and humanitarian action*, International Review of the Red Cross, Volume 87 Number 857, March 2005, p. 150.

55. Ekaterina Stepanova, *Terrorism in Asymmetrical Conflict: Ideological and Structural Aspects*, SIPRI Research Report No. 23, p. 5, available at http://books.sipri.org/files/RR/SI-PRIRR23.pdf (accessed 12 December 2014).

56. H. H. A. Cooper, "Evaluating the Terrorist Threat: Principles and Applied Risk Assessment," *Clandestine Tactics and Technology Series*, Gaithersburg, MD: International Association of Chiefs of Police (1974) p. 4.

57. Stepanova, at 5.

58. Robin Geiß, *Asymmetric conflict structures*, International Review of the Red Cross, Volume 88, Number 864 (December 2006) p. 758.

59. Toni Pfanner, *Asymmetrical warfare from the perspective of humanitarian law and humanitarian action*, International Review of the Red Cross, Volume 87 Number 857 (March 2005) p. 150.

60. Ibid. at 150.

61. Seth G. Jones, *The Future of Irregular Warfare*, Rand Corporation Testimony, presented before the House Committee on Armed Services, Subcommittee on Emerging Threats and Capabilities, 27 March 2012, p. 2, available at http://www.rand.org/pubs/testimonies/CT374.html (accessed 12 December 2014).

62. Charles Pena, *Winning the Un-War: A New Strategy for the War on Terrorism*, Potomac Books, Inc. (2006) p. 107.

63. Ibid. at 4-5.

64. Geoffrey Best, *Humanity in Warfare*, Columbia University Press (1980) p. 2.

65. Michael D. Gottesman, *Reciprocity and War: A New Understanding of Reciprocity's Role in Geneva Convention Obligations*, U.C. Davis Journal of International Law & Policy 14 (2007) p. 150.

66. Jeffrie G. Murphy and Jules L. Coleman, *Philosophy of Law: An Introduction to Jurisprudence* (Revised Edition) Westview Press (1990) p. 123.

67. Rene Provost, "Asymmetrical Reciprocity and Compliance with the Laws of War," in *Modern Warfare: Militias, Private Militaries, Humanitarian Organizations and the Law*, ed. Benjamin Perrin, UBC Press (2012) p. 17.

68. Ibid. at 18.

69. Geoffrey S. Corn, Victor Hansen, Richard B. Jackson, Chris Jenks, Eric Talbot Jensen, and James A. Schoettler, Jr., *The Law of Armed Conflict: An Operational Approach*, Wolters Kluwer (2012) p. 467.

70. Solis, at 8-9.

71. Robert Kolb and Richard Hyde, *An Introduction to the International Law of Armed Conflict*, Hart Publishing (2008) p. 25.

72. Sean Watts, *Reciprocity and the Law of War*, Harvard International Law Journal, Volume 50, Number 2, (2009) p. 366.

73. Kolb and Hyde, at 25.

74. Joshua Berlinger and Dana Ford, ISIS execution videos strikingly similar, CNN, 14 September 2014, available at http://www.cnn.com/2014/09/13/world/meast/isis-beheading-videos/ (accessed 26 November 2014).

75. Schmitt, at 42.

76. Charles J. Dunlap Jr., *The end of innonence: Rethinking noncombatancy in the post-Kosovo era.* Strategic Review (2000). pp.16-17.

77. Ibid. at 17.

78. Ibid.

79. "Common" in this context means that it appears in each of the four Conventions.

80. Geneva Convention (I) for the Amelioration of the Condition of the Wounded and Sick in Armed Forces in the Field." Geneva, 12 August 1949, art. 1.

81. Jean S. Pictet, Commentary to the Geneva Convention (I) for the Amelioration of the Condition of the Wounded and Sick in Armed Forces in the Field." Geneva, 12 August 1949, art. 1, International Committee of the Red Cross, Geneva (1952) p.25. See also, Watts, at 412. Professor Watts, in his article, raises thoughtful and sophisticated questions about the intent of the drafters specifically in terms of Article 1, and more generally about the concept of reciprocity in the Conventions. Watts suggests a more modest meaning for Article 1 than that offered by Jean Pictet.

82. Common Article 3 was a critically important development with the 1949 Geneva Conventions. Often characterized as a "Convention in miniature," it provided baseline humanitarian protections to non-international armed conflicts. That is, it provided international law and regulation to civil wars.

83. David Kennedy, *Of War and Law*, Princeton University Press (2006) p. 140.

84. Ibid. at 155.

85. Allen G. Breed and Julie Watson. "Desecration of war dead goes back centuries," Army Times, 13 January 2012, available at http://www.armytimes.com/article/20120113/NEWS/201130305/Desecration-war-dead-goes-back-centuries (accessed 6 December 2014).

86. Ibid.

87. Ibid.

88. Solis, at 9-10.

89. Human Rights Watch, Fighting Terrorism Fairly and Effectively, Released 16 November 2008, p. 12, available at. http://www.hrw.org/reports/2008/11/16/fighting-terrorism-fairly-and-effectively-0 (accessed.6 December 2014).

90. Ibid.

91. Ibid.

92. Mark Mazzetti, *Failure of Oversight Is Outlined – Agency Defends Program*, The New York Times, 10 December 2014, p. 1.

93. Senator John McCain's full statement on the CIA torture report, USA Today, 9 December 2014, available at http://www.usatoday.com/story/news/politics/2014/12/09/john-mccain-statement-cia-terror-report/20144015/ (accessed 12 December 2014).

94. The Judge Advocate Genearl's Legal Center & School, U.S. Army. *Operational Law Handbook, (2014) p. 11,* available at http://www.loc.gov/rr/frd/Military_Law/pdf/operational-law-handbook_2014.pdf (accessed 6 December 2014).

95. Solis, at 9.

96. John Fabian Witt,. *Lincoln's Code: The Laws of War in American History,* Free Press (2013) pp. 26-27.

97. Secretary State John Kerry's Remarks at the Counter-ISIL Meeting, 3 December 2014, availabale at http://www.state.gov/secretary/remarks/2014/12/234624.htm (accessed 6 December 2014).

Walzer *Contra* Walzer

*Uncovering the Pluralist Roots
of Walzer's Just War Theory*

Graham Parsons

INTRODUCTION

The contemporary debate about the legitimacy of humanitarian military intervention is usually framed by a deeper debate about the nature and importance of communal rights versus the nature and importance of individual human rights. When a regime in a foreign land is engaged in some brutal treatment of its own subjects, we, as citizens of the greatest military power on earth, may wonder if we have the right to use that power to end the brutality. Those who advocate for intervention usually argue that the protection of human rights is a just cause for war, even when the violations of human rights are occurring in foreign countries. Often, those who are against intervention accept this claim but argue that other more prudential concerns give us good reason not to intervene (e.g. the cost will outweigh the benefits). But sometimes those who are against intervention deny the claim: they argue that the rights of the community that the victims are members of prohibit military interventions even when their human rights are being violated by that community.

Michael Walzer surely falls into this last group and we will examine his particular position on intervention in this paper. But my real interest here is the above parameters of the debate about humanitarian intervention and how these parameters are, and are not, manifest in Walzer's theory. To follow his own description in his seminal work *Just and Unjust Wars* (2006 [1977]), he accepts the above parameters. According to him, the philosophical building blocks of his just war theory follow a pattern that goes back at least to Hugo Grotius and is found in all the great modern advocates of just war theory such as Pufendorf and Vattel. At its most basic level, we find in Walzer's theory a moral universalism in the form of a commitment to individual human rights. For Walzer, these are the rights of all people to life and liberty. Then, these foundational commitments are used to describe the creation of the rights of political communities and, in turn, states. Walzer, like his forebears in modern just war theory, calls this process of creation "the social contract." Then, we debate what the different communities owe each other and when, if at all, they may forcibly intervene in each other's territory and politics. This is just war theory in its modern form — hence the debate about humanitarian intervention framed as a debate about the rights of individuals versus the rights of states.

Regarding what different communities owe each other, Walzer, like many of his forebears, argues for a kind of political pluralism: the view that each group is entitled to constitute and conduct its own politics free from intervention by outsiders. For him, there is no universal form of political order that each group is expected to emulate, or at least not one that foreigners have a right to force them to emulate. Even a political culture that systematically violates individual human rights deserves to be tolerated by foreigners. Still, Walzer argues that one may (and should) demand that one's own political community live up to the demands of human rights. Thus, human rights are the ultimate judge of one's own community but not other's. Walzer refers to this as the "dualism" of state legitimacy (see 1985, 222-4). In this way, Walzer's just war theory is an attempt to combine a moral universalism in the form of human rights with a political pluralism in the form of an anti-interventionism even in the face of human rights abuses.

Walzer does acknowledge limits to his toleration of human rights abuses. He defends humanitarian intervention in cases of "massive violations of human rights" (2006, 101). In such cases, foreigners may intervene to stop the violations. However, he makes it clear that the violations of human rights must be overwhelming. The mere systematic violation of human rights is not a reason to intervene. To justify intervention, the violations must be "massive," something akin to genocide and enslavement. For Walzer, basic human rights abuses must cross a threshold of severity before constituting just cause for intervention. Speaking loosely, the abuses must move from more ordinary brutality to sheer barbarity. Thus, the vast majority of human rights abusing states are to be tolerated. Walzer has been criticized widely for this attempted combination of moral universalism and political pluralism (see Luban 1985a, 1985b). Walzer's critics argue that his moral universalism undermines his political pluralism and that regimes or cultures that systematically violate human rights are not entitled to toleration by others. Whatever value there is in communal integrity and political sovereignty, there is nonetheless a right to interfere forcibly in the politics of others to end basic human rights violations. In other words, Walzer is more tolerant of foreign political communities than the moral foundations of his own theory permit. According to his critics, human rights trump the rights of political communities. Thus, there should be no threshold human rights abuses must cross before they constitute just cause for intervention.

Though I do not agree with this view as a defense of interventionism, I do agree with Walzer's critics in one respect: Walzer's theory fails on its own terms. The moral foundations undermine the political pluralism. My goal here, however, is not to revisit the debate about humanitarian interventionism but, rather, to reread Walzer's theory and its position in the broader Walzerian corpus with this debate in mind. Reading his just war theory sympathetically, and with Walzer's other work on justice in view, reveals new things about the spirit of the theory and its problems. I believe there is a Walzerian way of reconstructing Walzer's just war theory that makes the theory more internally consistent and more interesting.

Few of the critics of Walzer's just war theory have made an effort to engage with the rest of Walzer's vast corpus. This is a big mistake. Not long after publication of *Just and Unjust Wars*, Walzer rather famously rejected universalism in the theory of justice and embraced a radical pluralism. I will argue that this later theory can be used to replace the universalist foundations of Walzer's just war theory. What we get as a result is a pluralist theory of just war all the way down. Seen this way, Walzer's theory departs fundamentally from the modern just war tradition, abandoning the conventional parameters of the debate about humanitarian intervention entirely. Walzer's just war theory is not based on individual human rights, but on a basic acceptance of cultural and political difference between groups and a fundamental commitment to the toleration of all communities. For Walzer, war is not a tool to enforce a universal morality—it is a tool to enforce a basic ethical duty to respect difference between groups.

HUMAN RIGHTS AND WALZER'S JUST WAR THEORY

Since the subject of this paper is not Walzer's theory of military interventions but the foundations of his just war theory as a whole, I will not confine myself to analyzing his views on intervention exclusively. In fact, there are many aspects of his just war theory that conflict with his professed commitment to human rights. In addition to his anti-interventionism, I can identify four other elements of Walzer's just war theory that cannot be based on individual rights to life and liberty.

1. The Domestic Analogy. Walzer describes his theory of *jus ad bellum*, or what he calls "the theory of aggression," as based on the view that political communities are analogous to individual persons. That is, states are morally like people in that they are bodies with rights that are not reducible to their parts. States have relations with each other in international society in much the same way as individuals have relations with each other in civil society. Though the political conditions of these interactions are importantly different, the moral character of the relations is not. "[S]tates actually do possess rights more or less as individuals do" (2006, 58).

But if states' rights are derived from the rights of their individual members as Walzer himself asserts, then state's rights should be reducible to the rights of individuals. Taking Walzer at his word, the domestic analogy would break down and relations between states would just be understood, at the most basic moral level, as relations between mere collections of individuals.

2. The Obligation of Soldiers to Fight and Die. Walzer argues that the rights of states are worth sacrificing individuals for. In particular, he argues that soldiers are obligated to serve in war upon command and that this obligation is based on the importance of the community itself. From the perspective of the members of political communities, aggression — the violation of a state's right to integrity and independence — is "morally as well as physically coercive." That is to say, when one's own political community is attacked, one's duty to fight to protect the community can be triggered. This is what, for Walzer, makes aggression such an extraordinary crime. As he says, "The wrong the aggressor commits is to force men and women to risk their lives for the sake of their rights. It is to confront them with a choice: your rights or (some of) your lives" (51). "The state that does resist, whose soldiers risk their lives and die, does so because its leaders and people think that they should or that they have to fight back" (52-3). "Aggression is a singular and undifferentiated crime because, in all its forms, it challenges rights that are worth dying for." The rights that are worth dying for are the rights of states to "territorial integrity and political sovereignty" (53).

But this puts greater value on the community than on the individual. The view expressed here holds that the rights of communities trump the rights of individuals. This cannot be reconciled with Walzer's insistence that the rights of communities are derived from the rights of individuals.

3. The Presumption in Favor of Resistance. Walzer argues that when a state is faced with aggression, that state ought to forcibly resist even when the likelihood of success is low. Thus, it is morally preferable for a state to fight for its rights and lose than for a state to forego resistance in order to spare the lives, health, and property of its members. Walzer clearly asserts this view in his discussion of the Finnish resistance against Soviet aggression in 1939. The Soviets demanded that their border with Finland be redrawn in order to prevent German shelling of Leningrad, should the Germans occupy Finland. The Finns refused to redraw the border and chose to go to war with the USSR instead, knowing the high risk of defeat. In the end, the Soviets won the war and redrew the border in a way even less favorable to the Finns than they had originally demanded. Additionally, thousands of Finnish soldiers were killed and hundreds of thousands of civilians displaced. Though Walzer stops short of claiming that the Finns ought to have resisted, he clearly asserts that the vindication of Finnish rights gave them good reason for resisting (70-2). As he says, "we do not measure the value of justice, apparently, in terms of lives lost" (67). In other words, a just war trades the interests of individuals for the rights of states.

But this puts the value of the rights of communities above the value of the rights of individuals. If state's rights were based on the rights of individuals, then the rights of individuals could not be traded for the rights of states. On the contrary, the rights of individuals would limit what could be done to protect states.

4. The Supreme Emergency Exception. Walzer argues that when a political community is in a supreme emergency, that is, when they are faced with an aggressor who not only seeks to violate their rights but seeks to exterminate them as a political community and the aggressor's victory is imminent, the victim community may deliberately attack noncombatants if it would help thwart the aggressor's victory. In other words, when faced with a choice between the survival of one's own community and the lives of innocent people, we are permitted to sacrifice the lives of the innocent for the sake of the community. As Walzer says, "Can soldiers and statesman override the rights of innocent people for the sake of their own political community? I am inclined to answer this question affirmatively, though not without hesitation and worry" (254).

But there should be no inclination to answer this question affirmatively given the basis of Walzer's own theory. If the rights of individuals underpin the substance of his just war theory, the rights of individuals should limit what states can do in their defense. One could not sacrifice individuals for the sake of communities. Walzer's exception to this general prohibition in supreme emergencies reveals, again, a conflict between his theory and its supposed moral foundations.

HINTS OF PLURALIST FOUNDATIONS
IN WALZER'S JUST WAR THEORY

We have now seen a number of places where the substance of Walzer's just war theory conflict with its supposed universalist foundations in individual human rights. In addition, we can find a number of places in his discussion of war where he seems to abandon the universalist foundations altogether and suggests instead an alternative pluralism grounded in a communitarian comprehension of the individual-community relation. These examples help make the case for considering Walzer's just war theory with a later-Walzerian pluralist foundation.

One place where a turn to moral pluralism appears to take place is in Walzer's defense of his anti-interventionism against his critics. A number of critics accuse Walzer's anti-interventionism of violating his own commitment of individual human rights. In his 1980 essay "The Moral Standing of States: A Reply to Four Critics," Walzer (1985) elaborates on the foundations of his just war theory and attempts to explain more clearly the "dualism" of his theory of state's rights. In this essay, Walzer does not appeal as explicitly to the individual rights to life and liberty as he does in *Just and Unjust Wars* to ground state legitimacy. Rather, he more consistently describes individuals as intimately connected with a particular political community and appeals to this connection as the basis of the rights of communities against foreign intervention. The one individual right he appeals to in order to ground the rights of states is a peculiar one, tailored specifically for people who are inheritors of a particular political culture, not for people who freely chose their own political obligations from a position outside of a particular historical community (e.g. the state of nature). What grounds the rights of political communities to integrity against intervention is "the rights of contemporary men and women to live as members of a historic community and to express their inherited culture through political forms worked out among themselves" (219).

These individual rights are very different from what it appeared Walzer was referring to as the rights of individuals to life and liberty in *Just and Unjust Wars*. Rather than choosing our political associations from a universal human standpoint, like the state of nature or the original position — and thereby exercising our liberty — what Walzer suggests here is underpinning our political obligations is membership in a particular political community that we do not choose, but merely inherit. The individual right to liberty which grounds our political obligations and, in turn, the rights of our communities to be free from interference by outsiders is ultimately the right of people, understood as essentially partisans in a particular historical moment in a particular political community, to live out this membership with those they share a common life with. In other words, individual liberty is the liberty to express one's authentic political identity with one's political fellows. I have the right to interfere with your politics only if I am one of your fellows by accident of birth. If I am not one of your fellows, e.g. you are Nicaraguan and I am Japanese, then I owe you (and all Nicaraguans) the freedom to work out Nicaragua's political future free from foreign interference (see 227-9).

This idea strongly suggests that Walzer is committed to a pluralistic ethics. When it comes to political justice, there simply is no universal standpoint from which to ground criticisms of others. The world is composed of irreconcilable and ineliminable political differences. Pluralism extends all the way down.

The most explicit rejection of the ethical universalist foundations, though, is found when tracing Walzer's discussion of the obligations of soldiers to fight in war upon command back to its origins. As mentioned above, Walzer argues that soldiers are obligated to fight and, perhaps, die to protect their community against aggression, because communities are worth dying for. This position clearly creates a problem for Walzer's professed commitment to the priority of individual rights. Prior to writing *Just and Unjust Wars*, Walzer grappled with this problem. In an essay titled, "The Obligation to Die for the State," first published in 1970, Walzer argues that liberal social contract theory cannot ground an obligation to fight in war for the sake of one's political community. For Walzer, the reason contract theory cannot ground such a duty is that it presupposes a clear distinction between the individual and his or her community and understands the community as a creation of the individual to serve his or her private interests. For the community to demand that its members die for it would be to reverse the priority of the individual over the community that liberal social contract theory presupposes.

Walzer, however, defends a non-liberal "contract" that would ground a duty to fight in war for the sake of the community. According to this "contract," the individual is transformed from a pre-political being into a person who is essentially a member of his or her particular political community. Following this transformation, the individual possesses a new identity and a new character. He or she is now a participant in a particular political history whose ethical virtue is inseparable from the good of his or her community. Now, the individual cannot distinguish his or her well-being from the survival of his or her political community. And, now, the individual can meaningfully be said to have a duty to fight for his or her community. As Walzer says,

> Into the state, according to this interpretation, a man brings the life which he has received from the bounty of nature and which is wholly his own. From the state, that is, from the shared experiences and general will of the political community, he receives a second life, a moral life, which is not his sole possession, but whose reality depends upon the continued existence of his fellow-citizens and of their association. (90)

And,

> A good society is one in which the new man, a moral member of a moral body, achieves his fullest development. The very instincts of pre-social man are overwhelmed and above all the instinct for self-preservation. When the state is in danger, its citizens rush to its defense, forgetful of all personal danger. They

die willingly for the sake of the state, not because the state protects their
lives—which would be...absurd—but because the state is their common life.
So long as the state survives, something of the citizen lives on, even after the
natural man is dead. The state, or rather, the common life of the citizens,
generates those "moral goods" for which...men can in fact be obligated to die.
The character of the political community obligates the citizen who participates
in it to die on its behalf and it simultaneously provides him with a motive for
dying. (92)

This is the understanding of the individual-community relationship that
Walzer uses to underpin the obligation of soldiers to fight in war in his earlier
work. Crucially, this view requires extending pluralism from the political
realm to the ethical. For, on this view, morality is based on one's attachment
to and participation in a particular historical political community. The good
life for the individual is inseparable from the virtuous engagement in the
politics of his or her society. Without that society, the good life is impossible.
For this reason, the community is worth dying for.

Importantly, Walzer refers us to this earlier essay in *Just and Unjust
Wars*. In the one place in the book where Walzer attempts to discuss the
foundations of the obligations of soldiers to fight in war, he points readers to
this earlier essay (2006, 54-5). This point implies that he believes the views
expressed in it are continuous with the views expressed in *Just and Unjust
Wars*. However, the views expressed in the essay do not, in fact, ground
political obligations and the rights of communities in a universal rights-based
morality. Instead, the essay departs from *Just and Unjust Wars* in that it
articulates a political and moral pluralism based on a communitarian conception of the individual.

WALZER'S PLURALIST TURN

In 1983, Walzer published his book *Spheres of Justice: A Defense of Pluralism and Equality*. This book articulates a theory of distributive justice for
modern capitalist societies. In doing so it self-consciously rejects universalism in the theory of justice. Walzer argues that justice is grounded in the
shared meanings that are embodied in a particular community's culture, institutions, and language. There is no universal standpoint from which to articulate and apply a theory of justice. Justice is always relative to a particular
place and time. Social criticism is therefore a matter of critically interpreting
the shared understandings of a particular community. As Walzer sums up his
position:

Justice is relative to social meanings...We cannot say what is due to this
person or that one until we know how these people relate to one another
through the things they make and distribute. There cannot be a just society

until there is a society; and the adjective *just* doesn't determine, it only mod-
ifies, the substantive life of the societies it describes. There are an infinite
number of possible lives, shaped by an infinite number of possible cultures,
religions, political arrangements, geographical conditions, and so on. A given
society is just if its substantive life is lived in a certain way—that is, in a way
faithful to the shared understandings of the members. (312-3)

This is a position that made Walzer known as a protagonist of the famed
"communitarian critique of liberalism" in the 1980s (see Kymlicka 2007).
Walzer would go on to defend versions of this position for at least the next
two decades in books like *Interpretation and Social Criticism* (1987) and
Thick and Thin (1994). As far as I am aware, to this day Walzer has not
abandoned this position.

But this is a dramatic change from the position Walzer takes in *Just and
Unjust Wars*. What we find in the later work is an abandonment of the moral
universalism that is used to underpin his earlier just war theory. This change
amounts to an abandonment of the dualism of political legitimacy that he
appeals to in defense of his anti-interventionism. As we have seen, Walzer
argues that one can demand that one's own culture and institutions live up to
the universal standards of justice, i.e. the respect for human rights. However,
one cannot demand that another's culture and institutions live up to those
standards. This is Walzer's moral universalism and political pluralism. But in
Spheres, there is no longer the claim that one can demand one's own culture
and institution live up to the universal standards of justice, because Walzer
has given up on the existence, or at least the usefulness, of those standards.
The appropriate standards to apply to one's own society are no longer universal, but are relative to the shared meanings embedded in that society. Walzer
is now a pluralist all the way down.

To some extent, Walzer seems to recognize the departure from *Just and
Unjust Wars*. In the preface to *Spheres*, Walzer distinguishes the approach he
takes to justice in it from the approach he takes in *Just and Unjust Wars*. He
says that while the theory he advances in *Spheres* proscribes "the use of
things for the purposes of domination," he adds, "This proscription has its
source, I think, less in a universalist conception of persons than in a pluralistic conception of goods." He continues,

> Some years ago, when I wrote about war, I relied heavily on the idea of rights.
> For the theory of justice in war can indeed be generated from the two most
> basic and widely recognized rights of human beings—and in their simplest
> (negative) form: not to be robbed of life and liberty. What is perhaps more
> important, these two rights seem to account for the moral judgments that we
> most commonly make in time of war. They do real work. But they are only of
> limited help in thinking about distributive justice. (xv)

Thus, Walzer distinguishes the theory of justice he uses in *Just and Unjust Wars* from the theory he advances in *Spheres*. Despite this, he appears to think both positions can be consistently maintained. According to him, the approach to distributive justice in *Spheres* need not affect the different approach to justice in *Just and Unjust Wars*.

This view of the divergence of the two approaches is difficult to accept. First, as we have seen, it is doubtful whether Walzer's theory of justice in war can in fact be generated from human rights. Second, the view presupposes a neat separation of the theory of war from the theory of distributive justice advanced in *Spheres* such that we could consistently talk about war in the terms of one kind of theory of justice and talk about distributive justice in the terms of another kind of theory of justice. But this isolation of the topics is not possible. Both topics engage with many of the same questions. In both *Just and Unjust Wars* and *Spheres*, Walzer relies on substantive commitments regarding the obligations of soldiers, the permissibility of conscription, the nature and distribution of sovereignty, the meaning of political membership, and the duties of non-interference in other communities. Thus, if two contradictory theories of justice are employed in each work, there will be trouble. Third, Walzer seems to have taken his pluralism one step beyond comprehension. Cross-cultural pluralism may be a coherent position but one cannot be a pluralist about everything. One cannot take a relativist position and combine it with a universalist position, for instance. This is nonsensical. Walzer's attempt at separating his theory of war from his theory of distributive justice would seem to amount to this kind of incoherence.

Walzer's turn to radical pluralism cannot be reconciled with the ethical universalism advanced in *Just and Unjust Wars*. Walzer must choose between the two positions. Given the elements of his theory of war that seem to deviate from his ethical universalism, as well as the moments where he explicitly relies on an ethical pluralism similar to that advanced in *Spheres* in defense of his theory of war, it is well worth considering what would happen to Walzer's just war theory if he abandoned ethical universalism in favor of his pluralism. In my view, by doing this his theory of just war is improved in the sense that it is rendered more internally coherent and its spirit is more accurately and powerfully captured.

A PLURALIST THEORY OF JUST WAR

There is not sufficient space here to fully articulate this new theory. I will only discuss how this theory generates the two most important tenets of his just war theory: the rights of political communities and the prohibition of attacks on civilians.

The Rights of Political Communities

According to Walzer, the only just cause for war is aggression, or the violation of a state's rights to political sovereignty and territorial integrity. When aggression has been committed, a state and its allies have a right to go to war to thwart or punish the aggressors. Walzer argues clearly in *Just and Unjust Wars* that the reason aggression gives others just cause for war is the overriding importance of the rights of political communities. For Walzer, the independence and integrity of political communities is worth going to war to protect.

What makes political communities so valuable is the "common life" that constitutes the identity of the people that make up the community. Political communities are more than just collections of individuals. They are political bodies, that is, groups of people who share a way of life. They have come together over long periods of time and formed an identity around "shared experiences and cooperative activity." Though Walzer calls this a "contract," he says it is not a literal contract. Rather, it is a metaphor for the slow, gradual coming together of individuals to form a nation or people.

At the core of Walzer's just war theory we find the obligation to respect people and their distinctive common lives. We must never violate the sovereignty of these communities. Each person is a member of one or more such communities and has the right to engage in the ways of life they find their identities expressed in and, hopefully, fulfilled in. We disrespect persons and their communities when we ignore the real political and cultural boundaries that separate us. This is not because people have, from the state of nature, elected to become members of one or another such community. Rather, it is because people are essentially political beings for whom membership in a political community is a non-negotiable part of who they are.

Walzer's just war theory is based on a basic commitment to acknowledging and respecting the different ways of life that humanity expresses in its different communities. In this way, it is a radically tolerant theory. It is not a pacifist theory, however. It holds that the one occasion for war is when it is needed to stop and punish political behavior that is intolerant of difference. For Walzer, all communities are to be left free to live out their own unique traditions. But if they should embrace policies or traditions that fail to allow other communities the same freedom, then we all have a right to use force to stop them. In a number of places in *Just and Unjust Wars,* Walzer states the heart of his theory in just this way. He says, for instance, "The theory of aggression presupposes our commitment to a pluralist world, and that commitment is also the inner meaning of the presumption in favor of resistance. We want to live in an international society where communities of men and women freely shape their separate destinies" (72). A just war is a war to protect and defend this international regime of tolerance. As such, it places the value of the pluralist character of the world above all else. As Walzer says, "the survival and freedom of political communities—whose members share a way of life, developed by their ancestors, to be passed on to their children—are the highest values of international society" (254).

Thus, from the radical pluralism Walzer commits himself to, he derives a universal principle of justice. This is a principle of anti-imperialism. It says, roughly (and in my own words), "do not impose one's own will on others who do not share the same political and cultural meanings as you." This view is articulated in *Spheres of Justice* and forms the heart of the theory.

> We are (all of us) culture-producing creatures; we make and inhabit meaning-ful worlds. Since there is no way to rank and order these worlds with regard to their understanding of social goods, we do justice to actual men and women by respecting their particular creations. And they claim justice, and resist tyranny, by insisting on the meaning of social goods among themselves. Justice is rooted in the distinct understandings of places, honors, jobs, things of all sorts, that constitute a shared way of life. To override those understandings is (al-ways) to act unjustly. (314)

It is this principle that prohibits aggression and justifies the use of force to stop it.

Noncombatant Immunity

If there is one place in *Just and Unjust Wars* where Walzer unambiguously relies on human rights it is his defense of noncombatant immunity. He argues clearly that, while the rights of communities can give us reason to go war, the rights of individuals cannot be overridden in war. For him, the rights of individual human beings limit what a state can do to protect the rights of a political community. To illustrate the point, Walzer discusses the Free French employment of mercenaries, who used rape as a military tactic in the Second World War. Walzer claims that no matter how useful such a tactic may be militarily, it is always immoral because it violates the rights of its victims (135).

If we give up on human rights as trumps against the interests of communities, as the proposed pluralist theory does, how can we maintain strict limits of the conduct of war such as noncombatant immunity? If we accept this new theory, won't every war be treated the way Walzer proposes we treat supreme emergencies? Won't we have justification to do anything to defeat the enemy?

I don't think so. I think the reformulated theory can generate an interest-ing and unified justification for *jus in bello* restrictions like noncombatant immunity. On the new theory we can say that the reason no one should deliberately attack noncombatants is the same reason one should go to war:

to preserve the integrity and independence of the world's different communities. If the purpose of the just war is only to thwart and repel aggression, then all wars must be limited in nature. The means employed in war must be consistent with the ends, and, since the ends are always to return to the *status quo ante bellum*, no just war has a reason to attack noncombatants, even those who are members of the aggressive community. A just war does not target noncombatants because a just war is carried out from a commitment to the preservation of all communities, even the enemy's. To deliberately target the enemy's civilians when the goal of the war is merely to end the enemy's aggression is to lose sight of what a just war is all about. To target noncombatants is to engage in wanton cruelty.

In a further sign that Walzer has had a pluralist foundation in mind for his just war theory, in a later essay, he defends the principle of noncombatant immunity in terms like this. Instead of saying deliberate attacks on civilians violate human rights he says,

> Implicit in the theory of just war is a theory of just peace: whatever happens to these two armies, whichever one wins or loses, whatever the nature of the battles or the extent of the casualties, the "peoples" on both sides must be accommodated at the end. The central principle of *jus in bello*, that civilians can't be targeted or deliberately killed, means that they will be—morally speaking, they have to be—present at the conclusion. This is the deepest meaning of noncombatant immunity: it doesn't only protect individual noncombatants; it also protects the group to which they belong. Just as the destruction of the group cannot be a legitimate purpose of war, so it cannot be a legitimate practice in war. Civilians are immune as ordinary men and women, disengaged from the business of warfare; they are also immune as members of a human community that is not a military organization. (2007, 266)

CONCLUSION

There is much more to be said both for and against this reformulated theory. The radical relativism of the theory, as well as the apparent ease with which it can generate the supreme emergency exception, should give us pause. My purpose here has merely been to show how Walzer's later theory of justice can be used to underpin his earlier just war theory. In fact, I have suggested that the new foundations do a better job underpinning the tenets of his just war theory than the old foundations. I have shown how the new foundations can be used to underpin the central components of his theory of *jus ad bellum* and *jus in bello*.

I hope I have succeeded in illuminating Walzer's thinking and revealing him to be much more interesting and innovative than he is normally thought to be. From this new perspective, Walzer is not working in the modern tradition of just war thought. That is, he is not building on a bedrock of human rights, working through a social contract to ground the rights of communities, and then articulating principles governing conflict between such communities. Rather, he is rejecting the foundational status of human rights, adopting an anti-liberal understanding of the individual and a relativist theory of justice, then articulating principles governing conflict between such nonliberal communities. Ultimately, he has much more in common with the pre-modern theorists such as Suarez and Vitoria and with 19th century realists such as Hegel than he has with the modern theorists such as Grotius, Pufendorf, and Vattel. That said, the truly Walzerian theory seems to me to be ultimately quite unique.

REFERENCES

Kymlicka, Will. 2007. Community and Multiculturalism. In *A Companion to Contemporary Political Philosophy*. 2nd ed. Edited by Robert E. Goodin, Philip Pettit, and Thomas Pogge, 463-77. Vol. 2. New York: Blackwell.

Luban, David. 1985a. Just War and Human Rights. In *International Ethics*. Edited by Charles Bietz, et al., 195-216. Princeton: Princeton University Press.

———. 1985b. The Romance of the Nation-State. In *International Ethics*. Edited by Charles Bietz, et al., 238-43. Princeton: Princeton University Press.

Walzer, Michael. 1970. The Obligation to Die for the State. In *Obligations: Essays on Disobedience, War, and Citizenship*, 77-98. Cambridge: Harvard University Press.

———. 1983. *Spheres of Justice: A Defense of Pluralism and Equality*. New York: Basic Books.

———. 1985. The Moral Standing of States: A Reply to Four Critics. In *International Ethics*. Edited by Charles Bietz, et. al., 217-37. Princeton: Princeton University Press.

———. 1987. *Interpretation and Social Criticism*. Cambridge: Harvard University Press.

———. 1994. *Thick and Thin: Moral Argument at Home and Abroad*. Notre Dame: University of Notre Dame Press.

———. 2006 [1977]. *Just and Unjust Wars*. 4th ed. New York: Basic Books.

———. 2007. Terrorism and Just War. In *Thinking Politically: Essays in Political Theory*. New Haven: Yale University Press.

The Hegemon's Dilemma

*Power Intolerance from Ancient Athens
to the United States of America*

Scott A. Silverstone

The modern international system was born in 1648 in what can be described as a declaration of *tolerance* among the major powers of Europe. For the previous thirty years these same powers, driven by ferocious *intolerance* of the Protestant or Catholic heresies of their neighbors, had brutalized each other in such vicious sectarian warfare that escape from the violence of intolerance was pursued through a compact – the Treaty of Westphalia. The consensus to emerge from the Thirty Years War was that intolerance of the other's religious practices, at least when it took the form of imposing your religion at the point of a sword – had to be controlled. The solution was a simple rule: *cuius regio, eius religio* – "his reign, his religion." In other words, escape from the tragic consequences of religious intolerance would hinge on respect for the rights of other sovereigns in the system.

More broadly, Westphalia codified the core principle that organizes the global political order we still live in: the system is constructed of sovereign states, and these sovereign states have the right to be free from external interference in their internal matters. But in an ironic twist, this progressive effort to bring *peace through tolerance* in the mid-17th century had the unintended effect of introducing a *new source of intolerance* among states that is potentially every bit as deadly as the religious wars of this era. Over 350 years later, we continue to wrestle with this particular form of intolerance and the dangers it can generate.

To explain this new form of intolerance, we must return to the basic rights that sovereign states are entitled to if the concept of sovereignty is to have any meaning in world politics. The right to freedom from external interference only makes sense if states also enjoy a higher right: the right to survive. Customary international law, the Just War tradition, and Article 51 of the United Nations Charter, all hold that self-defense is an "inherent right" for all states. In turn, survival depends on each state's right to equip itself with the physical tools – the weapons of war – that will make self-defense possible. After all, given that there is no higher authority above the states to protect them from predators, a condition called "anarchy" in the field of international relations, states must figure out how to provide for their own defense in what one scholar called a "self-help system."[1] Logically, then, tolerance of your neighbors' inherent right to survive also requires tolerance of the steps they might take to amass sufficient power to fend for themselves in the face of potential aggression.

But as students of international relations have long recognized, the character of the sovereign state system creates a trap in which tolerance of others' power might be impossible. The same power that can be used to protect might also be used to coerce and crush. As a result, tolerance for your neighbor's military power can actually produce grave dangers to your own security. While sovereign states might accept differences in religion, in ethnicity, national identity, or the political systems of others, fear might still lead them to see the mere existence of the power those other states possess to be an intolerable threat to their own survival. In other words, intolerance of the other's growing military power might be the key to safety. But in its most perverse form, this "security dilemma" finds states developing their power purely for self-defense, yet in turn, inadvertently producing such fear in others that all are caught up in spirals of competition and hostility as mutual intolerance leads down a dangerous road toward violent conflict.[2]

The objective of this chapter is to explore this power-intolerance trap in theory and practice. The ultimate goal is to shed light on the dilemma America now faces as China converts its astounding economic growth into military modernization and political influence in East Asia and beyond. Stated bluntly, what are the odds that America and China will get caught in this intolerance trap? For America, is intolerance of China's growing power a healthy reflex that will keep America and its allies safe; or will intolerance lead to conflict that should have been avoidable?

To understand the problem through a deeper historical context, we will start by reaching back in time to the Peloponnesian War among the Greek city-states of the 5th century B.C., a war centered around the two great rivals, Athens and Sparta. The Greek historian Thucydides left behind a brilliant contemporary account of this conflict. To this day, his *History of the Peloponnesian War* is considered to be the first work of international relations theory in view of its careful effort to extract general insights about human behavior that could be found useful by future generations struggling with similar security problems. While there are great differences between the world of the ancient Greeks and the 21st century, students of international relations routinely look back to this period to learn about war and peace, strategy, leadership and politics. It was a pre-Westphalian society, but it was also an anarchic system composed of independent city-states that experienced many of the dynamics we find in the modern era. For our purposes, the power-intolerance problem cuts across the key historical differences.

Athens takes center stage in this story, but not merely because Thucydides himself was an Athenian. It takes center stage because Athens was uniquely possessed by the power-intolerance phenomenon, which in turn drove the dynamism of shifting power in the ancient Greek system and a whirlwind of fear that generated the nearly three decades of bloodshed which followed. With this case in mind, we will then leap 2,400 years forward in time to consider our modern intolerance problem. Ultimately, the chapter will not promise a tidy solution to this dilemma. Its more modest objective is simply to highlight the importance of recognizing this form of intolerance as a prelude for mitigating its potentially devastating impact as states engage in the daily pursuit of security for their societies.

INTOLERANCE AND THE ATHENIAN EMPIRE

In 416 B.C., 38 warships carried 3,400 Athenian and allied soldiers into the inner bay of the small Greek island of Melos, about 100 miles south of the great imperial city-state. Their mission was to end Melian neutrality in the war that had ripped through the ancient Greek world for the previous fifteen years. An Athenian envoy sent from the invading force offered Melian leaders a simple choice: either submit to absorption within the Athenian empire without a struggle, or face a crushing blow that would produce the same results. In their brave reply, the Melians appealed to justice and reason. Please, respect our neutrality in this great power struggle with your Spartan enemies. While Melos had been founded by colonists from Sparta many generations earlier, the Melian negotiator pointed out that his city had never provided material or political support to Athens' adversary over the many years of this brutal conflict. If the Athenians would just leave Melos alone, he promised gratitude, even friendship. But most important, the Melians promised to remain a neutral city that Athens could ignore without danger.

The Athenians were unmoved by this seemingly reasonable request. The key fact here, the Athenian envoy insisted, is that we are very powerful, and you are weak. In this world, "the strong do what they can and the weak suffer what they must."[3] Despite the reality and logic of raw power that militated against them, which the Melians fully understood, they refused to concede. After a six month siege, treason within the Melian walls led to the city's fall:

in the aftermath, the entire male population was put to death, the women and children were sold as slaves, and five hundred Athenians were sent to colonize the island on behalf of the empire.

To this day, students of international relations still point to the fate of Melos as a reminder, or perhaps a warning, about the inevitable triumph of power over justice in the affairs of states. The most important reaction to this story, however, should be to ask why, why did Athens pursue this brutal course? Was this a particularly extreme example of what so-called classical realists would say is an innate human thirst for power as an end in itself?[4] Was it motivated by material greed, an act of imperial expansion in which a great state leveraged its structural advantages in the system to fill its treasury or the pockets of a privileged social class? Maybe it was an expression of a self-aggrandizing civic identity that led Athenians to believe they had the natural right to rule over other Greeks across the wider Hellenic world. As Pericles famously expressed the Athenian view in his funeral oration at the end of the first year of war, Athens is the "school" of Greece. Its virtues, perhaps, bestowed wisdom and civilizing superiority that should be spread through force if necessary.[5]

There is good evidence from Thucydides that each of these possible explanations, in general terms, has merit. Athenian citizens could be easily stirred by patriotic appeals to their civic virtues and superiority among the Greeks and the rights these virtues bestowed. The empire fed Athens' treasury and its wealthy and working classes alike; Athenians rarely refused an opportunity to increase the city's enormous wealth. And there are abundant examples that show how the idea of power alone could stoke the Athenian imagination and motivate action.

While each of these variables might have contributed to the brutal Athenian expansionism at Melos, the Athenians themselves point to a deeper cause at work: fear of vulnerability. The Melians had offered Athens friendly neutrality. So what was Athens afraid of? The Athenian retort to this offer makes the point bluntly: your friendship hurts us more than your hostility, because friendship is an indicator of weakness, hatred signals power. More precisely, the Athenians assert that if any state "maintain[s] [its] independence it is because [it is] strong and that if we do not molest them it is because we are afraid."[6] In other words, Melian *friendship* is *intolerable*. Melian *independence* is *intolerable*. For Athens it was a matter of safety, and safety could only be found in unchecked power over others.

This is among the most extreme expressions of the power-intolerance problem we find in history. According to one international relations school of thought – Offensive Realism – this Athenian perspective on power and security was the most sensible response to the potential dangers of an anarchic world. From this theoretical vantage point, states coexist in a very dark world in which they live in dread of the mere potential for others to use their physical power in highly aggressive ways. Even if your neighbors do not appear to have threatening intentions, a wise leader will remain hypersensitive to the inherent uncertainties of the future. Survival in anarchy is always precarious, warns John Mearsheimer, the most prominent Offensive Realist scholar, so the survival imperative demands that states assume the worst about others' future behavior. In contrast, a fool will remain complacently tolerant as potential rivals grow stronger. The only viable solution to the security dilemma, says Mearsheimer, is to amass so much more power than other states – to pursue hegemony, or dominance in the system – that you can fend off any threat the unknowable future might bring.[7] In sum, this is a worldview in which intolerance of other states' right to arm themselves is enshrined as a first principle.

In Thucydides' *History*, two particularly vivid passages perfectly illustrate this Offensive Realist understanding of security in an anarchic system. For the first, we return to the standoff between the invading Athenians and the resistant Melians. According to the Athenian antagonist, "of men we know, that by a necessary law of their nature they rule wherever they can." Look closely at the uncompromising language he uses here. It is a "*necessary law*" pushing men to "rule *wherever* they can." The Athenian insists that this is not a law for Athens alone. "And it is not as if we were the first to make this law or to act upon it when made," he continues. "We *found it existing before us*, and shall leave it to exist *forever after us*; all we do is to make use of it, knowing that *you and everybody else*, having the same power as we have, would do the same as we do."[8]

As a statement of scientific law – if X, then Y – the behavior we would expect to observe is simple: when states have the power to expand their rule over others, they will. To find a logical explanation for this expected behavior, however, we need to move beyond the Melian Dialogue to another infamous moment in Athenian history: the decision to launch an audacious expedition to conquer the island of Sicily, a decision reached in the summer of 417 B.C., just a few months after the fall of Melos. During the debate over this proposal in the Athenian assembly, the expedition's main champion, Alcibiades, reminded his fellow citizens what was at stake if Athens let this expansionist opportunity slip away. "We cannot fix the exact point at which our empire shall stop," Alcibiades warned. "We have reached a position in which we must not be content with retaining what we have but must scheme to expand it for, *if we cease to rule others, we shall be in danger of being ruled ourselves.*"[9]

Taken together, these two passages provide what seems to be the purest articulation from ancient texts of the Offensive Realist explanation for the power-intolerance phenomenon in anarchic systems, and the expansionist imperative this form of intolerance is said to produce. But as many readers may have already sensed, this theoretical claim about anarchy and the necessary law of expansion is controversial, among both international relations scholars and practitioners responsible for their states' security. Does anarchy and fear truly compel all major states to such extremes in their pursuit of survival? Is this radical level of intolerance for other states' right to arm themselves the most reliable way to secure your own survival? Does an objective "law of nature," described so confidently by the Athenian envoy at Melos, explain Athens' drive for hegemonic power in the fifth century B.C.?

Athenians certainly *believed* the world worked according to such a law. And given Athens' distinctive historical experience, this worldview is not so surprising. While Thucydides never develops this point explicitly, he suggests that Athens' empire building was rooted in its near-death experience of 480 B.C., during the great war against the Persian empire. To survive the Persian army's onslaught into the heart of Greece, the Athenians abandoned their city, took to their ships, and fled to the nearby island of Salamis. The invading "barbarians" torched the city. Two subsequent Greek victories in 480 and 479 B.C. sent a hobbled Persian force into retreat. Yet this desperate experience sparked a new vision of security for Athens, a vision that crystallized immediately after the Athenians reoccupied their ravaged city. The first component of this vision was purely defensive: thick walls were built around the city itself, but more important, walls were built around the Athenian port of Piraeus four miles to the west, and "long walls" enclosed the main road connecting Piraeus to the heart of the city.

Walls indeed bring a measure of security, but this certainly was no revolutionary shift in its pursuit. It was the leading Athenian citizen of the period, Themistocles, who rallied his people around the idea that security would not be found in a mere defensive crouch. Instead, Athens' safety would depend on unparalleled naval power, and naval power was the foundation for building an empire. The strategy would be to push outward, not hunker down at home. Thucydides tells us that Themistocles "was always advising the Athenians, if a day should come when they were hard pressed by land, to go down into Piraeus, and defy the world with their fleet."[10] And as we learn from an Athenian nearly fifty years after Themistocles set the Athenians on this course, "the nature of the case first compelled us to advance our empire to its present height, *fear being our principle motive.*"[11]

When reviewing the history Thucydides presents, hegemonic expansion does not appear as a "necessary" response to an intense yet nebulous fear that anarchy and uncertainty alone are said to produce. Instead, it was this concrete experience of such intense danger, a threat that brought Athens to the edge of actual extinction, which seems to have been the genesis of hegemony as the solution to the security dilemma. Rule everywhere, or be ruled yourself. With this experience in mind, Athens' extreme power-intolerance and its pursuit of hegemony to deny others the ability to cause harm is certainly understandable.

The pursuit of security through hegemony began when Athens and its remaining Greek allies chased the retreating Persians back into Asia Minor to break the empire's hold on the eastern Mediterranean and liberate Greek cities along the coast. But how well did this approach actually serve Athens' desire for security in the long run? For sure, the Persian Empire had been effectively thrown back and Athens' subsequent control of the eastern Aegean Sea kept the city safe from barbarian assault for generations. And for nearly 75 years, Athens had no peer in the Greek system that could threaten the city the way the Persians had in the early part of the century. Even with the terrible losses suffered during the 27 years of war with Sparta, Athens had what seemed like an inexhaustible ability to mobilize the treasure, manpower and political will to continue the fight. And it is also fair to point out that Athens' eventual defeat in the Peloponnesian War was not a given. So how can we judge Athens' choice to find security through hegemony and the power-intolerance that motivated it?

Fear was their "principle motive" for empire. Naturally, the Persians were their primary target in the early stages of expansion. But it did not take long for Athenians to convert their extreme and understandable intolerance for Persian power into *general* intolerance for *any* city or ruler that remained outside Athens' control. The story Thucydides tells of those fifty years after repulsing the last Persian invasion is one of seemingly continuous violent expansion. Expansionist momentum pushed their forces as far as North Africa, and for a time, Athenians were the "masters" of the Nile River.[12] But after the early victories over Persian forces in Asia Minor, Athens' power was most often directed against Greek cities still independent of its growing league and allied cities that were crushed as they tried to leave Athens' orbit. In the process, Athens converted what had been a voluntary alliance against the barbarian into a coercive empire of its own.

THE DEFENSIVE REALIST WARNING

It was now no longer intolerance for the barbarians alone, but intolerance for the independent power of fellow Greeks as well. Their suspicions of others ran amok, their perceptions of danger were easily inflated, and calculations of future threat defaulted to worst case scenarios that often did not reflect reality. Here we find the potentially fatal flaw residing within the hegemonic solution to the security dilemma. As Alcibiades warned, where do you draw the line in your expansionist quest for security? Is *all* power held by others an intolerable threat? And if so, are we doomed to endless conflict with those who push back in their own quest for security?

One of the most important debates within international relations revolves around this question. Interestingly, this is a debate within the realist camp –

those scholars of international relations who emphasize the impact of anarchy, uncertainty, and fear as motivating factors in the behavior of states. In contrast to Offensive Realists who contend that the only solution to the security dilemma is to dominate other states in the system (extreme power-intolerance), Defensive Realists assert that states will be more secure when potential rivals feel more secure themselves. For some realists, this sounds counterintuitive: after all, if power brings security, it seems that *more* power over others should bring *more* security.

But Defensive Realists point out that in many cases power intolerance and hegemony-seeking are no solution at all, because the tragic logic of the security dilemma suggests – and history demonstrates – that the move to dominate will simply provoke intense security fears in others, and this fear will compel a reaction. The paradoxical result of extreme power intolerance is that the state pursuing more security through more relative power will end up *less secure* in the end, as the play for dominance creates new rivals and deepens the hostility of existing rivals who will now push back harder than they would have before. Simply put, the more fear you create in others, the more your security can suffer as they rise up in opposition.

Defensive Realists provide a solution to this paradox, rooted in the claim that the intensity of the security dilemma can be moderated when states signal *tolerance* for other states' legitimate security interests. This insight depends on recognizing the fact that all states can suffer from uncertainty and fear generated within an anarchic system. Acknowledging that potential rivals are just as likely to experience and react to fear as you are puts leaders in a frame of mind to accept that the military capabilities other states develop might be a function of how much of a threat they think *you are*. Accepting other states' legitimate security interests, and tolerating the steps they take to protect those interests, can be the key to relaxing the level of fear and hostility, and avoiding unnecessary competition, in the international system.

One prominent Defensive Realist, Charles Glaser, does provide an important caveat to this argument: this strategy for reducing competition will not work with so-called greedy states.[13] Greedy states are those that have an appetite for aggression that springs from some internal motivation, rather than mere fear for their safety. Nazi Germany is the best example we have in recent history. Hitler's ideological commitment to Aryan superiority fueled a murderous drive to build an empire through violent conquest. The Nazi Party was certainly skillful in its manipulation of the German population's sense of vulnerability in the post-World War I system; Nazis used this perception of national weakness and external threats to rally domestic support for restoring Germany's place among the great powers. Yet Hitler's commitment to violent expansion was not a function of how threatening he believed other states to be. In this particular case, a policy of self-restraint by other European powers would not have diminished Nazi Germany's aggressive inclinations.

But as Glaser notes correctly, not all rival states are Nazi Germany. The key, then, is to distinguish between greedy states and legitimate security-seekers. While legitimate security seeking states will likely respond positively to signals of self-restraint and tolerance meant to reduce their level of fear, greedy states will not.

For the ancient Athenians, this would be the Defensive Realist message: not all other city-states are the Persian Empire. And to act as if they were truly as threatening as Persia risked provoking a terrible backlash against Athens that otherwise could be avoided. Thucydides' *History* demonstrates that this is exactly what happened. Relentless expansion, even if originally motivated by Athens' near-death experience at the hands of Persia, had the unintended consequences of stoking fear, hostility and a competitive spiral that directly led to the Peloponnesian War among the Greeks. And Athens had been warned beforehand about the effects of its behavior.

THE TRAGEDY OF ATHENIAN POWER INTOLERANCE

Thucydides begins the story of the immediate events that led to war with an account of a localized conflict between two rival city-states, Corcyra and Corinth. While the hostility that animated their dispute was the product of what can be considered a family feud over respect and rights between a mother city and its former colony, Athens was drawn in when the conflict turned into an opportunity to lock in its position as the undisputed naval hegemon of the eastern Mediterranean. Corcyra, victorious in its first naval clash with Corinthian forces, watched nervously as Corinth rebuilt its fleet and trained for a second round that would punish Corcyra for its insolence. To preempt Corinth's plan for retribution, the Corcyraeans approached Athens with a warning and an offer.

The warning was simple: if Corinth defeats us and absorbs our ships into its own fleet, Corinth will then have the most powerful navy among the Greeks. And since Corinth is allied with your rival Sparta, this power shift will become a terrible threat to you in the war with Sparta that is bound to come. The solution offered: join us in an alliance to defeat the Corinthians. This victory, they promised, will secure your naval supremacy and intimidate your adversaries, thus giving you confidence in safety for the future. [14]

A Corinthian representative at this meeting responded with a warning of his own, as if drawing directly from modern Defensive Realist theory: "there is no danger of our injuring you, as we are not enemies," but "you cannot become their auxiliary and remain our friend; if you join in their attack, you must share the punishment." And this notion of a future war with Sparta and its allies? There is no certainty of any such war, "and it is not worth while to be carried away by this [fear] *into gaining the instant and declared enmity of*

Corinth."[15] Corinth's advice: "Do not be seduced by the prospect of a great naval alliance. Abstinence from all injustice to other first rate powers," in other words, respecting their legitimate interests and tolerating moves to defend them, "is a *greater tower of strength* than anything that can be gained by the sacrifice of permanent tranquility for an apparent temporary advantage."[16]

The Athenian citizens debated this question during two assemblies; Thucydides tells us that the Corinthian's Defensive Realist logic of self-restraint, tolerance and continued tranquility had the upper hand during the first meeting. But the Corcyraeans had really played right into the fifty year legacy of Athens' near-death experience and its subsequent worldview: dominate or submit. The Athenians were willing to gamble that "the coming of the Peloponnesian War was only a question of time," so antagonizing the Corinthians in the short term was irrelevant in the face of the coming clash with Sparta.[17]

But it was this power-maximizing, power-intolerant, decision that propelled the Greeks toward war. Just as the Corinthian predicted, Athens' intervention – which led to Corinth's defeat in the second match with Corcyra – fired Corinth's hostility and determination to retaliate.[18] But most important, an assessment of the tragic nature of this decision for Athens begins with the abundant evidence Thucydides offers to show that Corinth's newfound hatred for Athens was not only decisive, it was necessary to shake Sparta out of its passivity. Thucydides emphasizes that the "Spartans, though fully aware of" Athens' aggressive expansion over many years, "remained inactive during most of the period" since the Persian War, "being of old slow to go to war except under the pressure of necessity." Thucydides, even though an Athenian himself, provides no evidence whatsoever to support the prediction that Sparta had hostile intent toward Athens. Instead, he shows that it was Athens' intolerance of Corinthian interests, laid bare through Corinth's merciless public badgering of Sparta for its neglect, which convinced Spartan leadership that "Athens' power could no longer be ignored." Athens' own intolerant behavior is what led the Spartans to recognize that "the time had come for them to throw themselves heart and soul upon the *hostile power* and *break it*."[19] And even though it took 27 years, Sparta did just that.

AMERICAN HEGEMONY AND THE RISE OF CHINA

Just as Athens and Sparta defined great power politics in the world of the ancient Greeks, the United States and China will define great power politics in the 21st century. And like Athens and Sparta, America and China are struggling with the fears and uncertainty generated within an anarchic state system. Arguably, the most important question embedded within this relationship is whether these great states can avoid being consumed by the security dilemma. Phrased another way, will the impulse toward mutual power-intolerance create a cycle of competition and hostility that hold the potential for a disastrous clash between them? The raw ingredients for such a clash are clearly evident on both sides. To probe these questions, it is most useful to start with the American side of the relationship.

Similar to Athens, the United States became a great power of system-wide proportions through war. At the turn of the 20th century the United States broke through the ranks of the major states with an industrial output that surpassed both the United Kingdom and Germany. America had massive power potential, mobilized briefly during the final years of World War I, yet until the late 1930s its power was more latent than actual. The United States military was small relative to many states in the world, and its political and economic influence waxed and waned unevenly in the 1920s and 1930s. But just like Athens, which responded to the Persian Empire's threat with a drive toward full mobilization of its power potential, the United States responded to the globe-girdling threat of German and Japanese aggression by drawing deeply on its potential to project power on a scale never before seen in history. Most important, also like Athens, America was determined to sustain its dominance – in regions far from home – after the enemy was defeated, "fear being our principle motive."

World War II generated strong consensus in the United States around a simple strategic idea: America could not tolerate other states in hegemonic control of either Europe or East Asia. To be sure, America was committed to safeguarding hegemony in its own region of the world. Conditions that would make this goal ultimately possible were established as early as 1823, when President James Monroe declared that America would treat any attempt by the great states of Europe to extend their power into any portion of the Western Hemisphere "as dangerous to our peace and safety."[20] As America developed sufficient power to back up this audacious claim with actual force in the early 20th century, dominance in the Western Hemisphere was a settled fact and widely-supported objective. But looking outward, America was not willing to tolerate a similar degree of hegemony by other great powers in Europe or Asia.

Intolerance of this condition was rooted in two fears. First, that rival hegemons could use their power to deny the United States access to the markets and resources of these two regions critical for continuing economic prosperity. A series of memoranda produced in the early 1940s by the War and Peace Studies group of the Council on Foreign Relations, which had been commissioned by an under-staffed State Department, demonstrated that for a robust American economy to survive it had to maintain access to European markets and critical resources from Southeast Asia. Co-existence with a Nazi-dominated Continent with its closed economic system in one critical part of the world, and Imperial Japan's Greater East Asia Co-Prosperity

Sphere in the other, would force the United States to fall back on hemispheric self-sufficiency. But as the War and Peace Studies group concluded, self-sufficiency was impossible.[21] An American economy that provided growth and opportunity for its citizens, for industry, labor and finance, demanded an open international economic order. The second fear is that once established as hegemonic in their own regions, these hostile states could project power around the world, perhaps even into the Western Hemisphere, thus radically altering the immense relative security enjoyed by the United States close to home. America guards its distinct position as the world's only regional hegemon with great jealousy.[22]

Wartime consensus on this strategic principle was cemented in the post-war years as Americans squared off against the next aspirant for hegemony in Eurasia. Like the United States, latent Soviet power was mobilized on a massive scale through total war. As the new postwar order emerged from the rubble, heavy Soviet forces sat right on the edge of Western Europe. And with its immense geographic scale covering 15 time zones, Soviet influence stretched to the edge of East Asia. American intolerance for further Soviet expansion produced what most Americans of the early Cold War saw as a logical next step in the pursuit of security: sustaining permanent American forces in both Europe and Asia to block others' power rather than throwing forces into the fight after the hegemonic threat had already launched its aggressive drive. America's worldwide military presence in the 21st century is a legacy of mid-20th century fears and the resolve to seek relief from uncertainty and the security dilemma through power-intolerance on a global scale.

This extreme power-intolerance was starkly evident during an embarrassing moment of unintentional clarity in 1992. On March 8, 1992, readers of the *New York Times* had a rare glimpse of the classified strategic vision of the Department of Defense when the newspaper ran excerpts from the draft Defense Planning Guidance (DPG) for 1994-1999. The DPG's central point: America would work to sustain a one superpower world. The timing was perfect. The Soviet Union had collapsed just two months earlier. For the first time since the rise of the sovereign state system at Westphalia in 1648, there was only one truly great power in the international system. The United States had no peer competitor, and the George H. W. Bush administration was working on how to keep it that way.

According to the draft DPG,

> Our first objective is to prevent the re-emergence of a new rival. This is a dominant consideration underlying the new regional defense strategy and requires that we endeavor to prevent any hostile power from dominating a region whose resources would, under consolidated control, be sufficient to generate global power. . . . We must maintain the mechanisms for deterring potential

competitors from *even aspiring to a larger regional or global role.* . . . There
are other potential nations or coalitions that could, in the further future, develop strategic aims and a defense posture of region-wide or global domination.
Our strategy must now refocus on precluding the emergence of any potential
future global competitor.[23]

Interestingly, once this objective became public it generated tremendous
political controversy. Without a global peer competitor to put the urgency
behind sustaining American dominance, many American political leaders
were not ready to pay the heavy costs this required. It was an election year
and the American economy was in recession. Americans had been eagerly
looking forward to a "peace dividend" with the end of the Cold War, and
there was strong support for the United States working collectively with
other states to address global security concerns, as America had done so
successfully in the war against Iraq one year earlier. In response to this
outcry, the administration removed the DPG language calling for extreme
intolerance of new great powers.[24]

Despite the drama caused by this blunt assertion of America's power
aims, there remained a broad underlying commitment in the United States to
the notion that America must remain the "indispensible nation" providing
"leadership" on a global basis. And leadership, as successive National Security Strategies from the George H. W. Bush and Clinton presidencies declared, demanded sustaining military supremacy in the years to come.

In 2002, the discomfort with declaring this objective out loud was washed
away in America's muscular response to the terrorist attacks of September
11th. The first National Security Strategy from President George W. Bush,
released in September 2002, made the point without flinching:

> The United States possesses unprecedented— and unequaled—strength and
> influence in the world . . . It is time to reaffirm the essential role of American
> military strength. We must build and maintain our defenses beyond chal-
> lenge . . . We know from history that deterrence can fail; and we know from
> experience that some enemies cannot be deterred. The United States must and
> will maintain the capability to defeat any attempt by an enemy . . . to impose
> its will on the United States, our allies, or our friends. We will maintain the
> forces sufficient to support our obligations, and to defend freedom. *Our forces
> will be strong enough to dissuade potential adversaries from pursuing a mili-
> tary build-up in hopes of surpassing, or equaling, the power of the United
> States.*[25]

In other words, the United States will not tolerate a peer power competitor, on the global or regional level.

Given this blunt objective, it is no surprise that the modernization of
Chinese military power and substantial improvements in its capabilities over
the past decade causes tremendous angst in Washington and among many

American strategic thinkers. But there are two questions that American leaders must contend with to assess the significance of Chinese growth: what is motivating China's investment in military modernization, and what does China intend to do with its military capabilities as it becomes increasingly more robust? Specifically, is China responding to the natural impulse to develop the *means for self-defense* in an anarchic system, or does China harbor *malicious or greedy intent* that will burst into aggressive acts as its capabilities reach critical mass?

Back in 1992, during the flap over the draft Defense Planning Guidance's call for extreme power-intolerance, the Defense Department spokesman, Pete Williams, hit the point squarely. According to Williams, America would not work to prevent other states in general from becoming prominent players in global politics. Instead, America was "concerned about *hostile powers* dominating any regions of critical interest to us."[26] So is China a hostile rising power, or is it a legitimate security seeking state?[27]

Interestingly, neither Offensive Realism nor Defensive Realism finds anything peculiar in China's military modernization. As Glaser puts it,

> If China were able to operate carrier battle groups near the U.S. coast and attack the U.S. homeland with long-range bombers, Washington would naturally want the ability to blunt such capabilities, and . . . it would try to catch up as quickly as it had the resources to do so. Those actions would not have been driven by any nefarious plan to subjugate the world, and so far there are strong reasons to believe that the same holds true for China's course.[28]

China and the United States coexist in an anarchic system, responsible for their own defense in an inherently uncertain world in which it is impossible to confidently predict the future behavior of potential adversaries. So on the one hand, China's reaction to its current vulnerability to American power – its intolerance for the current distribution of power – is easy to explain. On the other hand, the United States has no foolproof way to predict whether China, once it is much more powerful, will refrain from aggressive acts against the allies and the open order of East Asia that America is determined to defend.

WHAT TO DO?

Offensive Realism urges the United States to accept the tragic character of politics in anarchy, to make worst-case assumptions about future Chinese behavior, and respond by containing Chinese growth as vigorously as possible. In other words, exercise extreme power-intolerance and follow Athens' power-maximizing path to security, even if it leads to war. Defensive Realism warns us about the avoidable folly of this approach. Toleration of China's legitimate security needs, making room for China's prominent role in the region and the world, might provide a way to avoid the catastrophe that mutual power-intolerance is likely to produce. So in the end, the power-intolerance dilemma is at the heart of the decisions American leaders must make: is power intolerance a mechanism for survival, or a path to the tragedy of hegemonic war?

NOTES

1. Kenneth N. Waltz, *Theory of International Politics* (New York: McGraw-Hill, 1979).

2. John Herz, *Political Realism and Political Idealism* (Chicago: University of Chicago Press, 1959); Robert Jervis, "Cooperation under the Security Dilemma," *World Politics* 30 (January 1978).

3. Robert B. Strassler, ed., *The Landmark Thucydides* (New York: Free Press, 1996), 352.

4. Hans Morgenthau, *Politics Among Nations* (New York: Knopf, 1948).

5. Strassler, *Landmark Thucydides*, 114.

6. Ibid., 352-353.

7. John Mearsheimer, *The Tragedy of Great Power Politics* (New York: W. W. Norton, 2001).

8. Strassler, *Landmark Thucydides*, 354. Emphasis added.

9. Ibid., 372. Emphasis added

10. Ibid., 51.

11. Ibid., 43, emphasis added.

12. Ibid., 52-65.

13. Charles L..Glaser, "The Security Dilemma Revisited," *World Politics* (October, 1997): 171-201.

14. Strassler, *Landmark Thucydides*, 22-24.

15. Ibid., 26-27.

16. Ibid., 27.

17. Ibid., 28.

18. Ibid., 33.

19. Ibid., 65, emphasis added. Thucydides recounts a detailed Corinthian speech made during a conference of Peloponnesian League allies which draws a stark contrast between the inward looking, conservative Spartans and their Athenian rivals, who, the speaker claims dramatically, "were born into the world to take no rest themselves and to give none to others" (p. 40)

20. President James Monroe's Annual Message to Congress, December 2, 1823. Available at http://www.ourdocuments.gov.

21. The most detailed archival study of the War and Peace Studies memoranda has been conducted by Carlo Maria Santoro. See Carlo Maria Santoro, *Diffidence and Ambition: The Intellectual Sources of U.S. Foreign Policy* (Boulder: Westview Press, 1992), 75-82.

22. Scott A. Silverstone, "American Grand Strategy and the Future of Landpower in Historic Context," in eds. Isaiah Wilson III, Hugh Liebert, and Joseph DaSilva, *American Grand Strategy and the Future of U.S. Landpower* (Carlisle, PA: U.S. Army War College Press, 2014).

23. Excerpts from Pentagon's Plan: 'Prevent the Re-Emergence of a New Rival,' *New York Times* (March 8, 1992). Emphasis added.

24. Patrick Tyler, "Senior U.S. Officials Assail Lone-Superpower Policy," *New York Times* (March 11, 1992).

25. National Security Strategy of the United States of America, September 2002, pp. 1, 29-30. Emphasis added.

26. Tyler, "Senior U.S. Officials Assail Lone-Superpower Policy."

27. For China's public expression of its military posture and goals, see "China's Military Strategy," released by the State Council Information Office of the People's Republic of China in May 2015.

28. Charles Glaser, "Will China's Rise Lead to War? Why Realism Does Not Mean Pessimism," *Foreign Affairs* (March/April 2011). Mearsheimer the Offensive Realist says virtually the same thing in the 2014 version of *Tragedy of Great Power Politics*.

Means and Methods of Warfare

Towards an Objective Assessment for Selecting Military Targets–Beyond 'Enemy Thinking'?

Mirjam de Bruin[1]

"Philosophers and statesmen have long debated whether armed conflict within and between various organized communities constitutes an inevitable aspect of the human condition. Irrespective of one's viewpoint concerning this discussion, all would agree that armed conflicts are always costly in both human life and property. As such, throughout history, efforts have been made to limit these costs."[2]

INTRODUCTION

On February 22, 2015, the New York Times (NYT) reported that the Turkish Army sent troops into Syria "to recover the remains of a major historical figure and to evacuate the guards at his besieged tomb [..]."[3] The article goes on to explain that the tomb concerned is that of Suleyman Shah, grandfather of the founder of the Ottoman Empire, and that the Turkish government had received warning over the previous days of imminent clashes involving Islamic State, with the tomb 'possibly becoming a target.'[4] When referring to the success of the Turkish operation, the removal of the tomb, the NYT quotes the Syrian government in calling the 'Islamic extremists' "Turkey's puppets."[5]

Without further discussing the matter of sovereignty here and whether countries are allowed to mount military operations on each other's soil without permission beforehand; this recent example not only portrays how the media and parties themselves label parties or groups in armed conflict, 'puppets', 'extremists', it also reveals the current state of affairs in terms of warfare. Moreover, the issue raises questions as to what a permissible target actually is, e.g. would a tomb be a lawful target that can be attacked?

Over the past decades, violence has erupted in several regions particularly with a history of ethnic or religious antagonisms, often resulting in armed conflict. A view of the opponent as the 'enemy' with all its consequences and connotations seems inescapable in such a context. Striving for the submission of one's adversary in wartime seems contradictory to granting them protection or rights. Nonetheless this is what the law of armed conflict or international humanitarian law requires of all parties to a conflict. As will be discussed below, international humanitarian law has its foundations in the principles of humanity and military necessity. In practice this means that under the law of armed conflict, parties to a conflict ought to weigh and balance 'humanity' and 'military necessity' in designing their military operations or actions.

Therefore, this article takes the law of armed conflict as its point of study, as it is applicable in a context of 'us versus them' thinking, divisions, and 'difference-with-others.' By looking at the foundations of international humanitarian law, it explores how this branch of law challenges 'enemy thinking' in the context of warfare, where it seems inescapable. The paper will then briefly zoom in on the selection of military targets, i.e. those permitted to be attacked under the laws of war. As information about one's adversary may be one-sided or biased, this puts armies or armed groups in a most fragile objective position in interpreting an object as a military objective, factoring in 'humanity' and 'military necessity'. For the third part, the field of intelligence studies will be drawn from to look at situations that could occur from a tendency to think in terms of 'us versus them'. The article will argue how awareness of one's own tendencies could be looked at when orchestrating military operations against an adversary, while adhering to the laws of war.

INTERNATIONAL HUMANITARIAN LAW
AMIDST OF 'US VERSUS THEM'

International Humanitarian Law: Introduction to its Fundamental Principles

Often, international humanitarian law (hereafter: IHL)—according to some previously known as the law of armed conflict (LOAC)[6] —is viewed as a 'realistic' branch of public international law.[7] Such a label can be said to be earned twofold, first of all, because IHL rests on two primary fundamental principles, the principles of humanity and military necessity that balance each other: "[..] for the representatives of states to negotiate rules of international humanitarian law, and even to be convinced that in doing so they–often, the military officers on the list of states' delegations–have taken realities into account to such a degree that there will be no basis for invoking 'military necessity' *in justification of a deviation of the rules.*"[8] In the law of armed conflict realm, the principle of 'humanity' captures the protection of those who do not or no longer participate in hostilities, and aims to alleviate all human suffering in armed conflict–that of victims of armed conflict *and* of those taking part. The principle of 'military necessity' assumes that armed force be regulated, as such that it is only applied in the sense necessary for the war effort, and to that extent only.[9] Several say that every rule of IHL is a compromise between these two principles, between 'humanity' and 'military necessity'.[10] In the words of Schmitt: "[..] IHL represents a carefully thought out balance between the principle of military necessity and humanity. Every one of its rules constitutes a dialectical compromise between those opposing forces."[11]

The second reason why IHL or the "jus in bello" can be said to be realistic is related to the fact that it accepts the status quo as a given. After all, one could factually say that armed conflicts are taking place and IHL works with that as a fact without assessing its legitimacy. Still, IHL aims to alleviate the suffering that is caused through the regulation of warfare, without taking up the task of preventing a conflict as a whole–which is left to another branch of public international law, the "jus ad bellum", the regulation of the use of force under the legal framework of the United Nations Charter.

Historically it may be mentioned that a first codification of the laws of war is the Lieber Code or "Instructions", prepared in 1863 by German-American professor in New York Francis Lieber during the American Civil War. President Lincoln promulgated the Code, and although only binding on the forces of the United States, it is said to reflect laws and customs of war from that period of time.[12] Moreover, it furthered and inspired later codifica-tions in this field of law, such as for example the Hague Convention on land warfare in 1899. Article 14 of the Lieber Code already refers to military necessity: "Military necessity, as understood by modern civilized nations, consists in the necessity of those measures which are indispensable for secur-ing the ends of the war, and which are lawful according to the modern law and usages of war."[13] A few years before the Lieber Code came into exis-tence, on June 24th 1859 a battle took place in Solferino between Austrian forces and a French-Sardinian troop alliance.[14] Swiss businessman Henry Dunant (1828–1910) traveled through the village after the battle had taken place and witnessed the horrific effects: tens of thousands of wounded or dead left on the battlefield. "Oh. The agony and suffering during those days, the twenty- fifth, the twenty-sixth and the twenty-seventh of June!" he writes in his book 'A memory of Solferino'.[15] Each officer or soldier had to be helped, irrespective of the side they were on: "I could mention any number of isolated acts and incidents to prove the high character of the French Army and the courage of its officers and men, but mention must also be made of the humanity of simple troopers."[16] In order to help the wounded and collect the dead, he called in the help of women in the village of Solferino–a clear call for 'humanity'. It would mean the end of his business trip, and the beginning of what is now known as the Red Cross and Red Crescent Movement, consisting of the International Committee of the Red Cross (ICRC), International Federation of Red Cross and Red Crescent Societies, and 190 National Societies.

Other Fundamental Principles of IHL Derived from 'Humanity' and 'Military Necessity'

With the principle of humanity referring to the alleviation of suffering and the protection of those not or no longer participating in hostilities, and the principle of military necessity referring to permitting military considerations, the principle of distinction can be distilled from these two. The principle of distinction legally stands for the obligation of the parties to the conflict to distinguish between those who do and those who do not or no longer take part in the hostilities. Selecting those who fight from those who do not fight, such as civilians, requires parties to make a distinction between those two groups. Under this principle, combatants may be directly attacked, and civilians may not, as is nowadays codified in Articles 48, 51 (2), and 52 (2) of Additional Protocol I to the Geneva Conventions of 1949. Named as one of the "cardinal principles" of international humanitarian law by the International Court of Justice in the Nuclear Weapons Advisory Opinion[17] of 1996, the distinction between combatants and civilians was already set forth in the 1868 St. Petersburg Declaration, which read that "the only legitimate object which States should endeavor to accomplish during war is to weaken the military forces of the enemy."[18] The obligation to make a distinction between civilians or combatants logically includes a distinction between military objectives on the one hand and civilian objects on the other. Additionally, it is important to note that the weighing of 'humanity' and 'military necessity' relates to other core principles of IHL, i.e. the proportionality principle, the limitation of means and methods of warfare, and the prohibition of superfluous injury and unnecessary suffering.[19] For example, the prohibition of superfluous injury and unnecessary suffering shows how IHL attempts to alleviate the suffering of *all* of those in an armed conflict: civilians, but also combatants. It namely prohibits means and methods of warfare that cause physical impairment to an extent that is not justified by military necessity.[20]

There is an 'us versus them' way of thinking in times of armed conflict especially, meaning that opposing parties view each other as 'the enemy'. A difference-with-others, divisions and antagonisms all come together in the application of international humanitarian law, weighing two of its fundamental principles, aimed at 'limiting costs of warfare'. 'Enemy thinking' seems inescapable in situations where one or more states are opposing each other, or one or more parties opposing a government or each other, either party striving for the submission of the other. As Michael Walzer noted in his book *Just and Unjust Wars*: "[..] They can try to kill me, and I can try to kill them. But it is wrong to [..] shoot them down when they are trying to surrender. These judgments are clear enough, I think, and they suggest that war is still, somehow, a rule-governed activity, a world of permissions and prohibitions–a moral world, therefore, in the midst of hell."[21] IHL makes a 'counter-division' within the division that is inextricably correlated to warfare, i.e. that its rules require (1) a distinction to be made between those who do not or no longer take part in hostilities and combatants, hence not labeling *everyone* as to 'belong' to the other group or as 'the enemy', and (2) the prohibition of unnecessary suffering and superfluous injury, which requires limits to the means and methods of warfare on the basis of humanity and military necessity. The former requirement portrays how the distinction principle demands of parties to spare those who do not or no longer fight, despite seeing them as '(part of) the enemy'. The latter portrays how IHL grants protection–even to the 'enemy.' It will be discussed below how this poses challenges, as 'enemy thinking' may indeed seem inescapable in this context. This is most visible in the selection of a military objective that may lawfully be attacked.

MILITARY OBJECTIVES UNDER INTERNATIONAL HUMANITARIAN LAW

Defining a military objective

As could be concluded from the previous section, due to the obligation to make a distinction[22] between civilians or combatants on the one hand and therefore a distinction between military objectives and civilian objects on the other, parties to a conflict are obliged under IHL to direct operations against military objectives only.[23] What defines a military objective is stated in Article 52 (2) of Additional Protocol I to the Geneva Conventions: "Attacks shall be limited strictly to military objectives. For so far as objects are concerned, military objectives are limited to those objects which by their nature, location, purpose or use make an effective contribution to military action and whose total or partial destruction or neutralization, in the circumstances ruling at the time, offers a definite advantage." Both in Article 52 (1) of Additional Protocol I and the Customary Law Study of the ICRC, rule 9 is included, and states that "civilian objects are all objects which are not military objectives."[24] According to Oeter, the definitional boundary of what defines a civilian object and what a military objective "remains a critical problem," and according to him the general definition of 'military objective' has been one of the most heavily debated issues when concluding the Additional Protocol in 1977.[25] Oeter explains this by what is called the 'restrictive nature' of the definition.[26] When studying the elements of the definition of 'military objective', one is provided with a look at the kind of military objective that would be targetable under IHL, under which principles and whether there are exceptions.

First of all, the elements of the definition to determine what kind of an object may be a military objective; 'their nature, location, purpose or use' should be taken into account, which is arguably interlinked with the question if it 'makes an effective contribution to military action'. For example, "[l]ocation is a specific criterion by which an object gains military significance through its relationship with other places or objects," according to Jachec-Neale.[27] Although there is no exhaustive list of military objectives that may lawfully be attacked, Oeter does describe a set of what could be called classic or traditional examples, including e.g. armed forces; military aircraft and warships; buildings and objects for combat service support; and commercial objectives which make an effective contribution to military action–according to him: transport facilities, industrial plants.[28] It is argued that without such a list, the advantage is that practical implementation is more flexible, and a wide margin of appreciation of an object's targetability is mentioned as a disadvantage.[29] Hence, "[e]xact reconnaissance and the procurement of precise information by military intelligence services become key factors of lawful warfare."[30]

Secondly, in the application of the definition, the principles return. It can be argued that an attack on a military objective ought to be militarily necessary in the sense that it 'offers a definite advantage,' as the Article of the Protocol prescribes. 'Humanity' can be related here to the principle of proportionality, meaning the collateral damage–to civilians or civilian objects–cannot be excessive. Most important for the context of this article is the element that reads 'in the circumstances ruling at the time.' As was stated above, military intelligence is needed to determine whether an object makes 'by its nature, location, use or purpose' 'an effective contribution to military action' according to the Article in the Additional Protocol. Without a list of possible military objectives, an interpretation of what can be seen as a lawful target under IHL is required. In the 'us versus them' way of thinking that is inherent to armed conflict, this could produce one-sided or biased outcomes, since it may be unclear which circumstances may be *ruling* at the time of the assessment of an object for targeting decisions to be made.

Lastly, with room for interpretation in the definition, exceptions to classic examples of military objectives are not unthinkable, especially in contemporary conflicts: what if an object serves both military and civilians? Either way, in case of doubt a commander is required to treat the object as a civilian object.[31] Still, there are issues open to multiple interpretations.

The Responsibility of a 'Reasonable Military Commander'

Jachec-Neale points out that there are two features to the information which is to be considered in weighing a military objective and its 'anticipated military advantage': it is about information that is available at the time, and she states that the information must be timely and reliable.[32] However, above it was argued that there is room for interpretation of the definition, and "[i]t is unclear how much information is required to make an informed determination, as well as whether the information sought can be selective."[33] One could therefore argue that there is in fact a wide margin of appreciation of a certain object, which could lead to the conclusion that it is a lawful military objective, particularly if the available information is seen or interpreted in a certain way. The decision to select a military objective and target it is in the hands of the commander who is in charge of an operation, upon advise of a military legal advisor. It thus leads up to their assessment and decision whether an object qualifies as an objective that can be lawfully attacked, i.e. if it constitutes a military objective.[34]

Often, the case of the North Atlantic Treaty Organization (NATO) bombing campaign in the former Yugoslavia in 1999 is looked at in this realm, as it brings issues of proportionality to the front. In a report by the Committee Established to Review the NATO Bombing Campaign Against the Federal Republic of Yugoslavia prepared for the Office of the Prosecutor of the International Criminal Tribunal for the Former Yugoslavia (ICTY), the term "reasonable military commander" is brought forward.[35] When discussing issues of proportionality in attacking practice of the NATO, the Committee coins the term, but does not define it as such.[36] This is subject of interesting research by Broude, who applies behavioral psychology to this context in an innovative manner.[37] Thought-provokingly, Broude looks at the so-called framing effects that impact decision-makers' preferences. He applies this to the case of a military commander who decides upon military objectives, and how the information is phrased in a way that it influences his or her decision-making. This article, however, looks at how the previous stage, namely the analysis of information / intelligence, can occur under the influence of a certain settled mindset or bias, caused by 'enemy thinking,' also ultimately impacting a decision. This will be discussed in the next section.

In sum, the definition of a military objective comes from Additional Protocol I to the Geneva Conventions. It nevertheless does not define the elements of such a definition. This leaves room for interpretation, and the military commander has to decide based on the available information that is ruling at the time.

INTELLIGENCE AS SOURCE FOR SELECTION
OF A MILITARY OBJECTIVE

Intelligence failure

As was discussed earlier, a selection of military targets or objectives takes place 'in the circumstances ruling at the time,' based on information available to military commanders or decision-makers. With the room for interpretation there is in mind, it is worth looking into intelligence analysis for the purpose of military decisions regarding objectives that can be lawfully attacked.

The field of intelligence studies is a rather new discipline, which can easily be explained by the secrecy it operates under. Although a rather broad collection of memoirs of former agents have been published, and public investigations have taken place,[38] the field's literature and study is still developing in a mature, grounded direction–taking an interdisciplinary approach and adopting its own methodology. Some say, "[i]ntelligence analysis will never achieve the accuracy and predictability of a true science, because the information with which analysts must work is typically incomplete, ambiguous, and potentially deceptive."[39] Much of the focus of intelligence studies seems to be on failures, rather than successes of intelligence, as is also evidenced by media emphasis.[40] Although explanations for it may continue to be debated in a still to-be-fully-developed-discipline, one could argue that successes in this line of work are perhaps kept from the center of attention in order to 'pull the trick again'. Some say however, that failure "attracts more attention than success."[41]

Taking the literature in intelligence studies, the term 'intelligence failures' can be used in the context of selecting a military objective in times of armed conflict. Although the term is mostly coined in the relationship policy-maker-intelligence operative or at political level, the term may also be applied in the relationship between a military decision-maker and a military intelligence officer. After all, in both cases, intelligence is relied on to make these decisions, as was discussed earlier.

Examples of intelligence failure do not necessarily set a clear definition. For example, interviews with (former) field operatives in the United States[42] conducted by Johnston[43] show a lack of consensus about a definition, as answers vary greatly."[44] In this article, the definition Johnston developed in his work for the Central Intelligence Agency (CIA), will be used: "intelligence failure is systemic organizational surprise resulting from incorrect, missing, discarded, or inadequate hypotheses."[45] Intelligence failure can occur at all stages of what is called the 'intelligence cycle',[46] which refers to components such as 'planning and direction,' 'collection,' 'processing', 'analysis and production' and 'dissemination.'[47] One could narrow these categories down to 'collection', 'analysis' and 'dissemination', following Betts, who 'blames' decision-makers the most for intelligence failures, followed by analysts, whereas he rarely 'blames' collectors of intelligence.[48] For collectors of intelligence, it is important to decide what means they use and how they use it, namely "[..] the extent and type of collection have some bearing on success and failure."[49] Such decisions are nonetheless made by their management or through decision-maker's channels due to budget allocation. This could explain why Betts emphasizes the role of decision-makers; collectors of intelligence simply have to work within the boundaries they have been given. Under the heading of analysis, it can be stated that "strong pressure from policymakers can have a corrupting effect on the production of analysis."[50] If one is to read 'commander' or 'military decision-maker' where policymaker is mentioned, one could detect the similarly central role *any* consumer of intelligence has as a decision-maker, be it commander of a unit in times of armed conflict, or a policymaker at the level of strategic decisions. Like in any other context, (human) mistakes in analysis may occur. Specifically for the intelligence realm such mistakes may include: information overload;[51] which is closely linked to 'noise' posed by Wohlstetter[52] and 'groupthink posed by Janis.'[53] "Overload manifests itself also in the concept of 'noise', wherein the glut of extraneous material inhibits the analyst from focusing on the information that is central to the analytical problem or even prevents the analyst from spotting it."[54]

Lastly, the 'politicization of intelligence' is relevant for the role decision-makers play in intelligence, as they receive the information by means of dissemination. Such politicization can be described as "[..] the manipulation of evidence to fit preferred and pre-existing explanations, or the selection of evidence (involving omission as well as inclusion) to fit a known desired outcome [wanted by decision- makers[55]]."[56]

In conclusion, mistakes can be made at several levels, where management and decision-makers play a substantial role in each category. Intelligence failure does not have a set definition, yet explanations and examples thereof are multiple. Next, a brief case study will be offered.

THE CASE OF PEARL HARBOR

Pearl Harbor was under surprise attack by Japan on December 7th 1941, killing thousands and damaging important vessels to the U.S. Fleet.[57] Tensions between the U.S. and Japan had been ongoing many years before, starting at the Philippines, related to resource disputes.[58] The intelligence community had failed dramatically in not predicting Pearl Harbor would be attacked. The situation in Pearl Harbor has become so important for future generations that it is still used as a case study, used by the Kent School analyst trainers for example.[59]

Over the years, several researchers looked at the case in detail, including as Irving L. Janis, who examined "symptoms of groupthink that contributed to the wishful thinking displayed by the group of naval commanders in Hawaii during the weeks preceding the Japanese attack [whose] illusion of invulnerability seems to have been reinforced by [..] military decision-makers [..]."[60] Although some say collection lacunae also occurred,[61] the failure of intelligence on 'Pearl' mainly seems to have occurred at the level of analysis and dissemination. In relation to analysis, it ought to be mentioned that the warning analysts received only days prior to the attack, did predict *something* would happen. Japanese diplomats had begun to burn papers, presumably with codes on it.[62] Nonetheless, the location of an attack remained unknown until it actually happened.

At the dissemination level, Janis implies that naval officers were so certain of their own beliefs and interpretations that they did not (double) check information on the Japanese with the Washington command.[63] Due to this attitude, the context of the information never reached the appropriate highest level. Admiral Kimmel–the man in charge of the Pacific Fleet at the time of 'Pearl'–even argued that "[..] the warnings from Washington failed to correct the reasonable inferences he and his staff had drawn from the limited information available to them."[64] At the same time, Wohlstetter praises the capabilities of the Captain and Admirals involved in the Pearl Harbor situation, and she states: "The fact of surprise at Pearl Harbor has never been persuasively explained by accusing participants, individually or in groups, of conspiracy or negligence or stupidity. What these examples illustrate is rather the very human tendency to pay attention to the signals that support current expectations about enemy behavior."[65] In short, what this case study teaches us is that Pearl Harbor may have been predicted, had the signs and warnings been checked correctly–without a sense of invulnerability and with counterbalance–and had it been reported as such to the highest command.

INTELLIGENCE FAILURES' AWARENESS WHEN DECIDING UPON MILITARY OBJECTIVES

According to Herman, "[..] there is the obvious point that intelligence cannot be expected to be always right"[66] which may seem evident, but is in fact very relevant in the 'prediction' setting in which intelligence operatives work. "People interpret data through images, historical analogies, personal experiences and other hypotheses. There is a cognitive rigidity about the way they fit information into these patterns. They see what they expect to see; they come to conclusions too early and stick with them for too long. 'Groupthink'–in intelligence's relationship with its users, and within the intelligence community itself–reinforces these effects."[67] Such a view of expecting things, or 'knowing' what the opposing party does, could ultimately lead to intelligence failure, as was evidenced in the lack of a warning of the Japanese attack on Pearl Harbor.

With the room for interpretation as regards the definition of a military objective, and the reliance on intelligence as 'key factor' to determine a lawful attack, intelligence failure in such a situation can have impactful implications. After all, in the case of an object that has a 'dual-use', both civilian and military, groupthink could produce a one-sided or biased result, e.g. on an object that should have been regarded as civilian object, but was viewed as military objective. Ultimately, this could hurt the civilian population, which can be said to be the prime subject of protection under IHL. It is not said or argued here that mistakes cannot be made, nor that they would directly contribute to an unlawful attack. "A mind-set is neither good nor bad. It is unavoidable,"[68] states Heuer in his work "Psychology of Intelligence Analysis". Although allegedly unavoidable, Heuer and others do mention options for amelioration of 'groupthink' or other mistakes in intelligence collection and analysis. These include to avoid 'mirror imaging', meaning that an analyst may fill in gaps with his own perceptions or assumptions; 'thinking backwards'; and Devil's Advocate where one analyst deliberately takes the opposing or minority view to challenge the rest of the analyst team.[69] All methods share that they call for awareness of misconceptions and assuming too much, and: viewing the other as the 'enemy' to too large an extent.

In essence, one can make the claim that Janis' theory is still highly relevant today,[70] since some intelligence mistakes may continue to be made, particularly if those in the field are not (fully) aware of their 'us versus them' thinking. The inevitability of divisions does run deep in human nature, but with an awareness of one's 'groupthink' tendencies or mistakes in intelligence analyses, holding up a mirror to ourselves will reveal not one, not a double, but rather two images: the people we think we see and the people we see, i.e. two versions of the other. If one is aware of one's own (mis)conceptions, assumptions and difference-with-others towards the 'enemy' or opposing party, more objective assessments could be possible. This may impact decisions, and ultimately the targeting of military objectives. However, this does not answer the question if an act is unlawful, since one could argue that intelligence that may be viewed as one-sided or biased could still count as 'the available information' that was 'timely' and 'reliable.'

CONCLUSION

Over the past decades, violence has erupted in several regions particularly with a history of ethnic or religious antagonisms, often resulting in armed conflict. A prevalent view of the opponent as the 'enemy', 'us versus them' thinking, meaning that opposing parties view each other as the 'enemy', has its consequences in this context. Nonetheless is this the context in which international humanitarian law applies, and requires of all parties to a conflict to adhere to principles of humanity, military necessity and distinction.

The division that is inextricably correlated to warfare is 'counter-divided' by IHL, as it requires that a distinction is made between civilians and combatants, which is contrary to an 'us versus them' way of thinking: it prevents seeing the 'enemy' as a whole group, and obliges to distinguish within an opposing group. Additionally, IHL prohibits unnecessary suffering and superfluous injury. Based on the principles of humanity and military necessity, this results in limits to the means and methods of warfare in order to alleviate the suffering caused by warfare for *all*. Hence, IHL grants protection–even to the 'enemy.'

It was discussed above how 'enemy thinking' poses challenges in this context and is most visible in the selection of a military objective. Without a definition of (the elements of) 'military objective', or a list of possible military objectives, interpretation is left to the military decision-makers in the field who have to decide which objects can be targeted once labeled as an military objective. The 'enemy' way of thinking inherently to armed conflict could produce one-sided or biased outcomes, and it may be unclear which circumstances are ruling at the time of the assessment of an object. With the interpretation room that the definition of 'military objective' offers, and the reliance on intelligence as 'key factor' to determine a lawful attack, as Oeter indicates, intelligence failure in such a situation can have impactful ramifications. Due to intelligence failures and analysis mistakes in particular, circumstances may be interpreted differently than what they are because of a tendency in 'enemy thinking'. 'Groupthink' as example of an intelligence failure developed by Janis, could produce a 'biased' result, e.g. on an object that should have been regarded as civilian object, but was viewed as military objective. In sum, this article brings forward an awareness of 'enemy thinking'. If one is aware of one's own (mis)conceptions, assumptions, and difference-with-others, more objective assessments could be possible. This would benefit decisions, and therefore impact targeting processes.

BIBLIOGRAPHY

Arsu, Sebnem. "Turkish Military Evacuates Soldiers Guarding Tomb in Syria," *New York Times*, Feb. 22, 2015, http://www.nytimes.com/2015/02/23/world/middleeast/turky-syria-tomb-isis.html?_r=0.

Betts, Richard K. "Analysis, War, and Decision: Why Intelligence Failures Are Inevitable." In *Intelligence and National Security–The Secret World of Spies An Anthology*, ed. Loch K. Johnson and James J. Wirtz. New York: Oxford University Press, 2008.

Broude, Tomer. "In search of the "Reasonable Military Commander": Behavioral Framing Effects and Target Selection under International Humanitarian Law", accessed March 30, 2015. http://law.huji.ac.il/upload/5_TomeBroude_p.pdf.

Committee Established to Review the NATO Bombing Campaign Against the Federal Republic of Yugoslavia, "Final Report to the Prosecutor". http://www.icty.org/sid/10052.

Dunant, Henri. *A Memory of Solferino*. Geneva: International Committee of the Red Cross, American Red Cross, 1986.

Federation of American Scientists, FAS. "The Intelligence Cycle". Accessed March 30, 2015. http://www.fas.org/irp/cia/product/facttell/intcycle.htm

Gill, Peter and Mark Phythian. *Intelligence in an Insecure World*. Cambridge: Polity Press, 2006.Henckaerts, Jean-Marie, and Louise Doswald-Beck, *Customary International Humanitarian Law Volume I*. New York: Cambridge University Press, 2005.

Edited by Hensel, Howard M. *The Law of Armed Conflict–Constraints on the Contemporary Use of Military Force*. Berlington: Ashgate Published, 2005.

Herman, Michael. *Intelligence Power in Peace and War*. Cambridge: Cambridge University Press, 2010.

Heuer, Jr., Richards J. *Psychology of Intelligence Analysis*. Center for the Study of Intelligence, Central Intelligence Agency: 1999. https://www.cia.gov/library/center-for-the-study-of-intelligence/csi-publications/books-and-monographs/psychology-of-intelligence-analysis/PsychofIntelNew.pdf.

Heuer, Jr., Richards J. and Randolph H. Pherson, *Structured Analytic Techniques for Intelligence Analysis*. Washington: CQ Press, 2011.

International Court of Justice, "Legality of the Threat or Use of Nuclear Weapons", Advisory Opinion, July 8, 1996, I. C.J. Reports 1996, p. 226.

"Treaties, States Parties and Commentaries". *ICRC.org*. Accessed March 25, 2015, https://www.icrc.org/ihl/INTRO/110?OpenDocument.

Jachec-Neale, Agnieszka. *The Concept of Military Objectives in International Law and Targeting Practice*. New York: Routlegde, 2015.

Janis, Irving.L. *Victims of Groupthink–A Psychological Study of Foreign-Policy Decisions and Fiascoes*. Boston: Houghton Mifflin Company, 1972.

Johnson, Loch K. "The 9/11 Attacks and Iraqi WMD Failures." In *Intelligence and National Security–The Secret World of Spies An Anthology*, ed. Loch K. Johnson and James J. Wirtz, 497–505. New York: Oxford University Press, 2008.

Johnston, Rob. *Analytic Culture in the U.S. Intelligence Community*. Washington: Center for the Study of Intelligence, Central Intelligence Agency, 2005. https://www.cia.gov/library/center-for-the-study-of-intelligence/csi-publications/books-and-monographs/analytic-culture-in-the-u-s-intelligence-community/analytic_culture_report.pdf.

Joshi, Shashank . "Charlie Hebdo: a French intelligence failure?" *BBC*, Jan. 10, 2015, http://www.bbc.com/news/world-europe-30760656.

Kahn, David. "The Intelligence Failure of Pearl Harbor," *Foreign Affairs* (Winter 1991/1992), http://www.foreignaffairs.com/articles/47442/david-kahn/the-intelligence-failure-of-pearl-harbor.

Kalshoven, Frits, and Liesbeth Zegveld. *Constraints on the Waging of War–An Introduction to International Humanitarian Law*. New York: Cambridge University Press, International Committee of the Red Cross, 2011.

Lavoyer, Jean-Philippe. "Refugees and internally displaced persons: international humanitarian law and the role of the ICRC." *International Review of the Red Cross*, no.305, (1995), https://www.icrc.org/eng/resources/documents/article/other/57jmf3.htm.

Oeter, Stefan. "Methods and Means of Combat." In *The Handbook of International Humanitarian Law*, ed. Dieter Fleck, 166–187. New York: Oxford University Press, 2013.

Pieters, Boukje and Arjen Vermeer. *Inleiding Humanitair Oorlogsrecht.* The Hague: T.M.C. Asser Press, The Netherlands Red Cross, 2011.

Schmitt, Michael N. "Military Necessity and Humanity in International Humanitarian Law: Preserving the Delicate Balance", *Virginia Journal of International Law* 50, no.4, (2010): 795–839.

United States Senate Select Committee on Intelligence. "Report on the US Intelligence Community's Prewar Intelligence Assessments on Iraq." July 7, 2004, http://nsarchive.gwu.edu/ NSAEBB/NSAEBB254/doc12.pdf.

Walzer, Michael. *Just and Unjust Wars–A Moral Argument with Historic Illustrations.* New York: Basic Books, 2006.

Wohlstetter, Roberta. *Pearl Harbor: Warning and Decision.* Cambridge:Stanford University Press, 1962.

World War II History Info. Accessed March 30, 2015. http://worldwar2history.info/Pearl-Harbor/.

NOTES

1. The views portrayed in this article are those of the author alone, and in a personal capacity. The views are in no way binding upon the author's employer. De Bruin wishes to thank Ms. Lenneke Sprik, MA, LLM and Mr. Frédéric Casier, LLM in a personal capacity for their feedback; Ms Nádine Youhat is also thanked for her support at the early stages of this article.

2. ed. Howard M. Hensel, *The Law of Armed Conflict–Constraints on the Contemporary Use of Military Force* (Berlington: Ashgate Published, 2005), 39.

3. Sebnem Arsu, "Turkish Military Evacuates Soldiers Guarding Tomb in Syria," *New York Times*, Feb. 22, 2015, http://www.nytimes.com/2015/02/23/world/middleeast/turky-syria-tomb-isis.html?_r=0.

4. Ibid.

5. Ibidem.

6. As Michael N. Schmitt points out in: "Military Necessity and Humanity in International Humanitarian Law: Preserving the Delicate Balance", *Virginia Journal of International Law* 50, no.4, (2010): 806: "In the first half of the twentieth century, it [IHL] was known as the "law of war." The 1949 Geneva Conventions prompted a change to the " law of armed conflict", reflecting those instruments' use of the term "armed conflict" to emphasize that application of their humanitarian prescriptions did not depend on either a declaration of war or recognition by the parties of a state of war. More recently, this body of law has become known as "international humanitarian law", in great part through the efforts of the International Committee of the Red Cross (ICRC)." Both terms will be used here interchangeably, aimed at referring to the same: the law applicable in armed conflict. In this paper no explicit reference will be made to the different legal qualifications of armed conflicts, being 'international armed conflict' and 'non-international armed conflict.' The difference is nonetheless legally relevant for establishing which rules apply in each situation.

7. See for example, Jean-Philippe Lavoyer, "Refugees and internally displaced persons: international humanitarian law and the role of the ICRC," *International Review of the Red Cross*, no.305, (1995), https://www.icrc.org/eng/resources/documents/article/other/ 57jmf3.htm: "It is a 'realistic' law, which takes into account not only requirements stemming from the principle of *humanity*, upon which humanitarian law is based, but also considerations of *military necessity*."

8. Frits Kalshoven and Liesbeth Zegveld, *Constraints on the Waging of War–An Introduction to International Humanitarian Law* (New York: Cambridge University Press, International Committee of the Red Cross, 2011), 5. Emphasis added by author of this article.

9. An example that Kalshoven and Zegveld, ibid nt. 8, refer to is Article 12 of the First Geneva Convention (1949): "The Party to the conflict which is compelled to abandon wounded

or sick to the enemy shall, as far as military considerations permit, leave with them a part of its medical personnel and material to assist in their care."

10. Boukje Pieters and Arjen Vermeer, *Inleiding Humanitair Oorlogsrecht* (The Hague: T.M.C. Asser Press, The Netherlands Red Cross, 2011), 54.

11. Schmitt, ibid nt. 6, 798.

12. "Treaties, States Parties and Commentaries", *ICRC.org,* accessed March 25, 2015, https://www.icrc.org/ihl/INTRO/110?OpenDocument.

13. Ibid, Instructions for the Government of Armies of the United States in the Field (Lieber Code). 24 April 1863, Section I : Martial law — Military jurisdiction — Military necessity — Retaliation - Art. 14.

14. Henri Dunant, *A Memory of Solferino* (Geneva: International Committee of the Red Cross, American Red Cross, 1986), Introduction.

15. Dunant, ibid, 60.

16. Dunant, ibidem, 52.

17. International Court of Justice, *Legality of the Threat or Use of Nuclear Weapons*, Advisory Opinion, July 8, 1996, I. C.J. Reports 1996, p. 226, paras.74–87.

18. St. Petersburg Declaration, Preamble. The Customary Law Study of the ICRC cites it as such, Jean-Marie Henckaerts and Louise Doswald-Beck, *Customary International Humanitarian Law Volume I* (New York: Cambridge University Press, 2005), 3.

19. These will not be discussed in detail here.

20. Article 35(1) of Additional Protocol I to the Geneva Conventions reads: "In any armed conflict, the right of the Parties to the conflict to choose methods or means of warfare is not unlimited."Also, relevant in this respect is the second paragraph of that article: "It is prohibited to employ weapons, projectiles and material and methods of warfare of a nature to cause superfluous injury or unnecessary suffering." For example, certain weapons, such as dum dum bullets, cluster munitions, and chemical and biological weapons are prohibited.

21. Michael Walzer, *Just and Unjust Wars–A Moral Argument with Historic Illustrations* (New York: Basic Books, 2006), 35, 36. See how Walzer places this is in the context of contemporary context: "[..] the common features of contemporary combat: hatred for the enemy, impatience with all restraint, zeal for victory–these are the products of war itself whenever masses of men have to be mobilized for battle."

22. Article 48 of Additional Protocol I to the Geneva Conventions states: "In order to ensure respect for and protection of the civilian population and civilian objects, the Parties to the conflict shall at all times distinguish between the civilian population and combatants and between civilian objects and military objectives and accordingly shall direct their operations only against military objectives."

23. It stands out that in the jargon, the choice of words portrays quite clearly and strictly that something is a civilian *object*, whereas something military is an *objective*. A civilian object cannot be an objective in the international humanitarian law sense.

24. The Customary Law Study of the ICRC phrases it as such, Henckaerts and Doswald-Beck,, ibid nt.18, 32. The Customary Law Study is used for interpretation issues, as not every state is a Member State to Additional Protocol I to the Geneva Conventions. The United States for example, accepts the customary nature of the definition formulated in Article 52 (2) Additional Protocol I. This definition of military objectives was found to be customary by the Committee Established to Review the NATO Bombing Campaign Against the Federal Republic of Yugoslavia in its report, para.365.

25. Stefan Oeter, "Methods and Means of Combat," in *The Handbook of International Humanitarian Law*, ed. Dieter Fleck, (New York: Oxford University Press, 2013), 169.

26. Ibid.

27. Agnieszka Jachec-Neale, *The Concept of Military Objectives in International Law and Targeting Practice* (New York: Routlegde, 2015), 62. Jachec-Neale devoted an entire book to the concept of military objectives. This article by no means intends to describe as elaborately and eloquently what this fascinating study already affirms. Here, a mere focus is on one element, which is linked to the use of intelligence to select a military objective as a future target.

28. Oeter, ibid nt. 25, 171.

29. Oeter, ibid nt. 25, 170-1.

30. Ibid.

31. See Article 52 (3) of Additional Protocol I to the Geneva Conventions (1977).

32. Jachec-Neale, ibid nt. 27, 137.

33. See Jachec-Neale, ibid nt. 27, 141.

34. Obviously, in the context of an armed conflict where an armed group is party to the armed conflict, there may not be a set command structure such as in the armed forces of a State. Such a situation is worth linking to Oeter's findings: "[..] military actors without efficient means of reconnaissance and intelligence, [..], will encounter serious difficulties in meeting the requirements of Article 52 para.2 Additional Protocol I [the Article of 'military objective']", Oeter, ibid nt.25, 171.

35. Committee Established to Review the NATO Bombing Campaign Against the Federal Republic of Yugoslavia, "Final Report to the Prosecutor," http://www.icty.org/sid/10052, para.50.

36. Ibid, it reads: "[..] It may be necessary to resolve them on a case-by-case basis, and the answers may differ depending on the background and values of the decision maker. It is unlikely that a human rights lawyer and an experienced combat commander would assign the same relative values to military advantage and to injury to noncombatants. Further, it is unlikely that military commanders with different doctrinal backgrounds and differing degrees of combat experience or national military histories would always agree in close cases. It is suggested that the determination of relative values must be that of the "reasonable military commander"."

37. Tomer Broude, see his paper proposal from 2010: "In search of the "Reasonable Military Commander": Behavioral Framing Effects and Target Selection under International Humanitarian Law", accessed March 30, 2015, http://law.huji.ac.il/upload/5_TomeBroude_p.pdf.

38. See for example: United States Senate Select Committee on Intelligence (SSCI), Report on the U.S. Intelligence Community's Prewar Intelligence Assessments on Iraq, July 7, 2004.

39. Richards J. Heuer Jr and Randolph H. Pherson, *Structured Analytic Techniques for Intelligence Analysis* (Washington: CQ Press), 2011, 147. He goes on to say: "Intelligence analysis can, however, benefit from some of the lessons of science and adapt some of the elements of scientific reasoning."

40. Shashank Joshi, "Charlie Hebdo: a French intelligence failure?" BBC, Jan. 10, 2015, http://www.bbc.com/news/world-europe-30760656.

41. Michael Herman, *Intelligence Power in Peace and War* (Cambridge: Cambridge University Press, 2010), 224.

42. One could also look at other State practice. Yet in the context that this article was written in, American case studies seemed most relevant here.

43. Rob Johnston, *Analytic Culture in the U.S. Intelligence Community* (Washington: Center for the Study of Intelligence, Central Intelligence Agency, 2005), https://www.cia.gov/library/center-for-the-study-of-intelligence/csi-publications/books-and-monographs/analytic-culture-in-the-u-s-intelligence-community/analytic_culture_report.pdf.

44. Rob Johnston, ibid nt. 43, 6: Answers range from "I don't know;" and "There are no such things. There's only policy failure"; to: "You report what you know, and, if you don't know something, then it isn't error or failure. It's just missing information."

45. Rob Johnston, ibid nt. 43.

46. See Federation of American Scientists, FAS, "The Intelligence Cycle," accessed March 30, 2015, http://www.fas.org/irp/cia/product/facttell/intcycle.htm. This term is also used by Loch Johnson in his work on Iraq's possession of Weapons of Mass Destruction, "The 9/11 Attacks and Iraqi WMD Failures" in Loch K. Johnson and James J. Wirtz, *Intelligence and National Security–The Secret World of Spies An Anthology* (New York: Oxford University Press, 2008). That article is a reprint from Loch K. Johnson, "A Framework for Strengthening US Intelligence," *Yale Journal of International Affairs* I (2006).

47. Ibid.

48. Richard K. Betts, "Analysis, War, and Decision: Why Intelligence Failures Are Inevitable" in Loch K. Johnson and James J. Wirtz, *Intelligence and National Security–The Secret World of Spies An Anthology* (New York: Oxford University Press, 2008), 122.

49. Herman, ibid nt. 41, 231.

50. Peter Gill and Mark Phythian, *Intelligence in an Insecure World* (Cambridge: Polity Press, 2006), 118.

51. Gill and Phythian, ibid nt. 50, 85.

52. Gill and Phythian, ibid nt. 50, 85 refer to Roberta Wohlstetter, *Pearl Harbor: Warning and Decision* (Cambridge:Stanford University Press, 1962), 392, when stating: "Overload manifests itself also in the concept of 'noise', wherein the glut of extraneous material inhibits the analyst from focusing on the information that is central to the analytical problem or even prevents the analyst from spotting it."

53. Gill and Phythian, ibid nt. 50, 106 defines it as follows "[..] whereby analysts consciously or subconsciously accept dominant analyses or arguments and refrain from rocking the boat by registering their analytical dissent, for a variety of reasons". This term will be discussed further below, by means of the book of the inventor of 'groupthink', Irving.L. Janis, *Victims of Groupthink–A Psychological Study of Foreign-Policy Decisions and Fiascoes* (Boston: Houghton Mifflin Company, 1972).

54. Gill and Phythian, ibid nt. 50, 85.

55. Added by the author of this article.

56. Gill and Phythian, ibid nt. 50, 113.

57. World War II History Info, accessed March 30, 2015, http://worldwar2history.info/Pearl-Harbor/.

58. David. Kahn, "The Intelligence Failure of Pearl Harbor," *Foreign Affairs* (Winter 1991/1992), http://www.foreignaffairs.com/articles/47442/david-kahn/the-intelligence-failure-of-pearl-harbor.

59. See United States Senate Select Committee on Intelligence, Report on the US Intelligence Community's Prewar Intelligence Assessments on Iraq, July 7, 2004, 5, http://nsarchive.gwu.edu/NSAEBB/NSAEBB254/doc12.pdf.

60. Janis, see nt. 53, 75.

61. Wohlstetter, see nt. 52, 382: "Never before have we [the Americans] had so complete an intelligence picture of the enemy." Janis, see nt.53,77, disagrees with her by replying that "[..] MAGIC [decryption of Japanese code by Americans] was not enough" as it did show "[..] Japan was getting ready for massive military operations, but it did not inform the Americans exactly *where*." [emphasis added by author of this article].

62. Janis, see nt. 53, 79.

63. Janis, see nt. 53, 80.

64. Janis, see nt. 53, 83.

65. Wohlstetter, see nt. 52, 392.

66. Herman, ibid nt. 41, 226.

67. Ibid.

68. Richards J. Heuer Jr, *Psychology of Intelligence Analysis* (Center for the Study of Intelligence, Central Intelligence Agency: 1999), 66, https://www.cia.gov/library/center-for-the-study-of-intelligence/csi-publications/books-and-monographs/psychology-of-intelligence-analysis/PsychofIntelNew.pdf.

69. Ibid.

70. The author of this article takes the stance that the theories of both Janis and Wohlstetter are still highly relevant to present day, as mistakes of the same nature–as are described by these two theorists–continue to be made. The line of the Kent School is therewith followed.

II

Internal Divisions

From Slavery to Black Power

Racial Intolerance at West Point, 1778–2015

Ty Seidule

The United States Military Academy, like most American institutions, has a long history of intolerance. No chapter, no book could adequately describe a subject as large and multi-faceted as intolerance at an institution as old as West Point. Yet, even a cursory glance at episodes of intolerance in West Point's long history can help illuminate the subject. Racial intolerance pre-dates the founding of the Military Academy in 1802. This is no surprise. Slavery is America's original sin, going back to the earliest gatherings of Europeans in the New World. While "Life, Liberty, and the Pursuit of Happiness" provide a clarion call of tolerance in the Declaration of Independence, in practice, slavery gave the lie to soaring words.

The U.S. Constitution did not mention human bondage, yet it counted African American slaves as three-fifths of a human. For much of West Point's history, intolerance, especially racial intolerance, mirrored the American experience. Yet, cataloguing the practice of intolerance is impor-tant for an institution that needs clear thinking for its graduates, not self-congratulatory platitudes. While the prevalence of intolerance at West Point was and remains too high, the historical record shows clearly that when cadets and faculty act against intolerance, they can have a dramatic effect. In 1971, African American cadets demanded and achieved a dramatic increase in racial tolerance very quickly. While the Military Academy has had two centuries of intolerance, that does not preordain what will happen during its third century.

SLAVERY AT WEST POINT, 1778–1802

The story of racial intolerance at West Point begins before the United States Military Academy was founded in 1802. During the American Revolution, General George Washington called West Point the "key to the continent." He ordered his engineers to create a formidable defensive position to prevent the British from moving north from their perch in New York City and taking the Hudson Valley, thus cutting the New England colonies from the Mid-Atlantic and Southern States. [1]

Washington, one of the greatest military leaders in American history, occupies a special place at West Point. In 1783, he wrote a letter to Alexander Hamilton arguing for the creation of a military academy to prepare professionals for the rigors of combat leadership. [2] Today, West Point recognizes him throughout the campus. The mess hall, which hosts all 4,400 cadets for dinner on special occasions, is named after Washington. Outside its steps stands an impressive statue of Washington on horseback. As the cadets march through the barrack's sally ports and onto the plain during their dress parades, they pass Washington's statue and he seems to beckon them forward into battle.

Despite Washington's importance to the future United States Military Academy, there is only one painting of him at West Point. Jonathan Trumbull, an aide to Washington in 1776 and 1777, painted a portrait of the general with West Point in the background. Trumbull was studying in London in 1780 and painted the general from memory. Trumbull's painting was one of the first portraits of Washington seen in Europe and it was copied widely. Trumbull's Washington looks resplendent, wearing the uniform he picked for the Continental Army, blue and buff, the same blue that the U.S. Army wears to this day. Washington points toward West Point, while the American flag flutters high above Fort Putnam. Trumbull depicted the general with fortification plans in his hands, highlighting his genius as a strategist. With his sunburned face, Trumbull's Washington was no pampered politician or armchair general. He was the leader of the Continental Army on campaign, sharing hardship and danger with his soldiers. [3]

Yet, there is more to this picture. To Washington's left, his horse Nelson grazes contentedly. Holding the horse and looking at the general with admiration is Washington's enlisted aide, William Lee – a slave. The only painting of Washington at West Point includes an enslaved human being. Washington purchased Lee for 61 pounds, 15 shillings in 1768. In Washington's property book, he is identified as Mulatto Will, meaning that William Lee probably had a white father. Washington owned slaves for his entire life. At his death, the Washington estate listed as property 59 adults and 28 children. 83% of the adult male slaves were married to women who did not live at

Washington's Mansion House Farm. White slavemasters could and regularly did break families up by selling humans for profit. [4]

We know more about William Lee than about any other slave in the 18th century, because he accompanied Washington to every battle of the Revolutionary War. Lee was a "stout active man" and a superb horseman. Lee fixed Washington's hair each morning and slept outside his room every evening. We know that Lee carried Washington's telescope into battle. We know that Washington entrusted his slave with his most "precious papers." Washington freed Lee in his will and provided him with a yearly pension of thirty dollars for "his faithful services during the Revolutionary War." One veteran of the war called Lee the "faithful companion of his military years." [5]

Lee fought to create the country that enslaved him. The Continental Army veteran remained in bondage until Washington's death in 1799. After the general's death, veterans of Washington's campaigns would visit Mount Vernon to see Lee and reminisce about the war until his death in 1828. If Lee had been white, there would be towns and streets throughout the country named for him. Throughout the 19th century, Washington was seen as enlightened for freeing one slave upon his death. Yet throughout his life, Washington owned slaves and in one case went to great lengths to recover a runaway slave. In Philadelphia, he lied to make sure the slaves he brought there would not be freed under the laws of that state. [6]

SLAVERY AT WEST POINT, 1802–1861

William Lee was not the last slave at West Point. White officers had slaves at West Point until 1861, long after it was illegal in New York to own slaves. Scholar Walt Bachman has done groundbreaking work documenting the extent of slave owning among officers in the ante-bellum period. Few, if any, army officers mention that they owned slaves during this period. Because of the paucity of records, no history of West Point mentions slavery or any African Americans at West Point until black cadets arrived in the 1870s. Bachman, however, found an ingenious way to find black slaves and servants at West Point and throughout the army. He looked at tens of thousands of pay records in the National Archives. During the ante-bellum period, the army provided up to 30% extra pay for officers with servants. The Federal Government subsidized slavery for army officers even in states that had long since outlawed the practice. Therefore, every officer had a financial incentive to have slaves who were, of course, much cheaper than servants. [7]

Bachman's exhaustive research points to a large community of slaves and servants at West Point from 1802 through 1861. Sylvanus Thayer, called the father of the Military Academy, had several black servants, as did Dennis Hart Mahan and all of the senior professors. Or were they slaves? The pay stubs make it difficult to determine slave from servant. Each line from the pay stub lists the name of the servant, their skin color, and height. The description of skin color included, "light, mulatto, dark, and very dark."[8]

Officers often claimed the same servants and slaves on their pay records. Because each servant represented such a drastic pay increase, officers had an incentive to list as many as possible. Officers routinely "shared" servants, allowing multiple officers to reap the financial benefit without actually paying a servant or buying a slave. The practice was illegal but widely used by officers in the ante-bellum period. Although officers would gain a huge monetary advantage, there is no indication that African American servants saw additional money. Much of the domestic life of West Point depended on work done by black servants and slaves, yet no record remains of their lives.

THE CIVIL WAR AT WEST POINT, 1860–1865

Starting in the 1850s, West Point saw the same sectionalism based on slavery that affected the rest of the country. The Military Academy had always served as a national academy, helping to bridge sectional difference, but as the rest of the country moved toward conflict, so too did West Point. J.E.B. Stuart had praised the nationalizing influence of the Academy, saying that at West Point there was no north or south. By 1860, however, southern cadets had started an intimidation campaign against any cadets they thought supported Abraham Lincoln's Republican Party. As the 1860 campaign for president neared a vote, southern cadets held a straw poll, threatening anyone who supported Lincoln. Cadet Morris Schaff wrote later that it took more courage to vote for Lincoln at West Point than it did to face Pickett's Charge at Gettysburg. He would know. Schaff fought for the Union at that bloody battle.[9]

Intolerance at West Point extended not only to African Americans but also to those who championed their freedom. Few cadets openly advocated for the abolition of slavery prior to the Civil War. Avowed abolitionists were "cut" or "silenced," meaning that the rest of the corps of cadets would talk to them only if duty required. This practice was ordinarily directed at cadets whose behavior was considered ungentlemanly. The punishment was harsh indeed. In a place as isolated as West Point, with mountains to the north, south, and west, and the Hudson River to the east, there were few, if any, diversions other than the company of other cadets.

Many cadets silenced and hazed Emory Upton for his abolitionist beliefs. Upton had spent a year at Oberlin College in Ohio, the first college in the country to integrate. A cadet from South Carolina, Wade Hampton Gibbes, accused Upton of having sex with a black woman while at Oberlin. In the mid-19th century, accusing anyone publicly of having sex, much less with an

African American woman, was a grave affront. Gibbes would later resign from West Point, joining the Confederate Army and firing one of the first shots of the Civil War at Union forces inside Fort Sumter, South Carolina. Upton challenged the much larger Gibbes to a fight. As the cadets dueled with bayonets, the rest of the cadets eagerly cheered them on. Upton held his own, but would sport a five-inch scar from his ear to his lower jaw for the rest of his life. [10]

The U.S. Senate also saw West Point as a bastion of racial intolerance. In a number of speeches on the floor of the U.S. Senate, Republicans denounced the Military Academy in the most strident language. Senator Benjamin Wade from Ohio argued that "the evil tendencies" at West Point came from its support for slavery. Senator James H. Lane from Kansas decried West Point's "pernicious pro-slavery influence . . . in every department of the Government." If the Union were to perish, said Lane, the "epitaph will be 'died of West Point pro-slaveryism.'" [11] With more than a hundred cadets and graduates leaving West Point and the army to fight for the Confederacy, they had a point. The greatest leaders of the Confederacy were all West Point graduates, including President Jefferson Davis and almost all of the senior commanders. In the early years of the Civil War, the West Point graduates fighting against the United States, such as Robert E. Lee, James Longstreet, and Thomas "Stonewall" Jackson were more successful in the Eastern Theater than their hapless Union counterparts. The unsuccessful West Pointers fighting for the Union, such as George McClellan, Ambrose Burnside, and Joseph Hooker, added to the feeling that the best Academy graduates were on the Confederate side.

Cadets' and graduates' pro-slavery feelings, combined with defections to the Confederate Army, created the greatest crisis in the Military Academy's history. In 1861 and 1863, the Senate voted on bills to shutter West Point by stopping all appropriations. [12] While both bills failed, they rattled West Point's leaders, who feared for the Academy's continued existence. After 1863, superb West Point graduates such as Ulysses S. Grant, William T. Sherman, and Philip Sheridan led the Union to victory and changed the minds of many who had condemned West Point early in the war.

INTOLERANCE AT WEST POINT, 1865–1902

West Point basked in the afterglow of a tremendous victory led by Academy graduates. The U.S. Army struggled to translate victory over the South into economic and social gains by the recently freed African Americans. Nearly 200,000 black soldiers served in the U.S Army, with almost 40,000 dying for the Union cause. Few, however, served as officers. By 1869, only four segregated black regiments remained in the Regular Army: the 24th and 25th Infantry Regiments, and the 9th and 10th Cavalry Regiments who later became the famed Buffalo Soldiers. But the army did not allow any black Regular Army officers. Sending an African American to West Point would seed the army with black Regulars who would not only stay in the army for a career but might also lead white troops.

After the Civil War, Congressman Benjamin Butler from Massachusetts sought to appoint an African American to West Point. Butler served as a general in the Union army. While his competence as an army officer was low, his political skills were much stronger. Butler first used runaway slaves in the army, calling them "contrabands" of war. His embrace of black soldiers led to their later widespread use in the Union Army. As an officer, however, Butler had little regard for Academy graduates. In his memoirs he wrote, "The less of West Point a man has the more successful he will be." Butler argued that Ulysses S. Grant was successful, "because he was less like a West Point Man than any officer I ever knew." Butler found several young African American men to appoint, as did other members of Congress from 1870–1887. During this period, twenty-three black men received nominations to the Military Academy, eleven passed the nomination examination, but only three, Henry O. Flipper, John Alexander, and Charles Young graduated.[13]

West Point cadets and faculty subjected all African American cadets to virulent racism that featured both mental and physical abuse. The first two cadets, James W. Smith and Henry O. Flipper, took different approaches to the abuse. Some historians have blamed Smith, unfairly, for not accepting abuse quietly. Smith demanded equal treatment and protested to leaders inside and outside the Academy when he received abuse. He wrote a series of letters to newspapers detailing his treatment. President Grant changed the results of a court-martial for Smith, turning him back a year rather than accepting the verdict of expulsion. For demanding equal treatment, Captain George Andrew wrote that Smith was the "worst selection" for the first African American cadet, accusing him of being malicious, vindictive and untruthful.[14]

The criticisms of Smith smack of a double standard that historians of West Point have been too willing to accept. Some older histories of the Academy, like Stephen Ambrose's *Duty Honor Country*, seem to blame Smith for not being docile. As though a black cadet in the 19th century should not demand equal treatment. What were Smith's alternatives? One cadet dropped a full slop bucket (filled with human urine and feces) on his head.[15]

Nor were the faculty much better. Professor Peter Michie was the leader of the post-war West Point faculty. A decorated Civil War hero and a Republican, he nonetheless hated having African Americans at West Point, questioning if West Point was the right place to "solve the problem of social equality of the races."[16] Michie believed that black cadets at West Point contributed to ill-discipline and he approved of their silencing and ostracism. Michie wrote that black cadets "all displayed a marked deficiency in deductive reasoning."[17] He failed Smith in Natural and Experimental Philosophy (Physics) after a private examination for which Smith received no actual results and then Michie denied him a retest, both unusual practices at West Point at the time. Nor was Smith a marginal cadet. After his second year, he ranked fifteenth out of fifty-nine academically in his class. The evidence points to Michie railroading Smith out of West Point because of his race, and because Smith would not accept abuse. In a series of letters to the *New National Era and Citizen* after his expulsion, Smith detailed his severe mistreatment and mounted an effective defense of his academic performance.[18]

The seventh African American appointed and the fourth to enter, Henry O. Flipper, was the first to graduate. He tried his best to accept the institutional racism and abuse without complaint. Despite his ability to accept the insults and cruelty of cadets, Flipper remained completely isolated during his four years – "silenced" in West Point parlance – the target of a form of vigilantism by fellow cadets who felt he disgraced the Academy. No one spoke to the cadet outside the classroom or during official duties. As part of his silencing, Flipper ate alone, slept alone, and had no human-to-human contact for the majority of his four year experience. Yet in his memoirs, he tried to rationalize the cadets' malice, arguing that the majority would have liked to treat him as gentleman but that the "lowest classes," the "uncouth," held sway over the rest of the cadets. His memoirs are heartbreaking to read, as he tried desperately to make sense of his experience as the victim of unvarnished racism. He could not accept that the vast majority of West Point cadets and faculty hated him for no other reason than the color of his skin.[19]

Today, the Academy rightly recognizes Henry Flipper for his tremendous accomplishment as the first black graduate. Since the early 1970s, West Point has celebrated him in a host of ways: the annual Flipper Dinner and Award, the Flipper bust, and a small picture in the West Point Museum. Too often, however, the racism and abuse that makes his graduation such an incredible achievement are omitted from his story. Only by understanding the intolerance experienced by Flipper and Smith can we understand their courage.

Yet their treatment at West Point seems tame compared to the pressure experienced by Cadet Johnson Whittaker. Whittaker entered West Point in 1876 and roomed with Flipper for a year. When Flipper graduated, Whittaker remained the only black cadet, and the torture of emotional isolation wore on him. He wrote in a letter to Lieutenant Flipper, "Sadness creeps over me, for I am all alone." Whittaker attempted to emulate Flipper's approach of meeting abuse with silence. However, when a white classmate from Alabama hit him, Whittaker told the Academy's leadership of the assault, infuriating his fellow cadets. Again, the double standard of intolerance was the rule. White cadets would tolerate African American cadets' existence at West Point only when they accepted "their place".

Whittaker received a note warning him to stay awake at night because cadets had targeted him for retribution. On the morning of April 6, 1880, Whittaker missed morning reveille formation. The officer-in-charge Major Alexander Piper sent the cadet officer of the day George Burnett to see if Whittaker had overslept. Burnett found him gagged and trussed, like an animal, his ear and scalp cut by a straight razor, his bible burned. [20]

Racism so blinded West Point's leaders that they could not imagine that Whittaker's fellow cadets could plan and execute so horrific an assault. If white cadets could not hurt Whittaker, then perverse racial logic demanded that the only one who could have done this terrible deed was the black cadet himself. West Point's officers accused Whittaker of self-mutilation. They said he had bound and cut himself to garner sympathy. Defensive about external criticism, Academy leaders thought a black cadet attacked himself to aid the enemies of West Point.

Although the charges were ludicrous, the Superintendent John M. Scho-field ordered Whittaker court-martialed. The case was flimsy, resting on prejudice and wrongful assumptions. No inventory was taken of the room, which was cleaned before all the evidence was collected. The doctor botched the physical examination of Whittaker after the assault. The investigation was incomplete. Whittaker was nevertheless found guilty. Eventually, after an outcry in the national press, a presidential pardon cleared Whittaker. [21] He returned to the Military Academy briefly, but a faculty member failed him after a chemistry exam and he left the next day. The Whittaker case, the most publicized court martial between the end of the Civil War and World War I, showed the systemic and institutional racism at West Point.

Professor Michie and his colleagues at West Point saw a different victim in this case – the Academy's reputation, which Whittaker tried to slander. Many historians have concluded that Whittaker had bound and cut himself or that the evidence was unclear. Yet, Senator Daniel Voorhees, a Democrat from Indiana, had it right when he called for an outside investigation of West Point because of "brutality and barbarism" at the Academy. [22]

AFRICAN AMERICANS AT WEST POINT, 1890–1948

No African American graduated between 1890 and 1936 during the awful years of legal segregation and white terror called Jim Crow. At the end of Reconstruction in 1877, when the U.S. Army left the South, the gains made by freedman slowly eroded. Starting in 1890, the year after Charles Young left West Point, the last black graduate for 47 years, southern states began to amend their constitutions to limit the voting rights of African Americans.

Black participation in political life dropped to nearly zero as poll taxes, literacy tests, and other requirements first stripped African Americans of the vote and then from serving on juries or running for office. With no participation in politics, black schools and libraries, all segregated, became vastly underfunded. White terrorism served to enforce and expand the laws.

The election of 1912 saw almost no African American voters in the South, yet almost all white voters participated through grandfather clauses meant to include them and exclude black voters. Woodrow Wilson, the first Democrat elected president in fifteen years and the first southern-born president in fifty years, moved to segregate the federal work place. He appointed segregationist southerners and enforced Jim Crow laws throughout the government. In 1913, in a speech at Gettysburg for the 50th anniversary of that battle, Wilson removed all discussion of the purpose of the Civil War: to eliminate slavery. As the historian David Blight noted, the 1913 Gettysburg meeting, "was a Jim Crow reunion, and white supremacy might be said to have been the silent, invisible master of ceremonies."[23]

West Point and the Army reflected the commander-in-chief who demanded a completely segregated world, using law and terrorism to enforce it. Reading through the *Howitzer*, West Point's yearbook, is to see those terrible times in stark relief. The 100th Night Show was (and remains) a play written, directed, and acted by the graduating class of cadets celebrating and mocking their time at West Point. Performed with roughly 100 days left at the Academy, the play reflects both cadet experience and the wider world. The show always merits pictures and commentary in the *Howitzer*. Cadets painted in blackface and using racist language were prevalent for at least fifty years. While the worst examples occurred before World War II, even the class of 1953 featured cadets in blackface, despite the three African American cadets in that class. Intolerance is especially easy when a persecuted group is absent or present in vanishingly small numbers.[24]

No African American cadets graduated from West Point during Jim Crow, the period that included the worst examples of white terrorism in the United States since the Civil War. In 1932, Benjamin O. Davis, Jr. entered the Military Academy after two years of college at the University of Chicago. Davis' father was the only black Regular Army officer on active duty. At first, when Davis entered West Point, he found a few friendly faces willing to talk to him. One night, however, he heard a rap on his door and saw many cadets tromping to the latrines. There, the cadets asked what they should do about the African American cadet, though in far more racist language. Davis, realizing that they were discussing him, quickly stole back to his room. The cadets had decided to silence Davis. No one roomed with him. No one talked to him at meals. No one showed him even the slightest human decency. The silencing over the course of four years was emotional torture at the isolated West Point. Yet Davis refused to give in. As he later remarked in his autobiography, it would take more than silence to force him out. When he graduated, Davis hoped to become a pilot. The Army Air Corps refused his application despite Davis' high marks at West Point, because there were no segregated flying units for black pilots. Under no circumstances would the Army allow a black officer to command white troops or, especially, to command white officers.[25]

Davis was the fourth African American to graduate and the first in the 20th century. The next several African Americans had even worse experiences than Davis. Silencing continued. One white cadet said he was "advised to refrain from speaking to him (an African American cadet) and we were threatened with ostracism ourselves." Racism at West Point was institution-wide, not merely limited to a few rogue cadets. While silencing was bad, the graduates in the 1940s were subjected to more physical forms of punishment. Minton Francis, who graduated in 1944, later told a historian and his children that he was always the best-dressed cadet in uniform, maintaining a mirror polish on his shoes and wearing pants so heavily starched, they stood at attention by themselves. Francis, who roomed alone, would stand on his cot and ease himself into the pants to ensure he maintained the crease with no wrinkle. The other cadets knew he waited until the call out for formation to dress. As he put on his pants before one parade, he noticed that a cadet had defecated in his shoes. He could only dump the excrement out without enough time to thoroughly wash his shoes. When he lined up for formation, a cadet cruelly called out, "Why do Niggers stink?"[26]

The abuse heaped on Francis took many forms. White cadets routinely interrupted his study and sleep time in an attempt to hurt his academic standing. A lieutenant colonel named Samuels conducted thirty-minute interviews daily over two weeks to try to prove Francis unstable. Others accused him of taking money from the NAACP as a bribe to stay at West Point. Years later, Francis looked longingly at the isolation Benjamin Davis endured: "Although I have great empathy for Ben Davis's isolation, I am convinced that I would have thrived and prospered under such circumstances."

While cadets were the cruelest, the faculty maintained an unacceptable level of intolerance as well. None of the cadets in the 1930s and 1940s ever visited a faculty home while nearly all white cadets found invitations. About James Fowler, who graduated in 1941, one white cadet remarked: "Even we could distinguish between our treatment and that reserved for 'Mister Fowler'"[27] The commandant sent a letter to one black cadet, probably Fowler, telling him not to come to his house, despite the fact that his entire class was invited. Then the commandant told him not to go to the hop (dance) that followed the open house for fear of embarrassing himself.[28]

THE CIVIL RIGHTS ERA AT WEST POINT, 1948–1971

In July 1948, President Truman signed Executive Order 9981, which ordered the "the equality of treatment in the armed services without regard to race, color, religion or national origin." The president wanted the order implemented immediately, but the armed services, except for the Air Force, refused to act. The first Secretary of the Army, Kenneth Royal, a North Carolinian, refused to implement desegregation, and Truman fired him. The next Secretary of the Army, Gordon Gray, who was another North Carolinian, slow-rolled desegregation, doing just enough to keep his job. As a result, the Army did not desegregate its units until the high casualties suffered during the Korean War forced the army to act. However, the Korean War ended before the barracks at West Point desegregated. The three black cadets in the Class of 1953 roomed together in Company G2 for all four years, despite their protests. [29]

After the Supreme Court ruled in 1954 that separate was not equal in the famed court case, *Brown v. Board of Education*, West Point desegregated its barracks, but racism continued. No class had more than a few African Americans. The Class of 1951 called themselves the "Black Class," because they had four African Americans. [30] Campbell Johnson was a member of the Class of 1965. When he entered in the fall of 1961, he had the misfortune of joining M Company in the First Regiment of the Corps of Cadets. Company M1 had a group that called themselves the Alabama Klan. They conspired to run Campbell Johnson out of the Academy. Joseph Anderson was also a member of the Class of 1965. A star student, athlete, and a natural leader, the Academy gave Anderson prime leadership roles as a plebe (freshman). However, when the superintendent and commandant chose the leadership when Anderson was a senior, he was not selected for any position. Anderson and his classmates felt the decision was part of a pattern of institutional racism. [31]

In the nearly 100 years since the first African American cadet came to West Point in 1869, only sixty-eight black cadets had graduated. During the 1950s and 1960s, no more than twenty cadets attended West Point at any one time (all four classes included). At no time in the Academy's history before 1968 did the percentage of African Americans reach 1%. Most big changes at West Point come from outside pressure. The vast changes in Civil Rights throughout the country finally started to affect West Point. In 1968, the Assistant Secretary of Defense asked all the service academies to report minority, especially African American, enrollment. In response, the Military Academy created the Equal Admissions Program with one black officer called the Equal Opportunity Admissions Officer.

Even with such a small effort, the effect was immediate. The Class of 1971 had only four black graduates. The Class of 1973 admitted forty-four African Americans. By the fall of 1971, there were more black cadets then

there had been in the previous hundred years combined. The issues of tolerance that hurt black cadets – Confederate symbols, racist language, and segregation – now could be addressed, not by West Point's leadership, but by
African American cadets.

BLACK POWER AT WEST POINT, 1971–1976

The heyday of the 1968 and 1969 Black Power demonstrations went largely
unnoticed at West Point. The United States Military Academy, the nation's
premier college for educating future army officers, saw no protests in those
years. In fact, when African American cadets were interviewed in 1969, they
were asked if they expected to protest either educational or military policy.
They said no. Two years later, however, black cadets at West Point organized
quickly, protested dramatically, and forced a conservative institution to
change. At no other time in the Military Academy's 200-year history have
cadets protested so vehemently or so effectively. Ironically, the impetus for
change came from the very top. The commander-in-chief, President Richard
Nixon, sparked the cadets to action.[32]

On May 27, 1971, on a beautiful late spring day in New York's Hudson
Valley, President Nixon visited West Point. After a speech and a parade, the
superintendent, Major General William Knowlton took the president to Battle Monument, which lists the names of the Union Regular Army casualties
from the Civil War. Dedicated in 1897, the monument honors those who
"freed a race and welded a nation."[33] Just back from a trip to Alabama,
Nixon asked the MG Knowlton if he could see the Confederate monument.
Knowlton told Nixon that West Point memorialized only those who fought
for the nation, not against it. Nixon scoffed and told Knowlton that he needed
a Confederate monument.[34]

Back at the White House, Nixon sent a letter to Knowlton ordering the
superintendent to create a monument to "West Pointers who lost their lives
serving on the Southern side."[35] To track the Military Academy's progress,
Nixon assigned the project to the Deputy Assistant to the President for National Security Affairs, Brigadier General Alexander M. Haig, a 1947 graduate of West Point who had a reputation as the most political of generals, and
as a man who knew how to use power aggressively.[36]

Knowlton, presciently, worried about the "black cadets and graduates
reaction" to such a blatantly racist monument. West Point was trying to
increase the number of minority cadets to overcome the school's dismal
record of African American admissions. Knowlton knew that the negative
publicity surrounding a Confederate monument would devastate the Academy's recruitment efforts.[37] The year following the creation of the Equal
Admissions Office, West Point had admitted forty-four African American

cadets in 1969, far more than the four admitted in 1967.[38] By the fall of 1971, 119 black cadets were attending the Military Academy.[39]

Only eight were seniors. Their informal leader was Percy Squire, the highest-ranking black cadet in the corps. Squire, confident and charismatic, came from a strong African American community in Youngstown, Ohio. He understood the need to organize and he provided black cadets with a rallying point in 1971. Squire's good friend and fellow leader David Brice came from a starkly dissimilar background—a small rural town in South Carolina. When the local paper published an article about Brice coming to the Military Academy, members of the Ku Klux Klan burned a cross on his family's front lawn.[40]

On October 23, the superintendent asked Squire about the President's proposed Confederate monument. Knowlton described the reaction as "instant turmoil and chaos." Squire and Brice convened a meeting of all African American cadets on the night of October 25, 1971. Anger over the Confederate monument created seething resentment that bordered on mutiny. Some cadets argued for resigning en masse; others called for strikes, mass demonstrations, or sit-ins.[41]

After the meeting, the cadets wrote a "militant manifesto" (some called it the "black manifesto"). Modeled after the Attica prisoner demands written in September 1971, the cadets' manifesto listed the thirteen grievances against the Military Academy.[42] The manifesto was no mealy-mouthed protest, but a full-throated cry of Black Power demanding equality, respect, and understanding. Here was a mandate for tolerance. Squire wrote the manifesto, influenced by the book, *The Greening of America* by Charles A. Reich. The best-selling book trumpeted on its cover, "There is a revolution coming... the revolution of the new generation."[43] On November 8th, every African American cadet signed the manifesto and Squire delivered the six-page document to the superintendent the next day. As black Americans, they entered West Point with "awe and expectation." Their goal was to join the army and improve the quality of leadership for the "black military man." Instead, they found a "long train of abuses and usurpations" and "blatant racism."[44]

Nixon's Confederate monument proposal was the 13th and final grievance. The cadets charged that Nixon's proposal, more than any other, "seriously weakened the faith we had in the administration to understand our racial pride." They argued that Confederate graduates "abrogated their oath." The cadets noted that when they became officers, they might lead a military unit against a group of African American citizens like the radical Blackstone Nation. If, as officers, they left the army to accept positions of leadership among "rebelling blacks," they would be punished, even though "emotion, birth and racial ties" attracted them to this cause. If the cadets fought against the US Army, would they be immortalized with a monument? Or would they be court-martialed and thrown in the stockade?[45]

With the issuance of the manifesto, General Knowlton understood that he and the Academy were in crisis. If the monument process continued, he could face a mutiny. A savvy, intelligent officer who had previously served in diplomatic posts, he acted quickly. Knowlton wrote a letter to the Pentagon detailing the vociferous reaction of the African American cadets and arguing that a Confederate monument would hurt minority-recruiting efforts and cause a publicity nightmare.[46] On December 6, the Pentagon wrote back; the White House asked West Point to "terminate" the project. Nixon's Confederate Monument at West Point died. A hundred black cadets had defeated the President of the United States.[47]

The manifesto's effect did not stop with the demise of the Confederate monument initiative. West Point was a male enclave in 1971. The cadet hostess bused young women in from the surrounding area colleges for hops, as the cadets called dances, but few of those colleges had African American women. Those that did come were unimpressed. One black woman recalled her visit to West Point with horror, "We spent the whole evening square dancing!"[48]

The manifesto generated resources from the Academy to fix the problem. The superintendent provided a bus that Cadet David Brice sent to his uncle, a deacon in Hackensack, New Jersey who filled it with local women and sent it back to West Point. Brice and Squire arranged for use of the Superintendent's yacht. As the boat cruised the Hudson River to the melodious strains of soul music, black cadets danced – for one night, not that much different from college students anywhere in America. For many cadets, that was tolerance.[49]

Other grievances addressed broader issues. Memory plays an important role at West Point, home to many monuments recognizing America's military heroes. Yet no memorial on campus recognized the important role African Americans played in U.S. military history. The cadets demanded that the Academy recognize the 9th and 10th Cavalry, the Buffalo Soldiers, who had served at West Point for over forty years supporting the cadets' equestrian training. Soon, the old cavalry parade ground was named Buffalo Soldiers Field. More changes came: no more Confederate flags in rooms; no more playing of Dixie by the West Point band.[50]

Cadets searched for ways to use their newfound power to help all African Americans. Imbued with leadership and a sense of mission, they strove to show those outside the gates that they were not the instruments of white repression. At the time, sickle cell anemia, a scourge of the black community, had captured America's imagination. *The Washington Post* called it "the top attention getting disease of 1971."[51] Could the cadets create a fund-raising event to benefit all African Americans? Squire, Brice, and a black officer, Major Melvin Bowdin, brought the issue to the superintendent who by early 1972 needed no cajoling. The African American cadets were clearly in a position of power. With the full backing of the Academy, the benefit concert for sickle cell anemia research became a huge event.

"The Concert for the Blood" occurred on May 20, 1972, a week shy of a year from the date Nixon first mentioned the Confederate monument. Percy Squire sold the first ticket, priced at $5, to the newly promoted Lieutenant General Knowlton. African American cadets who earlier in 1971 had simply tried to have a soul-themed dance planned and executed an outdoor, Woodstock-like concert that featured soul royalty—Stevie Wonder and the Supremes.[52] The media predicted 50,000 people for the concert in West Point's football stadium. Heavy rain that day brought the total to fewer than 10,000.[53] Despite the wet conditions, "The Concert for the Blood" was a remarkable success. One white officer called the concert, "the first socially conscious event ever held at the Academy."[54] Later that month, cadets travelled to Washington, D.C. to visit Howard University, named after a former superintendent at West Point, and gave the Sickle Cell Anemia Research group the first proceeds check. By the final tally, the cadets had raised $41,000 for Sickle Cell Anemia research.[55]

The changes initiated by the cadets extended into 1972 as well. The Black History Week celebration became the highlight of the African American social calendar with speakers such as Representative Ron Dellums and Nation of Islam leader Louis Farrakhan. The reorganized and revitalized Race Relations/Equal Opportunity Office gave all cadets eight hours of mandatory race relations training, while faculty and staff trained for sixteen hours.[56]

Why were the African American cadets able to change the Military Academy's policies so quickly? Leadership made the difference. Percy Squire, David Brice, and the seniors in the class of 1972 knew how to lead. Well organized with a clear strategy, firm goals, and unity, the black cadets were a formidable force. Moreover, the cadets and officers did not want to discredit or disparage the Academy. They believed in the importance of having African American officers in the army's elite. They wanted to save the institution, not ruin it. West Point's African American cadets led the Academy toward a more tolerant position on race.

The cadets used President Nixon's politically cynical ploy at West Point to their advantage. African American cadets did not end racism or intolerance at West Point, but they did make a difference. Cadets in the 1976 yearbook paid for a two-page ad that featured two poems. The last line of the second poem provided an antidote to intolerance and an endorsement of diversity at the United States Military Academy:

"Once I was held in servitude, but now, it is my right to serve."[57]

GENDER INTOLERANCE AT WEST POINT, 1976–2015

Yet by 1980, that Black Power movement that filled African American cadets with racial pride began to wane. True, in that year an African American, Vincent Brooks, was appointed as First Captain, the highest-ranking cadet, but the racial pride so evident in the 1970s both at West Point and nationwide had dissipated. African American cadets had demanded and received more respect, but in 1976 a new group entered West Point – women. If African American men had spent a hundred years receiving poor treatment, now a new group competed with them and perhaps won the prize for intolerance from cadets and faculty. Racism remained at West Point, but intolerance towards women, through derogatory language, abuse, and disrespect, became endemic.

Women came to West Point in the fall of 1976 by Congressional mandate. An aggressive campaign to keep women out of the Military Academy by the Secretary of the Army, the Superintendent, and other army luminaries failed. General Matthew Ridgway, a World War II and Korean War hero, General William Westmoreland, the senior commander in Vietnam, and many former superintendents pronounced publically that the admittance of women would ruin West Point. The vast majority in Congress, however, felt differently. Republican Pierre S. "Pete" DuPont from Delaware argued that the exclusion of women from West Point was "ridiculous, wasteful, and anachronistic."[58]

When women arrived, they found overt and covert sexism from men who found their presence threatening to their own conceptions of masculinity and tradition. While leaders vowed publicly to support the decision, the early denunciation of women's inclusion left no doubt in the minds of male cadets of how their leaders really felt. The 119 women admitted in the class of 1980 found some male friendship, a few life partners, and plenty of abuse. While many men accepted women, a large number did not and those in leadership positions could and did make life hell for female cadets. One squad leader told women during their first weeks at West Point that, "I'm gonna' get everyone of you fuckin' bitches out of here!" Another man in a leadership role told his charges, "God did not make women to be soldiers." A cadet company commander held illegal formations every morning. The purpose of these hazing sessions, he told the women, was to eliminate every woman from his command. Women had condoms filled with water thrown at them. During physical training women were groped, and sexual slurs were commonplace both verbally and in graffiti all over campus.[59]

Intolerance in the form of sexism, sexual harassment, and sexual assault were prevalent for the first classes of women at West Point. Forty years later, are women treated better? The short answer is Yes. The early classes of women paved the way for greater acceptance, but problems – significant problems – remain. A survey taken in 2014 found that 91% of West Point women had suffered from sexism in the previous year, while 55% reported sexual harassment. West Point must work harder to change such awful statistics. While there has been movement from the Academy's leadership to address these significant issues, more must be done to document and discuss intolerance, and then fight it through education and leadership.[60]

Educating students on the prevalence of racial and gender intolerance provides one way to help combat this scourge. Strong leadership that promotes diversity can help as well. For more than two centuries, West Point has suffered from intolerance. The historical record can look bleak. Are there ways to combat intolerance? There are. When students and faculty acknowledge the systemic nature of intolerance, then they can demand fixes. In 2014, African American cadets petitioned the Academy's leadership to name the first barracks at West Point since 1971 after General Benjamin O. Davis, Jr., Class of 1936, the first black graduate in the 20th Century. With support from faculty and alumni, the cadets realized their goal. Davis Barracks is now a reality. African American cadets read about the example of Percy Squire and David Brice in 1971 and the effect they had in combating intolerance. Even within the military, people who demand equal treatment can receive it. Institutions, however, must do a better job of creating tolerant organizations and not rely on minority demands for equal rights.[61]

NOTES

1. John Bradley, "West Point and the Hudson Highlands in the American Revolution" (Unpublished, 1976). http://www.usma.edu/history/SitePages/West%20Point%20History.aspx

2. George Washington, "Sentiments on a Peace Establishment" letter to Alexander Hamilton, 2 May 1783.

3. The Trumball painting hangs in the Metropolitan Museum of Art, New York, NY. http://www.metmuseum.org/toah/works-of-art/24.109.88

4. Mary V. Thompson, "Slaves at Mount Vernon in 1799 and Slaves on the Mansion House Farm, 1799," March 31, 2015. Author's file. George Washington, Memorandum: List of Tithables and Taxable Property, *The Papers of George Washington, Colonial Series*, 8:104 and 104n.

5. Elkanah Watson, January 1785, in Jean B. Lee editor, *Experiencing Mount Vernon: Eyewitness Accounts, 1784-1865* (Charlottesville, VA: University of Virginia Press, 2006), 23. George Washington Parke Custis, *Recollections and Private Memoirs of Washington, By His Adopted Son, George Washington Parke Custis, With a Memoir of the Author, By His Daughter: and Illustrative and Explanatory Notes by Benson J. Lossing* (Bridgewater, VA: American Foundation Publications, 1999), 157 and 450-451. George Washington, Last Will and Testament, July 9, 1799, *The Writings of George Washington*, 37:276-277. *Accounts, 1784-1865* (Charlottesville, VA: University of Virginia Press, 2006), 23.

6. Gary B. Nash, "The African Americans' Revolution," in *Oxford Handbook of the American Revolution* (2012), ed. Edward G. Gray and Jane Kamensky, 250-70.

7. Walt Bachman, *Northern Slave Black Dakota: The Life and Times of Joseph Godfrey* (Bloomington, MN: Pond Dakota Press, 2013), 3-9.

8. Officer Pay Records, National Archives, courtesy of Walt Bachman. Author's files.

9. Morris Schaff, *The Spirit of Old West Point, 1858-1962* (New York: Houghton Mifflin, 1907), 149.

10. Ibid., 142-148. Upton also served as the Commandant of Cadets.

11. Congressional Globe, 37th Cong., 3d Sess., 325, 328.

12. James Tyrus Seidule, "'Treason is Treason:' Civil War Memory at West Point *Journal of Military History* (April 2012).

13. Benjamin Butler, *Butler's Book: Autobiography and Personal Reminiscences of Major-General Benj. F. Butler* (Boston: Thayer, 1892), 199.

14. Krewasky A. Salter I, *The Story of Black Military Officers, 1861-1948* (New York: Routledge, 2014), 28-30.

15. See Stephen Ambrose, *Duty Honor Country* (Baltimore: Johns Hopkins Press, 1966), 219-230.

16. Peter Michie, "Caste at West Point," *North American Review* 283 (June 1880): 604–13.

17. William S. Freely, *Grant: A Biography* (New York, 1981), 379.

18. Salter, *The Story of Black Military Officers*, 28-30.

19. Henry O. Flipper, *The Colored Cadet at West Point* (New York: Homer Lee & Co., 1878), 29-30.

20. John C. Marszalek, *Court-Martial: A Black Man in America* (New York: Charles Scribner and Sons, 1972), 47.

21. See Ambrose, *Duty Honor Country*, 222. Marszalek, *Court-Martial: A Black Man in America*, 241.

22. ibid., 75.

23. David W. Blight, *Race and Reunion: The Civil War in American Memory* (New York: Belknap, 2002), 9–11.

24. For examples see the 1915, 1923, and 1953 *Howitzers*.

25. Benjamin O. Davis, Jr., *American: An Autobiography* (New York: Penguin Press, 1992), 27-28.

26. Salter, *Black Military Officers*, 115. Interview with the Francis Family. Author's files.

27. Salter, *Black Military Officers*, 115. James Daniel Fowler, *Assembly Magazine* 46 (July 1988): 181-182.

28. Letter from Commandant of Cadets to unnamed cadet, 1938, Special Collections, USMA Library.

29. Interview with Cliff Worthy, West Point Center for Oral History, 2015.

30. Interview with Charles Ewing, Class of 1951. Author's files.

31. Interview with Joseph Anderson, Class of 1965. Author's files.

32. Martha Biondi, *The Black Revolution on Campus* (Berkeley: University of California Press, 2012), 1-12. Ibram H. Rogers, *The Black Campus Movement: Black Students and the Racial Reconstitution of Higher Education, 1965-1972* (New York: Palgrave MacMillan, 2012), 103-106. Student Survey, 1969, USMA Archives.

33. Charles Larned, "The Battle Monument at West Point," *Harper's Weekly*, 12 June, 1897, 594.

34. Memorandum to the Gifts Program Officer from Charles D. W. Canham, Assistant to the Superintendent, Subject: Memorial to West Pointers who served the Confederacy, 16 July, 1971. USMA Archives.

35. Letter from Richard Nixon to William Knowlton, 1 June, 1971. White House Central Files, Trip 20, West Point, New York, 5/28/1971, Box 56, Nixon Presidential Library.

36. Memorandum to the President dated 31 May, 1971 from Brigadier General Alexander Haig. Subject: Follow-up actions resulting from your visit to the US Military Academy, (Stamped "The President has seen"), National Security Files, Subject Files, President's West Point Speech, Box 377. Nixon Presidential Library.

37. Joel Morgovsky, "One Hundred Years of Blacks among the Grays," Office of Institutional Research, 1971. USMA Archives.

38. "Negro Cadets at the Academies Triple," *Washington Post*, 25 August 1967.

39. Fred S. Hoffman, "Record Total of Negroes Attend Service Schools," *Washington Post*, July 21, 1965. Four African American Cadets graduated with the class of 1965. West Point had a total of 29 African American cadets that year. James Ferron, "Blacks in The Long Gray Line," *New York Times*, 2 June 1991.

40. Interview with David Brice, July 27, 2012.

41. Memorandum to Deputy Chief of Staff for Personnel, Department of the Army from William Knowlton, Superintendent, United States Military Academy, Subject: Possible Civil War Memorial, 4 November, 1971. USMA Archives.

42. Joseph Ellis and Robert Moore, *School for Soldiers: West Point and the Profession of Arms* (New York: Oxford University Press, 1974), 216, 282. Richard C. U'Ren, *Ivory Fortress: A Psychiatrist Looks at West Point* (New York: Bobbs Merrill, 1974), 118.

43. Charles A. Reich, *The Greening of America* (New York: Random House, 1970).

44. "Manifesto." Author's files.

45. "Manifesto." Memorandum to Deputy Chief of Staff for Personnel, Department of the Army from William Knowlton, Superintendent, United States Military Academy, Subject: Possible Civil War Memorial, 4 November, 1971. USMA Special Collections. Interview with Peter Bailey, July 19, 2012; Interview with David Brice, July 27, 2012; Interview with Arthur Hester, July 24, 2012; Interview with Percy Squire, August 12, 2010.

46. Memorandum to Deputy Chief of Staff for Personnel, Department of the Army from William Knowlton, Superintendent, United States Military Academy, Subject: Possible Civil War Memorial, 4 November, 1971. USMA Archives.

47. Letter to Lieutenant General William Knowlton from Walter T. Kerwin, Jr., December 6, 1971. USMA Archives. Memorandum to President, Association of Graduates from William Knowlton, Superintendent, USMA, Subject: Possible Civil War Memorial, 6 January, 1972. USMA Archives.

48. Peter Bailey, "Getting It Together at 'The Point,'" *Ebony Magazine*, December 1971, Volume XXVII, No. 2, 136-144. Interview, David Brice, July 27, 2012. Ellis and Moore, *School for Soldiers*, 216.

49. Interview, David Brice, July 27, 2012.

50. "Progress Report on the 9th and 10th Cavalry Memorialization," March 31, 1972, Museum, Historical Memorialization Committee Files, West Point Museum.

51. "Group Sponsors Sickle Cell Anemia Tests," *Washington Post*, August 18, 1971.

52. *The Pointer View*, April 20, 1972. Interview, David Brice, July 27, 2012.

53. "Town Braces for Saturday, Crowds Could Reach 50,000," *New of the Highlands*, Highland Falls, New York, May 18, 1972. "Raindrops Dampened Saturday's Busy Schedule," *News of the Highland*, May 25, 1972, 1. George Basler, "Downpour Dampens USMA Festivities," *Newburgh Evening News*, May 20, 1972, 1.

54. U'Ren, *Ivory Fortress*, 119.

55. *Assembly: The Magazine of the West Point Association of Graduates*, October 1972.

56. Black Studies Report, September 1971. Superintendent's Annual Report, 1973. USMA Archives.

57. 1976 *Howitzer*, 406.

58. Lance Janda, "The Crucible of Duty: West Point, Women, and Social Change," in *West Point Two Centuries and Beyond*, ed. Lance Betros (Abilene: McWhiney Foundation Press, 2004), 348.

59. Janda, "The Crucible of Duty," 353-355.

60. Briefing to the Academic Board on Character Development, April 2015. Author's files.

61. Petition to the Superintendent on Barracks Naming, November 2014. Author's Files.

All Men Are Created Equal

Misogyny under Law[1]

Maritza Ryan

> The history of mankind is a history of repeated injuries and usurpation on the part of man toward woman, having in direct object the establishment of an absolute tyranny over her.—Declaration of Sentiments, 1848[2]

Throughout human history, to as many different degrees as there are points on the globe, women have been continually engaged in an ongoing struggle for their legal rights. Whether overt or subtle, some form of misogyny—originally defined as a hatred or fear of women and girls — is a common feature across national, religious and cultural borders in our world today. The American experience is no exception. This chapter takes a feminist jurisprudential look at the roots of gender discrimination that, still today, taints American law and society, and represents one of our greatest remaining challenges in fulfilling our national commitment to equal justice under law.

MISOGYNY: A UNIVERSALLY PRACTICED FORM OF INTOLERANCE

The word "misogyny" was first coined in the mid-17th century, and is rooted in the ancient Greek, combining *misos*, or "hatred," and *"gune,"* woman.[3] Today, the definition for misogyny encompasses not only a hatred of women, but also, as it is more commonly used today, a deeply entrenched prejudice against them.[4] Black's Law Dictionary, meanwhile, defines intolerance as inclusive of "bigotry and narrow-mindedness."[5] Indeed, misogyny may best be understood as a form of bigotry or prejudice against a group of people based on their feminine gender, or even on the characteristic of femininity itself. "The world's oldest prejudice," as misogyny has been characterized, is also its most persistent form of intolerance.[6] "Feminist Jurisprudence argues that we must look at the norms embedded in our legal system," and ask "how the law would be different if it took women's points of view and experiences into account."[7] Though there are many variations and streams of thought in Feminist Jurisprudence, all feminist legal theories do share a focus on the problem of patriarchy,[8] "a social system that is male-identified, male-controlled, male-centered,"[9] in which "power lies in men's hands and ...women are victimized as the permanent underclass."[10]

The obvious fruits of misogyny in law and culture are easily recognizable as the 24-hour news cycle confronts us with reports of girls attacked or killed for attempting to attend school;[11] terrorist groups who impose a severe and brutal form of *sharia* law in territories under their control, and take a particular interest in summarily executing educated and professional women;[12] the practice of selectively terminating female fetuses and even infanticide[13]; and the gang rape of suspected lesbians as a means of "curing" them of their homosexuality.[14] The list goes on, a practically daily reminder of the almost incomprehensible maltreatment and suffering visited upon more than half the world's population. As Americans, we look with horror upon these extreme examples of some men's inhumanity to women, and take small solace in the fact that these unspeakable acts seem to occur in distant lands, primarily in non-Western cultures, and under some other society's laws. Most fortunately for us, these forms of overt, extreme misogyny are not tolerated and practically nonexistent in the west today.

Nevertheless, as this chapter will explore, a more covert but still insidious variant survives within our own legal system and popular culture. Women have made undeniable gains, particularly in the attainment of higher education, where the percentage of women attending colleges and universities slightly exceeds that of men.[15] Every day, it seems, the doors of opportunity for women are opening, and the glass ceilings that once limited their progress and equal participation in employment and public life are shattering. Yet, they, and we as a society, still face numerous, gender-related challenges: among them, a persistent wage gap that cuts across practically every profession and workplace, from business to the law to Hollywood; the sexual assault of women in schools and in the workplace and high rates of domestic violence; and growing legal attacks on women's access to reproductive health services, are but a few examples. Misogyny, whether to a slight or great degree, "finds social expression in the concrete behavior" of a given society, in its "cultural institutions, in writings, in rituals, or in other observable activity," to include the law.[16] Misogyny is, therefore, the crucial ingredient of the gender discrimination which still disadvantages women and girls in our own country, and which cannot be corrected until its roots are first recognized and understood.

THE AMERICAN EXPERIENCE

"From the beginning of the United States experiment in democracy, we have faced the same enduring contradictions: the yearning for fulfillment of idealist claims to individual liberty and prosperity, versus the reality of inequalities of race and of gender..."[17]

The leaders of the American Revolution well understood that in calling for independence, they were summoning a radically new political ideal: one which championed individual rights and the rule of law, and upended the divine right of kings to rule over their unwilling and voiceless subjects. As is clear, if still uncomfortable for us to note today, women—along with slaves of African ancestry and Native Americans of both genders—were simply not included in this bright new paradigm of self-governance and personal liberty. In April, 1776, future-President John Adams wrote a letter to his wife, Abigail — with whom, by all reports, he shared a happy and egalitarian marriage – in which he replied rather lightheartedly to her request that, "in the new code of laws," he should "remember the ladies."[18] "As to your extraordinary code of laws, I cannot but laugh," he wrote, "Depend upon it, we know better than to repeal our masculine systems."[19] With tongue firmly in cheek, he argued that men were women's masters in name only, as "in practice, you know we are the subjects." Abigail's tone nevertheless remained serious in her next letter to her husband, revealing her frustration with his dismissive attitude:

I cannot say that I think you are very generous to the ladies; for, whilst you are proclaiming peace and good-will to men, emancipating all nations, you insist upon retaining an absolute power over wives.[20]

THE DOCTRINE OF COVERTURE

Despite Abigail Adams' warnings to her husband, "there is no evidence that the nation's founders gave much thought to women's rights during their deliberations over independence or the nation-building process."[21] The "masculine system" of "absolute power over wives" to which both remarkable correspondents referred was *coverture*, a feature of British common law that survived the American Revolution essentially unchanged, and became an integral part of American law.[22]

Sir William Blackstone, the renowned jurisprudentialist and expositor of British common law, included a section on the principle of coverture in his influential 1765 classic, *Commentaries on the Laws of England*, in which he noted:

> By marriage, the husband and wife are one person in law: that is, the very
> being or legal existence of the woman is suspended during the marriage, or at
> least is incorporated and consolidated into that of the husband; under whose
> wing, protection, and cover, she performs every thing; and is therefore called
> in our law-French a *feme-covert, foemina viro co-operta*; is said to be *covert-
> baron*, or under the protection and influence of her husband, her baron, or lord;
> and her condition during her marriage is called her coverture.[23]

Or, in other words, "upon marriage the husband and wife became one —
him."[24] The "condition" of a married woman as a *feme covert* essentially
rendered her legal status equivalent to that of a child[25] or servant, protected
under the "cover" provided by the outstretched "wing" of her husband. Indeed, under the doctrine of coverture, the legal relationship between a husband—as Blackstone refers to him, "her baron or lord"— and wife was
analogous to that of nobleman and feudal serf or slave.[26] Because "a woman's marriage resulted in the extinguishment of her independent legal identity, self-determined interests, and autonomous rights,"[27] she was legally
"disabled," from entering into business contracts, bringing a case to court for
resolution in her own name, or inheriting, acquiring or disposing of property.
Marital status dictated that not only did her personal and real property now
belong to her husband, but "her person" as well.[28] Consequently, a husband
could, in cases involving wifely "misbehavior," administer "moderate correction" through "domestic chastisement, in the same moderation that a man
is allowed to correct his servants or children."[29] Moreover, a married man's
legal right to have sexual relations with his wife could "be exercised forcibly
if necessary, because the legal definition of rape specifically excluded husbands and wives."[30]

FOR HER PROTECTION AND BENEFIT

> "These are the chief legal effects of marriage during the coverture; upon which
> we may observe, that even the disabilities which the wife lies under are for the
> most part intended for her protection and benefit: so great a favourite is the
> female sex of the laws of England."— Sir William Blackstone

It is also true that the law of coverture imposed certain duties and responsibilities on the husband in regards to his wife, as—having been stripped by
law of her ability keep her own earned income, convey property, apply for
credit, etc.— she was now "totally dependent" on him for her and her children's basic necessities of life.[31] The common law "Doctrine of Necessaries," therefore, provided that neglectful husbands could be held liable to third
parties for debts incurred by their wives in obtaining necessary food, cloth-
ing, shelter and medical services.[32] A husband also assumed liability for his
wife's pre-marital debts,[33] and, although title devolved to him upon mar-

riage, he could not sell any real property inherited through her without first obtaining her consent.[34] Under the doctrine of coverture, wives could be tried and punished for their own individual criminal offenses, but— as the dim-witted bureaucrat, Mr. Bumble, discovered in the Charles Dickens classic, *Oliver Twist*— a husband could also be held personally liable for his wife's crimes, even when she was the actual criminal mastermind of the pair:

> "That is no excuse," replied Mr. Brownlow. "You were present... and indeed are the more guilty of the two, in the eye of the law; for the law supposes that your wife acts under your direction."
>
> "If the law supposes that," said Mr. Bumble, squeezing his hat emphatical-ly in both hands, "the law is a ass- a idiot. If that's the eye of the law, the law is a bachelor; and the worst I wish the law is, that his eye may be opened by experience - by experience."

THE FEMININE SPHERE

As Mr. Bumble's protest illustrates, "the common-law doctrine of coverture was a legal fiction, a theory that was expanded to define the relationship of a married couple to the outside world, their families, their children, and them-selves."[35] Under the guise of protecting women by placing them under their husband's authority, coverture divested women of their individual agency and constrained their ability to engage in business and public life. Unmarried and widowed women, however, were also subject to the same prejudices as their married sisters, even though the "legal fiction" of coverture never ap-plied to them. In practice, all women in the United States — whether married or single, possessed of their individual legal identities or "civilly dead" – were routinely "denied significant legal, political, and economic rights" "solely on the basis of their sex."[36] A "long series of slow steps"— begin-ning with the adoption by the states of Married Women's Property Act stat-utes in the mid-1800s[37] — eventually overcame coverture's presumption of a marital "unity" founded on the wife's "civil death."[38] Motivated by econom-ic pressures rather than any concern for gender equality, these state reforms succeeded in removing at least some of a wife's "disabilities" under cover-ture by restoring her right to contract and convey property.[39]

Nonetheless, "the social and legal consequences of the doctrine of cover-ture" for all women, regardless of their marital status, were "pervasive" and persist even into the present day.[40] In applying the doctrine of coverture, the courts had, after all, classified women in the same category as "children and imbeciles, denying their capacity to think and act as responsible adults and enclosing them in the bonds of protective paternalism."[41] Coverture eventu-ally faded away as binding legal principle, but its underlying presumptions— which strictly limited women due to their purported biological and psychological characteristics as well as the rigid social, religious and cultural mores of the Victorian era— remained. Women were no longer considered akin to chattel owned by the men in their lives, but the Victorian "ideal of woman-hood" prevalent in late nineteenth century America nevertheless demanded that they occupy a "separate sphere" than men. "Men were responsible for all public activities and relationships outside the family," while "women were responsible for the household and the children and the private world of the home."[42] By the end of the 19th century, and indeed "[f]or at least six decades into the twentieth century," as borne out by case law, "there had been little progress in dismantling the near universal belief in separate spheres - the idea that women's place was in the home and men's in the public, commercial world."[43]

In an 1870 letter, the powerful Queen Victoria herself based her opposition to giving English women the vote on the "separate spheres" theory (which evidently did not apply to her):

> The Queen is most anxious to enlist everyone who can speak or write to join in checking this mad, wicked folly of 'Woman's Rights,' with all its attendant horrors, on which her poor feeble sex is bent, forgetting every sense of womanly feeling and propriety. Lady —ought to get a good whipping. It is a subject which makes the Queen so furious that she cannot contain herself. God created men and women different—then let them remain each in their own position... Woman would become the most hateful, heartless, and disgusting of human beings were she allowed to unsex herself; and where would be the protection which man was intended to give the weaker sex? [44]

THE ERA OF "ROMANTIC PATERNALISM"

The "separate spheres" doctrine, coverture's wily descendent, was regularly wielded by American courts to "protect" women and their tender virtue by excluding them from the workplace, the halls of higher education, the professions, and public life in general. Examples of cases in which such restrictions on women's rights were unsuccessfully challenged include:[45]

- *Bradwell v. Illinois* (1872): Excluding women from the practice of law.[46]
- *Minor v. Happersett* (1875): Denying women the right to vote.[47]
- *Muller v. Oregon* (1908): Upholding "protective legislation" prohibiting women from working more than 10 hours a day.[48]
- *Goesaert v. Cleary* (1948): Restricting women from serving as bartenders.[49]
- *Hoyt v. Florida* (1961): Exempting women from serving on juries.[50]

In each of these cases, the courts rested their decisions on ostensibly benevolent and unabashedly paternalist reasons. In *Bradwell*, the court reiterated the "wide difference in the respective spheres and destinies of man and woman," noting that "[t]he natural and proper timidity and delicacy which belongs to the female sex evidently unfits it for many of the occupations of civil life."[51] In *Minor*, the unanimous court — applying a cramped interpretation of the privileges and immunities clause of the 14th Amendment— held that voting was never "one of the absolute rights of citizenship." States alone, not the Constitution, had the power to confer the right to vote, and the states' decision to "commit that important trust to men alone"— and not to "[w]omen and children" — was not for the court to question.[52] *Muller* cited the need to protect women's frail constitutions— and their fertility— from the effects of overwork, thus making "the physical well-being of woman… an object of public interest and care in order to preserve the strength and vigor of the race."[53] The *Goesaert* court agreed with the state of Michigan that allowing women to bartend, as opposed to just waitressing, could "give rise to moral and social problems against which it may devise preventive measures," to include "drawing a sharp line between the sexes." The statute, interestingly, did not forbid the wives and daughters of male bartenders from bartending, presumably because their vulnerability and virtue could be protected by their husbands and fathers working nearby.[54] And in *Hoyt v. Florida*, a 1961 case, the court found that it was reasonable to "relieve" women of compulsory jury duty, since "woman is still regarded as center of home and family life" and service as a juror might not be "consistent with her own special responsibilities."[55] Evidently, the courtroom, in which jurors are frequently confronted with the uglier side of human nature in all its depravity and cruelty, was no place for the state's delicate and emotionally fragile women. Ironically, defendant Geraldine Hoyt was convicted by an all-male jury of beating her husband to death with a baseball bat.

FROM THE ERA TO A LITIGATION STRATEGY

"Equality of rights under the law shall not be denied or abridged by the United States or by any state on account of sex."—Equal Rights Amendment, Section 1.

In 1972, the passage of a national Equal Rights Amendment (ERA)—an initiative with tremendous bipartisan backing at the time—seemed a certainty. That same year, Congress had passed Title IX, which opened the doors of even the most elite "vocational, professional, and graduate schools and most undergraduate schools" to women across America, although it "fell short of a comprehensive attack on gender discrimination in education, leaving major gaps in admissions and athletics."[56] Also in 1972, Congress had extended the coverage of the Civil Rights Act of 1964 — which, as a result of an amendment proffered "in a spirit of satire and ironic cajolery," banned gender as well as racial discrimination in the workplace — to more employers and unions.[57] Emboldened supporters now promoted the ERA as providing a more comprehensive "constitutional basis from which changes in the American legal structure could be made,"[58] a far more preferable alternative to the piecemeal approach of fighting the "long, expensive, and difficult political and legal battles"[59] that would be needed to challenge each individual discriminatory state or federal law, one case at a time.

By the early 1980's, however, "opposition to the national amendment appeared insurmountable," and the law that had been cruising toward ratification was now suddenly adrift in deep waters. [60] The anti-ERA movement was led by a prominent conservative woman attorney, Phyllis Schlafly, who became the prime spokeswoman for the anti-ERA coalition. Effectively "repackag[ing] nineteenth-century gender constructs," Ms. Schlafly hauntingly "championed separate spheres, motherhood and republican domesticity" [61] and cast the ERA so proudly championed by feminists as "a threat to the nuclear family, and thus a threat to the stability of the society at large." [62] She and her grass-roots organization, STOP-ERA—the "STOP" standing for "Stop Taking Our Privileges"— claimed that its passage would not only strip women of special protections in state and federal law regarding alimony, child custody, and Social Security benefits, but also lead to unisex bathrooms, women in combat, and homosexual marriage. [63] In effect, according to Ms. Schlafly, ERA would "rip society apart," [64] bringing a frightening, genderless dystopia from the realms of science fiction into the reality of hometown America.

STOP-ERA and Ms. Schlafly, still a forceful voice in conservative politics today at the age of 90, were resoundingly successful, ensuring the ERA's narrow defeat in 1982, a mere three states short of ratification. The ERA failed to become part of the U.S. Constitution (although efforts to revive the amendment at the national level continue [65]), but the ERA did raise Americans' consciousness about the legal obstacles faced by women due to gender discrimination: despite the failure at the national level, about half the states have added ERA-like language to their own state constitutions. [66]

Meanwhile, during this same turbulent period of the 1970s, the battle over gender discrimination had already commenced in the courts. A coordinated legal campaign—devised and primarily executed by Columbia Law professor, and later director of the ACLU's Women's Rights Project, Ruth Bader Ginsburg – sought to use the 14th Amendment's Equal Protection clause[67] to dismantle discriminatory laws "by bringing a series of cases that were clear winners."[68] Professor Ginsburg's "aim was to strike down laws that relied on outdated stereotypes about men and women" which "unfairly penalized individuals—" men as well as women— "who did not conform to traditional gender roles."[69]

From 1972 to 1979, Ruth Bader Ginsburg argued six cases before the Supreme Court — winning five— and "filed petitions for review and amicus curiae briefs in many more."[70] The "clear winners" in those early days included:

- *Reed v. Reed* (1971): Striking down a state law—the first time ever on the basis of unconstitutional gender discrimination — that mandated a preference for male executors, thus denying a grieving mother the opportunity to serve as administrator of her son's estate.[71]
- *Frontiero v. Richardson* (1972): Invalidating military regulations under which married male service members were automatically granted higher housing allowances at the "with dependents" rate, while female service members were instead required to submit proof that their husbands were financially dependent upon them.[72]
- *Weinberger v. Weisenfeld* (1975): Voiding Social Security Administration regulations that denied widowers—such as the plaintiff, a sole parent whose wife had died during childbirth—the same survivor benefits afforded to widows.[73]
- *Craig v. Boren* (1976): Striking down an Oklahoma law that permitted women to purchase beer at age 18, while requiring that men be at least 21 years old.[74]

This string of influential wins eventually paved the way for further landmark decisions in the Supreme Court such as *United States v. Virginia* (1996), which struck down the male-only admissions policy then in effect at the Virginia Military Institute (VMI) as violative of the equal protection clause. The Court declined to hold that gender was a "suspect classification," such as race, color, or religion, which would have triggered the most rigorous level of judicial review, strict scrutiny. The Court nevertheless demanded of the state "an exceedingly persuasive justification" for disparate treatment based on gender: rationales dependent on "overbroad generalizations about the different talents, capacities, or preferences of males and females"[75] failed to meet this "heightened" legal test. Reflecting on the nation's "long and unfortunate history" of discrimination against women on the basis of gender, the Court, in a majority opinion written by Justice Ruth Bader Ginsburg, held that "categorization by sex may not be used to create or perpetuate the legal, social, and economic inferiority of women."[76]

THE LEGACY OF MISOGYNY

"Ensuring women's full participation in society requires that— in addition to law — change occurs on a number of fronts, including the transformation of political, social, and economic institutions that often (still) relegate women to second-class citizenship."[77]

The courts' more robust enforcement of the Equal Protection clause as to gender; Congressional action to prevent and address discrimination in the workplace and in education by statute; and the undeniable surge in the number of women in practically all areas of public life once closed to them, are all incontrovertible signs of legal and social progress. Over the last several decades, women have entered both institutions of higher learning and the work force at an unprecedented pace. "Between 1970 and 2005, the gender composition shifted to the extent that women now make up the majority—54 percent—of the 10.8 million young adults enrolled in college."[78] In 2009, for the first time in U.S. history, women made up half of all American workers, with "mothers [as] the primary breadwinners or co-breadwinners in nearly two-thirds of American families."[79] These numbers show that women have been *admitted* to the public sphere that was once forbidden to them; whether they have been *accepted* in the public sphere — as equal citizens— is subject to debate. Other, more sinister numbers may provide some evidence that a deeply entrenched, if much more covert, prejudice against women— one that undervalues their economic worth, their right to physical autonomy and personal safety, even their freedom of agency and capacity to make reasoned decisions— still lingers.

A PERSISTENT WAGE GAP

Though its exact numerical value is the subject of some controversy, statistics consistently show that the gender wage gap in America is real. The work that women do across the spectrum of the labor force— from pink to blue to white collar— appears to be "worth less" than that of men, regardless of their marital status or whether they have children.[80] The United States Census Bureau reported that in 2013, the female-to-male earnings ratio was 0.78 (i.e., women earned $0.78 for every dollar earned by men).[81] Despite their success in attaining higher levels of education than their male peers, "women are still paid less than men at every educational level and in every job category,"[82] a discrepancy that first appears at the start of young workers' careers, and yawns wider as they age.[83] A recent survey of full-time workers' salaries, all college graduates in their first year in the workforce, revealed that women were already being paid just 82% of what their similarly-situated male counterparts earned.[84] Nearly all of these young women just starting out in their working careers were still childless, yet it is true that American working women literally pay the price when they become mothers: among industrialized nations, the United States stands alone in failing to legally mandate paid maternity leave.[85] A woman's decision to take time off — if she is even permitted to do so — without pay in order to recover from childbirth or care for a new baby can thus deliver a range of "devastating long-term financial consequences," to include negatively impacting her career and lifetime earnings.[86] The cumulative effect of the gender wage gap over a lifetime of work is substantial, and contributes to "higher rates of economic insecurity" for women and their families, who as a result face a higher likelihood of living in poverty— 14.5 % of women as compared to 11.0 % of men.[87]

VIOLENCE AGAINST WOMEN

In the realm of physical security and personal safety, women also still face a significantly higher risk of sexual assault on college campuses and in the military, at their places of work and in and around their homes, than men do. Although a grossly underreported crime—more than 90% of sexual assault victims on college campuses do not report the assault[88] — the best estimate appears to be that one in five undergraduate women (for men, 1 in 66) has been the victim of attempted or completed sexual violence during their college years.[89] For female nonstudents, the rate of rape and sexual assault is higher— 1.2 times during the ages of 18-24,[90] and 1 in 5 over a lifetime — than for college students (for men, the rate is 1 in 71).[91] A reported 28% of women in the military experienced rape during their military service,[92] though some reports place the number even higher, at twice the civilian rate.[93] The Department of Justice estimates that 8% of rapes of women are committed in their places of work.[94]

Women also face unique dangers to their health and safety within the domestic sphere, in the confines of their own homes. Per the Justice Department's Bureau of Justice Statistics (BJS), intimate partner violence declined from about 2.1 million victimizations in 1993 to around 907,000 in 2010, a 64 percent drop over the 18-year data collection period.[95] Nevertheless, according to a 2011 survey, the lifetime prevalence of physical violence by an intimate partner was still an estimated 31.5% among women; in the 12 months before taking the survey, an estimated 4.0% of women experienced some form of physical violence by an intimate partner.[96] From 2003 to 2012, domestic violence, of which the majority of victims were female (76%), accounted for 21% of all violent crime in the United States.[97] Shockingly, the number of American women who were murdered by current or former male partners from 2001 to 2012 — 11,766 — was "nearly *double* the amount of casualties lost in war during that same period of time."[98]

REPRODUCTIVE RIGHTS

Fifty years ago, the Supreme Court ruled in *Griswold v. Connecticut*[99] that a state ban on the use of contraceptives by wives and husbands (later to include unmarried individuals in *Baird v. Eisentadt*[100]) violated a constitutional, fundamental right—the right to privacy. Forty-two years ago, the Court's much more controversial decision in *Roe v. Wade*[101] held that the right to privacy also encompassed a woman's decision whether to terminate a pregnancy. That landmark case, however, spawned a strong movement to reverse the right to abortion, and in the intervening decades, anti-abortion rights/ "pro-life" groups have deployed a highly effective combination of litigation and legislative strategies designed to significantly limit women's access to legal abortion services.

The Court's 1992 decision in *Pennsylvania v. Casey* upheld the "central holding" of *Roe v. Wade*, noting that "[t]he ability of women to participate equally in the economic and social life of the Nation has been facilitated by their ability to control their reproductive lives."[102] The majority opinion, authored by Justice Sandra Day O'Connor, noted that the common-law principle "that a woman had no legal existence separate from her husband, who was regarded as her head and representative in the social state" was today inconsistent with "our understanding of the family, the individual, or the Constitution."[103]

Casey, however, permitted states to "enact regulations to further the health and safety of a woman seeking an abortion," beginning at the moment of conception, so long as they were not an "undue burden."[104] State legislatures, rather than the courts, became the new battlegrounds for practically undermining if not legally overruling *Roe*: in 2013 alone, "22 states adopted 70 different restrictions on abortion;"[105] more than 100 bills regulating abortion services and access have already been introduced in the 2015 state legislative sessions.[106] Americans United for Life, an anti-abortion group, has described the wave of new laws as "life-affirming legislation designed to protect women from the harms inherent in abortion."[107]

The new restrictions have included requiring female patients to undergo an invasive sonogram by transvaginal probe at least 24 hours prior to the abortion procedure;[108] requiring them to view or read anti-abortion materials, to include claims that abortion may lead to suicide and mental illness in women;[109] lengthening mandatory "waiting periods" designed to give them an opportunity to fully consider their decisions to 72 hours, with no exceptions for victims of rape or incest;[110] and bans on all abortion procedures beginning at 20 weeks, and in some cases earlier, with limited or no exceptions for pregnancies involving rape or incest, severe fetal abnormalities, or to save the life or health of a woman.[111] A federal antiabortion bill introduced in January of 2015 would have banned abortions nation-wide past 20 weeks, but was withdrawn following controversy over a provision that would only have exempted rape victims if they could show a police report verifying the attack.[112]

In March of 2014, the Michigan legislature passed a law banning private insurers from including coverage of abortion services in their policies, to include cases involving rape or incest, or when critical health concerns force women to terminate their pregnancies. [113] In June of 2014, the Supreme Court ruled in *Burwell v. Hobby Lobby* that corporations controlled by religious families can refuse to include contraceptive coverage in the insurance policies of their female workers. [114] The owners of Hobby Lobby Stores, Inc., and the Conestoga Wood Specialties Corporation, had argued that several contraceptive methods function by "prevent[ing] a fertilized egg from implanting in the woman's uterus, and therefore were a type of abortion," to which they objected on religious grounds. [115] In a fierce dissent, Justice Ginsburg argued that the Court's ruling would "deny legions of women who do not hold their employers' beliefs access to contraceptive coverage," in effect eclipsing a woman's right to make her own "autonomous choice, informed by the physician she consults," as to whether and when to bear children and other intimate decisions regarding her own health. [116]

CONCLUSION

"We hold these truths to be self-evident:
that all men and women are created equal…"
—Declaration of Sentiments, 1848

From the earliest days of the founding of the United States as a nation, American law and culture reflected deeply ingrained prejudices against women — i.e., misogyny — that denied them full citizenship rights alongside men. Perhaps more so than other forms of bigotry, misogyny has always been a double-edged sword: under the doctrine of coverture, the same perceived biological differences that cast women in exalted roles as virtuous wives and mothers, also rendered them vulnerable and in need of "protection" from their own physical, emotional, and intellectual frailties. With the benign purpose of shielding women from harm, the law excluded them from higher education, denied them entry into the professions and many occupations, and essentially banished them from public life.

Today, coverture has all but "faded from the legal scene,"[117] although remnants of patronizing and even contemptuous attitudes towards women, the underlying foundation for the structure of coverture, remain. It is the misogynistic mind-set that condones paying women less for the same work, justifies sexual assault and domestic violence in the minds of its perpetrators, and seeks to remove from women the ability to make vitally important decisions as to their own lives, health, and well-being. Only a clear-eyed recognition of the continuing legacy of misogyny— which oddly coexists with tremendous progress in the fight against gender discrimination — will allow the eventual fulfillment of our nation's highest aspirations to equal justice under law for every American.

NOTES

1. BG Maritza Ryan, US Army, Retired, is a former Professor & Head, Department of Law, U.S. Military Academy (USMA) at West Point, New York. The views and opinions expressed in this article are those of the author alone, and do not necessarily state or reflect those of USMA, the Department of the Army, the Department of Defense, or the United States Government.

2. Elizabeth Cady Stanton, primary author, *Declaration of Sentiments and Resolutions*, Woman's Rights Convention, 19-20 July 1848, Seneca Falls, New York. See The Elizabeth Cady Stanton and Susan B. Anthony Papers Project, Rutgers University, at http://ecssba.rutgers.edu/docs/seneca.html

3. Webster's Dictionary.

4. Oxford's English Dictionary, 2002; William Safire discusses the slight but significant change in the meaning of "misogyny" in his "On Language" column entitled, "Irregular Warfare, Beyond the Unconventional," *The Times Magazine*, June 8, 2008.

5. Black's Law Dictionary.

6. Jack Holland. *Misogyny: The World's Oldest Prejudice.* Avalon Publishing Group, 2006.

7. Ann Juergens, "Feminist Jurisprudence: Why Law Must Consider Women's Perspectives"(1991). William Mitchell College of Law, *Faculty Scholarship*. Paper 111. http://open.wmitchell.edu/fasch/111

8. Jeanne L. Schroeder, "Feminism Historicized: Medieval Misogynist Stereotypes in Contemporary Feminist Jurisprudence," *Iowa Law Review,* 75 Iowa L. Rev. 1135 (July, 1990).

9. Mary Becker, "Patriarchy and Inequality: Towards a Substantive Feminism,*" The University of Chicago Legal Forum,* 1999 U. Chi. Legal F. 21 (1999), at p. 24.

10. Holland, at 275.

11. Robert Mackey, "Pakistani Activist, 15, Is Shot by Taliban," October 9, 2012, The New York Times, at http://thelede.blogs.nytimes.com/2012/10/09/pakistani-activist-14-shot-by-taliban/, regarding the assassination attempt on future Nobel Prize winner Malala Yousafzai.

12. Nick Cumming-Bruce, *"Women's Rights Activist Executed by ISIS in Iraq,"* September 25, 2014, at http://www.nytimes.com/2014/09/26/world/middleeast/womens-rights-activist-executed-by-islamic-state-in-iraq.html?_r=0

13. "Gendercide: The war on baby girls," *The Economist*, March 4, 2010, at http://www.economist.com/node/15606229

14. Jennifer Pfalz, "Rape as Cure for South African Lesbianism," The Guardian Liberty Voice, January 5, 2014 , http://guardianlv.com/2014/01/rape-as-cure-for-south-african-lesbianism/#i9ER3EPCjRfTFhoK.99

15. Mark Hugo Lopez & Ana Gonzalez-Barrera, "Women's college enrollment gains leave men behind," Pew Research Center, March 6, 2014, at http://www.pewresearch.org/fact-tank/2014/03/06/womens-college-enrollment-gains-leave-men-behind/

16. David D. Gilmore, *Misogyny: The Male Malady.* Penn Press, 2001, at p.9.

17. Carmen Vazquez, "Equality: Through the Looking Glass." *8 N.Y. City L. Rev. 463*, speech delivered at the Symposium in Honor of the Work of Professor Ruthann Robson at the City University of New York School of Law on November 5, 2004.

18. Susan Gluck Mezey, *Elusive Equality: Women's Rights, Public Policy, and the Law.* Lynne Rienner Publishers, Inc., 2003, at p. 5.

19. Letter from John Adams to Abigail Adams, April 14, 1776, Massachusetts Historical Society, Adams Family Papers, at http://www.masshist.org/digitaladams/archive/doc?id=L17760414ja&
bc=%2Fdigitaladams%2Farchive%2Fbrowse%2Fletters_1774_1777.php

20. Letter from Abigail Adams to John Adams, May 7, 1776, Massachusetts Historical Society, Adams Family Papers, at http://www.masshist.org/digitaladams/archive/doc?id=L17760507aa

21. Mezey, p. 6.

22. Mary Elizabeth Borja, "Functions of Womanhood: The Doctrine of Necessaries in Florida," *University of Miami Law Review,* 47 U. Miami L. Rev. 397, November, 1992, at 398.

23. William Blackstone. *Commentaries on the Laws of England, Vol, 1* (1765), p. 442.

24. Zaher, at 461.

25. Because of this diminished legal status, married women, even upon widowhood and return to *a femme seule* (single) status, could not take custody or guardianship even of their own children. *See* Joanna L. Grossman, "Book Review: *Separated Spouses - Man and Wife in America: A History, by Hendrik Hartog, 2000,*" *Stanford Law Review* 53 Stan. L. Rev. 1613 (July 2001), footnote 177.

26. Kristi Lowenthal, *Conservative Thought and the Equal Rights Amendment in Kansas,* (Ann Arbor: ProQuest LLC,, 2008), at p. 35.

27. Sabrina Balgamwalla, "Bride and Prejudice: How U.S. Immigration Law Discriminates Against Spousal Visa Holders" *29 Berkeley J. Gender L. & Just. 25 (*Winter, 2014), at 32.

28. Zaher, at 460.

29. Blackstone, p. 444. See also, Reva B. Segal, "'The Rule of Love': Wife Beating as Prerogative and Privacy"(1996). Yale Law School, *Faculty Scholarship Series*. Paper 1092, January 1, 1996.

30. Clare Cushman, Supreme Court Decisions and Women's Rights, 2nd Ed., CQ Press, 2011, p. 1.

31. Borja, at 397.

32. Borja, at 397.

33. Catherine Bishop,"When Your Money Is Not Your Own: Coverture and Married Women In Business in Colonial New South Wales," *Law and History Review*, Vol. 33, No. 1, 181-200, February 2015, at 181.

34. Borja, at 397. Upon widowhood, women also had the right of "dower," under which they could claim any property they brought into the marriage, as well as a life tenancy in one-third of the husband's estate. *Harvard Business School*, "Women, Enterprise & Society: Women and the Law," at http://www.library.hbs.edu/hc/wes/collections/women_law/

35. Zaher, at p. 463.

36. Zaher, at 459.

37. Borja, at 401.

38. Zaher, at 462.

39. Borja, at 401.

40. Zaher, at 462.

41. Barbara A. Brown et al., " The Equal Rights Amendment: A Constitutional Basis for Equal Rights for Women," *80 Yale L.J. 871, 872 (1971).*

42. Zaher, at 461.

43. Grossman, at 1662.

44. Lytton Strachey, *Queen Victoria*, Harcourt-Brace, 1921, at p. 409.

45. Grossman, at footnote 199.

46. *Bradwell v. Illinois*, 83 U.S. 130 (1873).

47. *Minor v. Happersett*, 88 U.S. 162 (1875).

48. *Muller v. Oregon*, 208 U.S. 412 (1908).

49. Goesaert v. Cleary, 335 U.S. 464 (1948).

50. *Hoyt v. Florida*, 368 U.S. 57 (1961).

51. *Bradwell v. Illinois*, 83 U.S. 130, 141 (1873).

52. *Minor v. Happersett*, 88 U.S. 162, 173 & 178 (1875).

53. *Muller v. Oregon*, 208 U.S. 412, 421 (1908).

54. *Goesaert v. Cleary*, 335 U.S. 464, 466 (1948).

55. *Hoyt v. Florida*, 368 U.S. 57, 62 (1961).

56. Mezey, p. 47-48.

57. Mezey, p. 70-71. Representative Howard Smith, D-VA, had hoped to derail passage of the entire bill by including women.

58. Borja, at 403.

59. Michelle Fadeley, Carol Heisler and Mary Kubasak, "Equal rights for women long overdue," *The Daily Herald*, November 21, 2014, at http://www.dailyherald.com/article/20141121/discuss/141129813/

60. Borja, at 403.

61. Kacey Calahane, "Women Against Women's Rights: Anti-Feminism, Reproductive Politics, and the Battle for the ERA," *Thinking Gender Papers,* Spring 2014,, UCLA Center for the Study of Women, p. 7, at http://www.escholarship.org/help_copyright.html#reuse .

62. Calahane, at pp. 1-2.

63. Clare Cushman, *Supreme Court Decisions and Women's Rights* (CQ Press, Washington D.C.: 2011), at p. 27.

64. Calahane, at p. 5.

65. David Crary, "90 years on, push for ERA ratification continues," Associated Press, August 10, 2014, http://www.news.yahoo.com/90-years-push-era-ratification-continues-162622942.html .

66. Amelia Templeton, "Is an Oregon Equal Rights Amendment Necessary?" *Oregon Public Broadcasting*, 25 September 2014, http://www.opb.org/news/article/is-an-oregon-equal-rights-amendment-necessary/

67. "[N]or shall any state… deny to any person within its jurisdiction the equal protection of the laws." 14th Amendment to the Constitution of the United States, Section 1 (1866).

68. Cushman, at p. 64.

69. Cushman, at 64.

70. Cushman, at 259.

71. Reed v . Reed , 404 U.S. 71 (1971).

72. *Frontiero v. Richardson*, 411 U.S. 677 (1973).

73. *Weinberger v. Wiesenfeld*, 420 US 636 (1975).

74. *Craig v. Boren*, 429 U.S. 190 (1976).

75. *United States v. Virginia*, 518 U.S. 515 (1996), at pp. 532-533.

76. *United States v. Virginia*, 518 U.S. 515 (1996), at pp. 531-534.

77. Mezey, at p. 3.

78. Mark Mather and Dia Adams, "The Crossover in Female-Male College Enrollment Rates," *Population Reference Bureau*, February 2007, at http://www.prb.org/Publications/Articles/2007/CrossoverinFemaleMaleCollegeEnrollmentRates.aspx

79. Maria Shriver, *The Shriver Report: A Woman's Nation Changes Everything*, October 2009, accessible at http://shriverreport.org/special-report/a-womans-nation-changes-everything/

80. An exception that may be surprising to some is the U.S. military, which generally pays every soldier, sailor, marine or airman according to his or her rank and years in service without regard to gender. See Defense Finance and Accounting Service, http://www.dfas.mil/militarymembers.html.

81. United States Census Bureau, Carmen DeNavas-Walt, Bernadette D. Proctor, "Income and Poverty in the United States," Report Number: P60-249, September 16, 2014).

82. Amanda Hess, " Women Make Less Than Men at Every Education Level," March 3, 2012, citing US Census Bureau Report, *Good Magazine*, http://magazine.good.is/articles/women-make-less-than-men-at-every-education-level

83. Pew Research Center, Social & Demographic Trends, "On Pay Gap, Millennial Women Near Parity – For Now," December 11,2013, at http://pewrsr.ch/1fiyqoJ

84. The American Association of University Women, "The Simple Truth about the Gender Pay Gap," Spring 2015, at http://www.aauw.org/research/the-simple-truth-about-the-gender-pay-gap/

85. Susanna Kim, "US Is Only Industrialized Nation Without Paid Maternity Leave," *ABC News*, May 6, 2015 at http://abcnews.go.com/Business/us-industrialized-nation-paid-maternity-leave/story?id=30852419. A notable exception is the U.S. military, which provides for 6 weeks of paid convalescent leave to the mother, and up to 10 days of paid paternity or parental leave.

See Department of Defense, Instruction Number 1327.06, "Leave and Liberty Policy and Procedures," June 16, 2009, Incorporating Change 2, effective August 13, 2013. Per a January 2016 Presidential Proclamation, all federal agencies will offer their employees 6 weeks of "advanced sick leave," while Congress considers a bill that specifically provides for paid "administrative" maternity or paternity leave along the lines of the Department of Defense policy. *Eric Yoder,* " Democrat bill would give federal workers paid parental leave," *The Washington Post,* January 26, 2015, at http://www.washingtonpost.com/blogs/federal-eye/wp/2015/01/26/paid-parental-leave-for-federal-workers-proposed/

86. Ibid.

87. National Women's Law Center, "Insecure and Unequal: Poverty and Income Among Women and Families," 2000-2012 (Sept. 2013), at http://www.nwlc.org/resource/insecure-un-equal-poverty-among-women-and-families-2000-2012

88. National Sexual Violence Resource Center, "Statistics About Sexual Violence," 2012, 2013, 2015, at http://m.nsvrc.org/sites/default/files/publications_nsvrc_factsheet_media-packet_statistics-about-sexual-violence_0.pdf

89. Centers for Disease Control and Prevention, "Sexual Violence: Facts at a Glance" (2012) at http://www.cdc.gov/violenceprevention/pdf/sv-datasheet-a.pdf .

90. Bureau of Justice Statistics, "Rape and Sexual Assault Among College-Age Females, 1995-2013," December 11, 2014, at http://www.bjs.gov/index.cfm?ty=pbdetail&iid-5176

91. National Sexual Violence Resource Center, "Statistics About Sexual Violence," 2012, 2013, 2015, at http://m.nsvrc.org/sites/default/files/publications_nsvrc_factsheet_media-packet_statistics-about-sexual-violence_0.pdf

92. One in Four, "Sexual Assault Statistics," accessed March 4, 2015, at http://www.oneinfourusa.org/statistics.php

93. Megan N. Schmid, Captain, United States Air Force, "Combating a Different Enemy: Proposals to Change the Culture of Sexual Assault in the Military," *Villanova Law Review,* 55 Vill. L. Rev. 475 (2010), at 475.

94. National Sexual Violence Resource Center, "Statistics About Sexual Violence," 2012, 2013, 2015, at http://m.nsvrc.org/sites/default/files/publications_nsvrc_factsheet_media-packet_statistics-about-sexual-violence_0.pdf

95. Shannan Catalano, Ph.D., "Intimate Partner Violence, 1993–2010," *Bureau of Justice Statistics*Special Report, November 2012.

96. Centers for Disease Control and Prevention (CDC), "Prevalence and Characteristics of Sexual Violence, Stalking, and Intimate Partner Violence Victimization — National Intimate Partner and Sexual Violence Survey," United States, 2011.

97. Jennifer L. Truman, Ph.D., and Rachel E. Morgan, Ph.D., "Nonfatal Domestic Violence, 2003–2012," *Bureau of Justice Statistics* Special Report, April, 2014.

98. Alanna Vagianos, "Remind Us It's An Epidemic," *The Huffington Post,* October 23, 2014.

99. *Griswold v. Connecticut,* 381 U.S. 479 (1965).

100. *Eisenstadt v. Baird,* 405- U.S. 438 (1972).

101. *Roe v. Wade,* 410 U.S. 113 (1973).

102. *Planned Parenthood of Pennsylvania v. Casey,* 505 U.S. 833 (1992) at 835.

103. *Planned Parenthood of Pennsylvania v. Casey,* at 897.

104. *Planned Parenthood of Pennsylvania v. Casey,* at 837.

105. Erik Eckhom, "Access to Abortion Falling as States Pass Restrictions," *The New York Times,* 3 January 2014, at http://www.nytimes.com/2014/01/04/us/women-losing-access-to-abortion-as-opponents-gain-ground-in-state-legislatures.html?_r=0

106. Public Health Watch, "GOP Lawmakers Have Already Introduced More Than 100 Abortion Restrictions in 2015," February 16, 2015, citing the Kaiser Family Foundation.

107. Erik Eckholm, "Access to Abortion Falling as States Pass Restrictions," *The New York Times,* 3 January 2014, at http://www.nytimes.com/2014/01/04/us/women-losing-access-to-abortion-as-opponents-gain-ground-in-state-legislatures.html?_r=0

108. Erik Eckholm, "Ultrasound: A Pawn in the Abortion Wars," *The New York Times,* February 25, 2012.

109. David Bailey, "Appeals court upholds South Dakota abortion law's suicide advisory," The Chicago Tribune, July 24, 2012, at http://articles.chicagotribune.com/2012-07-24/news/sns-rt-us-usa-abortion-southdakotabre86n1dm-20120724_1_sarah-stoesz-consent-law-abortion-provider

110. John Eligon, "Missouri Enacts 72-Hour Wait for Abortion," *The New York Times*, September 11, 2014.

111. Jennifer Ludden, "States Continue Push to Ban Abortions After 20 Weeks," *NPR*, January 22, 2015, at www.npr.org/blogs/health/2015/01/22/378852507/states-continue-push-to-ban-abortions-after-20-weeks

112. Megan Thielking, "Republican leadership pulls anti-abortion bill that was tearing the caucus apart," *Vox*, January 21, 2015, at www.vox.com/2015/1/21/7867225/abortion-ban-congress

113. Louise Knott Ahern, "Abortion insurance law taking effect in Michigan," *Detroit Free Press*, March 12, 2014, at http://archive.freep.com/article/20140312/NEWS06/303120050/Abortion-insurance-law-taking-effect-in-Michigan

114. *Burwell v. Hobby Lobby Stores, Inc.*, 573 U.S. __ (2014).

115. Adam Liptak, "Supreme Court Rejects Contraceptive Mandate for Some Corporations," *The New York Times*, June 30, 2014.

116. *Burwell v. Hobby Lobby Stores, Inc.*, dissent, J. Ginsburg.

117. Zaher, at 462.

III

Religious Intolerance

On Religious (in)Tolerance

Nelly Lahoud

Over the past few decades, an emphasis on promoting religious tolerance has emerged in public discourse in response to a large number of terrorist attacks carried out in the name of religion. Various conferences promoting interfaith dialogue and understanding are organized by academic, diplomatic, governmental, and non-governmental organizations. Many people believe that the more people learn about the religious beliefs and cultures of others, the better understanding and appreciation they would have of the "other," and that ultimately this understanding would engender peaceful co-existence among people of different faiths.

While respecting the noble intentions underpinning this enthusiasm, it is nevertheless important to inquire whether people of different faiths are disposed to tolerating or disagreeing over religious beliefs. Exploring the monotheist traditions, this essay contends that, despite the common beliefs shared by Judaism, Christianity, and Islam, there are differences fundamental to the core values of each of these traditions. Accordingly, it will argue that promoting religious toleration is a facile approach towards peaceful co-existence; instead, that accepting disagreement over religious beliefs would serve as a stronger building block for co-existence.

MISTAKING SIMILARITIES FOR COMMONALITIES

Concerned by militancy in the name of religion, contemporary discourse in support of religious tolerance is keen to highlight similarities over differences among religions. If people were to attain a deeper understanding of their common teachings, this discourse holds, it would make it more conducive for people from these traditions to co-exist in peace. Remarking on post-

9/11 relations among Jews, Christians, and Muslims, John L. Esposito holds that "appreciating their shared beliefs and values . . . is a matter no longer simply of interreligious relations and religious pluralism but of international politics."[1]

In line with this spirit of religious rapprochement, the three traditions are often described as part of the "Abrahamic tradition" to emphasize their single origin and the common thread that unites all three. The designation of "Abrahamic tradition" is indeed an accurate description, highlighting the key role that Abraham plays in all three. As Francis E. Peters neatly observes, the three faiths

> were born of an event that each remembers as a moment in history, when the One True God appeared to an Iron Age sheikh named Abram and bound him in a covenant forever. Abram is the later Abraham, the father of all believers and the linchpin of the faith, and indeed the theology, from which the three communities of that God's worshipers emerged.[2]

But a closer appreciation of the teachings of Judaism, Christianity and Islam reveals that not all three are equal as far as their respective share of common beliefs. Perhaps for this reason Peters compares these children of Abraham to siblings who "in their maturity . . . stand apart and regard their family resemblances and conditioned differences with astonishment, disbelief, or disdain."[3] As will be discussed, the distinction between *shared* and *similar* beliefs can be fundamental when it concerns the core beliefs of these religious traditions.

CHRONOLOGY AS THE DETERMINANT OF SHARED BELIEFS

While the three monotheist traditions have some beliefs and Prophets in common, their shared beliefs are asymmetrical rather than reciprocal. As far as commonalities are concerned —and from the vantage point of Muslims — Islam incorporates Jewish and Christian teachings into its beliefs. In addition to holding that Muhammad, the founder of the Islamic faith, is a Prophet, a Messenger of God sent to preach to all of humanity about the One God and His Word, observant Muslims also believe in the Jewish prophets. The Qur'an even considers Islam to be *millat Ibrahim*, "the religion of Abraham," which enjoys a unique status among faiths as being God's *khalil*, "friend" (Q. 4: 125). According to Islamic teachings, Abraham dissociated himself from his family and his community on account of their polytheistic beliefs and chose to submit (*aslama*) to the One God; this submission is both the literal meaning of "Islam" and the essence of its teachings. Islam incorporates some aspects of the Christian faith, recognizing Jesus and describing him as a

Prophet (Q. 2: 87). The Qur'an also has a chapter about Mary, the mother of Jesus, and attests to the Virgin birth (Q. 66: 12).

Moving back in history, shared beliefs progressively decrease. From the vantage point of Christians, the Christian faith does not recognize Islamic teachings. It does, however, recognize Judaic teachings as its own and considers that Jesus "came not to abolish the law but to fulfill it" (Matthew 5:17). The earliest tradition is even less disposed to being receptive of the other two's beliefs. From the vantage point of Jews, Judaism recognizes neither the Christian nor Islamic creed; nor does it recognize their respective founding figures.

At first glance, one may be inclined to guess that of the three traditions, Islam is most disposed to being receptive of the other two's beliefs, followed by Christianity then Judaism. Yet a closer reading of these traditions' teachings reveals that the reason Islam appears to be more receptive of Judeo-Christian heritage has largely to do with chronology. More precisely, viewing these traditions from an historical lens, it is not surprising for Islam to incorporate Judeo-Christian teachings, given that it emerged in the seventh century in a milieu where Judaic and Christian influences already existed.

It stands to reason that Christianity should build upon the Judaic tradition given that it was founded by a Jew, but that it would be impossible for it to incorporate the teachings of a tradition that emerged some seven centuries later. Continuing with this chronological reasoning, the fact that Judaism precedes both Islam and Christianity by centuries makes it logical that, even though some of its beliefs serve as core teachings of the traditions that follow it, its own teachings are least receptive.

SHARED BELIEFS IN CONTEXT: THE ISLAMIC CASE

Exploring some of Islam's core teachings, one cannot escape the profound appreciation that the Islamic faith has for Judeo-Christian figures. One is also struck, however, by the way in which Islam appropriates these figures, diverging from Jewish and Christian core beliefs. Anthony H. Johns captures this tension:

> It [*i.e.*, Islam] is something *out there*. Yet paradoxically almost, something *here* as well: a monotheistic religion that has transformed its Judaeo-Christian hinterland, and separated itself from the Hebrew ethnicity from which in part it sprung. It is a religion that . . . is a realisation of Arab genius and carries a universalisation of the Arabic language in a way that transcends any Arab ethnicity associated with it, by colouring with loan words from it the vernaculars of diverse peoples and cultures, and establishing it as a language of intellectual discourse alongside these vernaculars in every country of the Muslim world.[4]

A few examples illustrate what seem to be both *"out there"* and *"here"* at the same time. For instance, the Qur'an and early Muslim sources attribute to Abraham (and other Jewish prophets), as well as to Jesus, biographies that are not entirely founded on canonical Judeo-Christian sources. Their point of departure is virtually the same, relating the Biblical story that presents Abraham as the father of two nations, one from his wife Sarah through his son Isaac, and the other from the maid Hagar through his son Ishmael. Muslim sources, however, impart an additional role to Abraham, one that concerns his son Ishmael. They relate that after Hagar and Ishmael left Canaan, heading south toward Arabia, Abraham had visited them; following God's command, he and Ishmael built the Ka'ba, a celestial stone in Mecca, and proclaimed the pilgrimage.[5]

Islam's appropriation of Christian beliefs also diverges from Christian canonical sources. For instance, while Jesus is revered by Muslims as a prophet, he is not considered to be the Son of God. Instead, Jesus' status is on a par with that of Muhammad and Jewish prophets, who are all believed to be messengers of God. Diverging further from Christian teachings, the Qur'an states that Jesus was not crucified; instead, it appeared to those who witnessed the crucifixion as if he was (Q. 4: 157). Among the verses that highlight these differences are those to be found in Sura 23 (chapter), entitled *al-Mu'minun* ("the Believers"):

> He [Muhammad] brought them the truth,
> But most of them detest the truth.
> Were the truth to align itself with their fancies,
> Heavens and the earth would be in disarray. (Q. 23: 70-71)[6]
> We have brought them the Truth,
> and yet they lie!
> God has not taken a son!
> And there is no god beside Him.
> Were this so, each god would claim primacy
> for what He had created, and each would strive
> to outdo the other . . . (Q. 23: 90-91)[7]

Islam explains the divergence among the various Scriptures not on the basis of plurality of interpretations, but also on faulty transmission. The Qur'an considers the Torah and Gospels (Q. 3:3) as legitimate Scriptures, but the reason why the Qur'an differs from them is attributed to the fact that human recordings of Judeo-Christian Scriptures have corrupted some of the original contents (Q. 5:15). The Qur'an, in Muslims' views, did not undergo similar corruptions by humans, for it is God's Word, revealed to Muhammad in Arabic (Q. 4: 82; 12: 2).

Some scholars highlight that to appreciate the divergences between the Qur'an and Judeo-Christian Scriptures, one needs to be mindful of Muhammad's role in the Qur'an. In addition to addressing all of humanity, God in the Qur'an reminds Muhammad "of the vast design of the divine economy of salvation in which Muhammad has been chosen for a central role."[8] Viewed from this perspective, Judeo-Christian prophets provided Muhammad solace when his people rejected his preaching. As the teachings of earlier prophets were rejected by their people (e.g., Q. 2: 53; 2: 87; 23:44), the rejection of the message Muhammad preached by his Jewish, Christian and pagan contemporaries would come to pass. At the same time, since Muhammad is depicted in the Qur'an preaching the same message as his Jewish predecessors, Islam gains a heritage that antedates the 7th century.

COMBINING UNDERSTANDING AND DISAGREEMENT

The previous section argues that engaging in a deeper understanding of the monotheist traditions is bound to bring out not just shared beliefs, but also profound differences. As John Locke observed in relation to the differences among Christian Churches, "every Church is Orthodox to it self; to others, Erroneous or Heretical. For whatsoever any Church believes, it believes to be true; and the contrary unto those things, it pronounces to be Error."[9] It would be a presumption to assume that interreligious dialogues would automatically lead to religious toleration.

But if a deep understanding of others' belief systems is meant to be the purpose of interfaith dialogues, then the rich intellectual heritage of the classical era furnishes us with examples that highlight the value of acknowledging differences between different faiths. Some of the great classical texts produced by scholars from the monotheist traditions reveal a rich understanding of other people's religious beliefs driven by eagerness to highlight the differences not just between religious traditions, but also within each tradition.

The corpus of al-Shahrastani (d. 1153), considered a significant contribution to the history of religions up to the 18th century, is one such example. In the preface to his *Kitab al-Milal wa-al-Nihal*,[10] al-Shahrastani explicitly states that his study of "the religious beliefs of different peoples" was to "seek out both the *familiar* and the *unfamiliar* [emphasis added]."[11] He made no attempt to reconcile the differences; rather, since he believed that "salvation belongs to only one sect,"[12] he wanted his book "to provide a lesson to one who can reflect and a means of reflection for one who can draw a lesson."[13]

Others, in their spiritual quests, learned about the beliefs of others and refuted them until they found fulfilment that responded to their inner needs. In *The Incoherence of the Philosophers*, Abu Hamid al-Ghazali (d. 1111), who once served as the head of the Nizamiyya madrasa at Baghdad, refuted the teachings of Greek philosophers and their Muslim heirs, but not in support of traditional Islamic orthodoxy. Instead, after a long search that caused him to abandon his post at the Nizamiyya madrasa, Ghazali came to realise that truth can be found through a direct experience of God, through the Sufi Way of life. It is be learned from "the effect of a light which God most High cast into my breast . . . From that light, then, the unveiling of truth must be sought."[14]

Similarly, and in pursuing a defense of natural law, Christian theologian Peter Abelard (d. 1141) was comfortable bringing out differences of beliefs by unpacking what appeared to him to be their outward similarities. In his *Dialogus inter philosophum, Judaeum et Christianum,*[15] consisting of dialogues (that appeared to him in a dream) among a philosopher, a Jew, and a Christian, Abelard is keen to unmask their differences of beliefs. The three men explain that they are "inclined to different religious faiths . . . to be sure, we all alike confess that we are worshippers of the one God, but we serve him by different faiths and different kinds of life."[16] The philosopher proceeds to relate that he applied himself to the doctrines espoused by both the Jew and the Christian, and "I found the Jews fools and the Christians crazy."[17]

Religious differences were not always expressed in subtle ways. In the 8th century, the Byzantine theologian John of Damascus rejected Jesus' depiction in the Qur'an as a prophet. In countering Islam's rejection of Jesus' divinity in support of a purer form of monotheism, John of Damascus argued that Muslims were the "cutters of God," because they cut away from God the Logos and the Spirit.[18] Similar disagreements are recorded to have taken place during the Abbasid era (750-1258), an era that is considered of the richest intellectual phases in Islamic history. It was in the 9th century in Baghdad where the Caliph Harun al-Rashid established the House of Wisdom (*bayt al-Hikma*) where people from different faiths came together in the pursuit of learning. As they built upon and developed Greek, Indian and Persian sciences, they appear to have relished disagreement. The following passage comes from an account by a Spanish theologian who witnessed two sessions conducted by Muslim theologians (*mutakallimun*) in Baghdad during the Abbasid era, and decided never to attend another:

> The first session, which I attended, there were not only Muslims of all sorts, orthodox and heterodox, but also religious deviants, Zoroastrian (guèbres), materialists, atheists, Jews, Christians; in short, there were unbelievers/skeptics (incrédules) of all kinds. Each sect had its own leader, entrusted with the task of defending the opinions they professed . . . one of these unbelievers would address the gathering: "we are gathered here to reason, he would say. You all know the rules. You Muslims shall not invoke arguments from your Book [i.e., the Qur'an] or based on the authority of your prophet, because we believe in neither. Each one should limit his arguments to reason." Everyone

applauded. – You understand, continued the Spanish theologian, after listening to such things, I didn't return to these assemblies. They proposed that I should visit another, I did, but it was just as scandalous. [19]

Texts such as these may well offend modern sensitivities, for the ultimate objective of the author is to refute others' belief systems and defend his own. Yet their seeming insensitivity did not detract from the seriousness with which the authors approached these subjects. A common feature of their intellectual exercises is the authors' willingness, even eagerness, to unmask some of the differences that underpin the outward similarities between their own system of beliefs and those of others. This eagerness is not driven by militancy, but by the pursuit of learning and understanding.

CONCLUDING REMARKS

In view of the profound differences among the three monotheist traditions, is promoting religious tolerance among people feasible and conducive to peaceful co-existence? As the preceding discussion shows, even a basic understanding of the teachings of the monotheist traditions is likely to bring out some irreconcilable differences. In the age of the Internet and social media, masking common beliefs as similar will likely lead to exploitation by those promoting militancy and clashes of civilizations.

Scripture and our medieval ancestors both lacked our modern seemingly neutral designations; they used *infidels* instead of *non-citizens* or *alien*. They certainly lacked the subtlety of using inverted commas to use offensive language with immunity as well. Instead, Muslims, Christians and Jews wrote treatises that were saturated with expressions like *infidels, may God bury their souls*, or *crush their bones* etc... directed at those who did not share their beliefs. They were not composed with a view that centuries later they would be quoted on CNN, al-Jazeera and posted on anti-Semitic websites, as representing the teachings of their respective religious traditions.

Since promoting knowledge on a mass scale is feasible in the modern era, it would be more constructive to promote not just the commonalities between different religions, but also the differences. Differences are bound to be uncomfortable for many, but an epistemic community is better served by honest disagreement than by a shallow tolerance that is bound to be vulnerable to militant intolerance. Religious tolerance is constructive when it is exercised by the state. For just as citizens' opinions, personalities, and habits do not determine their responsibilities and rights within a state, so should their religions.

Locke's wisdom on this matter is as relevant today as it was during his time. In his view, toleration is not the natural extension of religions when they are in power, but when they lack it. "Where they have not the Power to carry on Persecution, and to become Masters," he remarked, "there they desire to live upon fair Terms, and preach up Toleration."[20] Cognizant of the dangers of combining religion and political power, Locke asserted that toleration is to be exercised by the state with respect to all religions. But exercising toleration is not a product of the state's authority in matters of religion; instead, "As the Magistrate has no Power to impose by his Laws, the use of any Rites and Ceremonies in any Church, so neither has he any Power to forbid the use of such Rites and Ceremonies as are already received, approved, and practiced by any Church: Because if he did so, he would destroy the Church it self."[21]

BIBLIOGRAPHY

Abelard, P., *Ethical Writings*, Hackett Publishing Company (October, 1995).

Esposito, J. L., 'Foreword', in F. E. Peters, *The Children of Abraham*, Princeton: Princeton University Press, 2006.

Al-Ghazali, Abu Hamid Muhammad, in *Al-Ghazali Deliverance from Error: Five Key Texts Including His Spiritual Autobiography, al-Munqidh min al-Dalal*, (translated and Annotated by R.J. McCarthy), Louisville, KY: Fons Vitae, 1980.

Johns, A. H., 'On encountering the other in Islam: Reflections, reminiscences and hope,' in Morris, Shepard, Tidswell & Trebilco (eds), *The Teaching and Study of Islam in Western Universities* London: Routledge, and New York: Routledge, 2014, pp. 46-62.

——. 'Sura al-Mu'minun: A Reading and Reflection,' *Journal of Qur'anic Studies*, forthcoming October 2016.

Lings, M., *Muhammad – His Life Based on the Earliest Sources*, Rochester: Inner Traditions, 2006.

Locke, J., *A Letter Concerning Toleration*, Indianapolis: Hackett Publishing Company, Inc., 1983.

Meyendorff, J., 'Byzantine Views of Islam,' *Dumbarton Oaks Papers,* Vol. 18 (1964), pp. 113-132.

Peters, F. E., *The Children of Abraham*, Princeton: Princeton University Press, 2006.

Renan, E., *Averroes et L'Averroisme, Oeuvres Complètes*, Paris: Calmann-Levy, 1952, Tome III.

Shahrastani, Muhammad ibn 'Abd al-Karim, *Muslim Sects and Divisions: the section on Muslim sects in Kitab al-milal wa'l-nihal*, trans. by A. K. Kazi and J. G. Flynn, London: Kegan Paul International, 1984.

NOTES

1. John L. Esposito, 'Foreword', in F. E. Peters, *The Children of Abraham*, Princeton: Princeton University Press, 2006, p. xii.

2. F. E. Peters, Ibid. p. 1.

3. Peters, Ibid., xvii.

4. Anthony H. Johns, 'On encountering the other in Islam: Reflections, reminiscences and hope,' in Morris, Shepard, Tidswell & Trebilco (eds), *The Teaching and Study of Islam in Western Universities* London: Routledge, and New York: Routledge, 2014, pp. 50-51.

5. Martin Lings, *Muhammad – His Life Based on the Earliest Sources*, Rochester: Inner Traditions, 2006, chapter: 'House of God.'

6. Translation by Anthony H. Johns, 'Sura al-Mu'minun: A Reading and Reflection,' *Journal of Qur'anic Studies*, forthcoming October 2016. My gratitude to the author for sharing his unpublished article with me.

7. ibid.

8. ibid.

9. John Locke, *A Letter Concerning Toleration*, Indianapolis: Hackett Publishing Company, Inc., 1983, p. 23.

10. Shahrastani, Muhammad ibn 'Abd al-Karim, *Muslim Sects and Divisions: the section on Muslim sects in Kitab al-milal wa'l-nihal*, trans. by A. K. Kazi and J. G. Flynn, London: Kegan Paul International, 1984.

11. ibid., p. 8.

12. ibid., p. 10.

13. ibid., p. 8.

14. Abu Hamid Muhammad Al-Ghazali, in *Al-Ghazali Deliverance from Error: Five Key Texts Including His Spiritual Autobiography, al-Munqidh min al-Dalal*, (translated and Annotated by R.J. McCarthy), Louisville, KY: Fons Vitae, 1980, pp. 57-8.

15. Peter Abelard, *Ethical Writings*, Hackett Publishing Company (October, 1995).

16. ibid., p. 59.

17. ibid., p. 60.

18. John Meyendorff, 'Byzantine Views of Islam,' *Dumbarton Oaks Papers,* Vol. 18 (1964), pp. 111.

19. Cited in Ernest Renan, *Averroes et L'Averroisme, Oeuvres Complètes*, Paris: Calmann-Levy, 1952, Tome III, p. 950.

20. Locke, op. cit., p. 33.

21. ibid., p. 41.

Theological Complicity in Religious Violence

Ellen T. Charry

Both state-sponsored and spontaneous impersonal violence against persons and property stemming from communal fear, resentment and anger always have and now are not infrequently tied to theological commitments.[1] Consider some recent examples. On Purim 1994 (25 February), Baruch Goldstein, an Orthodox Jew, American physician and founding member of the far right-wing Jewish Defense League that began in Brooklyn in 1968, fired upon Palestinian Muslims at prayer in the Ibrahimi Mosque/ Cave of the Patriarchs in Hebron, sacred to both Jews and Muslims, murdering 29 people and injuring 125 others. Goldstein chose Purim because it commemorates the date in the Book of Esther that permitted Jews to "assemble and defend their lives, to destroy, to kill, and to annihilate any armed force of any people or province that might attack them, with their children and women, and to plunder their goods on a single day throughout all the provinces of King Ahasuerus, on the thirteenth day of the twelfth month, which is the month of Adar" (Esther 8:11-2). The Book of Esther reports that on the permitted day Jews killed 300 people in the capital city.

Goldstein selected Purim because he was persuaded that these Palestinian Muslims were, by definition, terrorists who threatened Jewish lives and believed that that gave him biblical authorization to commit mass murder of people at prayer. He picked Hebron, a Palestinian city in the occupied West Bank, because it was the first Jewish religious incursion into the Occupied Territories with a settlement deemed illegal by international law but advanced and protected by the Israeli government.[2] Goldstein was beaten to death by survivors on the premises and is revered as a martyr by some ultra-Orthodox Jews. He picked the Tomb of the Patriarchs because it is sacred to

Jews and he believed it should belong to Jews only, not to Muslims. His murderous action was both politically and theologically motivated. He was protesting both the right of Arabs to live on land that he believes belongs exclusively to the Jewish people on biblical grounds and the Muslim claim to worship the God of Abraham, that is, the God of Israel.

In 2012, Rakhine Buddhists in western Myanmar/Burma engaged in what appears to be ethnic cleansing of Rohingya Muslims. In the spring of 2014, in the Central African Republic, loosely organized violent militias, populated by young, violent, uneducated Christians called anti-balaka raped, pillaged, tortured, mutilated, burned, dismembered and evicted "foreigners" that is, Muslims, from their homes in the country's capital, Banguie, marauding with impunity in the presence of an ineffectual government. Reestablishing the Muslim caliphate in retaliation, devoted Muslims employ beheading, amputation, slavery and mass murder testified to by mass graves discovered in Tikrit in what they believe is obedience to God's will. The great preponderance of this violence is carried out by young men with high testosterone levels. It is a good time to be an old woman like me.

The Fort Hood massacre (2009), Boston Marathon bombing (2013), even the siege and slayings in Sydney (2014) and certainly the Paris and Brussels bombings in 2015 and 2016 all have theological undercurrents even when political or even personal considerations complicate understanding. That is to say, religious beliefs shape behavior even unselfconsciously. What people assume about themselves, God and others and the shape of an orderly world has behavioral implications.

At the same time, all these religions, Judaism, Buddhism, Christianity and Islam claim to be civilizing agents. They all believe that their religious way fosters virtuous character and behavior that when well-inculcated in the young will nurture pious individuals who would structure socially stable societies, indeed societies accountable to the will of God or whatever term functions with that authority. An interfaith version of this belief comes from my Islamics professor who seeks common cause with Christians against secularism that he argues is the common enemy of the Abrahamic faiths (Nasr 2002).

Religious fervor mixes easily with ethnicity and modern nationalism can add further fuel to various fires. The modern western experiment in religious toleration with its lighter touch has been hard won as modern European and English history show only too well. Modern religious pluralism based on the separation of "church" and state has not taken hold across the globe. Secular government is still a threatening notion for many, perhaps including my westernized Islamics professor and understandably so where weak governments, even if secular in name, may be beholden to religiously entrenched structures for legitimacy, as in Iran and Israel.

CHRISTIAN COMPLICITY

Christians are not without blood on their hands as the situation in the Central African Republic reminds us. Quite apart from that, Christian contempt for Judaism is embedded in its scriptures and violence against Jews has been part of the Christian landscape since its legalization in the fourth Christian century. Christian violence, both church sponsored and spontaneous, was carried out both against non-Christians and against dissident Christians. The church's twenty year-long crusade against the Albigensians in Languedoc (1208 – 29) basically eliminated them. The Crusades are indelibly embedded in Muslim and Jewish memory as a time of Christian violence against them. The Iberian Reconquista that led to the expulsion of Jews and Muslims/ Moors is still preserved in their memories and kept alive in their young while faithful Christians are often unaware of atrocities committed by their forbearers in God's name. Institutional memory tends to memorialize being victimized and forget being victimizers. Conflicting and self-justifying narratives of history run all down the line and continue to shape the identities of millions of religious people.

Indeed, there is little in the practices of ISIS that Christians have not also employed on occasion, although instead of beheading, Christians sometimes burned their opponents alive, as in the autos-da-fe of the Spanish Inquisition in the fifteenth century that may have been more barbaric than beheading as burning is slower.

Christian history is studded with intra-Christian violence as well. Maximos the Confessor had his tongue cut out and his right hand amputated by other Christians as punishment for his interpretation of the doctrine of the incarnation in the seventh century in order to stop him from preaching and writing. John Calvin sent Michael Servetus to his death for abjuring trinitarianism. Catholics were martyred for their faithfulness to Rome until late in the seventeenth century (1680 to be exact).

To address intra-Christian violence following the Protestant Reformation, the Peace of Augsburg negotiated between Roman Catholics and Lutherans in 1555, established the principle of "cuius regio, eius religio," (the religion of the ruler dictates the religion of the ruled), was observed throughout the Holy Roman Empire and institutionalized a century later in the Peace of Westphalia (1648) that extended toleration to Calvinists and created the basis for national self-determination to end both the Thirty Years War in the Holy Roman Empire and the Eighty Years War between Spain and in the Dutch Republic. "Let he who is without sin cast the first stone" (John 8: 7).

THEOLOGICAL ACCOUNTABILITY

Religion's dark side is that in order to solidify the identity and formation of the community it may come to hold other traditions in contempt, especially if they emerged out of struggle with the older tradition. Thus, Jewish scripture holds the Canaanites in contempt (enter Goldstein) Christianity holds Judaism in contempt, Islam has some contempt for Judaism and Christianity (hence ISIS executing Copts), Protestantism held Catholicism in contempt, Protestants who baptized only adults held pedo-baptists in contempt and so on. Such religious contempt is usually scripturally backed and theologically driven although economic, social and cultural differences feed it, as was the case of "the troubles" in Northern Ireland.

With inter- and intra-religious violence now escalating it is needful that the theological sources of contempt fueling it be understood and perhaps addressed. While each must address its theological and scriptural resources on its own terms, leaders from the traditions should be able to come together on the common ground of concern for the contempt in which they hold others so that in one another's presence they can offer mutual counsel based on their learnings from sustained reflection on their own history of contempt over time. My suggestion is the reverse of what my Islamics professor proposed: not that the traditions should join forces against a common external enemy but that they should join forces against a common internal enemy, contempt for the different other.[3]

Against the binary on which contempt for otherness rests I want to posit the notion of theological friendship or perhaps partnership, strange as it may sound. Aelred of Rievaulx eloquently articulated the idea nine centuries ago.

> First, there should be a mutual caring; friends should pray for each other, blush and rejoice for one another, each should weep over the other's lapse as though it were his own, and look on his friend's progress as his own. In whatever ways he can, he should encourage the timid, support the weak, console the sorrowful and restrain the hot-tempered. Moreover, he must respect the eyes and ears of his friend, and never presume to wound them with an unseemly act or an unfitting world. A becoming reserve is friendship's best companion: take reserve away from friendship and you deprive it of its greatest ornament. How often has a sign from my friend damped down or quenched the smoldering fire of anger, already on the point of flaring out! How many times have his graver features checked the undignified remark already on the tip of my tongue! How often when I have needlessly dissolved into laughter, or fallen into idle chatter has his arrival restored me to a proper gravity! Besides, if there is something that needs saying, it comes better from a friend and leaves a deeper mark. A recommendation must carry real weight when the giver is known to be loyal and yet not given to flattery. Therefore between friends sound advice should be given confidently, candidly and freely. Mutual admonishment is an integral part of friendship; it should be kindly and not roughly given, and patiently, not

resentfully, received. For believe me, there is no scourge of friendships like flattery and complaisance, the characteristic vices of the light-minded and smooth-tongued, those who say what's sure to please and never what is true. To let there be no hesitation between friends, none of the pretence [sic] that is so utterly incompatible with friendship. One owes a friend the truth; without it the word friendship has no meaning. (Rievaulx 1993, 187)

Here I adapt Aelred's commendation of personal spiritual friendship for rethinking the relationship between religious traditions. This is different from the common understanding of interfaith dialogue where representatives of traditions may come together to address specific theological disagreements or even to see the other as the other sees him-herself. It is rather the task of assisting the other tradition(s) to grow into its best self on the ground of what I take to be the fundamental theological task: the work of sustained reflection on God and the things of God.

Theology is a self-critical discipline, using discipline in both senses of the word. Bringing Jewish, Christian and Muslim theologians together confessing their common burden of contempt for one another would provide the grounds for partnership needed to hold one another's hand, so to speak, through these painful minefields. Perhaps a helpful adage for such an undertaking is found in Irving Greenberg's most riveting sentence: "No statement, theological or otherwise, should be made that would not be credible in the presence of the burning children" (Greenberg 1977), be they children burning in Auschwitz in 1944, children burning in Gaza seventy years later, or children maimed in Syria after that.

Driving religiously inspired violence, be it between or within traditions, is a binary opposition that assumes an either/or approach to those labeled "other". Perpetrators of religiously inspired contempt blaze with fear and anger that may dangerously combine as righteous indignation. It may be that the "other" humiliates one's identity and honorable commitments or competes for one's own access to resources needed for basic well-being. But in addition is some form of the idea that the other's theological convictions compete with and thereby threaten one's own and with it one's notion of a rightly ordered universe. Should such thoughts spread among society it could disrupt the social order understood to be ordained by God. To combat the threat of social disruption the "other" is objectified, perhaps seen as a social contaminate, dehumanized, demonized, even animalized. What may begin as an understandable theological argument may deteriorate into *ad hominem* polemics as we see clearly in Christian theology all along the line.

Closing the door on theological contempt will be difficult; opening new doors even more so. Here I propose theological grounds for a model of theological partnership between Christianity and Judaism in order to advance each one's struggle with its own form of disdain. In so doing, I will speak from but not for both Judaism and Christianity. In such a setting Islam, must speak from and for itself.

THE JEWISH-CHRISTIAN CASE

The 2000 year long enmity between Judaism and Christianity (not necessarily between Jews and Christians who may choose to look away from the theological enmity that obtains between them) is theological and has been variously identified. Some would say the traditions disagree on whether Jesus of Nazareth is the expected messiah of the Jews. Others would say that they disagree on the doctrine of God, whether God is properly understood as triune or as a strict monotheistic unity. Still others would point to disagreements on how to interpret Hebrew scripture or how to be obedient to God. All of these considerations find their place in the general notion that each tradition claims that it worships God truly while the other worships God wrongly in one or more ways. That is, each community believes that it alone is the people of God and therefore the other cannot be and to do so lays claim to that title falsely.

While not all binary oppositions between communities are vulnerable to this dynamic, my own task is now to argue that the exclusive claim to God's affection that each one makes is theologically untenable because such a claim threatens other claims that each also holds. That is, each of these traditions needs to acknowledge the theological legitimacy of the other in order to make sense of its own claim about God's universal goodness and sovereignty. In the case of Judaism, embrace of Christianity (not Jews becoming Christians but embracing God's embrace of gentiles through Christ) would secure the universal goodness and sovereignty of God for Judaism. In the case of Christianity, the challenge is two-fold. It must secure its claim to worship the God of Israel and it must secure its claim of the goodness of creation that exists quite apart from the church. Embrace of the theological validity of Judaism, (not Christians becoming Jews but embracing God's embrace of Jews through Judaism) would secure both that Christians worship the God of Israel, the maker of heaven and earth, and the goodness of creation.

IN JEWISH TERMS

To the Jewish case first. Jewish theology claims that God is both the God of Israel and the sovereign of the universe. Yet unless Jews seek to evangelize the world for Judaism, the claim of divine universality remains contentless. As long as Jews do not seek to Judaize the nations—and they have not since Christianity was legalized and empowered—their theological disinterest in gentiles implies a tribal doctrine of God that eviscerates the belief that God is maker of heaven and earth. If the one who spoke and brought the world into being is the God of the Jews only, this is a local, even cruel God indeed who loves and cares not for 99.9% of the world's population.

If, on the other hand, God *is* the maker of heaven and earth and the nations are not called to become Jews, Judaism must consider carefully how God is the God of the nations. Theological indifference is theological neglect and that neglect impinges on its basic theological convictions. That problem was addressed by Saul/Paul of Tarsus whose understanding of the people of God embraced the nations. Paul, or at least the dominant readings of him, went on to argue that in doing that Christ so reshaped Judaism that it was no longer recognizable as Judaism to most Jews. As the binary took hold Christianity became a separate religion. Whatever Paul may have envisioned for a proper relationship between Jews and Christians, if he could have envisioned such a division is now a moot point given the subsequent unsightly history.

With the exception of Franz Rosenzweig in the early twentieth century, Jews have not taken up the challenge that Paul saw or the solution that he offered. Rosenzweig suggested that Christ provided a way to God for the nations and that that did not entail the dissolution of Judaism as Jews practiced it, going back as far as Paul's day where circumcision, dietary restrictions and holy days were central to Jewish obedience to God.

Rosenzweig proposed that Judaism faces inward, deaf to the flow of history. It does not adapt or change in response to changing circumstances. At the same time, however, Christianity is the light of God that shines out from Judaism to the nations. Christ is the way to God for gentiles. Rosenzweig did not seem to realize that the gentile embrace of the Jewish Messiah was something that Jews should embrace as central to Judaism's own theological coherence and that that **was** Judaism's outward turn. While Rosenzweig's stunning proposal of one people of God in two forms has not been embraced by Jews, it or some refinement of it, stands as a powerful theological opportunity for Jews to make sense of the universal sovereignty of God that would address the danger of theological tribalism that compromises divine sovereignty and goodness to end the debilitating competition for divine favor that has spurred the longest war from the Jewish side.

IN CHRISTIAN TERMS

If Judaism's theological challenge to internal coherence is to make sense of the universality and goodness of God, Christianity's theological challenge is to make sense of its claim to worship the God of Israel, maker of heaven and earth who avows the goodness of creation. Over and again, Christians have been tempted to sever Jesus Christ from the God of Israel and especially from God's relationship to the Jewish people, a position known as supersessionism.

Augustine of Hippo put the supersessionist position succinctly in his comment on a phrase in the long superscription of our Psalm 34 that reads "he forsook him and went away." Augustine reads Christ for David and then asks "Whom did he [Christ] forsake" He forsook the Jewish people and went away . . . they clung to the old sacrifice after the order of Aaron, and did not grasp the sacrifice according to the order of Melchizedek; so they lost Christ, and the Gentiles came to possess him" (Augustine 2000b, 18). Without Christ, Augustine and the rest of the tradition with him holds, the Jews are without God.

Although carefully developed trinitarian doctrine identifies Jesus as the Son of the Father in God in order to claim that Christians worship the God of the Jews and not a Jewish man, the temptation to concentrate knowledge of God in Christ, sometimes Christ alone, threatens to obscure God's reach beyond Christ. The temptation is enshrined in the basic Christian creeds that, while identifying God as creator, skip over the entire biblical history of Israel to proclaim Jesus Christ as the Son of God. Two-thirds of the Christian Bible that recounts the history of God's dealings with humanity through Israel is disregarded.

The danger implicit in the christological concentration was evident early on in the proposals of Marcion of Sinope and Manichaeism that while officially repulsed continue to haunt Christian theology and preaching from time to time. While these heresies are quite different from one another, they share distrust in the goodness of creation and by implication God's goodness outside of a strictly Christian environment upon which Genesis 1 insists. Indeed, both the Hebrew Bible and the Jewish people (sometimes represented as the synagogue) have frequently represented disobedience, sin, evil, and Satan in Christian rhetoric and art. Opposition between the church and "the world" has provided an excuse to demonize whatever the church may find troubling at any point in history limiting the reach of God's goodness to church members.

Another way of putting the problem is to say that with the christological insistence, creation is severed from redemption apart from Christ. Here, the idea is that good resides in the world only as connected to the redeeming work of Christ. In its own turn, this view limits divine goodness and promotes fear and suspicion of all that is not sanctified by Christian confession. Again, Jews who have resisted Christianization have represented resistance to God and been denigrated for insisting on religious autonomy. On this model, proper Christian action calls for opposition to the forces of darkness that lie outside Christian control. The result is the squeezing of divine goodness and grace into Christianly controlled landscapes, be they psychologically, culturally or politically construed. This separation of creation from redemption may express itself in a desire to transform creation Christianly for the sake of its redemption, but it cuts Christians off from what has been called common grace, the goodness of God that is embedded in the world by virtue of being creature.

The danger that accompanies the separation of creation from redemption and can amount to a denial of common grace is that Christianity may become spiritually fastidious, dwelling in a pure spiritual realm of ideas that at best cannot see God's goodness operating in the world apart from Christ and at worst sees demonic forces at work beyond the church. Thus, christomonism carries the temptation of a residual Marcionism and Manichaeism that undermine Christianity's commitment to divine goodness. As was also true in the Jewish case, the danger here is to Christian theological integrity itself; it is not a matter of special pleading on behalf of the crucified Jewish people.

CONCLUSION

In sum, in the case before us, I have proposed that because both Judaism and Christianity believe in the goodness and universality of God (that Islam also of course believes) by looking to the other Jews and Christians can assist the strengthening, or I should say the straightening out of their own tradition as theological partners in the task of enabling the traditions to become sources of blessing in the world.

Backing up now from this particular case, the larger suggestion is that given that theology is a self-critical discipline undertaken for the well-being of the societies in which religious communities are located, engaging in self-criticism in one another's presence can establish theological friendship both to support and assist the several traditions reflect on their own vulnerabilities in a broad context. Watching one another consider and address concern for internal coherence around issues like the goodness and sovereignty of God will advance the well-being of members of the religious communities by targeting contempt for others as well as of the larger communities. It will weaken the fear that religious contempt from the "other" might impact them negatively.

WORKS CITED

Armstrong, Karen. 2015. *Fields of blood: religion and the history of violence*. NY: Alfred A. Knopf.

Augustine. 2000b. *Expositions of the Psalms: 33–50*. Translated by Maria Boulding. Edited by John E. Rotelle. v. vols. Vol. 2, *Works of Saint Augustine: A Translation for the 21st Century*. Hyde Park, NY: New City Press.

Greenberg, Irving. 1977. "Cloud of Smoke, Pillar of Fire: Judaism, Christianity, and Modernity after the Holocaust." In *Auschwitz: Beginning of a New Era?*, edited by Eva Fleischner, 7–55. New York: KTAV.

Nasr, Seyyed Hossein. 2002. *The heart of Islam: enduring values for humanity.* 1st ed. [San Francisco]: HarperSanFrancisco.

Rievaulx, Aelred of. 1993. "Selections from On Spiritual Friendship." *In Cistercian World: Monastic Writings of the Twelfth Century*, edited by Pauline Matarasso, 169–90. London; New York: Penguin Books.

Sacks, Jonathan. 2003. *The dignity of difference: how to avoid the clash of civilizations.* Rev. ed. London ; New York: Continuum.

NOTES

1. Karen Armstrong has defended religion against the charge that it foments violence because it has been allied with political systems that require the use or at least the threat of the use of force to maintain civil society. While she is correct to note that religious thinkers have also abjured violence and sought to employ their beliefs and practices compassionately and for peaceful purposes, there is no doubt but that religious beliefs grounded in univocal understandings of truth are readily aroused to justify violence. The theological dimensions of religious violence remain to be addressed on their own terms. (Armstrong 2015)

2. Jewish settlers in the West Bank now number in the hundreds of thousands with whole cities now gobbling up Palestinian land.

3. This carries Jonathan Sacks's plea for tolerance beyond his poignant vision (Sacks 2003)

"And who is my neighbor?"

American Liberators in Transnational Context

Stephen F. Barker

INTRODUCTION

Within the entangled relationships of intolerance that can lead to extraordinary evil, the perspective of the bystander provides insight in to the role of human agency. Presumed to be neutral and usually exonerated due to their distance from the crime, these individuals can be reconsidered within the historical framework of Holocaust and genocide studies and lose their moral opacity. The last "bystanders," or immediate witnesses to these crimes, were the liberators who through force of arms released the victims from the perpetrators' grasp and therefore separated themselves from simply "seeing" the crimes. So in their act of witnessing they became something else because of their role and how they reacted when presented with the horror of the Holocaust. By examining the theoretical and practical lines of the identity of these figures of liberation we can better understand the complicated relationships that exist in the context of mass atrocity. This entangled nature can best be seen in the unique stories of Germans (mostly Jewish Germans) who emigrated to the United States before World War II, joined the U.S. Army, were sent back to fight in Europe, and then encountered some manifestation of the Holocaust. The personal identities and intentions of these particular liberators affect how they view themselves in the encounter: as the uniformed men-at-arms eliminating bondage and then alternatively as its possible victims.

A diverse representation of history can be balanced through the use of personal accounts. These testimonies provide alternative perspectives to traditional sources since "listening closely to the witnesses allows us greater depth and nuance than can be derived from the tendentious obfuscation of official accounts."[1] They confirm and contribute to the descriptions of survivors when compiling evidence of massive slavery and genocide as well as providing an on-the-ground perspective that expands our understanding of the events when coupled with official sources. It is important to hear from these former soldiers according to their own subjective viewpoint, i.e. how they saw themselves at the time and then how they represent themselves at the time of the interview. Unique perspectives are offered by German-Americans who have renegotiated their nationality. These transitional figures present interesting questions about how they understand their identities given the experience of emigration and return. This paper will examine what motivated their actions at the time, how they saw themselves, how they felt about returning under arms to the country of their birth, and then their witnessing of the consequences of the Shoah. Referencing these oral histories in combination with official sources will aid in understanding the complex period at the end of World War II.

When Raul Hilberg describes the Holocaust as "experienced by a variety of perpetrators, a multitude of victims, and a host of bystanders...Each saw what had happened from its own perspective, and each harbored a separate set of attitudes and reactions."[2] Liberators do not fit into this formulation because, by their very nature, as soon as liberators enter this tangled relationship they end it. But this paper contends that not only should we consider liberation voices in relating the history of the end of World War II but also reconsider how we conceptualize the idea of the liberator using their first-person accounts. Hilberg also spoke passionately of the importance of the perspective of the witnesses:

> The victims in the camps and the liberators who stumbled upon them have a different view, a different impression, and a different remembrance from that which generations henceforth will have—the pictorialization of the camp network. They saw it; they smelled it; they felt it; they suffered from it. Their view was microscopic, immediate. They saw the detail as no one else will see it.[3]

The war categories of perpetrator, victim, and bystander can be contrasted with the postwar labels of witnessing: war criminal, survivor, prisoner, liberator, rescuer, war crimes trial participant, etc. These latter titles have a more legalistic formulation while the former are more experiential. But these labels belie the fact that violence persisted after the war ended and thus the former relationships described by Hilberg are still in play and are indeed blurred into those of witnessing in the aftermath and occupation. Both sets of categories must be considered and the two roles are bound together in these accounts of liberation.

Most of the liberators examined here can be placed into the categories of Jewish survivor *and* liberator if one considers refugees who left prior to the outbreak of World War II as survivors.[4] Nevertheless, these different categories of analysis illustrate how the story and study of the Holocaust has grown from the core groupings of perpetrators, victims, and bystanders. By studying Jewish German-Americans and their hyphenated identity, one can expect them to possess a deep ambivalence regarding their return to Germany, how they see themselves, and how they view others involved in the Holocaust.[5] Much has been made, and rightly so, of the courage and care of American army and Red Cross medical personnel who entered the camps and sought to save lives. Heroic narratives have recently dominated the popular representations of this period of the conflict—but these narratives tend to elide the emotional earthquake of the encounter, omit episodes of residual violence, obscure the surprise of initial reactions, and do not address long term impacts of the experience. Here, in the closing months of the war, existed a time between times. The traditional categories of Holocaust violence such as perpetrator, victim, and bystander become blurred by the rush of events, the shifting of power, and the introduction of new players. In this context, the popular ideal of the morally just liberator and savior do not appear as neatly bound up in the victors' post-war narrative. The Allies entered Germany as a conquering army whose liberating action in the country was secondary to the overriding mission of defeating the Germans militarily and occupying them after victory.[6]

Harry Adler, a German-American GI, reflected on the application of post-war labels in his interview: "They call us 'liberators.' In my opinion that's a misnomer. We basically stumbled onto these places because the German guards just ran away and left the gates wide open…there was no fire fight, so the word 'liberator' I don't think applies—we just arrived on the scene and saw this monstrosity."[7] At Buchenwald, Guy Stern recalls thinking, "I'm not a liberator" when telling how prisoners embraced him the day after their liberation.[8] Additionally, Si Lewen notes the "misconception" of liberation as something that happened often with "shooting and fighting—nothing of the kind…this whole business of liberation was not as glorious as what the media makes it out to be."[9] When and how should the term "liberator" be used then? On two simultaneous levels: first and foremost, it describes those individual soldiers who by force of arms, or by their military presence alone, caused the German gaolers to relinquish their death grip on the lives and locales in their possession. Secondly, liberators were those soldiers who directly witnessed the process of breaking open the bonds of the concentration camp universe; they caused or saw the result of death marches and death trains from camp evacuations. Liberators are witnesses. Their experience as witnesses of and participants in liberation mark them as significant historical figures.

Kurt Klein, a German-American Jew who emigrated prior to 1938, survived by leaving Germany before Kristallnacht. He escaped the fate of his parents at Auschwitz and was able to subsequently save others through his actions as a soldier when he returned to the country of his birth. This combined experience of survival, early escape, and then return under arms creates an interesting perspective and led Klein to advise the audience of his videotaped testimony to, "Be aware of the plight of others and help them because ultimately you are not doing it just for them, you're doing it for yourself as well."[10] Klein's testimony shows how personal stories can illuminate and clarify broad categories of protagonists by revealing complexities that aid our understanding of the events. Similarly, Robert Weil saw the inside of Dachau as a prisoner for three months after *Kristallnacht* in 1938; and then, after emigrating and being drafted, he helped liberate the camp of Woebbelin with the 8th Infantry Division seven years later.[11] In addition to being first on the scene from the outside world, some of the liberators also had the cultural propinquity to make the experience all the more significant. Accounts from these individuals, with an outsider's insider view, provide a unique perspective of the events. For these reasons of proximity, Robert Abzug accurately describes all liberators as the "most compelling witnesses."[12]

Additionally, there were some soldiers who came to the camps simply to see them, voluntarily or responding to senior officers' orders to do so. For example, after seeing Ohrdruf (discussed further below) on 11 April 1945, General Eisenhower ordered every nearby unit not actively engaged at the front lines to see the camp. While it may be problematic to label all of these particular soldiers as liberators, all were *witnesses* to liberation—only different aspects or phases of it. Mostly, the liberation of the camps was a function of the institutional actions of the army. While the liberation of the camps should correctly be seen as fitting into the larger narrative of liberating Europe from Nazi oppression—too often, however, the story of camp liberation is lost in the larger story which obscures how liberation actually rolled out on the ground.

These conquering soldiers became occupiers, but in the changing heroic narrative of the post-war era, highlighted in generous treatments in some recent books, their role as liberators has become predominant.[13] This heroic interpretation has also been applied to the more focused treatments of Jewish soldiers. Identifying as a Jewish American while in army uniform had a significant effect upon how these soldiers experienced the war in Europe, especially when they liberated Jewish prisoners. Abzug describes how the experience was more complex for Jewish GIs and states how,

In many cases they experienced deep conflict between fear and sympathy, as if on each survivor's face they could read the unavoidable comparison: 'It could have been you.' At the same time, an overwhelming sense of kinship between such strangely different human beings sometimes grew up, a connection built upon the simple but powerful mutual recognition of Jewishness.[14]

Abzug's essay stresses how the sight of the camps increased camaraderie across religious lines while others note how the Jewish religion facilitated building kinship along national and ethnic lines. A closer look at the liberation experience will demonstrate this unique instance of identity distinction and understanding in times of trauma.

LIBERATIONS

Albert Rosenberg, another German-American Jew working in military intelligence, entered Buchenwald, near Weimar, five days after its initial liberation. There were still piles of corpses outside the crematoria; he also saw burned skeletons in the ovens, which he says had a capacity of cremating 400 bodies a day.[15] Tasked to prepare a report on Buchenwald, Rosenberg spent over a month in the camp with former prisoners, including Eugene Kogon, collecting information and writing the report in German—the language everyone involved knew best. While interviewing prisoners in the *kleine Lager* section of the camp reserved mostly for Jews, Rosenberg pinned a cardboard Star of David to his uniform in order to relate to and build rapport with the survivors he spoke with. The conditions of the *kleine Lager* were much worse than the rest of camp due mostly to neglect. It had an "incredible stench" and there was "nothing human about the place," according to Rosenberg.[16] He says his report was never published because of its "political implications" until he gave a copy of it to David Hackett who translated, edited, and published it as *The Buchenwald Report* in 1995.[17] Many people worked on the lengthy report, but Rosenberg, after spending over 30 days interviewing, compiling, and editing, signed his name on the cover letter.[18] While Rosenberg was at Buchenwald he used his past and present background to connect with the survivors and report on their experiences.

Harry Adler worked as a driver and interpreter for a colonel in charge of civil affairs for 5th Corps. Arriving in Weimar, his boss decided to see the "stockade" that he had heard about. "We didn't realize what was going on," Adler says as they drove into the camp and saw a "mountain of cadavers" at Buchenwald.[19] After they witnessed American military policemen forcing German civilians to dump bodies into trenches dug by the army engineers, he could not stay to watch. "And today I ask myself," Adler continues, "what reaction I had—I was a 20-year-old soldier—looking at this, not understanding what it was all about. I had already by that time seen a lot of blood and guts—war is not a very pleasant thing—but this…I couldn't explain it, I had no idea where we were."[20] Si Lewen, too, tried to comprehend the camp world, but failed: "I only sank to my knees and broke down and wept seeing the remains and reminders of what could have been my fate—had I come to Buchenwald not as an American soldier but as a doomed prisoner."[21]

Fifty-six miles to the northwest of Buchenwald on the same day of 11 April, Americans encountered the Dora-Mittelbau concentration camp outside of the city of Nordhausen. Gunther Plaut, a Jewish army chaplain and German-American, was "right up front" with the first troops of the 104th Infantry Division as they rolled into Dora on 11 April.[22] Plaut says he *did* have knowledge of the camps and the Nazi designs of extermination through slave labor: "By the time I got to Dora, I knew what was going on. But when you see it, you know that that you didn't know anything. When you find 4,000 people dead lying around and 400 skeletons crawling around half alive, then you know that you are in the presence of evil incarnate."[23] He relates how his chaplain's jeep, with its Star of David and flag, attracted the survivors. While of course some of them wanted food, Plaut says, "Many of them, the first thing they wanted was not food…what they wanted was identity."[24] They wanted "Jewish religious items, and for our troops to get in touch with their relatives in the United States or somewhere in the world."[25] He then tells about how they cared for the dead:

> Nordhausen, we were only there for a few days and I happened to be in charge of burying the dead. And I commandeered, the general put me in charge, I commandeered the best citizens—they had to come in their Sunday clothes, and the women, and bring spades, forks, spoons, whatever it took to dig graves—and they had to wash the bodies, too. And one of them said to me that I'm asking them to do something inhuman and that's really when I exploded…when they told me that *I* was doing something inhuman to bury the dead—people that *they* had killed.[26]

Plaut saw grave duty as a just desert to atone for the crimes of the camps. This kind of retribution would be seen at other camps as well.

American soldiers were no longer simply shocked by what they saw, their shock gave way to violent reprisal. Chaplain Plaut describes the change, "By this time the whole army was waking up to what was going on, and if the soldiers had not understood before why we were fighting Germany, now they knew. And they started hating them with gusto."[27] The interviewer goes on to ask him about whether or not he was inclined toward revenge: "Feelings of revenge? Yes, of course, how could you not have them? But, um, I was also a religious person [inaudible]…there was a guy some of the inmates at one of the camps recognized as an *SS* man who had persecuted them and he was in our custody at the time. And I told the guys to let him loose, let the people take care of him."[28]

Plaut also went to Willingshausen, where his father was from, with an M3 half-track vehicle to "liberate" the village, but found white flags already flying so he collected all the guns in the town.[29] But he also wanted to bring to justice the men who had wronged his family, so he announced he was on official legal business and read from a fake document:

> I have orders from the War Department in Washington to find out who the people were who on the 9 and 10th of November 1938 beat a certain Levi Plaut....I held a court martial there in the village because I knew that on *Kristallnacht* they had beaten up my uncle, the one surviving uncle who still lived in the village, and his wife. And I went to go find who did it. It was a little difficult in the beginning, but when I threatened the mayor of the village that he would be taken instead...and my assistant nudged him with his sawed off shotgun, his memory returned magnificently and he surrendered the two guys who had beaten up my uncle.[30]

His uncle survived after spending time in Theresienstadt but Plaut does not know what happened exactly to the men he arrested. He also reports that his father was very happy when he received a letter relating the above events. Plaut's revenge acted itself out as a form of victor's justice in and outside the camp, as an attempt to balance out the egregious results of Nazi policies of violent persecution, extermination through labor, absolute neglect of the prisoners' health, and their callous disregard for life. In a way, it was justice through victory—only in a personal dimension. These actions, outside the scope of normal soldiering, show a different manifestation of justice delivered to a defeated Germany. What Plaut did not see at Dora, however, were the prisoners who had been recently evacuated to Dachau.

When U.S. Army soldiers encountered the Dachau camp outside of Munich, they would not just be spectators to acts of revenge as seen at Buchenwald and Dora. Fritz Schnaittacher, as a member of the 157th Infantry Regiment, 45th Infantry Division, entered Dachau on 29 April 1945 as shots were still being fired and says, "I would be inclined to think that it was our men that were doing the firing...any Germans being killed because of the rage within our troops—I wouldn't doubt it for one moment because when you could only feel the deepest of rage and hatred for what human beings could do to each other..."[31] Schnaittacher says he did not know much at all about the camps before he entered Dachau. Parked on the tracks outside the camp, he came across the remains of one of the last evacuation trains from Buchenwald. Its thirty-nine open and closed box cars contained 2,310 corpses which had taken a maze-like route over a twenty-two day ride from Weimar; forced to meander through Czechoslovakia and Austria before being able to find an open track to Dachau.[32] "Death has an ugly face on these people," Schnaittacher had written in a letter to his wife in 1945, "they were starved to death—the position they were lying in show that they succumbed slow-ly..."[33]

Upon entering the camp to conduct an interrogation, Schnaittacher saw what he described as "living cadavers."[34] And the gun fire he heard was, in fact, Americans shooting Germans they found in the camp. Soldiers of I Company, 3rd Battalion, 157th Regiment (45th Infantry Division) were the first to scale the walls of Dachau and they quickly became enraged by what they found in the camp, especially after seeing the death train themselves. As they captured several German soldiers who had remained in the camp hospital, noncommissioned officer school, and a finance center, they collected them near the hospital and guarded them with a machine gun. The American machine gunner, acting under orders to shoot the prisoners if they tried to escape, fired on them claiming they were making moves to flee. Karl Mann, however, a German-American interpreter working for the battalion com-mander, Lieutenant Colonel Felix Sparks, contends that "the I Company officers decided that they were going to shoot these Germans."[35] The official army investigation of the events contends that at least 17 German soldiers were killed and that GIs should be charged for their actions. None were charged, probably due to conflicting testimonies regarding another group of German guards who were taken from the towers and allegedly shot by the 42nd Infantry Division soldiers who had also entered the sprawling camp.[36] This episode is the one of the most controversial of the war in terms of the alleged execution of POWs by Americans and it shows how liberators, in the chaotic and emotionally charged moment of discovery, could perpetrate vio-lence against the Nazi perpetrators while the original victims looked on.

Herman Cohn tells of visiting Dachau as a chaplain's interpreter three days after its liberation by reading the account he gave his wife in a letter after leaving the camp. He reads, "it would take days to count the bodies I saw...and now there are dead *SS* men all around the camp, killed by our troops or by some of the inmates who got a hold of their guns. Just as well done."[37] Later in the letter Cohn adds, "I was hoping there would still be some guards that we could kill...I kicked some of dead guards to make sure they were dead."[38]

In his letter, Cohn had folded up a newspaper report on Dachau that provided him the first news of the camp and motivated him to see it for himself. *The Stars and Stripes* is a soldier paper that published the following account, read by thousands like Cohn,

> American soldiers and reporters were mobbed, kissed and thrown into the air
> and carried on shoulders high through a sea of weeping, cheering, laughing
> prisoners of the notorious Dachau concentration camp late today in one of the
> maddest and most heart-rending liberation scenes of the war...The extent of
> the horror at this camp is beyond description. There is no way to put into

words the stench of thousands of corpses lying in the crematorium, or the death chamber in the 'hospital.'[39]

Such reports encouraged many soldiers to see the camps shortly after their discovery or because they were ordered. What they witnessed deeply affected them, as seen in Cohn's letter.

Another German-American, Willy Herbst, experienced both sides of the fence after he was sent to the labor camp at Paderborn in 1939 but managed to use a hospitalization to avoid returning as ordered. He emigrated to the U.S. instead and was drafted in 1943. Upon entering Dachau a few days after liberation, he states, "When I arrived, bodies were still lying around; the sight was horrible. Even though I had been in a concentration camp before, I never realized what might have been in store for me...My sister and everyone on my father's side were killed at Dachau."[40]

Soldiers' experiences of revenge varied—while most felt it acutely, only some actually acted on it. Although Robert Sternberg, for example, remarked to a German he was interrogating, "You know you threw me out of your country, this is one way to pay you back," he did not actively seek revenge. At Dachau, Sternberg states in his testimony that he actually stopped other GIs from killing the guards, "If we want to be like them, we shoot them."[41] Harold Baum, another German-American Jew, relates such a story after entering the camp at Flossenburg around April 23rd, where he saw "scores of dying, starving prisoners," but found a couple men who stuck out:

> There were also well-fed prisoners who had on the same inmate uniforms. I unsuccessfully tried to communicate with them in German; one kid in my company spoke Russian and Polish to them and they did not understand that either. We could not figure it out. My captain decided to strip them down and discovered that they had their blood type tattooed under their arm, which was customary practice among SS troops. They went into the mass graves and helped to dispose of the all the corpses, but they did not last to face a war criminal trial. The justification for their demise was that they switched uniforms, which under the Geneva Convention is a punishable offense. They remained in the pits with the corpses.[42]

This episode illustrates the danger of masquerade during World War II as well as how retributive justice was meted out by the liberators. Each encounter was different as each man made different decisions about how to handle the situation.

Dachau, as a main camp, had an elaborate system of subcamps that were based around Mühldorf and Kaufering—which in turn also had subcamps.[43] The network focused its slave labor on excavating tunnels and workspace underground to facilitate the production of jet-fighters and long-range rockets. Walter Monasch states that while he had heard of the large prison camps, he was unaware of the "extermination element" of the camps so he was horrified by the conditions of a Dachau satellite camp in southern Bavaria called Hurlach (also known as Kaufering IV) that the Nazis had attempted to liquidate before abandoning. His unit was the first to reach Hurlach in late April. The slave labor camp had no barracks but rather tin-roofed trenches six feet deep, 20 feet across, and 60 feet long, which had been locked down, drenched in gasoline, and set alight as the *SS* guards fled. Horrible as that sight was, Monasch says Mauthausen was worse.[44]

Located near Linz, Austria, Mauthausen was built shortly after the *Anschluss* in 1938 and its first prisoners were brought there from Dachau. These prisoners formed the first slave laborers of a company founded by the *SS* called the German Earth and Stone Works Incorporated (*Deutsche Erd- und Steinwerke, GmbH*-DESt), in order to mine the generous granite deposits at the site of the camp.[45] Monasch's mother had exhorted him to search for his aunt there (he later found out that she had died in Auschwitz) and he describes Mauthausen with "living dead walking around...the terrible noise of silence...you could still smell the smell of death...even today I don't know if I can deal with it. It's incomprehensible."[46] Werner Ellman entered Mauthausen the day of its liberation and first recalls how the survivors he met on the road approaching the camp were scared of him because he spoke German.

> We don't know what the hell's going on. The first thing I saw, skeletons walking in certain kinds of uniforms. I go up to three or four of them, and I say, 'What goes on?,' and it's in German: *'Was ist los hier?'* And they died in front of me, in fright. Yeah, God, they were so close to dead anyway. All of sudden the guy collapses. In the meantime, my driver's feeding somebody, and he dies on him. He just falls down, and he's gone. We're in such amazement and such confusion; we don't know how to make anything out of this...It's hard to describe because the condition of these people—they are obviously civilians and not soldiers. They don't have guns; we do. And they look at us, and they think we're Germans. I speak German, I'm in uniform, and I got a gun. And they're scared shitless.[47]

In the camp, Ellman explored Mauthausen's rooms with meat hooks, gas chambers, furnaces, and the infamous quarry. He then witnessed the discovery of several German guards and tells how other GIs took away their boots and socks and told them to "scram," then turning to the prisoners, they said, "they're escaping, go catch them...they brought back pieces."[48] Ellman continues, "You become a beast when you are in a beast environment long enough. The GIs really wanted to punish these guys."[49] Leaving in shock, he confronted a local farmer in a nearby field who denied he knew what was going on in the camp—Ellman says he wanted to kill him because he was so upset at the farmer's denial and what he saw.

Leonard Linton, of the 82nd Division's Military Government section, had a mother who was Christian and a father was Jewish. Russian refugees from the Bolshevik Revolution, they settled in Berlin shortly after their son's birth in 1922 but fled in 1938. Linton could speak Russian, German, and French—in addition to English. In reaction to encountering the Woebbelin camp near Ludwiglust in northeastern Germany (a subcamp of Neuengamme) he remarks feeling, "the hatred of everything German even more accentuated, if that was possible."[50] When his commanding officer brought in the Ludwiglust mayor for a haranguing, Linton served as translator: "Deep emotional indignation poured out of [my commander], without any four letter words, but in the most erudite terms I had heard since entering the army. It filled me with pride and humility at the mere fact of being alive and wearing the uniform of the U.S. Army. On finishing, my CO turned away in disgust from the silent mayor."[51] The mayor, who had portrayed himself as an ignorant bystander to the events happening in right outside his town, was then taken to see the camp. He committed suicide with his family the following day.

Linton also describes how the Woebbelin experience hollowed out the men imprisoned there long enough:

> One thing we learned: There comes a point in their life when they don't want to live any more. We call them zombies. Because they are emaciated. Their eyes are bulging. Because all the skin, all the flesh, collapses. ...They look right through you with those sad, huge eyes. They don't care about anything. They have lost the will to live. There is nothing worse than that, because you can't cope with it. And they will die, even though they are free. We could give them food, but they will die.[52]

These prisoners were referred to as *Muselmänner*—an odd nickname derived from the German word for Muslim—for those listless, apathetic prisoners who were resigned to their fates. Primo Levi mentions it in his book *Survival in Auschwitz*, "This word '*Muselmann*', I do not know why, was used by the old ones of the camp to describe the weak, the inept, those doomed to selection."[53] Linton took a small group of French prisoners, some of whom were *Muselmänner*, to an undamaged office in the town's railway station. There he provided them with food instead of taking them to the crowded hospital because he thought it would increase their chance of survival. Sure enough, "[a]fter a few more days of intermittent visits, the former zombies started talking and I admired the one responsible for saving his colleagues' lives."[54] He then found out through talking with them more that one of the recovering survivors had been a classmate of his when he had lived in France, a journalist imprisoned for subversive writing. Liberators such as Linton were profoundly affected by their experiences of dealing with the victims, bystanders, and perpetrators.

CONCLUSIONS

The men studied in this project have identities imbricated from several angles. First, by its nature, liberation is a witnessing act compelled into being by the presence of the outsider at the site of imprisonment and in contact with the prisoners, i.e. the soon-to-be liberated. But what is the relationship between the sight of the crimes and the reaction they provoke? Breaking the plane separating the outside world from the horrors inside the camps is a seminal moment of liberation. When stumbling upon and then stepping into the camps, the liberators cross over into the realm of the witness and witnessing. Their descent into this macabre world changes them and stays with them when they leave via traumatic memory. Having seen the hidden face of a hideous humanity, many liberators resolve to never allow such a thing to happen again and speak out in response to those who now deny its existence in the past. Their exposure to the inhuman made them reevaluate their own humanness.

Additionally, their ethnicity and nationality also affected how liberators saw themselves. Joseph Eaton says they "couldn't touch the Jewish issue in 1944" and they did not really talk about being Jewish until later.[55] Walter Monasch speculates about what would be different if he had not been born Jewish, saying, "I hope I would have been on the right side. I might have been a Nazi, who knows?"[56] He acknowledges the influence of being from Germany by saying, "clearly I have things with me, in me, that come from my German heritage," what he refers to as his "Teutonic background…that's who I am." This nod to an ethnic and cultural legacy from Germany indicates that he considers himself both Jewish and German. Earlier in the interview, he shared an ironic story of how he was once picked out by a Hitler Youth Leader in early high school as a good example of an Aryan. But by questioning whether or not he would be on the right side if he had born as a non-Jewish German, he points to the contingency of past events which sometimes dictate roles to play or situations to live that may not be under the control of the protagonist. His comment also encourages us to question the nature of ethnicity as a fixed part of one's identity and consider it perhaps as a function of one's social and cultural milieu. Regardless, Monasch does not consider Germany as his homeland any longer: "The Germans took it away."[57] He then emphatically states, "I'm an American and a Jew. And I see no contradiction in that."[58] While retaining traces of his German identity, he has firmly replaced it with his American identity while remaining Jewish.

As American soldiers, they faced the sordid reality of warfare in the frozen foxholes of the Ardennes and Hurtgen Forests. As Germans, they faced the ambivalence of returning to the country of their youth as an enemy along with the suspicions of their comrades. And as Jews they faced a possible death in the concentration camps if they had never left or were captured.

That is why these men were considered victims and survivors, as well as liberators, after the war.

Reactions of soldiers varied when encountering the camps but as seen at Dachau and Mauthausen, some acted on the urge to exact vengeance for the horrible deeds they uncovered. Alternatively, Leonard Linton concludes his testimony in awe of the survivors: "I must say, what amazes me is that so few of [the survivors] are vengeful. I am more outraged, personally, at what the Nazis have done, and I would like to see bloody revenge, if possible...than the survivors themselves."[59] Lee Merel, who witnessed the aftermath of the massacre at Gardelegen on 13 April 1945 and interrogated many Germans prisoners, perceived no regret from the perpetrators. These perceptions reinforced the soldiers' attitudes towards the Germans: "They [Germans] couldn't care less...I found the feeling very widespread."[60] These poignant observations are effectively contextualized with their unique German-American perspective as soldiers and participants in these traumatic encounters.

Issues of identity formation, assertion, and dissonance fill the first-person accounts of these men. Overlapping dimensions of their identity during the war come up against the cold realities of combat, as when Eric Leiseroff remembers how he felt as a German-American Jew:

> And I used to get a great kick out of telling them I was Jewish. 'Ich bin ein Jude.' When you come as a G.I., you feel protected, you know, it's a completely different picture. Even in those days I felt myself Americanized. I'm talking about '44, '45. To see American soldiers dead had a much bigger impact on me. I would see somebody lying there with boots, our boots. If I saw a German lying there, a bunch of Germans, I didn't care. But to see your own![61]

The experience seemed to make the men hyper-aware of who they were and who they used to be. John Herman, who does not appear to be Jewish from his interview, tells of how he was the object of anti-German sentiment in the army, "I had one sergeant who gave me hell, 'If it wasn't for people like you we wouldn't be in this war.'" When asked by the interviewer how it feels to be German-born, Herman reacts vociferously: "Hey, I'm not German. I'm American. That's why I got pissed with that sergeant....I was no longer German by the time I went into the army."[62] These realizations were tied closely to their former position as refugees or émigrés and then later as their role as conquering soldiers, or liberators, and then later still as occupiers of a defeated Germany and Austria. These experiences shaped the differences between their German and American identities, with most indicating they felt more American and less German by the end of their European deployment with the army. Therefore we should see liberators as complex historical figures given their diverse backgrounds, intentions, and actions in order to resist the idea of a totalizing, triumphant liberator.

As liberators, these historical figures tell the story of the Holocaust in a new way that reveals a perspective of unpreparedness, shock, and trauma at the tactical level. If these returned émigrés—who experienced the persecution and sometimes were even interned in the camps before the war—felt this horrible shock, then it could be argued that *no one* on the ground was prepared, familiar, or properly informed regarding the nature of the camps.

SOURCES FOR FIRST-PERSON ACCOUNTS

Adler, Harry. Library of Congress, Veterans History Project, AFC 2001/001/78488 VHP MV02 (REF).

Baum, Harold. In *The Enemy I Knew: German Jews in the Allied Military in World War II.* Minneapolis: Zenith Press, 2009.

Cohn, Herman. *Visual History Archive*, USC Shoah Foundation, 24 December 1996, Chicago, Illinois. http://sfi.usc.edu/

Eaton, Joseph. USHMM archive testimony, audio recording, RG-50.030*0581.

Ellman, Werner. *Visual History Archive*, USC Shoah Foundation, 6 June 1997, Chicago, Illinois. http://sfi.usc.edu/

Ettlinger, Harry. Library of Congress, Veterans History Project, AFC/2001/001/51210.

Herbst, Willy. *GIs Remember: Liberating the Concentration Camps.* Washington, DC: Museum for American Jewish Military History, 1994.

Herman, John E. Library of Congress, Veteran's History Project, AFC/2001/001/53763, (SR02 REF) audio recording.

Klein, Kurt. *Visual History Archive*, USC Shoah Foundation, 7 December 1995, Scottsdale, AZ. http://sfi.usc.edu/

Leiseroff, Eric. In *The Liberators*, edited by Yaffa Eliach and Brana Gurewitsh. New York: Center for Holocaust Studies, Documentation, and Research in Brooklyn, 1981.

Lewen, Si. Interview with the author, 17 August 2012, Gwynned, PA.

"Reflections and Repercussions: the Memoirs of Si Lewen," accessed online at http://www.silewen.com/script/chapter16.html on 19 December 2012.

Linton, Leonard. In *Holocaust Testimonies: European Survivors and American Liberators in New Jersey*, edited by Joseph J. Preil. New Brunswick, NJ: Rutgers University Press, 2001.

In Stafford, David. *Endgame, 1945: The Missing Final Chapter of World War II* (New York: Little, Brown, and Company, 2007). The author cites an unpublished memoir written by Linton entitled "Kilroy Was Here" found in the archives of the Allied Museum in Berlin.

Mann, Karl. In *The Liberators: America's Witnesses to the Holocaust.* New York: Bantam Books, 2010.

Lee, Merel. In *Holocaust Testimonies: European Survivors and American Liberators in New Jersey*, edited by Joseph J. Preil. New Brunswick, NJ: Rutgers University Press, 2001.

Monasch, Walter. *Visual History Archive*, USC Shoah Foundation, 14 May 1998, Novato, California. http://sfi.usc.edu/

Ottenheimer, Fritz. Library of Congress, Veterans History Project, AFC/2001/001/57012 *Escape and Return: Memories of Nazi Germany*, 2nd edition. Kearney, NE: Morris Publishing, 2000.

Plaut, W. Gunther. *Visual History Archive*, USC Shoah Foundation, 28 September 1995, Toronto, ON. http://sfi.usc.edu/

"Nordhausen," *GIs Remember: Liberating the Concentration Camps.* Washington, DC: National Museum of American Jewish Military History, 1994.

Rosenberg, Albert. *Visual History Archive*, USC Shoah Foundation, 10 August 1998, El Paso, TX. http://sfi.usc.edu/

Schnaittacher, Fritz. United States Holocaust Memorial Museum (USHMM) archive testimony, video recording, RG-50.030*0325, 9 May 1995.

Stern, Guy. USHMM videotaped testimony, 1 May 1990, RG-50.030*0223.

Sternberg, Robert. *Visual History Archive*, USC Shoah Foundation, 18 November1996, Harts-
dale, NY. http://sfi.usc.edu/
From There to Here and Back Again. New York: Carlton Press, 1995.

BIBLIOGRAPHY OF SECONDARY SOURCES

Abzug, Robert H. *GIs Remember: Liberating the Concentration Camps*. Washington, DC:
National Museum of American Jewish Military History, 1994.
Introduction to *The Liberation of the Nazi Concentration Camps 1945: Eyewitness Accounts of
the Liberators*, edited by Brewster Chamberlin & Marica Feldman. Washington, DC: U.S.
Holocaust Memorial Council, 1987.
Bartov, Omer. "Wartime Lies and Other Testimonies: Jewish-Christian Relations in Buczacz,
1939-1944." *East European Politics and Societies* 25, No. 3 (August 2011).
Berenbaum, Michael. "The Rescuers: When the Ordinary is Extraordinary," *The Routledge
History of the Holocaust*, edited by Jonathan C. Friedman, 315-325. London: Routledge,
2011.
Chamberlin, Brewster & Marcia Feldman, eds. *The Liberation of the Nazi Concentration
Camps 1945: Eyewitness Accounts of the Liberators*. Washington, DC: U.S. Holocaust
Memorial Council, 1987.
Eliach, Yaffa and Brana Gurewitsh, eds. *The Liberators*. New York: Center for Holocaust
Studies, Documentation, and Research in Brooklyn, 1981.
Furst, Peter. "Joyous, Sobbing Prisoners of Dachau Mob, Kiss Liberating Yank Troops." *The
Stars and Stripes*, 2 May 1945. (Delayed from 29 April).
Hackett, David A., editor and translator. *The Buchenwald Report*. Boulder: Westview Press,
1995.
Hilberg, Raul. *Perpetrators, Victims, Bystanders: The Jewish Catastrophe 1933-1945*. New
York: HarperPerennial, 1993.
Hirsh, Michael. *The Liberators: America's Witnesses to the Holocaust*. New York: Bantam
Books, 2010.
Karras, Steven. *The Enemy I Knew: German Jews in the Allied Military in World War II*.
Minneapolis: Zenith Press, 2009.
Kogon, Eugene. *The Theory and Practice of Hell: The German Concentration Camps and the
System behind Them*, translated by Heinz Norden. New York: Farrar, Straus and Giroux,
2006.
Megargee, Geoffrey P., ed. *The United States Holocaust Memorial Museum Encyclopedia of
Camps and Ghettos, 1933-1945: Early Camps, Youth Camps, and Concentration Camps
and Subcamps Under the SS-Business Administration Main Office (WVHA)*, vol. 1, parts A
and B. Bloomington, IN: Indiana University Press, 2009.
Levi, Primo. *The Drowned and the Saved*. New York: Vintage Books, 1989.

NOTES

1. Omer Bartov, "Wartime Lies and Other Testimonies: Jewish-Christian Relations in
Buczacz, 1939-1944," *East European Politics and Societies* 25, No. 3 (August 2011): 506.

2. Raul Hilberg, *Perpetrators, Victims, Bystanders: The Jewish Catastrophe 1933-1945*
(New York: HarperPerennial, 1993), ix. For post-war "entangled relationships," see Atina
Grossman, *Jews, Germans, and Allies: Close Encounters in Occupied Germany* (Princeton:
Princeton University Press, 2007).

3. Raul Hilberg in *The Liberation of the Nazi Concentration Camps, 1945: Eyewitness
Accounts of the Liberators*, Brewster Chamberlin and Marcia Feldman, eds., (Washington, DC:
U.S. Holocaust Memorial Council, 1987), 84.

4. Sixteen of the oral histories came from the Visual History Archive (VHA) at the University of Southern California's Shoah Foundation Institute. "Liberators and Liberation Wit-

nesses" and "Rescuers and Aid Providers" are two of the tags. The default category for the Shoah Foundation's interviews is "Survivor" and thus one needs to look closer for more detail.

5. For more on fragmented Jewish identity prior to World War II, see Marsha L. Rozenblit, *Reconstructing A National Identity: The Jews of Hapsburg Austria During World War I* (New York: Oxford University Press, 2001).

6. Nora Levin scathingly addresses the absence of Allied rescue efforts when she writes, "An immense abyss lay between the instruments of death and the instruments of salvation." She blames the Allies for not doing more and not having a plan to rescue the Jews from extermination, for possessing knowledge of the atrocities but doing nothing to stop it. "The liberation of the Jewish survivors," Levin argues, "was a fortuitous by-product of military victory, an accidental consequence which taxed many Allied officers with sticky problems for which they had neither the time nor taste." Nora Levin, *The Holocaust: The Destruction of European Jewry 1933-1945* (New York: Thomas Y. Crowell Company, 1968), 683, 689. Also, see General Eisenhower's 1945 "Proclamation No. 1" whose first line declares, "We come as conquerors, not oppressors."

7. Harry Adler, Library of Congress, Veterans History Project, AFC 2001/001/78488 VHP MV02 (REF).

8. Guy Stern, USHMM videotaped testimony, 1 May 1990, RG-50.030*0223.

9. Si Lewen, interview with the author, 17 August 2012, Gwynned, PA.

10. Kurt Klein, Shoah Foundation videotaped testimony, 7 December 1995, Scottsdale, AZ.

11. *GIs Remember: Liberating the Concentration Camps,* (Washington, DC: National Museum of American Jewish Military History, 1994), 48.

12. Robert Abzug, "Jewish American Liberators," *GIs Remember: Liberating the Concentration Camps,* (Washington, DC: National Museum of American Jewish Military History, 1994), 4.

13. See Deborah Dash-Moore, *GI Jews: How WWII Changed a Generation* (Cambridge, MA: Belknap Press, 2004);Steven Karras, *The Enemy I Knew: German Jews in the Allied Military in World War II* (Minneapolis: Zenith Press, 2009); Michael Hirsh, *The Liberators: America's Witnesses to the Holocaust* (New York: Bantam Books, 2010).

14. Abzug, "Jewish American Liberators," *Liberating the Concentration Camps: GIs Remember,* 7.

15. Albert Rosenberg, USC Shoah Foundation testimony, 10 August 1998, El Paso, TX.

16. Ibid.

17. Ibid.

18. David A. Hackett, ed. and trans., *The Buchenwald Report,* (Boulder: Westview Press, 1995), 377.

19. Harry Adler, Library of Congress, Veterans History Project, AFC 2001/001/78488 VHP MV02 (REF).

20. Ibid.

21. Si Lewen, "Reflections and Repercussions" at http://www.silewen.com/script/chapter16.html, accessed on 19 December 2012.

22. W. Gunther Plaut, Shoah Foundation testimony, 28 September 1995, Toronto, Ontario.

23. Ibid.

24. Ibid.

25. W. Gunther Plaut, *Liberating the Concentration Camps: GIs Remember,* 20.

26. W. Gunther Plaut, Shoah Foundation testimony.

27. W. Gunther Plaut, Shoah Foundation interview. Compare with Eisenhower's letter to Marshall.

28. Ibid.

29. Ibid.

30. Ibid.

31. Fritz Schnaittacher, USHMM archive video testimony, RG-50.030*0325, 9 May 1995.

32. Hirsh, 194.

33. Fritz Schnaittacher, excerpted page from a hand-written letter dated May 1945, USHMM Photo Archives, Desig. # 16.517, W/S # 35537.

34. Ibid.

35. Quoted in Hirsh, 203.

36. Ibid.; Felix Sparks, SIF VHA testimony, 17 September 1996, Denver, CO.

37. Herman Cohn, Shoah Foundation videotaped testimony, 24 December 1996, Chicago, Illinois.

38. Ibid.

39. Peter Furst, "Joyous, Sobbing Prisoners of Dachau Mob, Kiss Liberating Yank Troops," *The Stars and Stripes*, 2 May 1945 (Delayed from 29 April).

40. Willy Herbst, *GIs Remember: Liberating the Concentration Camps*, (Washington, DC: Museum for American Jewish Military History, 1994), 43.

41. Sternberg, Shoah Foundation testimony. For a similar sentiment (among others), see the novel by Hanoch Bartov, *The Brigade*, trans. David S. Segal (Philadelphia: Jewish Publication Society of America, 1967), 232.

42. Harold Baum, in Steven Karras, *The Enemy I Knew: German Jew in the Allied Military in World War II* (Minneapolis: Zenith Press, 2009), 164.

43. *The United States Holocaust Memorial Museum Encyclopedia of Camps and Ghettos,* vol. 1, part A, 488-490. See also http://www.ushmm.org/wlc/en/article.php?ModuleId=10006171 for more information.

44. Walter Monasch, Shoah Foundation videotape testimony, 14 May 1998, Novato, California.

45. See "Mauthausen" at http://www.ushmm.org/wlc/en/article.php?ModuleId=10005196 as well as *The United States Holocaust Memorial Museum Encyclopedia of Camps and Ghettos,* vol. 1, part B, 905.

46. Walter Monasch, Shoah Foundation videotape testimony, 14 May 1998, Novato, California.

47. Werner Ellman as quoted in Hirsh, 257.

48. Werner Ellman, Interview 29715, *Visual History Archive*, USC Shoah Foundation, 6 June 1997, Chicago, Illinois.

49. Ibid.

50. Stafford, 310.

51. Ibid., 310-311.

52. Leonard Linton, *Holocaust Testimonies: European Survivors and American Liberators in New Jersey*, ed. Joseph J. Preil (New Brunswick, NJ: Rutgers University Press, 2001), 277.

53. Primo Levi, *Survival in Auschwitz* (New York: Touchstone, 1996), 88n; see also Primo Levi, *The Drowned and the Saved*, trans. Raymond Rosenthal (New York: Vintage International, 1989), 83-84.

54. Stafford, 312. Linton also comments on the unforgettable smell of the camp, as many liberators do, and the deep olfactory impression it made on his memory.

55. Joseph Eaton, USHMM archive testimony, RG-50.030*0581.

56. .Walter Monasch, Shoah Foundation videotape testimony, 1998, Novato, California.

57. Ibid.

58. Ibid.

59. Leondard Linton, *Holocaust Testimonies*, 276.

60. Lee Merel, *Holocaust Testimonies*, 280.

61. Excerpts from interview with Eric Leiseroff, ed. Yaffa Eliach and Brana Grewitsch, *The Liberators: Eyewitness Accounts of the Liberation of Concentration Camps*, 2.

62. John E. Herman, Library of Congress, Veteran's History Project, AFC/2001/001/53763, (SR02 REF) audio recording.

Poisoned Virtue

Child Sacrifice in Abrahamic Scriptures
and Interpretation

Bruce Chilton

INTRODUCTION: THE PROBLEM

Søren Kierkegaard in "Fear and Trembling" portrayed Abraham as heroic, a true knight of faith whose belief suspended ethical judgment, "transforming a murder into a holy act well pleasing to God."[1] This reading gives classic expression to a view common to existentialist philosophy and modern Christian thought alike, conveyed with Kierkegaard's sweeping phrase, much quoted in philosophical discussion, "the teleological suspension of the ethical." For some reason, perhaps having to do with the existential anxiety with which Kierkegaard imbued Abraham, this principle has escaped identification as another version of saying that the ends justify the means.

In addition to offering a questionable logic of ethics, Kierkegaard's interpretation perpetuates a cultural misapprehension common throughout the West. After the biblical period, especially from the fourth century C.E. on, hagiography had its way with Abraham. As the founder of ideals that Judaism, Christianity, and Islam, all strive to realize within their societies, Abraham's image is typically burnished to make him into a model of what every believer should be. Yet when Abraham is taken to be above reproach and his behavior as depicted in Genesis 22 is assumed to be noble, the result is to commend violence: the virtue of the patriarch is poisoned by a lack of reflection, as three examples – all involved with the Crusades and all tied by their authors to the story of Abraham's offering – amply illustrate.

147

Pope Urban II toured his native France between 1095 and his death in 1099 in order to preach the Crusade, appealing to the common conviction that bloodshed purifies the faithful and pleases God. He called for warriors who would literally bear the sign of the cross on their chests during their journey to Jerusalem, as pilgrim cross-bearers (*croisés* in French, crusaders in English) who could celebrate their release from sin as they went to battle. If they died in their struggle against the heathen, Urban guaranteed with his authority as pope, their sins would be forgiven.

Urban grounded his argument for why Crusaders should go forth to battle with an assessment of their present, sinful condition at home, which could be cured, he promised, by battling abroad. He added a practical edge to his appeal, amounting to an attempt at social engineering. He predicted that a good war against a common foe would at last resolve the problem of internecine squabbles among the bellicose knights of Medieval Europe.

Yet Urban was thinking, not only politically, but also in terms of the supernatural virtue of giving one's life for the Catholic faith. He believed that fractious knights at home could be transformed into heroic martyrs in the crucible of holy war. By means of both the blood they offered and the lives they took on the way to Jerusalem, he explicitly stated that each Crusader became "a living, holy and pleasing sacrifice"[2] to God.

Urban also made the connection between the Crusaders and the Maccabees before them, comparing Maccabean combat "for rituals and the Temple" to the new and nobler struggle for the *patria*, the "fatherland." Historians have often remarked that the Crusades successfully combined medieval hunger for pilgrimage, penitence, and spoil with assertions of national and papal power. Those observations are valid, but the popular energy unleashed by the Crusades has nonetheless puzzled historians, chiefly because they have not adequately factored in the sacrificial dimension of Urban's appeal. Self-*sacrifice*, more than self-interest, is the hidden hand guiding this strange and relentless history.

Popular response to Urban's call exceeded all expectations, in numbers and in zeal. Crusaders became notoriously difficult to control, because they included not only knights, but also hosts of untrained enthusiasts, especially from the peasantry. They took the papal grant of forgiveness to very much to heart, because Urban promised a reward for the present[3] as well as the future: "he absolved all the penitent from all their sins from the hour they took the Lord's cross and he lovingly released them from all hardships, whether fasting or other mortification of the flesh." Crusading was a license, not only to kill, but also to eat one's fill and indulge other appetites, absolved in advance from the sins of greed, theft, and lust. Battle took the place of the penance, payment, and stringent disciplines usually required for forgiveness.

Pope Urban sought to persuade "men of all ranks, knights as well as foot soldiers, rich as well as poor, to carry aid promptly to those Christians [in

Muslim lands] and to destroy that vile race from the lands of your brethren." The response gave him more than he had asked for. In the First Crusade alone, between 60,00 and 100,000 people[4] —men, women, and children— answered Urban's call. Thousands of them, especially the badly trained, amateurs, and the young, were served up to their Muslim enemies for slaughter in modern day Turkey, far short of the goal of their "pilgrimage."

Retribution and pilgrimage were combined in the Crusades, as has often been remarked, but the aim was salvation. A monk of the time, Guibert of Nogent, appreciated and repeated Urban's aim, saying, "God has instituted in our time holy wars, so that the order of knights and the crowd running in their wake, who, following the example of ancient pagans, have been engaged in slaughtering one another, might find a new way of gaining salvation." Violence had been baptized as the route to heaven for men and women and children who wished to find a way to be free of the corruption of this world despite their own worldly, violent proclivities, and to win their place in heaven with Christ.

Sinners could not make up for their sins personally, of course, but recourse to penitential discipline, or the violent short cut of joining the Crusades, demonstrated sorrow and faith in Christ's atoning gift. Middle English poetry is filled with examples of lyrics recited at the time one paid a recompense for sin, such as the "Invocation to the Cross:"[5]

> O blissful Crosse, teche us al vertu
> Plesyng to god for oure salvacion,
> Quenchyng alle vices in the name of Ihesu
> Raunson payng for oure dampnacion.

That Cross, portrayed as the fulfillment of the sacrifice of Isaac and the supernatural altar of God's eternal offering of his Son to himself, was now literally taken up in the Crusades by ordinary sinners, so they would be cleansed of sin for eternity. They grasped the opportunity in their tens of thousands.

The Crusaders' zeal targeted *all* those who rejected faith in Christ. Many militants took out the full vigor of their initial fervor against Jews in their own communities before they left for the Holy Land, as well as against Jews who lay along their path to Jerusalem. Although their pogroms might seem a grotesque perversion of Urban's aim, the Crusaders were convinced of the family resemblance among all infidels, and it seemed madness to leave the enemy undisturbed at home while fighting them abroad.

In addition to their rejection of Christ, circumcision represented a common bond between Muslims and Jews, designed according to the Crusade's propagandists to give "free rein for every kind of shameful behavior."[6] Peter the Venerable, a learned monastic abbot who had the Qur'an translated into

Latin in order to refute it, came to the conclusion in 1146 (or 1147) that God rejects "the Jews like the hateful Cain, the Muslims like the worshippers of Baal."

Pogroms became international Christian practice during the centuries of the Crusades. Describing the crowning of Richard the Lionhearted in 1189, Richard of Devizes offers an account that is as chilling in its rhetoric as the atrocities against Jews in England that it depicts were inhuman. Richard refers to the Eucharist that solemnized the coronation as the sacrifice of Christ. He links that sacrifice to another, the slaughter by Christian mobs of Jews described as "vermin:"[7] "On the very day of the coronation, about that solemn hour, in which the Son was immolated to the Father, a sacrifice of the Jews to their father the devil was commenced in the city of London, and so long was the duration of this famous mystery, that the holocaust could scarcely be accomplished the ensuing day."

The Crusaders' taste for the torture and decapitation of their victims emerged during a pogrom against the Jews in Worms according to written records. But the holy warriors took to their method with eagerness, and they used it against their enemies generally; later in their campaign, they unearthed Muslim dead so as to decapitate them, too. In the case of armed opponents in the field, however, the Crusaders had to face the inevitable outcome that when the fortunes of war shifted, their grisly tactics could be turned around and used against them. Nonetheless, the decapitation of enemies remained a standby Crusader practice, especially useful when heads could be catapulted into besieged cities, in order to demoralize their inhabitants.

By the time the First Crusade ended, Crusaders had engaged in cannibalism at Marrat in 1098, and beheading seemed compassionate compared to other means of killing at their hands. Raymond of Aguilers wrote of the taking of Jerusalem on 15 July 1099: "Some of the pagans were mercifully beheaded,[8] others, pierced by arrows, plunged from towers, and yet others, tortured for a long time, were burned to death in searing flames. Piles of heads, hands and feet lay in the houses and streets, and men and knights were running to and fro over corpses."

Raymond portrayed this pornographic bloodshed in terms of sacrifice, specifying that "in the Temple our men were wading up to their ankles in enemy blood," that some 320 corpses were set ablaze as a burnt offering, and that the slaughter began on Good Friday at the ninth hour, when Jesus was crucified. The Crusaders gathered for Mass in the alleged place of Jesus' burial, the Church of the Holy Sepulcher, while the blood of their victims was still on them, so that their devotion was enhanced by the blood that had been shed—their victims', their comrades', their own – and Christ's.

While Muslim armies could turn the Crusaders tactics against them, and Muslim theologians articulated teachings of *jihad* to address the new situation, Jewish families and communities had no recourse to military defense. A Christian chronicler, Albert of Aachen, recorded that in Mainz in 1096, "The Jews, seeing that their Christian enemies were attacking them and their children, and that they were sparing no age, likewise fell upon one another, brothers, children, wives, and sisters, and thus they perished at each other's hands. Horrible to say, mothers cut the throats of nursing children with knives[9] and stabbed others, preferring them to perish thus by their own hands than to be killed by the weapons of the uncircumcised."

A Jewish chronicler made both the actions and the motivations involved even more explicit in his description of collective suicide: "Each one in turn sacrificed and was sacrificed, until the blood of one touched the blood of another. The blood of husbands mixed with that of the wives, the blood of fathers and their children, and the blood of brothers and their sisters, and blood of rabbis and their disciples, the blood of bridegroom and their brides... the blood of children and nursing infants and their mothers. They were killed and slaughtered for the unity of God's glorious and awesome name."

From the perspective of the biblical and Judaic tradition, the question had to be asked, and it was asked (using the term "Aqedah" to designate Genesis 22): "Were there ever 1,100 Aqedahs on one day – all of them like the Aqedah of Isaac, son of Abraham?" In the face of this carnage, "Why did the heavens not grow dark and the stars not hold back their splendor?" Isaac ben David, warden of the Jewish community in Mainz, put into brutal action the theology that explained innocent sacrifice that had been current since the time of the Maccabees. He killed his children in front of the ark of the Torah in the synagogue, and said, "May this blood be atonement for all my sins."

The horror of the images makes them difficult to believe, and the force of legend and oral retelling is palpable in many stories of the Crusades' Jewish victims. In one famous story, a young mother named Rachel killed her children, one of them named Isaac:

> She took her young son Isaac – he was most pleasant—and slaughtered him.... As for the lad Aaron, upon seeing that his brother had been slain he shouted, "My mother, my mother, do not slay me;" and he went and hid under a box. Rachel then took her two daughters Bella and Madrona and sacrificed them to the Lord, God of hosts, who commanded us not to compromise our untainted fear of him and to be totally wholehearted with him. When the righteous woman finished sacrificing her three children to our Creator, she raised her voice and called out to her son, "Aaron, Aaron, where are you? I shall not have mercy to spare you either." She pulled him by his leg out from under the box where he had hidden and sacrificed him to God the powerful and the exalted.

Crusaders, enraged that they had been cheated of young lives to kill, beat the sacrificial mother to death.

In perhaps the most disturbing, darkly described tale of pre-emptive slaughter within a Jewish community, a Rabbi and prospective father-in-law takes the lives of both his son, named Abraham, and his son's bride to be, tragically named Sarit (a diminutive form of the name Sarah). When she tries to escape her Aqedah by running away, the Rabbi intervenes:

> But when her father-in-law, Master Judah ben Rabbi Abraham the pious saw that such was his daughter-in-law's intention, he called to her, "My daughter, since you did not have the privilege of wedding my son Abraham, you will not marry any Gentile either." He caught hold of her... kissed her on the mouth, and raised his voice, wailing together with the maiden. He cried out in a loud voice, bitterly, to all those present, "Behold, all of you, this is the wedding my daughter, my bride, that I am performing today." They all cried, sobbing and wailing, mourning and moaning. The pious Master Judah said to her, "Come and lie in the bosom of Abraham our father, for in an instant you will acquire your place in the next world and enter into the company of the righteous and pious." He took her and laid her upon the bosom of his son Abraham her betrothed and, with his sharpened sword, he cut her up the middle into two parts; then he also slaughtered his son."

The resonance of these stories with the Aqedah is as obvious as their unremitting violence, inspired by biblical descriptions of cutting sacrificial victims in half. The narratives' total dedication to the ideal of sacrifice pushes aside moral objection to taking the lives not only of one's children, but also of young people who wanted no part of self-sacrifice.

Jihad with its connexion to martyrdom proved effective within a context of tribal warfare, and brought Islam international conquests long before the Crusades. In December of 627, the Byzantine emperor Heraclius put an end to what he thought was the greatest threat to his empire, the Persian super-power that Greece and Rome had elevated to mythic proportions, when he defeated the Sassanid dynasty's army at Nineveh. Heraclius took back Jerusalem and returned sacred relics that the Sassanids had plundered. But he overlooked the quarter from which his greatest defeat was impending.

In 630 Heraclius triumphantly returned the "Holy Cross" (wood on which Jesus had allegedly been crucified) to the Holy City, but he then saw his army, tens of thousands strong, defeated by the new Muslim forces at Yarmuk during August of 636. Jerusalem fell two years later, and the Holy Cross had to be shipped to Constantinople, while the "Holy Lance" that allegedly killed Jesus was removed to Antioch.

The Muslim doctrine of the "four swords" emerged during the early centuries of spectacular triumph:

> Allah gave the Prophet Muhammad four swords: the first against the polytheists, which Muhammad himself fought with; the second against apostates, which Caliph Abu Bakr fought with; the third against the People of the Book

[Christians and Jews], which Caliph 'Umar fought with; and the fourth against
dissenters, which Caliph 'Ali fought with.

This teaching by Al-Shaybani, who died in 804 CE, helps explain what
motivated the enormous success of Muslim raiders, especially during a time
when the two super-powers of the era, the Byzantine Empire and the Sassanid Empire, had largely exhausted themselves in confrontation with one another. Centuries prior to Urban II, Islam had found a way to turn lethal
squabbles among clans outward into productive conquests for the *umma*, the
community.

Jihad by no means precluded peaceful relations with Christianity. In 800,
eastern monks presented Charlemagne with keys to the Church of the Holy
Sepulcher, the standard of the city of Jerusalem, along with sacred relics,
after long negotiations with the Muslim Abbasids in Baghdad led by Isaac, a
Jew whom Charlemagne had sent as part of a contact group. But once the
Crusades became the norm, resort to anything but violence to gain access to
Jerusalem seemed a betrayal to many Christians. Frederick II, the Holy Ro-
man Emperor, led his Crusade more by diplomacy and his own knowledge of
Arabic than by force of arms, and arranged for Jerusalem, Bethlehem, and
Nazareth to be placed under Christian control in 1229, but Frederick, called
"the Infidel Emperor" saw his settlement rejected by the papacy.

The resilience of the Qur'anic teaching is such that it proved adaptable to
the cessation of conquest as well as to extension into new territories. The
jurist al-Shafi'i (who died in 820 C.E.) taught that *jihad* was a *collective*
responsibility, not required of all Muslims, during the period that Islam settled into relatively stable borders with Christian lands. The Crusades, of
course, as well as attendant actions such as the Christian "reconquest" of
Spain, meant the end of relative stability, and signaled the need for a militant
definition of *jihad.*

No single figure better represents the Muslim response to the threat of the
Crusades than Saladin, the general born in Tikrit who welded disparate Muslim kingdoms in the eastern Mediterranean basin into a single force, dedicated to Sunni Islam. The triumph of Saladin over the Crusaders was triggered
by the ill-advised attempt of the Crusading knight Reginald de Châtillon,
beginning in 1182, to destroy Mecca and Medina. This brought to the land of
the Ka'ba a threat that neither Muhammad nor the Qur'an had foreseen, but
one that clearly justified *jihad*, serving to help Saladin forge a united opposition.

Reginald at first succeeded to the fateful extent that he kidnapped Saladin's sister in 1187. Saladin vowed he would decapitate Reginald with his
own scimitar. After the battle of Hittin later the same year, he did just that,
ordering the execution of 200 Templars and Hospitallers at the same time.
During his campaign, which included the liberation of Jerusalem, Saladin

learned of the death of his little son, named Isma'il. On the Feast of Sacrifice, which commemorates Ibrahim's offering of his son, Saladin made a vow in Jerusalem[10] that would influence the understanding of *jihad* ever after: "I think that when God grants me victory over the rest of Palestine I shall divide my territories, make a will stating my wishes, then set sail on the sea for their far-off lands and pursue the Franks there so as to free the earth of anyone who does not believe in God, or die in the attempt." One of his biographers, when describing Saladin's victory at Tiberias, relates both the grisly conse-quences of *jihad* and the deep conviction that the land needed to be purified of Christianity: "The field of battle became a sea of blood; the dust was stained red, rivers of blood ran freely, and the face of the true Faith was revealed free from those shadowy abominations." In a chilling throwback to the Crusader's pogroms against the Jews, 'Imad ad-Din observes that "the humiliation proper to the men of Saturday was inflicted on the men of Sun-day." *Jihad* had been unleashed for defensive reasons, but with an intensity and an extension in its reach which, in theory, no one could escape.

A century later, the jurist Ibn Taymiyah (1268-1328 CE), responding partially to confrontation with Crusaders but chiefly to Mongol invasions from the east, articulated a definition of *jihad* that made it the literal pinnacle of Muslim faith,[11] based on the Prophet's analogy of dedication to Allah to a camel, "the head of the affair is Islam, its central pillar is the *salat* [prayer], and the tip of the hump is the *jihad*." This made Ibn Taymiyah say, as he is still quoted in militant websites today: "Now, it is in *jihad* that one can live and die in ultimate happiness, both in this world and in the hereafter."

The bloodied Crusader, the Jewish child literally called an Aqedah, the *shahid* who dies in the midst of the *jihad*, have confronted one another in battle and met one another in sacrifice – not continuously, but with sporadic intensity—since the eleventh century of the Common Era. Woven into texts and traditions that combine metaphor, archetype, and direct identification with martyrs of the faith, they reach into the symbolic depths of culture, where people can be moved to act for reasons they are often in no position to understand.

TURNING GENESIS 22 INTO A SACRIFICIAL TEXT

On its surface, Genesis 22 could not sustain many of sorts of interpretation it has been made to serve. After all, its climax is reached with the angel's intervention in v. 11-13 that leads Abraham to sacrifice, not his son, but a ram. A text that is opposed to the sacrifice of young human beings has been used to support offering them up in warfare.

To some extent, that transformation was possible because, in the environ-ment in which Genesis 22 was produced, human offering was a current activity. The inscription called "The Moabite Stone" (carved during the middle of the ninth century BCE) on behalf of Mesha, king of Moab, shows that the ideology of holy war was not limited to Israel.[12] Mesha relates that his god, "Kemosh said to me, 'Go, take Nebo against Israel.' And I went by night and fought against it from the break of dawn until noon, and I took it and slew all, seven thousand men and boys and women and girls and female slaves; for to Ashtor-Kemosh I had devoted it. And I took from there the vessels of Yhwh and brought them before Kemosh."

The transition from sacrifice to child sacrifice left enough traces in ancient sources to permit us to see how it occurred. In Israelite and ancient Near Eastern practice, as well as in the rituals of Greece, Rome, India, and South America, specified parts of any sacrificial animal were offered to the flames, for the deity alone, while the participants enjoyed the rest. At times, the whole victim belonged to the god, typically when a community felt that their collective behavior had brought about divine disfavor: then those who sacrificed would offer a feast for the deity alone, and not take part themselves. The food might all be consigned to flame, or a part distributed among the priesthood, but the point was that when the usual, festal communion between divine and human participants had been interrupted, the deity alone would benefit from a sacrifice in order to re-establish a broken relationship.

Once the offering of sacrifice went to the god alone as a valuable gift of restitution, and the connection with human consumption was broken, then the preciousness of human flesh could make it seem an ideal medium of worship in crisis. That is exactly how the offering of children is presented in the Hebrew Bible. In a narrative even sparer than the prose of the Aqedah, Mesha, the king of Moab, in the thick of battle against the kings of both Judah and Israel, "took his firstborn son who was to reign in his stead, and offered him for a burnt offering upon the wall." Instead of condemning this action, the passage goes on to narrate, "A great wrath came on Israel; they pulled back from him and returned to their own land" (the Second Book of Kings 3:27). In other words, the human sacrifice worked. Mesha, a contemporary of the Elohist source that produced Genesis 22 (during the ninth century BCE), actually did what Abraham did not, and benefited as a result.

Mesha's sacrifice of his son, near the same time that the Elohist source crafted the Aqedah, shows how deeply, without any connection to Abraham, the appeal of child sacrifice had worked into the consciousness of the ancient Near East. From the point of view of the god Kemosh, all the destruction of battle came as a sacrifice that he rewarded with victory for his people Moab. From the point of view of the story in the Second Book of Kings, the sacrifice of Mesha's son in particular was so effective that divine "wrath" came upon Israel: apparently Yahweh either took pleasure in the human offering himself, or did not stand in the way of the pleasure Kemosh took in Mesha's sacrifice. The success of the desperate ritual, however it was explained, posed a disturbing question. If other peoples cherished their gods so much that they are willing to offer their children, could Israelites show themselves less devoted to their deity?

Time and again when dealing with sacrificial and ritual texts and then comparing them to archaeological evidence, it becomes plain that ancient sources downplay or deny the violence involved in killing, although slaughter of some kind is an indispensable act within most rites. During the first century B.C.E., Diodorus Siculus reported on the ancient practice at Carthage,[13] revived during time of war, to offer children to the local god (20.14.6): "A bronze statue of Cronos among them extended its hands, palms up and inclining toward the earth, so that the children set on it rolled down and fell into a chasm filled with fire." According to Diodorus' account, two hundred children were selected for this treatment, and another hundred were volunteered for the rite. Here there can be no doubt but that child sacrifice was practiced ritually, and Diodorus refers to human sacrifice among Egyptians (1.88.5), Celts (5.31.3-4; 5.32.6; 31.13.1), and Messenian Greeks (8.8.2), as well. But archaeological investigation at Carthage in particular both confirms Diodorus' account with skeletal remains and inscriptions and uncovers another, related feature of child sacrifice. The inscriptions so far discovered refer to the gifts offered to the various gods of Carthage, rather than to who was offered in the flames or the method of killing the children, most of whom were less than two years old.

Inside the Iron Age fortress at Arad, archaeologists found remains of a temple used for several centuries during the time of the Divided Monarchy (ninth century BCE).[14] Though worship centers outside of Jerusalem were forbidden by the Law of Moses (Deuteronomy 12), high places flourished throughout the land according to the Bible. The sacrificial altar is visible in the outer courtyard. Sanctuaries of Israelite communities were often local operations serving one or more clans or villages, or at most one or two larger clan groups (or tribes). Individual families could even set up their own shrines, altars, or temples. Although the compilers of Genesis—2 Kings present Shiloh as the principal religious and political center of pre-monarchic Israel, important sanctuaries seem to have been located in several towns during the settlement period. These early cultic centers included Shechem, Shiloh, Nob, Kadesh, Beersheba, Dan, Penuel, Bethel/Mizpah/Gilgal, Hebron, Gibeon, and Ophra.

By the time the Elohist source was first crafted,[15] during the ninth century B.C.E., the united kingdom of David and Solomon had been torn apart by civil war. Judea remained under the control of David's successors, but the bulk of the country – which appropriated the name of Israel – went a separate way, with its own king, altars, rituals of sacrifice, and ideas of what God truly desired. This Israel (called the Northern Kingdom in modern scholarship, to distinguish it from Judea) was more prosperous than its southern counterpart, more able and willing to trade and make alliances with sur-rounding countries and empires, and therefore more open to influences from cultures whose worship differed radically from the standards set out by the prophets of Yahweh. In this syncretistic environment, Israelites in the north embraced gods alongside Yahweh. Child sacrifice, one of the practices known from before, during, and after this period, became a pressing issue for the Elohist. The Aqedah represents the Elohist's response to the possibility that offering a son would seal a father's devotion to God.

Linguistic choices that went into telling the story give it its unique voice, alive with the exceptional nature of the events recounted:

> Then after these things God tried Abraham. He said to him, Abraham. And he said, Look—me. He said, Take now your son, your cherished one, whom you love, Isaac, and go your way to the land of Moriah, and offer him up there, an offering by fire on one of the hills that I say to you.
>
> Abraham awoke early in the morning, saddled his ass and took two young men with him, as well as Isaac his son, split the wood of the offering by fire, and arose and went to the place that God said to him. On the third day Abra-ham lifted up his eyes and saw the place from afar. Abraham said to the young men, Stay back here with the ass. I and the young man, we will go there. We will worship. We will come back to you.
>
> Abraham took the wood of the offering by fire and put it on Isaac his son, and took in his hand the flint and the knife, and the two of them went, together. Isaac spoke to Abraham his father. He said, My father. And he said, Look – me, my son. He said, Look—the flint and the wood, but where is the lamb of the offering by fire? Abraham said, God will himself see the lamb of the offering by fire, my son. And the two of them went, together.
>
> They came to the place that God said to him, and Abraham built there a slaughter pit, and arranged the wood, bound up Isaac his son, and put him on the slaughter pit above the wood. Abraham sent back his hand, took the knife to kill his son.

The routine of sacrifice permeates this narrative, determining the content of every action, punctuating each gesture, and grounding the whole plot in a relentless rhythm. That is why Abraham needs no more than the initial com-mand by God —what to sacrifice, how and where – to proceed along his way. Abraham knows what to do; inexorable ritual seems to drive him to a foregone conclusion.

Knowledge of the sacrificial sequence underlies the horror that the story evokes, as well as its action. Once Isaac is identified as the victim God wants, each move – ordinarily an anodyne increment in shedding animal blood for divine festivity—ratchets toward infanticide. Isaac focuses the narrative and its horror when he asks, "Where is the lamb of the offering by fire?" He knows what needs to happen, yet doesn't know Abraham's intent; his knowledge and his ignorance together make him the most acute observer of the events, as well as their innocent victim.

When Isaac, who is about to be sacrificed, asks innocently about the lamb, his question encapsulates the full power of Genesis 22. Its emotional impact derives, not merely from a masterful style of narration, but also from a fearless investigation of the connection between sacrifice and infanticide.

By the time of the Elohist, human sacrifice had been practiced for millennia. The end of the Stone Age saw the first urban communities and, in some cases, the institutional killing of children. Cities were the basic unit of human civilization, generating large markets, the production of surpluses that could be used to trade with other cities, specialized activities, armies, wars and casualties, the practice of victors taking multiple wives from the women of fallen enemies and comrades alike, central government, royal courts, and a central altar of sacrifice.

The urban temple, the foundation of the whole city, had to be seen as holier and more powerful, more attractive to the gods, than any other altar. Human sacrifice emerged as the price required to assure divine favor in building a city,[16] the means of making the urban temple the ultimate altar. Several ancient myths depict the founder king of a city as sacrificing his own child, his first-born son, by slaughtering him on the foundation stone of the city in order to secure prosperity, and especially victory over enemies.

Before the Exodus of the people Israel from Egypt, human sacrifice had been practiced on the land that Israel eventually occupied, and was practiced after Israelite settlement. When God "tried Abraham," that trial was in no way hypothetical. Abraham climbed Moriah to worship his deity with his most cherished possession, following time-honored practices of peoples far more ancient than Israel, the Elohist source, and Abraham himself. But this narrative equally illustrates that sacrificing a person clashes with the usual practice and purpose of sacrifice in general. That's what makes the story a trial. Isaac's question about the lamb for the offering speaks from the heart of Genesis 22, posing the crucial issue: what is the fundamental difference, if any, between sacrificing a person and sacrificing an animal?

In the original text of Genesis 22, although it is God who tries Abraham (v. 1), an "angel" rather than God himself intervenes to prevent the sacrifice (v. 11). The Elohist source substitutes the angel for God in order to avoid any implication of God's physical intervention; the source characteristically avoids anthropomorphism. The ancillary result, however, emerges in the suspicion that the angel denies what God had actually wanted. Although not the intent of the Elohist, this shadow of doubt has fed subsequent interpretation.

The Book of Biblical Antiquities represents a transitional moment, fueled by the reality and the remembrance of martyrs who really did die, *when Isaac was seen as an actual sacrifice*, and had been intended as such by God. This is the moment, very early in the second century C.E., when the term "Aqedah" came into its own, because it was a reference to the way a sheep or a ram was tied up for slaughter[17] , foreleg to hind leg. Isaac became a ritual offering and his death appeased God for the sins of Israel, and "Aqedah" became the designtion of Genesis 22 within Rabbinic interpretation.

This human sacrifice emerged as the paradigm of all sacrifice at a crucial moment in Israelite history. The Romans had burned the Temple when they occupied Jerusalem in 70 C.E., preventing the public practice of the sacrificial ritual that had until that time been the principal seal of the covenant. How could God allow this place, the intersection of heaven and earth, to be defiled by Gentiles? The fundamental challenge of the Romans to Israelite identity made a second great revolt, during 132-135 C.E., as inevitable as it was inevitably disastrous. The *Book of Biblical Antiquities,* written either between these two wars or after them both, has Isaac say that his willingness to die at Abraham's hand proves that God has made human life a worthy sacrifice (32:3): only the prototype of offering remained after the Temple's destruction, and it became imperative within Judaism that Isaac's offering should be seen as complete and perfect. That interpretative move permitted Jews to conceive of the covenant continuing even after the most visible sign of the covenant, sacrifice in the Temple, had been wiped off the face of the earth.

When Abraham placed Isaac on the altar as a burnt offering, both father and son were rejoicing as well as ready to act (*Liber Antiquitatum Biblicarum* 40:2-3). Here the older theology of the Maccabees finds its capstone. Although the *Book of Biblical Antiquities* stops short of saying that Isaac died on Moriah, it stands as the earliest reference to Isaac's "blood" (*Liber Antiquitatum Biblicarum* 18:5): "on account of his blood I chose them." The intention of father and son was so perfect, their offering was accepted as if it had been completed, and that "blood" seals the election of their progeny. In the case of Genesis 22, we can clearly see that the turn toward the primordial reflex of child-sacrifice is the consequence of violent external forces (the Roman demolition of the Temple) combined with a theology designed to enable the community to survive in desperate circumstances (Maccabean martyrdom).

Isaac's "blood" in the Aqedah stood for sacrifice, and – because the Romans had burned the Temple down in 70 CE and then razed the remaining masonry in 135 C.E.—Isaac came to embody the only sacrifice that God would or could accept. During the second century (see the Mishnah, Ta'anith 2:5), some Rabbis taught that the sound of the ram's horn with prayer and fasting would cause God to answer the community as he had once answered Abraham on Moriah. The Aqedah eventually took the place of the offering of the daily sacrifice required in the Temple, the Tamid lamb, when blood was poured into the altar's flames. Centuries later, around 450 C.E., the Rabbinic *midrash*, or interpretation, of the Book of Leviticus explained that, when any Israelite reads about the Tamid, God remembers the Aqedah (Leviticus Rabbah 2:11). Because the Aqedah is presented as the true ideal that the offering of the daily lamb recollects, Isaac and the martyrs took the place of the discontinued ritual in the Temple.

The Aqedah, produced with the resources of Judaism in its confrontation with Hellenistic culture (and quite apart from Christianity until this time), demonstrates that the offering of children is not a primordial instinct that "civilized" culture controls. To the contrary, the capacity of literate civilizations, the inheritors of Stone Age cities, to conflate children and sacrifice and war and religious duty into a single myth or metaphor such as the Aqedah, assures that no developed society in the Abrahamic tradition has ever perished for a want of willingness to shed innocent blood.

Once the connection between Isaac's Aqedah and ritual sacrifice had been made, it was possible for it to be articulated in other sacrificial contexts. A second-century midrash, for example, called the *Mekilta*, has God explain in Exodus 12:13 why he will pass over houses where he sees blood at the threshold of Israel's houses during the first Passover: "when I see the blood, I see the blood of Isaac's Aqedah." In this creative reading, typical of the ancient genre of midrash and quite unlike a strict commentary in the modern sense, the association of the Aqedah extends into a new paschal connexion without breaking the earlier connexions with the Tamid sacrifice.

The precise reasons for this innovative association with Passover only become plain when Christian claims during the second century, which presented Jesus' death at Passover as the true sacrifice foreshadowed by Isaac, are taken into account. But Isaac's status as the prototype of martyrdom and sacrifice made that Christian theology possible, and enabled Rabbinic Judaism to reply to the association between Christ and Isaac on the part of those whom the Rabbis considered heretics.

In his role of the prototypical martyr offering his life, Isaac crossed the line from readiness for sacrifice into sacrifice itself. When sacrificial blood is at issue, what God sees might be considered metaphorical or literal, and there is good evidence that Rabbinic interpretation took the image both ways. Perhaps, some interpreters said, Abraham went so far as nick Isaac's carotid artery[18], so that he lost a quarter of his blood before his father was stopped in the course of his sacrificial routine.

As this trajectory of interpretation developed (in Genesis Rabbah 55-56), Isaac's awareness about all the events around him also sharpened. Now he was no longer twenty-five years old (as Josephus portrayed the heroic young man in *Antiquities* 1 § 227), but thirty-seven, and he approached the sacrifice, not as a zealous martyr, but in mournful humility, tears falling from his eyes as—contradicting Philo's picture (*On Abraham* 176)—he asks his father to bind him fast, so that he will not struggle and blemish his body, which had to be perfect to be acceptable as a sacrifice. When the classic midrash Genesis Rabbah came to completion during the fifth century, Isaac's determination became quieter and deeper than in earlier interpretations, and for good reason. By then Constantine's recognition of Christianity put Judaism as a religion in a more perilous position than ever before within the Roman Empire.

The sacrifice that Abraham made of his son by this stage meant to some interpreters, not only that Isaac's blood was shed, but also—in the presentation of the Babylonian Talmud (Ta'anit 16a)—that he had been *reduced to ashes*. No more extreme statement of the completion of the ritual could be imagined. By the same token, means could be imagined by which Isaac would appear again in the biblical narrative: God must have raised Abraham's son, the child of promise, not merely from death, but from the ashes of a sacrifice by fire. Isaac symbolized a human offering that pleased God, but at the same time the will of God for Israel's survival by any means necessary, including physical resurrection from the dead. Isaac was redeemed from Moriah, no matter how far the sacrifice had gone, just as the people Israel had returned from what seemed certain extinction in Babylon.

Genesis Rabbah (chapters 55-56) in its present form took several centuries to evolve, and it interleaves many different traditions. Once these changes were incorporated within the Aqedah, Isaac was furnished with a temperament, character, and spiritual experience commensurate with his resurrection. By that stage, *Isaac*'s Aqedah had taken on a literary fullness such that Isaac nearly eclipsed Abraham within the narrative of events on Mount Moriah. Isaac carrying the wood was like a man carrying his cross (Genesis Rabbah 56.3)

STRATEGIES OF REDEMPTION FROM SACRED VIOLENCE

God has good reason to doubt the man he is trying in Genesis 22. Within the Book of Genesis by this stage, Abraham is not the noble figure of later tradition, but the subject of testing because his actions and their motivations have become suspect. They are dubious within the presentation of Genesis itself, not merely from a modern perspective. Men by the time Genesis was written were not supposed to pimp their pregnant wives (Genesis 20:1-16), desert their children and their children's mothers (Genesis 21:8-21), or enter into covenantal relationship with human rulers and their divinities rather than with God (Genesis 21:22-34).[19]

Within chapter 22, taken in its own terms, Abraham plods along on automatic pilot from beginning to end, neither complaining when told to carve up his child and burn him, nor celebrating when he gets to keep his son. He had bargained with God for the lives of the people of Sodom (Genesis 18:22-33), but says nothing at all to preserve the life of his child. He is not a Kierkegaardian "knight of faith" at all. He is a brute, and everything about his brutish behavior towards his family – by this point a deliberate theme in Genesis – emphasizes by contrast God's compassionate intervention. It is God who "saw" in the ram a way out of the dilemma posed by Abraham's character, and God who "was seen" by Abraham, so that the patriarch in the end spares his son's life.

The climax of the story, which delivers its message, insists both that Abraham and his progeny will enjoy the covenantal promise of Yahweh (vv. 16-18) and that Abraham is not to do anything whatever again to threaten harm to Isaac (vv. 12-14). When Abraham returns to Beersheba at the close of chapter 22 (v. 19), he does so on the basis of his covenant with Yahweh, rather than with Abimelech, and with a complete and enduring dedication to Isaac as his son and Sarah's. Just as he never came close to threatening the lives of his children again, so he never again offered his wife to Abimelech or anyone like him, and desisted from making covenants that competed with the divine covenant. Abraham came down from Moriah a changed man.

The test of the Aqedah put Abraham back on the track of the covenant. Only a reading of Genesis 22 out of context, with the assumption of Abraham as a stereotypical hero of faith, makes his character and his behavior noble. Traditional *midrashim* of Judaism fell under the sway of the hagiographic portrait of Abraham, and yet they also found ways, implicit and explicit, to explore their awareness that Abraham's character was more complex and flawed than that of a conventional hero. Ancient interpreters on the whole proved themselves more sensitive than their modern counterparts, Kierkegaard included, to the remorseless logic of this biblical text.

Implicit criticism of Abraham is embedded in the elevation of Isaac's participation and importance, *the son's* emergence as the principal human actor in the story, rather than the father. This comes out vividly in the interpretation that at the moment Abraham raises his knife to slay his son, Isaac saw directly into heaven,[20] and perceived the angels there. Abraham saw them only indirectly, reflected in his son's eyes. At the heart of the story, the disclosure of divine compassion that makes human life and Israel's survival possible, Isaac's vision is clearer than Abraham's.

Some *midrashim* factor Sarah into the Aqedah of traditional Judaism— although she is excluded from the biblical text of Genesis 22—in order to criticize Abraham explicitly. After speaking of the events on Moriah, Genesis 23:1-2 reports with only incidental explanation that Sarah died. A classic Midrash, Leviticus Rabbah, makes what Abraham did responsible for her death. At the same time, this interpretation embeds the story in the commemoration of the New Year, when the ram's horn, the *shofar*, is to be blown as the Aqedah is remembered.

In the *midrash* contained in Leviticus Rabbah, Isaac returns home after the Aqedah and tells his mother what happened on Moriah. Despairing and bewildered, she asks, "Had it not been for the angel you would have been slain?" When Isaac confirms that, the scene becomes searing: "Then she uttered six cries, corresponding to the six blasts of the *shofar*. It is said, She had barely finished speaking when she died." Absent from Mount Moriah, Sarah is the only parent emotionally present to her son, and the ram's horn that is blown every new year conveys her grief. Every time the *shofar* sounds, those who are aware of this *midrash* remember both Sarah's love and Abraham's hardness of heart.

Not content with this overt preference of Sarah to Abraham in terms of moral integrity and basic humanity, this *midrash* goes on to caricature Abraham as a compulsive sacrificer. Posing the question of where Abraham had been prior to the burial of Sarah, Leviticus Rabbah goes on:

> Where did he come from? Rabbi Judah son of Rabbi Shimon said, He came from Mount Moriah. Abraham harbored doubts in his heart and thought, Perhaps some disqualifying blemish was found in him and his offering was not accepted.

So while his wife has just died of grief at the realization of his heartlessness, Abraham is still caught up with the impulse to kill Isaac *after God has told him to stop threatening his son's life.*

Abraham is stuck in his understanding before the angelic intervention, in this *midrash*, fretting that his child wasn't pure enough to be sacrificed, instead of rejoicing that the son of the covenant had been spared by divine compassion. Sarah wasn't there, but she understands what Abraham cannot grasp, even after a divine vision and voice had shown him the truth. The insight that the impulse to sacrifice his son came from the patriarch himself, rather than from God, links the interpreter who composed this *midrash* in Leviticus Rabbah directly with the Qur'an, which knew that the impetus for the sacrifice came from Ibraham's atavism, not from Allah's will.

These *midrashim* take up in their own ways the clear imperative of Genesis 22 itself: to tame the impulse to offer one's children in sacrifice with the awareness that it comes from a false, prideful, and self-interested understanding of divine will. If you want to know what God wants, it is reflected more directly in Isaac's eyes than in Abraham's, in the perspective of the victim rather than the slayer. And the wisdom to act on what is disclosed on Mount Moriah, to blow a *shofar* of grief that will drive away the compulsion to sacrifice innocent human life, comes from the parent who cares, not from the parent who commands.

Similarly, in a scene of haunting power, the Gospels give the lie to any claim that discipleship of Jesus involves giving in wholesale to the ethic of self-sacrifice or child sacrifice. At the decisive moment prior to his arrest and crucifixion, the Gospels insistently portray Jesus, not as heroic, determined, or even stoical, but as doubtful and uncertain, beset by human weakness.

Mark, the earliest of the Gospels, sets out the scene most vividly of them all (Mark 14:32-43):

> And they come to a tract whose name was Gethsemane, and he says to his students, "Sit here while I pray." And he takes along Peter and James and John with him, and he began to be completely bewildered and distressed, and he says to them, "My soul is mournful unto death: remain here and be alert." He went before a little and fell upon the ground and was praying so that, if it were possible, the hour might pass on from him. And he was saying, " *Abba* , Father: all things are possible for you. Carry this cup on, away from me! Yet not what I want, but what you!" And he comes and finds them sleeping, and says to Peter, "Simon, are you sleeping? You were not capable of being alert one hour? Be alert and pray, so that you do not come into a test. The Spirit is willing, but the flesh is weak." He again went away and prayed. Having said the same thing, he again came and found them sleeping, because their eyes were weighed down; and they did not know what to reply to him. And he comes the third time and says to them, "Sleep for what remains and repose: it suffices. The hour has come, Look: the son of man is delivered up into the hands of sinners. Be raised, we go. Look: the one who delivers me over has approached." And at once while he is still speaking Judas, one of the Twelve, comes along, and with him a crowd with swords and clubs from the high priests and the scribes and the elders.

This scene, first written in Mark's crabbed, inelegant Greek (which I have put into the closest correspondence to English possible) achieves its power by what it says about Jesus, and by how it weaves his experience of human weakness into the experience of his followers.

Jesus openly admits his weakness, his "soul is mournful unto death," and he wants his disciples near to comfort him. His words are not just a general admission of grief; rather, he speaks in the words of Jonah at Nineveh (Jonah 4:9), another case of a prophet who sorrowed at the vocation given him by God. That is what makes Jesus' anguish at this moment arresting from the outset. Although depicted from the beginning of Mark's Gospel as God's Son, here he is not even sure he can complete his work as a prophet.

Jesus asks for the "hour" to pass him by—and to leave him alive. The term "hour" refers both to his personal fate (the time of his death), and to the moment when everything he as done will reach its climax in the disclosure of God's kingdom. How can God's Son be praying to elude that climactic realization of what he has done and who he has always been? An ancient critic of Christianity, the second-century classicist Celsus,[21] picked up on the scene in Gethsemane, asking how Jesus could possibly "mourn and lament and pray to escape the fear of death." The contrast in Celsus' mind was between Jesus and philosophical heroes such as Socrates, who faced their deaths with a noble calm.

Had Celsus known the Gospels better, he could have sharpened his criticism—and he no doubt would have. When Jesus asks for "this cup" to be taken from him, that reflects the Aramaic idiom, the "cup of death:" yet in Mark he has been predicting his death, and speaking of its necessity, with greater and greater specificity, and explaining to his followers that they had to be prepared to take this same path (Mark 8:31-38; 9:30-37; 10:32-45). He has already said that they would drink the cup that he drinks (10:39) and that his purpose was to give his life for redemption (10:45). His hesitation now, unless it has some deeper purpose, seems not only a matter of cringing in the face of pain and death, but also of denying his divine mission and misleading his disciples. This passage represents a searching challenge to the belief that suffering is necessary, and the way this challenge is posed is key to the whole Gospel's meaning.

This section of Mark belongs to one of the earliest oral sources in all the Gospels – the account of Jesus' passion and death crafted by Peter and his companions. Prayer featured vitally in this proto-Gospel, and Peter stressed the importance of intense repetition in prayer. In Gethsemane, Jesus brings his anguish to his *Abba* three times. Peter's source spoke of Jesus' prayer in order to model for believers how they themselves should pray when in distress, not merely to give information about Jesus.

That is the reason for which liturgical rhythms and antiphonal dialogue ripple through the story of Gethsemane. It is designed as part of Peter's passion narrative, the story of Jesus' suffering up to and including the moment of his death. Those events were particularly commemorated and recited by Christians every year prior to Easter, the Sunday of the resurrection, the Sunday when converts were baptized after extensive preparation by means of study, vigils of prayer during the night, and fasting. Those converts joined Jesus liturgically in Gethsemane, and searched themselves to see whether they were ready for the "hour"—the decisive moment of potential danger and revelation—that their baptism represented.

In Peter's narrative, the human failing to be avoided prior to this decisive moment was not an agonized plea for one's life like Jesus', but the languor that came to disciples during their vigils (Mark 14:37-38). By contrast, Peter's story *commends and endorses* Jesus' open expression of fear and doubt. This is prayer as it should be—directed to God as one's *Abba*,[22] which in Aramaic means both "father" and "source," and completely open in its acknowledgement of human weakness.

Peter's understanding, although shaped to suit the needs of liturgy, corresponds well to the historical circumstances that Jesus faced. His campaign against the high priestly administration in the Temple—climaxing in his violent expulsion of animals and their vendors – had put him in danger. But the complexities of power politics eluded him. He could not have known that the execution of Pilate's protector in Rome would dispose Pilate to put his military resources and might at the disposal of the high priest, Caiaphas.

Even a few weeks prior to Jesus' action in the Temple, an alliance between Pilate and Caiaphas seemed unimaginable. In Gethsemane, the unthinkable became real. The imminent danger of crucifixion – deliberately the most painful and shameful of deaths, which Roman authority alone could command – only became fully apparent to Jesus when Roman soldiers as well as police from the Temple joined in the attempt to capture him.

In the Gethsemane scene, Peter conveys the moment when Jesus in his mind's eye confronted the might of Rome, not only the anger of the high priest, and asked his God whether such a fate was truly necessary. Peter's portrayal of Jesus' agony of doubt contradicts the conventional view of Jesus as the all-knowing Messiah who is in complete control of his passions. That view gained traction within the development of the New Testament over time, as one can see by comparing how later Gospels handle the same scene in Mark. Comparing all the accounts, it is obvious that, as time went on, Christians became less and less comfortable with Jesus being indecisive or fearful in the face of death.

Yet as the Gospels progressively insulated Jesus against his own humanity, a process that continued for centuries after the Gospels were written, each still insisted in its own way that Jesus had a choice, whether to remain in Jerusalem and risk death, or to flee with the hope of survival. Even John's Gospel, the latest, and the most stylized of them all in the New Testament where Jesus' humanity is concerned, emphasizes this crucial element of informed decision.

When, in John's Gospel, Jesus speaks of himself as the "good shepherd" who "lays down his life on behalf of the sheep" (John 10:11), that is with a specific understanding (John 10:18): "No one takes it from me, but I lay it down of myself." In principle, Jesus might have learned, as Ibrahim did in the Qur'an, that intention alone sufficed for his sacrifice.

Automatic martyrdom, or acquiescence to an abstract command despite one's fear and indecision, is not the portrait of Jesus that the Gospels convey. Instead, they insist that Jesus, fully aware of the emotions and doubts that were running though him, great and small, made a choice to offer his life for his sheep or, as he goes on to call his followers in John, his "friends" (John 15:12-17). Insight, commitment, and an assessment of circumstance all contribute to his strategic choice. It is *his* choice, and it is unquestionably noble: there is no doubt whatever but that the Christian tradition endorses the model of martyrdom that it inherited from Maccabean Judaism, and further develops that model.

But a crucial aspect of that development—too often overlooked, with grievous consequences—is that the martyr fully deals with his own emotional state, as well as with the external conditions he confronts. Martyrdom must always be a matter of one's insight into oneself and into the world at one and the same time. Attempting to mimic a single, heroic gesture—despite one's feelings and whatever the circumstances—amounts to play acting, because it does not represent the self-giving on behalf of others that is the purpose Jesus clearly states, by word and by deed.

Muhammad, in contrast to Jesus, was a prosperous merchant at the time the Qur'an started to be revealed to him, surah after surah. His considerable means, together with his resourcefulness and his willingness to use physical force, assured his survival and prosperity, and that of his movement, against considerable odds.

The fact that the Medinan surah that spells out the religious obligation to fight when occasion demands is entitled "Repentance" indicates how vital combat was to loyalty to Allah in Muhammad's circumstances. In effect and in fact, war became an article of faith (9:19, 20, *Al Tawbah*): "Do you make the giving of drink to pilgrims or the maintenance of the sacred mosque equal to him who believes in Allah and the last day and struggles for Allah's way? They are not equal in the sight of Allah.... Those who believe and leave home and strive with property and life in Allah's cause have the higher rank in the sight of Allah."

Because the striving of *jihad* had become a paramount religious virtue, Muhammad's concern over the years to specify that there should be "no compulsion in religion," becomes understandable. He needed to insist, and he did insist in *Al-Baqara* 2:256, that *jihad* was a requirement to preserve the freedom to make Islam possible, but emphatically *not* a form of authorization to compel Islam, a compulsion which he taught amounted to a contradiction in terms. True submission to Allah was between Allah and the believer, not a matter of public policy.

Later interpreters for the most part correctly understood Muhammad's stance and systematized his disparate teachings into a doctrine of just war that, in turn, influenced Christian thinkers such as Thomas Aquinas during the Middle Ages. Yet the everlasting rewards promised to those who "struggle" in physical combat link up together into a tantalizing thread within the Qur'an, comparable to the heavenly benefits promised at a later period to Christian Crusaders. That comparison is not coincidental, since Muslim portrayals of the joys of heaven and the pains of hell deeply influenced Christian thought, and inspired poets such as Dante.

Those who are slain in the way of Allah will enjoy the heavenly garden prepared for them according to another Medinan surah (47:4-6, *Muhammad*). That revelation, written at a time of threat of invasion from Mecca, also reveals Muhammad's frustration when the call to *jihad* was not heard: the faithful say they are awaiting a word of revelation, and when Muhammad gives them one (47:20, *Muhammad*), they look as if they are about to faint dead away.

The example of Ibrahim became sharper in surahs composed in Medina, although the patriarch had featured centrally in Muhammad's long thought before that. But in Medina Muhammad interacted with interpretative traditions of Jewish communities, including traditions involving the Aqedah. In the midst of his forceful call to physical engagement with enemies, warranted by the threat of annihilation and pursued even at the risk of life, the temptation must have been strong for Muhammad to associate Ibrahim's offering of his son with the dispatch of young men to war.

The Qur'an instead portrays the patriarch's deep attachment to his sons (14:39, *Ibrahim*). In view of the deaths of Muhammad's small sons and the strong identification he felt with Ibrahim, these words are especially touching. It would have been a very small step for Muhammad to see the loss of his own children reflected in the Aqedah, and to use Ibrahim's sacrifice as the basis to demand that believers should sacrifice their children in the cause of Allah. But that is just the step Muhammad did not take.

The Qur'anic Aqedah (37:84-111, *Al Saffat*) instead insists that, as a prophet, Ibrahim followed Allah's lead away from the conventions of idolatry, but also against the impulse to assume that Allah required human sacrifice. Muhammad saw Ibrahim and his sons as models of resistance against idolatry (14:35, *Ibrahim*), more than as paradigmatic martyrs. Ibrahim with his son Isma'il is the hero of the cleansing of the Ka'bah in particular, and its establishment for the pure worship of Allah (22:26, *Al Hajj*, the surah on pilgrimage, written both before and after the *hijrah*). This is the task that Muhammad himself completed, when – having taken control of Mecca in 630 CE—he dedicated the Ka'ba to the exclusive worship of Allah, removing and destroying the idols that he believed polluted it.

The purpose of cleansing the Kab'ah was not only to permit pilgrimage there to be free of idolatry, but also to assure that sacrifice was offered to Allah alone. Muhammad explicitly associated the duty of pilgrimage with *animal* sacrifice (22:27-28, *Al Hajj*). The location of this sacrifice is crucial (22:33, Al Hajj): it is Mina, where Ibrahim's vision took place, and showed what should be offered, and what should never be offered, to Allah.

The association between the Qur'anic Aqedah and the sacrifice at Mina links Ibrahim to every believer. For that reason, it is crucial for any and all Muslims that Ibrahim's submission to Allah and his son's came out of their vision according to the Qur'an, not any literal attempt to go through with human sacrifice. All their action and experience focuses on the single recognition (37:106, *Al Saffat*) that "this was an obvious trial."

God intervened with an "immense sacrifice" of an animal (37:107), so that *only* animals are ever to be considered for sacrifice again. Allah wants only these animals, and their physical offering does not please him, "Their flesh and blood does not reach Allah; your devotion reaches him" (22:37, *Al Hajj*). Only evil people could mistake the giving of a child as a duty; Muhammad described (70:11-14, *Al Ma'arij*) sinners willing to sacrifice children, wives, brothers and kin to save themselves from divine punishment, like Mesha in the Hebrew Bible.

The Qur'an makes the demand for sacrifice categorical: "Therefore to your Lord turn in prayer and sacrifice," says one of the last surahs (108:2, *Al Kawthar*). But in making that requirement, Muhammad could not have been clearer that the means of sacrifice could never be a human offering and that Allah enjoys, not any particular victim that is offered, but the devoted intention that motivates offering.

Islam, the most recent of the monotheisms, is also the most rooted in the primordial impulse of sacrifice, because literal, animal offerings are a regular part of its continuing practice. In the light of the Muslim Aqedah, believers should know, however, that Allah has never desired, and that they should never offer, any human victim.

Within the tangled strands of interpretation that have issued from Genesis 22 and the interpretative possibilities of the Aqedah, patient alternatives of reading Abraham more critically than is traditional (Leviticus Rabbah), of holding up the example of discernment rather than conventional heroism (the scene of Gethsemane in Mark 14), and of observing that God himself never truly wanted or commanded human sacrifice (*Al Saffat* in the Qur'an) have held out the prospect of redemption from sacred violence. Whether these alternatives will prevail over the endorsement of conventional devotion of children to military sacrifice is a decision that lies in the hands of interpreters.

NOTES

1. *Fear and Trembling and The Sickness unto Death* (tr. Walter Lowrie; Princeton: Princeton University, 1941) 64. The same portrayal permeates the analysis of Hugh C. White, *Narration and Discourse in the Book of Genesis* (Cambridge: Cambridge University Press, 1991) 191, and has become a staple of literary criticism. Jo Milgrom cogently attacks Kierkegaard's position as convenient to "justify almost any atrocity;" *The Binding of Isaac. The Akedah – A Primary Symbol of Jewish Thought and Art* (Berkeley: Bibal, 1988) 19-23. Jon D. Levenson rightly attributes Kierkegaard's interpretation to the Pauline tradition of portraying Abraham as a hero of faith; *The Death and Resurrection of the Beloved Son. The transformation of child sacrifice in Judaism and Christianity* (New Haven: Yale University, 1993) 125-142.

2. Thomas Asbridge, *The First Crusade. A New History* (Oxford: Oxford University, 2004) 66, quoting Robert the Monk, *Historia Iherosolimitana*. Sources are helpfully presented in Edward Peters, *The First Crusade. The Chronicle of Fulcher of Chartres and Other Source Materials* (Philadelphia: University of Pennsylvania, 1998) and Robert Levine, *The Deeds of God through the Franks. A translation of Guibert de Nogent's Gesta Dei per Francos* (Rochester: Boydell, 1997).

3. As the historian Orderic Vitalis said of Urban in 1135; see Jonathan Riley-Smith, *The First Crusade and the Idea of Crusading:* The Middle Ages Series (Philadelphia: University of

Pennsylvania, 1986) 28. The following quotation is from Aziz S. Atiya, *Crusade, Commerce and Culture* (New York: Wiley, 1966) 21, citing Fulcher of Chartres.

4. See Asbridge, 40. Anna Comnena, the Byzantine emperor's daughter, is the source of the most specific estimate, of 10,000 knights, 70,000 infantry, and many, many camp followers made it as far as Constantinople. Casualties and desertions were enormous. Asbridge estimates at only 13,300 the Crusader force that finally took Jerusalem (p. 300), smaller than the tragic 30,000 of the "Children's Crusade" of 1212, who set off for death and slavery (Atiya, 85).

5. Frank Allen Patterson, *The Middle English Penitential Lyric. A Study and Collection of Early Religious Verse*: Columbia University Studies in English (New York: Columbia University, 1911) 138.

6. See John V. Tolan, *Saracens. Islam in the Medieval European Imagination* (New York: Columbia, 2002) 135, citing Guibert de Nogent. On Peter the Venerable, see Jeremy Cohen, *Sanctifying the Name of God. Jewish Martyrs and Jewish Memories of the First Crusade* (Philadelphia: University of Pennsylvania, 2004) 3-4.

7. From J. A. Giles, "Chronicle of Richard of Devizes," *Chronicles of the Crusades* (London: Bohn, 1848) section three.

8. Asbridge, 316, cf. 87, 193, 273-274. The following citation is taken from Atiya, 61-62. Among other informative and readable histories, see Jonathan Riley-Smith *The Crusades. A history* (New Haven: Yale University, 2005); Christopher Tyerman, *God's War. A new history of the Crusades* (Cambridge: Belknap, 2006).

9. These and the following examples come from Jeremy Cohen, *Sanctifying the Name of God.* 5-6, 13, 61-64, 74, 107-108, 143-144; see also Shlomo Eidelberg, *The Jews and the Crusaders. The Hebrew Chronicles of the First and Second Crusades* (Madison: University of Wisconsin, 1977) and Robert Chazan, *In the Year 1096. The First Crusade and the Jews* (Philadelphia: JPS, 1996).

10. According to Saladin's hagiographer, Baha' ad-Din, quoted in Francesco Gabrieli (translated by E. J. Costello), *Arab Historians of the Crusades*: The Islamic World Series (Berkeley: Univeristy of California, 1984) 100-101, cf. 104. The next citation is from 'Imad ad-Din, 18-29; see Gabrieli, 134-135.

11. Atiya, 133, makes the case that pilgrimage had provided a major dimension of this teaching, as in the case of the Crusades. See also Richard Bonney, *Jihad. From Qur'an to bin Laden* (Basingstoke and New York: Palgrave Macmillan, 2004), 116.

12. The inscription has been published many times since its identification in 1868. See R. F. Klein, *The Recovery of Jerusalem. A Narrative of Exploration and Discovery in the City and the Holy Land* edited by Walter Morrison; New York: Appleton, 1872) 389-402; Klaas A. D. Smelik, "The Literary Structure of King Mesha's Inscription," *Journal for the Study of the Old Testament* 46 (1990) 21-30.

13. Didorus goes on to compare Euripides' presentation of the sacrifice of Iphigeneia. See also 13.86.3 and the discussion in Joyce E. Salisbury, *Perpetua's Passion. The death and memory of a young Roman woman* (New York: Routledge, 1997), 51-4, who also cites Plutarch Tertullian, and Minucius Felix to this effect. On the archaeological evidence, see Lawrence E. Stager, "Carthage: A View from the Tophet," *Phönizer im Westen* (edited by Hans Georg Niemeyer; Mainz: Zabern, 1982) 155-166; Lawrence E. Stager and Samuel R. Wolff, "Child Sacrifice at Carthage -- Religious Rite or Population Control?" *Biblical Archaeology Review* 10 (1984) 30-51.

14. Yohanan Aharoni, "Arad: Its Inscriptions and Temple," *The Biblical Archaeologist* 31.1 (1968) 1-32.

15. Good arguments have been made for dating elements of the Elohist source, or even the source as a whole, much later. But its characteristic concern with prophecy reflects a setting in the ninth century B.C.E. Even those, particularly in Europe, who express skepticism about an early dating of the Elohist source agree that this prophetic emphasis animates Genesis 22. See Friedhelm Hartenstein, "Die Verborgenheit des rettenden Gottes. Exegetische und theologische Bermerkungen zu Genesis 22," *Isaaks Opferung (Gen 22) in den Konfessionen und Medien der Frühen Neuzeit*: Arbeiten zur Kirchengeschichte (edited by Johann Anselm Steiger and Ulrich Heinen; Berlin: de Gruyter, 2006) 1-22.

16. This is well described in *Understanding Religious Sacrifice. A reader*: Controversies in the Study of Religion (edited by Jeffrey Carter; New York: Continuum, 2003); *Sacrifice in Religious Experience*: Numen Book Series XCIII (edited by Albert I. Baumgarten; Leiden: Brill, 2002); Jon D. Levenson, *The Death and Resurrection of the Beloved Son. The Transformation of Child Sacrifice in Judaism and Christianity* (New Haven: Yale University, 1993); Paul Wheatley. *The Pivot of the Four Quarters. A preliminary enquiry into the origins and character of the ancient Chinese city* (Chicago, Aldine, 1971).

17. See Tamid 4:1 in the Mishnah and one of the most useful works ever written on the Aqedah, Shalom Spiegel's *The Last Trial* (tr. Judah Goldin; New York: Random House, 1967) xix-xx. See also Aharon (Ronald E.) Agus, *The Binding of Isaac and Messiah. Law, Martyrdom and Deliverance in Early Rabbinic Religiosity*: SUNY Series in Judaica: *Hermeneutics, Mysticism and Religion* (Albany: State University of New York, 1988).

18. See J. Mann, *The Bible as Read and Preached in the Old Synagogue* (Cincinnati: Union of American Hebrew Congregations, 1940) 67; H. J. Schoeps, "The Sacrifice of Isaac in Paul's Theology," *Journal of biblical Literature* 65.4 (1946) 385-392; Eduard Lohse, *Märtyrer und Gottesknecht* (Göttingen: Vandenhoeck & Ruprecht, 1963).

19. The possibility of Abraham's idolatry is at Beersheba is raised by Mishael Maswari Caspi and Sascha Benjamin Cohen, *The Binding [Aqedah] and its Transformations in Judaism and Islam. The Lambs of God*: Mellen Biblical Press Series 32 (Lewiston: Mellen Biblical, 1995) 7.

20. This interpretation is found in the Targums Pseudo-Jonathan and Neofiti at Genesis 22:10. For a treatment, see P. R. Davies and B. D. Chilton, "The Aqedah: A Revised Tradition History," *Catholic Biblical Quarterly* 40 (1978) 514-546. For the *midrash* that follows, see Leviticus Rabbah 20.2 in *The Midrash Rabbah. Leviticus* (translated by J.J. Slotki, edited by H. Freedman and Maurice Simon London: Soncino, 1977). These interpretations anticipate Wilfred Owen's.

21. Quoted in Origen's work of the third century, *Contra Celsum* 2.24; see Henry Chadwick, *Contra Celsum. Translated with an introduction and notes* (Cambridge: Cambridge University, 1953). On the Aramaic idiom of the "cup," see Roger Le Déaut, "Goûter le calice de la mort," *Biblica* 43 (1962) 82-86. For a technical discussion of the Gethsemane scene and its sources, see Raymond E. Brown, *The Death of the Messiah*: The Anchor Bible Reference Library (New York: Doubleday, 1994) I:146-234.

22. See Chilton, *Jesus' Prayer and Jesus' Eucharist His Personal Practice of Spirituality* (Valley Forge: Trinity Press International, 1997).

Plagues and Politics

Epidemics and "Re-Framing"
in Modern American History

Andrew J. Forney

On October 30, 2014, Kaci Hickox decided to defy the government of Maine and went for a bike ride. Hickox had recently volunteered for Doctors Without Borders and returned from spending five weeks in Sierra Leone, helping to stem the rising tide of Ebola-related deaths in West Africa. Upon her return, Hickox had loudly agitated against a forced quarantine at the Newark airport where she had re-entered the country. Kept for three days in a tent off the airport's tarmac, and guarded by an assigned – and armed – security detail, Hickox claimed that she was being held "as a prisoner." She showed no signs of Ebola and pointed out that the disease was only transferrable through the body fluids of a patient that already evinced the tell-tale early symptoms of the disease – fever, nausea, and joint ache. Finally allowed to leave New Jersey and return to her home state of Maine, Hickox found herself further quarantined by that state. The government of Maine ordered her to stay quarantined in her boyfriend's residence for twenty-one days, not to interact with people, and to avoid all public places. They also detailed a twenty-four hour police surveillance unit to her residence to ensure that the quarantine stayed in place and that her whereabouts were never in question. Simply by putting foot to pedal, Hickox broke the law.[1]

The events surrounding Hickox quickly became politicized. During her initial quarantine she clashed with New Jersey Governor and potential 2016 presidential candidate Chris Christie, calling him a "bully" and threatening to sue him. He replied, in a brusque manner that belied the obvious political considerations, stating, "Whatever. Get in Line." An editorial about "Ebola-panic politics" in *The Nation* stated that Hickox had "struck a blow for all the teachers, nurses, public employees, minimum-wagers and workers of all kinds that Christie has bullied, belittled and silenced over the years." Christie did relent after three days of public criticism, including a White House lawn reprimand from President Barack Obama. Once having left New Jersey, Hickox wrangled with another governor, Maine's Paul LePage. Seeking re-election in 2014, LePage faced stiff competition from two outside candidates. The governor decided to take a hard-line against Hickox, declaring that he would use "the full extent of his authority allowable by law" to enforce the twenty-one day quarantine. By Election Day, the bike ride had split the state. When questioned who he had voted for in the gubernatorial election, Hickox's boyfriend said, "You can guess who we voted for."[2]

The political drama surrounding the quarantine surprised many. Prescient observers should have known better. Natural disasters, and the responses to them, tend to become politicized, be it by the actions of the state or local government or the grassroots actions of various groups to assist survivors. Epidemics, a unique form of natural disaster, also engenders political responses, but to varying degrees. Unlike tornados, hurricanes, earthquakes, or floods, epidemics lend themselves to social separation. The fear of contagion breeds notions of quarantine, be they official or self-imposed, which specifically limit individual and group interactions. Claims can be made that breaking quarantine, as Hickox did, is tantamount to using lethal force against others, a blatant disregard for community safety. At the least, many claim such actions represent an irresponsibility that could rend the social fabric and delegitimize the communal understandings that bind nations and peoples together.

The eminent medical historian Charles Rosenberg defined the politicization and socialization of epidemics as "framing." Society "frames" diseases within a socio-political context that measures the epidemics spread and impact alongside of previously held moral beliefs and value assessments. "What is often lost sight of [when discussing disease]," Rosenberg argued, "is the process of disease definition itself, and second, the consequences of those definitions once agreed upon in the lives of individuals, in the making and discussion of social policy, and in the structuring of medical care." Outbreaks never occur within a vacuum and the perception of their spread, quarantine, and treatment all reflect the core beliefs of a given society or nation.[3]

American history is replete with such examples. Epidemics – be it the contagion that decimated 90% of the Native American population upon first contact, the smallpox that helped determine the American Revolution, or the cholera that blossomed during America's early industrialization – shaped the United States and its history. And this shaping entailed more than just sickness and death; the political response to these instances inflamed pre-existing social and political divisions while helping establish new ones. A democratic society based on community participation and political connectivity possesses a unique fragility towards epidemics that strain social bonds.[4]

Such a strain exposes another socio-political process that takes place during periods of disease outbreaks. This can best be understood as "reverse-framing," or the defining of individuals within a society based on the same "framing" qualifiers identified by Rosenberg, but including social exclusion and inequality as distinct characteristics. Whereas framing places disease within a socio-political context, reverse-framing analyzes the response and characterization of a particular disease and its victims to draw conclusions about the formulation of social hierarchies and conceptions of "ideal citizens." More than just an academic exercise, reverse-framing of historical epidemics expose the sharp dissimilarities in terms of medical response, access, and care among the most marginalized within a society or nation.

This study will examine epidemics and their socio-political ramifications in modern American history, specifically during the twentieth century. An analysis of the 1918 – 1920 influenza outbreak and the appearance of AIDS during the early 1980s show the continuation of the trends discussed above. Both diseases exposed and exacerbated existing political differences in the American societies in which they appeared. Further study shows how the impact of these diseases fell most severely on marginalized communities outside the pale of "normal society." A recounting of the important historical works on disease in history will precede these case studies, and the study will conclude with some thoughts on the recent Ebola crisis.

HISTORICAL ANTECEDENTS

Thucydides wrote about the "Plague of Athens" in his *History of the Peloponnesian War* sometime during the fourth century BCE. While he decided not to comment about the medical or scientific aspects of the epidemic, he did feel qualified to recount the appearance and impact of the sickness. Most historians believe the plague was a type of bubonic plague akin to the "Black Death" that ravaged Europe during the Middle Ages. Going beyond a simple recitation of the disease's symptoms, Thucydides told of the social impact of the disease on Athenian society.

> By far the most terrible feature in the malady was the dejection which ensued when any one felt sickening, for the despair into which they instantly fell took away their power of resistance, and left them a much easier prey to the disorder; besides which, there was the awful spectacle of men dying like sheep, through having caught the infection in nursing each other. This caused the greatest mortality. On the one hand, if they were afraid to visit each other, they perished from neglect; indeed many houses were emptied of their inmates for

want of nurse: on the other, if they ventured to do so, death was the consequence.

Even generally homogenous Athens experienced the social schisms that the plague created. And Thucydides knew this first hand, for he himself fell ill during the worst of the plague year.

Two oft-overlooked elements of Thucydides' account of the plague deserve further note: the role played by war-related demographic shifts and the plague's impact on marginalized communities. The Athenian traced the plague's spread from the Sahel, through the Nile Delta, across the Mediterranean, and through his city's walls. Thucydides called the movement of displaced people into the safety of Athens an "aggravation of the existing calamity," most likely unaware that the population shifts ushered in by the war's advent led to the plague's spread. He did understand that these displaced persons suffered the most. "As there were no houses to receive them," he wrote, "they had to be lodged at the hot season of the year in stifling cabins, where the mortality raged without restraint." In these quarters, "The bodies of dying men lay one upon another, and half-dead creatures reeled about the streets and gathered round all the fountains longing for water."[5]

The 1970s saw the publication of two books crucial to creating our modern understanding of the relationship between disease and history: Alfred Crosby's *The Columbian Exchange* (1972) and William H. McNeill's *Plagues and Peoples* (1976). Crosby's work focused on the global biological effects of the exploration and colonization of the American continents by the Spanish Empire in the century after Columbus set foot on Hispaniola. As opposed to the traditional retelling of *conquistadors* and Technotitlan, Crosby instead put a non-human actor at the center of the conquest narrative: disease. Building off of contemporary census-based studies that had slowly begun to postulate a "demographic collapse" in the indigenous populations following first contact, he modeled how the introduction of zootic diseases spelled the complete rupture of many native societies. Disease ran rampant throughout the American continents for approximately a century, denuding the far-away New England coast and leaving it a veritable ghost land for the arrival of the Pilgrims during the 1620s. Epidemics had precipitated political chaos and rupture, shattered the bonds of very powerful empires in Meso-America, and prevented the native population from being able to build a coherent socio-political response to future European incursions.

While Crosby did spend a sizeable portion of his work focusing on the disease impact that Spanish explorers brought to the Americas, he also analyzed the movement of other biological and cultural life ways across the Atlantic, be they types of agriculture, fruits and vegetables, and herding. Most importantly, he exhibited the two-way (or three-way if one includes Africa) nature of the Atlantic Exchange. European and African farmers quickly began transplanting fruits and vegetables in their native biomes, creating new agricultural and environmental realities. Potatoes, yams, and cassava became dietary staples in the Eastern Hemisphere. In his most contentious chapter, Crosby claimed that syphilis had actually originated among the indigenous people of the Americas and rapidly spread among Spanish explorers and conquerors. While many scientists and historians still debate his notion, it is clear that the idea of syphilis travelling eastward across the Atlantic is rife with socio-political ramifications.[6]

Plagues and Peoples built on Crosby's work but focused solely on epidemic diseases and their impact in world history. McNeill had built a strong academic foundation as a "global historian" apt to analyze centuries of history where others might dissect the impact of a decade. His history of disease was epic in scope, charting an evolutionary duality between men and microbes. The transition to farming and sedentary lifestyle brought humanity into direct contact with diseases, through faulty sanitation measures or zootic transmission by living in close proximity to domesticated animals. This new biotic reality created "disease pools" uniquely intertwined with local populations; upon the occurrence of a significant demographic shift, these disease pools would intermingle and new epidemics would flare up until a new stasis had been reached. For McNeill, the grand movement of peoples over space – Alexander's march into the Indian subcontinent, the Mongol surge across Asia, and European expansion into the Americas – heralded new waves of epidemic disease. The sweep of history witnessed the intermingling of disease and human interaction; as he closed his work, he stated:

> In any effort to understand what lies ahead, as much as what lies behind, the role of infectious disease cannot be properly left out of consideration. Ingenuity, knowledge, and organization alter but cannot cancel humanity's vulnerability to invasion by parasitic forms of life. Infectious disease which antedated the emergence of humankind will last as long as humanity itself, and will surely remain, as it had hitherto, one of the fundamental parameters and determinants of human history.[7]

This paragraph, however, came at the end of McNeill's discussion of medical achievements that transpired during the eighteenth and nineteenth centuries. Many historians, scientists, and social commentators often overlook the implications from *Plagues and Peoples'* last paragraph and instead focus on the rapid gains made by science in the modern era. The development of germ theory, the research done into mosquito-born-diseases, the discovery and implementation of antibiotics – all seem to indicate a progressive advancement in humanity's ability to counter epidemics that had ravaged and paralyzed humanity for centuries. As the twentieth century opened, many prominent Western observers could point to the new field of "sanitation" as a panacea to the diseases of the past. Cleanliness and proper planning could forestall disease outbreaks prior to their blossoming into raging epidemics. As we will see, this did not prove to be the case.

DANCING WITH THE "SPANISH LADY": THE INFLUENZA EPIDEMIC OF 1918 – 1920

Historians still debate the origins of the "Spanish Influenza" that struck the globe between 1918 and 1920.[8] Most scientists do agree that that influenza strain first appeared in the Midwestern states sometime in the early spring of 1918. Some go even further and label the new Army cantonment at Camp Funston, just outside Manhattan, Kansas, as ground zero for the initial contagion. Soldiers first started falling ill from traditional flu-like symptoms there during late February and early March. While the flu appeared to be widespread throughout the training base, it did not appear to be particularly fatal. Those that did perish, though, provided doctors with a conundrum: the majority of those that died appeared to be in the prime of their lives and had succumbed to an acute pneumonia that turned their lungs into a spongy mass of phlegm and blood. Most doctors, however, saw these initial anomalies as outliers or curiosities and focused instead on the majority of cases that resembled the traditional malady.

The likelihood that Camp Funston, or another similar Army cantonment, became ground zero for the first wave of influenza is revealing in many regards. By the spring of 1918, the United States approached the one year anniversary of its declaration of war against the Central Powers. The intervening year had witnessed the mass mobilization of the American population as the U.S. government sought the most efficient means to both mass produce war materiel and rapidly build an army that many estimated would reach one million soldiers. The realities of both projects created wide-ranging demographic shifts as families moved to the Midwest and New England to fill new positions in the now-bustling factories and young men, volunteers and draftees alike, reported to initial army training. To meet this need, the army built dozens of camps to in-process and train their new charges, preparing soldiers eventually to serve on the Western Front. Camp Funston, one of these news camps, arose from the Kansas prairie in a matter of weeks.[9]

Those that ascribe to the Camp Funston/Ground Zero hypothesis posit that a young farm hand, either by volunteering or being drafted, arrived a Camp Funston sometime during late winter 1918 and carried the influenza strain that precipitated the first wave of the epidemic. The influenza strain most likely crossed from an animal (probably a pig or chicken) that he had been in close contact with prior to his arrival at Funston. Our patient zero may never have become sick; his proximity to the vector animals may have allowed him to build immunity due to repeated exposures. Once at Funston and surrounded by a rapidly shifting population of young men that had never been exposed to that specific influenza strain, patient zero became a twentieth century "Typhoid Mary." And the nation's mobilization played a ready accomplice, packing trains with soldiers for Europe, unaware that several of them were slowly becoming feverish. The path of the influenza's progression followed the train tracks, appearing in New York, the primary embarkation hub for Europe, by March.[10]

As noted above, many people, both soldiers and civilians, fell ill that spring, but not many died. Influenza, carried on troop ships across the Atlantic, landed in France with the doughboys, quickly infecting belligerents on both sides of the trenches. From there, it spread throughout the globe, new advances in ocean travel making it easier for infected individuals to arrive at new destinations without having presented with influenza symptoms during their transit. This first wave, running from approximately early-spring to late-summer 1918, presented similar symptoms around the globe: heightened communicability but low mortality, with those few that died being young and healthy. While institutions like the military and the government did track the rising wave of sickness, they also noticed its clear abatement and foresaw no indications of a greater biological conflagration.

This all changed during the last week of August 1918. A new and deadlier strain of the influenza virus appeared in three geographically distinct locations that week: Freetown, Sierra Leone; Brest, France; and Boston, Massachusetts. This disease varied significantly from the first wave that had recently spun across the globe. While still highly contagious, this version of the virus had a higher mortality, with five to ten percent of a stricken population rapidly reaching life-threatening levels; three percent of Freetown's population died from the epidemic during the month of September, 1918. Those infected, to include those that survived, degraded rapidly, often going from healthy to bed-ridden and feverish in a matter of hours. One patient claimed that falling sick made him feel as if he "had been beaten all over with a club."[11]

In a striking resemblance to the first wave of influenza, the disease culled the young and healthy in large numbers. Once considered a statistical aberration, the death of society's most vibrant members now presented a startling reality to the doctors and scientists struggling to understand how best to stem the flood of disease. They gradually determined that the lethality of the virus directly related to a victim's health. Infection in robust patients heralded an overactive immune response, leading to the overproduction of mucus and near-constant coughing that resulted in the spongy-blood soaked lungs of the earlier victims. Later researchers hypothesized that the influenza virus from the first wave, travelling the globe and rapidly reproducing, mutated into the more virulent form that led to the massive death and social rupturing of the second and third waves of 1919 and 1920.

American society reeled. Most large urban areas ran out of coffins, forcing morgues and "slab houses" to pile bodies on cooling floors to prevent
their rapid decomposition. The Red Cross sought to step into any institutional
and infrastructure gaps, but the healers quickly became the sick, increasing
the sense of social distance as volunteers became harder and harder to find.
Many cities prohibited large outdoor gatherings, although many still held
large parades and rallies to engender support for the war effort. City and
county governments passed any number of ordinances to protect their citizens, from forcing all weddings and funerals out of doors, to conscripting
doctors and nurses to serve on emergency influenza wards. Such measures
often included commissioning local clothiers to mass-produce cotton face
masks for public servants, and in some locales, all residents.

The ubiquitous cotton masks became the symbol of the government's
response to the influenza crisis, and its lack an indicator of rebelliousness and
insurrection. Many cities required all its citizens to wear the masks when out
in public, making the decision not to wear one punishable by arrest. San
Francisco passed an ordinance on October 18th, 1918, stating that "surgical
masks" would be worn by all those travelling in public starting November 1st.
The Red Cross and others took out a full page ad on October 22nd to let the
city know that they would be making 5,000 masks available to the general
public for free the next day; by noon, they were all gone. The Red Cross then
distributed over 40,000 masks the next day and would count over 100,000
gone over the course of the first four days.

The long arm of the law rounded up those that either chose not to wear a
mask or who pushed theirs off their nose and mouth, even briefly. Wide
spread "stings" took place in San Francisco's busy hotel district throughout
the first weeks of November, nabbing hundreds of people without masks and
levying punishments that ranged from a five dollar fine to thirty days in jail.
Interestingly enough, those localities throughout the nation that did mandate
mask wear adopted a unique name for those that did wear masks: "slackers."
Today a common place slang label for the lazy, the word first appeared
during the initial stages of the United States' war-time mobilization to designate those men that either did not register for the draft or "dodged" the draft
call-ups. Thus, in the fall of 1918, American society slowly equated not
doing one's duty in terms of the military service with not following the terms
of masking laws. While not viewed as legally the same, social norms ostra-
cized those that did not take the necessary sanitary steps.[12]

The influenza epidemic, beyond drawing political lines in terms of mask-
wearing, also exacerbated pre-existing social divisions in society. If one drew
expanding concentric circles surrounding white middle-class America during
the fall of 1918, with each ring representing the ethnic and racial stratification of American society, one could easily chart which groups experienced
the greatest impact from the disease. In the first circle, recent European

immigrants died in numbers far higher than the middle-class citizens that lived mere blocks away in America's expanding cities. Huddled in tenement houses and lacking the medical infrastructure in their neighborhoods that would have allowed rapid diagnosis and treatment, these newcomers to America tended to rely on familial and ethnic networks that unknowingly spread the disease rather than ameliorate its affects. Not until the Red Cross and other volunteer charities began making their way into these communities did they begin to discover the ravages of the epidemic: an apartment housing close to a dozen people, all dead; babies suckling at dead mothers' breasts; and fathers, now bereft of families, trying to build coffins from old furniture. The expansion of urban medical services into these lower-class ethnic neighborhoods, while somewhat stemming the tide of death, did little to erase the memory of the early days of the epidemic.

Jim Crow and empire best define the latter circles of our model of American society and disease impact. African Americans, barred through segregation from hospital beds in the South, often fell ill and died in their homes. Much as the case with immigrants in urban tenements, this practice of home treatment helped spread the disease among familial and kinship networks. Influenza would take huge swaths out of the immediate, and often extended, family, leaving no one to provide care and treatments to those that fell ill. The few professionally-trained black doctors and nurses rose to the challenge, but often felt daunted combating both a microscopic killer and a racial hierarchy. Those in American society that suffered the worst from the epidemic tended to be the "newest" Americans – those most recently incorporated into the nation by late nineteenth century expansion. Native American mortality topped nine percent; most estimate that two percent of their entire population died from influenza. At one point during the fall of 1918, 100,000 Puerto Ricans (out of a total population of 1.25 million) would fall ill from influenza. And in the recent American territorial addition of Samoa, over twenty-two percent of the island's small population would perish from influenza. While many at the time would claim these heightened mortality figures resulted from "weaker breeding" (what we might call today genetic predispositions), most modern-day researchers believe they resulted instead from cultures still reeling from integration into the United States, social and geographic isolation, and a general lack of interest from the American public.[13]

By early 1920, the influenza epidemic appeared to have run its course. The numbers from the influenza pandemic of 1918 – 1920 almost defy comprehension. Across the globe, between twenty and one hundred million people died from the disease in approximately two years. Most areas lacked institutional mechanisms for proper recordings of influenza deaths, leading to the wide variance in the low- and high-end estimates. That said, it is important to remember that during the four years of World War I approximately twenty-four million soldiers and civilians died, while about sixteen million combatants died in the six years of World War II. An average of 2.5 percent of all those infected by influenza died, a seemingly insignificant number unless one considers that one-fifth of the global population fell ill during this time period. U.S. life expectancy dropped by twelve years in 1918. If a like-virulence pandemic broke out today, 1.5 million people would perish in American alone.[14]

THE "GAY" DISEASE: HIV AND AIDS, 1980 – 2014

During late 1980, a series of young to middle-aged homosexual men began arriving at hospitals in Los Angeles and San Francisco with a bevy of abnormal diseases. Most prominent among them were *Pneumocystis carinii* pneumonia (PCP), a rare pneumonia mostly seen in babies and the elderly, and Kaposi's sarcoma, a version of skin cancer often found in elderly men. Interestingly enough, most of the initial twenty-six patients that reported these two illnesses often presented with several others, and they all tended to be diseases or symptoms not seen in young men. Further analysis indicated the reason why: their immune systems provided no defense against or reaction to these infections, preventing the patients from recovering. These men died from illnesses thought reserved to infants, the aged, and chemotherapy patients. Doctors in California scrambled to discern the trends among the chaos. And as they peered through their microscopes, more gay men began arriving in their clinics, all suffering from the same conglomeration of illnesses, and without any explanations.[15]

Researchers, unclear about what exactly caused this mysterious illness but sure that it was something new, labeled the disease Gay-Related Immunodeficiency Disease (GRID) during 1981. This moniker, later shed for AIDS, greatly influenced the course of not only the epidemic, but also the research and treatment of the disease. At the same time, the GRID label overlooked other striking findings appearing not just in California, but also in New York, Miami, and Newark. Patients in these areas also included gay men, but included more heterosexual men and women. And the connections between these individuals seemed less distinct than sexuality: hypodermic drug users, Haitian immigrants, and hemophiliacs. Clearly, these incidences of the disease were not "Gay-Related."[16]

Beyond the hemophiliacs, the markedly higher rates of infection among homosexuals, hypodermic drug users, and Haitian immigrants boded ill for their care and the chances of halting the disease. These three groups represented a unique *trifecta* of marginalized Americans during the 1980s. Ronald Reagan, elected in 1980, had campaigned on two core principles: shrinking government and a return to American values. These ideals appealed to a sizable portion of American society that viewed the post-Watergate era as a period of individual excess, government subversion, and national decline. Reagan sought to build an electoral base that included evangelicals, Christians that often viewed world events through a moralistic lens, and traditionalists, conservatives that believed in the promise of American values domestically and internationally. These two groups cemented a platform for Reagan that sought moral consensus on American/family values at home with a robust presence abroad. This movement also included several fringe elements that appealed to xenophobic notions of corruption within American society, a vocal minority that helped steer future conversations about GRID/AIDS.[17]

For these political groups, illness and death among "homos," "druggies," and "boat people" stirred few notions for government action. In the case of the first two groups, few conservative legislators and observers believed that these "moral failures" necessitated wide-ranging government action. These "lifestyle choices" could merely be corrected through self-discipline, family connections, and prayer. As the epidemic worsened, several leading evangelical ministers proclaimed that "AIDS is a punishment from God" for "perverted lifestyles" and "immoral choices." It did not help that early epidemiological studies that sought to determine the vector of the new disease, when left grasping at straws, could only point to "promiscuity" as a clear connective factor. Drug addicts fared little better; Reagan's rhetoric of morals and values led to a significant increase in funding and legislation for the "War on Drugs." Little more than a verbal flourish under Nixon, this "War" grew under Reagan. The eruption of crack into inner-city neighborhoods occurred symbiotically with the beginning of the AIDS epidemic. National advertising and education campaigns often painted drug addicts as depraved criminals, leaving little room for compassion, or at the very least treatment, in American society.[18]

This conflation of GRID/AIDS with marginalized groups in American society occurred at a transitory point in American politics. As mentioned above, Reagan promised significant cuts to governmental programs on the campaign trail. Once elected, he ushered in a tax cut and reduction in government bureaucracy. Successive budgets cut funding from the National Institutes of Health (NIH), the Centers for Disease Control (CDC), the Food and Drug Administration (FDA), and other organizations and institutions directly responsible for researching and analyzing the new epidemic. And this proved to be no case of benign neglect. In 1982, the CDC spent approximately $1million on GRID/AIDS research, while at the same time spending $135 million on swine flu investigation and vaccine development. And the release of these budgetary findings brought forth much criticism...for taking money away from research in venereal disease and "other vital public health problems." In 1985, when the death of famous actor Rock Hudson to AIDS alerted the general public to the already 12,000 people who had died from AIDS (as well as the hundreds of thousands infected), Reagan appointees to the Department of Health actually slashed the AIDS research budget by over $10 million. This stubborn trend in funding did not change until more AIDS patients came from outside the marginalized sections of American society.[19]

Despite these fiscal reverses, dozens of scientists, doctors, and researchers heroically fought to stem the tide of AIDS deaths while at the same time working to isolate the microbe responsible for the disease. By the mid-1980s, they finally isolated the human immunodeficiency virus (HIV). Interestingly, it appeared to be a mutated form of a virus found in monkeys, predominantly ones from the Great Lakes region of Central Africa. Once the news of this reached the American public, a wave of xenophobic and racist notions swept the nation. Many observers, pointing to the initial prevalence in the Haitian immigrant population, blamed the Haitian exodus from the late 1970s and early 1980s turmoil in that nation for bringing the virus to the United States. Many also blamed increased globalization and connectivity with central Africa for the arrival of AIDS. At the first international conference on AIDS, taking place in Atlanta during April 1985, a reporter asked one of the leading Zairian AIDS researchers "Is it true that Africans have sex with monkeys?"[20]

Such popular misconceptions and sublimations clouded the public discussion of HIV and AIDS throughout the 1980s and into the early 1990s. Several municipalities forbade children infected with HIV from attending school, even though they had been infected at birth unknowingly by their mothers or been a recipient of a blood transfusion from HIV-infected blood. It would take a Supreme Court decision in 1990 to fully forbid this practice. Budget cuts to the FDA limited the amount of surveillance the organization could do in terms of the nation's blood supply. Once the word got out that hospitals, blood banks, and the Red Cross may have HIV-infected blood, a panic swept the nation. Public education and information campaigns did eventually placate the nation's nerves, but not before many thousands died, oftentimes alone or misunderstood.[21]

Placing "blame" for the origin of AIDS took on a particularly vehement tone during the 1990s. As stated above, scientists quickly traced the genetic origins of the virus to Central Africa. Many Westerners pointed to the lack of governance and general "backwardness" of African nations to explain how such a globally destructive event could simmer and then explode onto the world. Then, in 1999, British scientific journalist and researcher Edward Hooper published his massive book, *The River*. Over the course of a thousand pages, Hooper claimed to draw evidence that well-meaning polio vaccination teams actually brought HIV to Africa during the 1950s. The World Health Organization's plan to vaccinate the world's population against polio actually backfired when testing of the vaccine on chimpanzees led to the introduction of Simian Immunodeficiency Virus (SIV) into Central Africa's human population. This controversial theory, now basically disproven, ignited controversy not just within African nations, but also in the now-gaining-momentum anti-vaccine movement within the United States. Subsequent research has shown how the genetic heredity of the HIV viruses trace back to Central Africa from well-before Hooper's oral polio vaccine incident, invalidating his claims for the most part. But this research does claim that the social fractures and upheavals created by turn-of-the-century imperialism helped set the condition for the diseases mutations and later global transmission. Such conclusions only add to the contested political legacy of the epidemic's origin.[22]

By the mid-1990s, the education and information campaigns had begun to pay off. Incidences of HIV exposure began to decline and reach a level of stasis in American society. Tragically, this same trend did not extend around the globe. The fall of the Soviet Union, the liberalization of China, and the resource exploitation of Africa opened new regions to travel, global connectivity, and HIV. By 2010, HIV infected thirty-three million people around the world. And while current trends indicate a leveling off in terms of per capita infection, the long-range impact of this pandemic will be hard to determine. While many point to the relationship between HIV/AIDS and the cultural change within American society during the 1990s and 2000s in terms of LGBT acceptance and civil rights, such a transition does not automatically translate to all areas impacted by AIDS. Some observers postulate that the recent waves of homophobic killings and increased rates of female circumcision in Sub-Saharan Africa have AIDS paranoia as at a least tangential cause. Large-scale global campaigns to alleviate AIDS-related suffering in Africa did slowly pay dividends during the twenty-first century, but not before generations of HIV-exposed youth contracted the disease. The social ruptures created by this new epidemiological reality may take decades to realize.[23]

WHAT NOW? EBOLA IN THE TWENTY-FIRST CENTURY

At the time of this chapter's writing, hospitals have not reported any new Ebola cases within the United States in several months. The summer's hysteria has waned, and new crises have caught the attention of the American public. But for a period of several weeks, the disease looked poised to follow the historical trends of the epidemics that had preceded it. Ebola, and the nation's response, became heavily politicized. As the situation in West Africa worsened, many politicians and commentators called for a region-wide travel ban. Such a legislative idea stirred up foes of immigration already gnashing their teeth over a crisis several months earlier. Children fleeing violence in Central America flocked to the U.S.-Mexican border, creating logistical issues and legal headaches for the Immigration and Naturalization Service (INS) and the Obama administration. The dire threat of Ebola in West Africa only appeared to accentuate the porous nature of America's borders, an example of a xenophobic reflex akin to the response to AIDS among Haitian immigrants during the 1980s.[24]

As nurses and care-givers fell ill, it became clear that the CDC's guidance for protection did not meet the most stringent guideline. As the public began to harangue the CDC, and by extension the NIH, these institutions fired back, showing how budget cuts and austerity measures enacted by the sequestration plan authorized by Congress in 2012 had slashed their budgets and their effectiveness. Some Democratic lawmakers targeted the Republican Senate for holding up the nomination process of a new Surgeon General. How could one deal with a potential epidemic, they claimed, without a Surgeon General to lead the fight? Finally, in an attempt to quell the hysteria, President Obama very publicly met with many of the nurses and caregivers responsible for treating the Ebola patients, ensuring to shake their hands or give them hugs. This very personal close contact sought to calm those that assumed the virus could jump easily into the greater American population.[25]

As Ebola petered out in the United States, it still ravaged West Africa, with the World Health Organization (WHO) claiming that the potential existed for it stay at epidemic levels of morbidity and mortality for the next twelve to thirteen months. With deaths possibly reaching into the tens of thousands, the United States felt forced to act. President Obama committed troops to West Africa, assigning them to security and transportation roles. He also discussed a "Marshall Plan for Africa," the allotment of $6 billion for recovery and development in the wake of the epidemic. Although a noble idea, administration officials have released few specifics concerning the planned aid.[26]

By the 2014 holiday season, most Americans had let Ebola fall out of their day-to-day vocabulary. This may be the most ready similarity between this disease and its precursors, influenza and AIDS. Historians studying both epidemics commented on the ability of American society to rapidly expunge these traumatic national events from their communal psyche. Given the enormity if the influenza epidemic, the lack of any literary retelling of the disease is shocking, particularly so since the 1920s marked the flowering of American letters. While an influenza vaccination campaign does show a commitment to preventing another epidemic from occurring, every few years an abnormal influenza strain will appear that has travelers putting on their surgical masks and the local pharmacy selling out of hand sanitizer. And for all the attention brought to AIDS during the 1990s, the decrease in the disease's incidence rate has allowed it to fall off the general social radar. As AIDS enters it fourth decade of endemic status globally, no new activists campaigns exist that ultimately would threaten the disease's termination.

These two examples provide evidence to a stark reality of American communal memory. Epidemics do not have a long shelf life in the American mind. The lack of an arbitrary nature, when coupled with the apparent rejection of technological and medical progress, allows an epidemic to create social schisms easier to forget than to plan for. Future public health officials, politicians, and planners must contend with these realities, no matter their unsettling nature. And this preparation does not solely contain a medical reaction, but the totality of the socio-political components that epidemics either usher in or exacerbate further. If not, cities may, yet again, begin running out of coffins.

NOTES

1. Jeff Brady, "Nurse Kaci Hickox Takes a Bike Ride, Defying Maine's Quarantine," *NPR.org*, October 30, 2014, www.npr.org/2014/10/30/360179356/nurse-kaci-hickox-takes-a-bike-ride-defying-maines-quarantine (accessed June 16, 2015); "Nurse Describes Ebola Quarantine Ordeal: 'I was in Shock. Now I'm Angry.'," *CNN.com*, October 27, 2014, http://www.cnn.com/2-14/10/26/health/new-jersey-quarantined-nurse/ (accessed June 16, 2015).

2. Leslie Savan, "Nurse Kaci Hickox Takes on Bully Governors Christie, Cuomo and LePage," *The Nation*, October 29, 2014, http://m.thenation.com/blog/186681-nurse-kaci-hickox-takes-bully-governors-christie-cuomo-and-lepage (accessed June 16, 2015); Matt Acro, "Chris Christie to Maine Nurse: Go Ahead, Sue Me over Ebola Quarantine," *nj.com*, October 29, 2014, http://www.nj.com/politics/index.ssf/2014/10/chris_christie_to_maine_nurse_go_ahead_sue_me_over_ebola_quarantine.html (accessed June 16, 2015).

3. Charles Rosenberg, "Disease in History: Frames and Framers," *The Milibank Quarterly*, vol. 67, sup. 1 (1989): 1–15 (quote pg. 4); see also Charles Rosenberg, "Explaining Epidemics," in *Explaining Epidemics and Other Studies in the History of Medicine* (Cambridge: Cambridge University Press, 1992), 293–304; and Elena Conis, *Vaccine Nation: America's Changing Relationship with Immunization* (Chicago: The University of Chicago Press, 2015).

4. Alfred Crosby, "Virgin Soil Epidemics as a Factor in the Aboriginal Depopulation in America," in *The William and Mary Quarterly*, vol. 33, no. 2: 289–299; Elizabeth A. Fenn, *Pox Americana: the Great Smallpox Epidemic of 1775–1782* (New York: Hill and Wang, 2002); and Charles E. Rosenberg, *The Cholera Years: The United States in 1832, 1849, and 1866*, 2nd ed. (Chicago: University of Chicago Press, 1987).

5. Thucydides, *The Peloponnesian War*, trans. John H. Finley, Jr (New York: Random House, 1951), 110–113.

6. Alfred Crosby, *The Columbian Exchange: Biological and Cultural Consequences of 1492* (New York: Greenwood Publishing, 1973).

7. William H. McNeill, *Plagues and Peoples* (Garden City: Anchor Books, 1976); quote from 257.

8. The historiography of the Influenza Pandemic of 1918–1920 grew substantially after the turn of the Twenty-first century. The best overall works are Barry's *The Great Influenza* and Crosby's *America's Forgotten Pandemic*; see John M. Barry, *The Great Influenza: The Story of the Deadliest Pandemic in History* (New York: Penguin Books, 2005) and Alfred W. Crosby, *America's Forgotten Epidemic: The Influenza of 1918* (Cambridge: Cambridge University Press, 1989). For other treatments of the epidemic see Nancy K. Bristow, *American Pandemic: The Lost World of the 1918 Influenza Pandemic* (Oxford: Oxford University Press, 2012); Ana Luisa Martinez-Catsam, "Desolate Streets: The Spanish Influenza in San Antonio" in *The Southwestern Historical Quarterly*, vol. 116, no. 3 (January 2013), 287–304; Ed Coss, "World War I, the Spanish Flu, and Memory," in *The Eisenhower Clearinghouse Journal* (Winter 2004); and Gina Kolata, *Flu: The Story of the Great Influenza Pandemic of 1918 and the Search for the Virus that Caused it* (New York: Farrar, Straus, and Giroux, 1999). For a

discussion of the epidemic in Canada, see Mark Osborne Humphries, *The Last Plague: Spanish Influenza and the Politics of Public Health in Canada* (Toronto: University of Toronto Press, 2013).

9. Coffman does an admirable job outlining the mass mobilization and infrastructure improvements needed to generate the necessary manpower for the American Expeditionary Force (AEF); see Edward M. Coffman, *The War to End all Wars: The American Military Experience in World War I* (Lexington: University Press of Kentucky, 1998).

10. Barry's popular work on the Influenza Pandemic is currently the most popular book on the epidemic. He advances the "Camp Funston Epicenter" theory in his book as the primary explanation. This is not a fully agreed upon theory.

11. Crosby's work on the Influenza Pandemic is still the best scholarly treatment of the epidemic. For his treatment of the inauguration of the "second wave" of global influenza, see 37–41.

12. For a discussion of San Francisco during the Influenza Pandemic, see Crosby, *America's Forgotten Pandemic*, 91–120.

13. For a good overview of American perceptions of its newest citizens, see Matthew Frye Jacobson, *Barbarian Virtues: The United States Encounters Foreign People at Home and Abroad, 1876–1917* (New York: Hill and Wang, 2001).

14. All data from Crosby, 202–294.

15. Historical accounts of the AIDS Epidemic take up book shelves, if not book cases, at libraries. While not discussing all of them, this study will attempt to build a narrative of the diseases emergence within the United States and the later implications of the disease in American and global society. As such, the scope of the books covered in this chapter may appear narrow, but for purposeful reasons.

The most compelling account of the conflict between Reagan-era conservatism and AIDS in the gay community is still Shilts' *And the Band Played On*; see Randy Shilts, *And the Band Played On: Politics, People, and the AIDS Epidemic* (New York: St. Martin's Press, 1987). While the intellectual verve of the book has lasted a generation on, scientific inquiry has invalidated some of the work's conclusions. For a readable overview see Laurie Garrett, *The Coming Plague: Newly Emerging Diseases in a World Out of Balance* (New York: Penguin Books, 1994), 281–389; and David Quammen, *Spillover: Animal Infection and the Next Human Pandemic* (New York: Norton Books, 2012). Rosenberg sought to describe the "framing" of AIDS in the mid-1980s; see Charles E. Rosenberg, "What is an Epidemic? AIDS in Historical Perspective," in *Explaining Epidemics and Other Studies in the History of Medicine*. Harden provides a nice overview as well, although she incorporates a much more global aspect; see Victoria A. Harden, *AIDS at 30: A History* (Washington, D.C.: Potomac Books, 2012).

16. Garrett, 280–310.

17. Numerous historical works chart the rise of late-twentieth century American conservatism in general. See Jefferson Cowie, *Stayin' Alive: The 1970s and the Last Days of the Working Class* (New York: The New Press, 2012); Daniel T. Rodgers, *Age of Fracture* (New York: Belknap Press, 2012); Robert O. Self, *All in the Family: The Realignment of American Democracy since the 1960s* (New York: Farrar, Strauss and Giroux, 2012); and Rick Perlstein, *The Invisible Bridge: The Fall of Nixon and the Rise of Reagan* (New York: Simon and Schuster, 2014).

18. Self, 383–395.

19. Garrett, 298–304; see also Charles E. Rosenberg, "Disease and Social Order in America: Perceptions and Expectations," in *Explaining Epidemics and Other Studies in the History of Medicine*.

20. Garett, 348–360.

21. Verghese's *My Own Country* gives a heart-rending account of the social fractures created by the AIDS epidemic in small-town America; see Abraham Verghese, *My Own Country: A Doctor's Story* (New York: Vintage Press, 1995).

22. Edward Hooper, *The River: A Journey to the Source of HIV and AIDS* (Boston: Back Bay Books, 1999). For a summation of the research that invalidated most of Hooper's conclusions, see David Quammen, *The Chimp and the River: How AIDS emerged from an African Forest* (New York: W. W. Norton and Company, 2015).

23. Greg Behrman, *The Invisible People: How the U.S. Has Slept Through the Global AIDS Pandemic, the Greatest Humanitarian Catastrophe of Our Time* (New York: Free Press, 2004); and Lawrence O. Gostin, *The Aids Pandemic: Complacency, Injustice, and Unfulfilled Expectations* (Chapel Hill: University of North Carolina Press, 2004).

24. Jad Mouawad, "Experts Oppose Ebola Travel Ban, Saying it Would Cut Off Worst Hit Countries," in *New York Times*, October 17, 2014, http://www.nytimes.com/2014/10/18/business/experts-oppose-ebola-travel-ban-saying-it-would-cut-off-worst-hit-countries.html (accessed June 18, 2016); Greg Sargent, "Scott Brown: Anyone with Ebola can 'Walk Across' our 'Porous Border,'" in *The Washington Post*, October 14, 2014, http://www.washingtonpost.com/blogs/plum-line/wp/2014/10/14/scott-brown-anyone-with-ebola-can-walk-across-our-porous-border (accessed June 18, 2016).

25. Paul Callan, "We Need a Surgeon General, not an Ebola Czar," *CNN.com*, October 20, 2014, http://www.cnn.com/2014/10/15/opinion/callan-ebola-surgeon-general-frieden/index.html (accessed June 18, 2016); Michael Tanner, "Budget Cuts and Ebola," in *National Review*, October 15, 2014, http://www.nationalreview.com/article/390311/budget-cuts-and-ebola-michael-tanner (accessed June 18, 2016); and Brett Norman, "Ebola Highlights CDC Funds Crunch," *Politico.com*, October 2, 2014, http://www.politico.com/story/2014/10/ebola-dcd-funding-111556.html (accessed June 16, 2015).

26. "Report: 11 US Treatment Centers Treated only 28 Patients," *Military.com*, April 13, 2015, http://www.military.com/daily-news/2015/04/13/report-11-us-ebola-treatment-centers-treated-only-28-patients.html (accessed June 18, 2015); "Ebola: Liberia's Johnson Sireaf urges 'Marshall Plan,'" *BBC.com*, March 3, 2015, http://www.bbc.com/news/world-africa-31705594 (accessed June 15, 2015); Maggie Fox, "Why It's Not Enough to Just Eradicate Ebola," *NBCnews.com*, November 2, 2014, http://www.nbcnews.com/storyline/ebola-virus-outbreak/why-its-not-enough-just-eradicate-ebola-n243891 (accessed June 18, 2016); "When Disasters Like Ebola Hit, the World Needs the World Health Organization. And It's Failing," *Vox. Com*, May 22, 2015, http://www.vox.com/2015/5/22/8640607/ebola-WHO-reform (accessed June 2, 2015); and "World Health Organization's Ebola Response Draws Criticism," *voanews.com*, November 20, 2014, http://www.voanews.com/content/world-health-organization-ebola-response-criticized/2528251.html (accessed May 14, 2015).

IV

Political and Philosophical Considerations

Residue of Intolerance

Polluting Civil Rights

Robert J. Goldstein[1]

Intolerance is anything but a momentary wrong, it is an enduring evil that persists well-beyond the lives of its initial victims and perpetrators. The residuals of intolerance take many forms and can impede generations from achieving social and economic progress. Environmental *in*justice is but one of those many forms, but *its* consequences perpetuate and aggravate the disadvantages of second-class citizenship, extending inequities and deepening their ramifications.

Civil rights are the basic necessities of empowerment. Without civil rights, inequality is certain, but even with those basic rights, equality is not assured. The Civil Rights Movement of the 1960s demonstrated that to attain actual empowerment in the fight to eliminate legal discrimination, much more than a mere moral imperative was required. Organization, planning, strategy, and fortitude were key to each and every incremental success along with the tears and blood that were the price of victory. The elimination of *de jure* inequality was only the start of a long climb from slavery. The question posed herein is whether a movement is needed to highlight and eradicate instances of environmental *in*justice, an often neglected aspect of the *de facto* inequality that has become unbridled in our time, and threatens to undo much of the progress made toward true equality.

ONE OF MANY ENVIRONMENTAL DISASTERS . . .
AND A FOOTNOTE

In 2008, five million cubic yards of coal ash, a toxic by-product of burning coal, spilled from the Tennessee Valley Authority's Kingston Fossil Plant in Tennessee into the surrounding wealthy community (Dewan). A CBS News *60 Minutes* segment about the spill focused on the lack of federal regulation of coal ash and the impact of the spill on the affluent homeowners nearby, describing "a billion gallons of muck [that] shot into the Emory River like a black Tsunami" (CBS 60 Minutes Report, 2010). Sadly, pollution disasters are an all too frequent scenario. A one-line mention in that segment footnoted the final destination of the coal ash as a "dry landfill in Alabama" (5:33).

Similar incidents involving coal ash have focused attention on the existence of what has been termed "America's coal ash crisis" (Sierra Club, 2014). As recently as February 2, 2014, according to the United States Environmental Protection Agency, "up to 39,000 tons of coal ash spilled into the Dan River at Eden" North Carolina (U.S. EPA, 2014), from a Duke Energy facility (Trip, 2014). The environmental organization Earthjustice lists 208 "known cases of contamination & spills" (Earthjustice, 2014). According to the Southern Alliance for Clean Energy, the Southeast "is home to 40% of the nation's coal ash impoundments" (SE Coal Ash, 2014).

A chance visit to that "dry landfill in Alabama," and what was ultimately learned on the journey frames this perspective of the status of modern day civil rights, and the continued need to pursue goals still unattained despite a half-century of progress.

STUDYING DISCRIMINATION IN ITS MANY FORMS

Fifty years ago the federal Civil Rights Act was passed to put an end to legalized segregation and discrimination (Civil Rights Act of 1964). Starting in 2013, the West Point Center for the Rule of Law instituted a Civil Rights Staff Ride, an interdisciplinary educational journey for cadets from the United States Military Academy who will graduate as officers in the U.S. Army. A staff ride is a method of educating officers about a particular battle by visiting the battlefield. The mission of the Staff Ride was to study the law and history of the Civil Rights Movement, but more importantly, to understand its contemporary meaning. This Staff Ride was an interdisciplinary vehicle to teach law, history, and diversity by creating empathy in understanding and appreciating diversity, and the struggle for civil rights in America. The Staff Ride is a carefully constructed teaching project that consists of both time in the classroom and a two-week long trip to meet individuals involved with the civil rights struggle, collect oral histories based on their experiences, while visiting "battlefields" instrumental to the course of the Civil Rights Movement.

The learning goals and objectives of the Staff Ride was to have cadets: (1) gain specific knowledge of both the legal principles that allowed civil rights to be denied for a significant portion of American history, and the legal tools used to ultimately remedy those wrongs; (2) understand the historical context for the evolution of the law; and (3) appreciate the cultural milieu that paralleled those changes.

The teaching and learning activities were geared toward each of these goals and objectives. In the classroom, instructors employed a variety of pedagogical practices to examine the complexity of civil rights issues both in the past and the present day. These practices included primary document assessment, case review, role-playing, and multimedia analysis (particularly films and music) that helped provide a conceptual understanding and contextual backdrop to the civil rights period.

During the Staff Ride itself, the cadets engaged with all outside participants and were responsible for developing discussion questions that would help build a cogent narrative for the entire staff ride. Participants were chosen from three age-related groups, including: (1) Veterans of the Civil Rights Movement; (2) their children; and (3) their grandchildren. Meetings with members of these three groups allowed cadets the opportunity to witness first-hand the generational differences that they, in their own experience, could relate to. While the first two generations resembled their grandparents and parents respectively, the third were their peers.

The 2014 West Point Civil Rights Staff Ride was a great success. Travelling throughout the South, cadets were able to meet with civil rights legends like Robert Parris Moses (Dumas, 2003), Medgar Evers widow, Myrlie Evers (Evers-Williams, 1967), and Fred Gray (Gray); but perhaps their biggest success was understanding that there is still a great need for the Movement to continue.

Teaching diversity is an important part of the educational needs at USMA, and the Civil Rights Staff Ride proved to be a vehicle to test innovative interdisciplinary techniques to approaching this issue in the classroom. It is fitting that West Point takes the lead in diversity education; as was learned during the Staff Ride, much of the impetus for the Civil Rights Movement was generated by veterans who had returned from the Second World War. Teaching diversity is also a mandate for the Army in order to foster cohesion and enhance team work.

CIVIL RIGHTS AND ENVIRONMENT

Among the many places the Staff Ride visited on the journey to the South to understand the issues of the Civil Rights Movement was the Atlanta boyhood home of Dr. Martin Luther King, Jr. In the family room a partially played game of Monopoly™ is on display. When asked, the Park Ranger who acts as tour guide noted that it was Dr. King's favorite game. Interesting, especially since many educators use Monopoly™ to teach Affirmative Action to students (Dierringer, 2013). In Monopoly™, if you start the game in the middle, or if you are playing with different rules, your chances of winning are very, very poor. Monopoly™ can be used as a metaphor for the recovery from inequality.

Living in a safe and healthful environment is not a luxury, it is a human right. Clean water and air, and access to healthful food are important components of this right. The nexus between environment and civil rights is the subject of environmental justice. According to the EPA, "Environmental Justice is the fair treatment and meaningful involvement of all people regardless of race, color, national origin, or income with respect to the development, implementation, and enforcement of environmental laws, regulations, and policies" (USEPA EJ). Environmental justice is a critical civil right.

Environmental *in*justice is most certainly not the only "residue of intolerance" that is the legacy of legal, or *de jure* discrimination. At least equally compelling are the dangers faced by young black males whom, one recent analysis places at more than 20-times greater "risk of being shot dead by police than their white counterparts" (Gabrielson, 2014). The "mass incarceration" of African Americans, affording them permanent criminal-class status also belies the existence of a "post-racial" era in the United States (Alexander, 2010). Fundamental to these and other latent manifestations of injustice is the continued segregation of schools (Carter, 1964) (Clotfelter, 2001), and the severe economic divide that plagues African Americans (Shapiro, 2013).

But environmental justice cases are also pernicious, and deal with the most basic of human rights, and critically, they are easily hidden and often overlooked. "Environment has its impacts on behaviors" (Alkhatib, 2014), in fact studies have indicated a relationship between crime and exposure to lead. A study conducted in Jordan found that "prisoners have about double concentration of blood lead and it is highly possible that our findings supported the environmental hypothesis which explained the effects of removal of lead from gasoline in lowering crime rates" (Alkhatib).

"Exposure to lead has both class and race correlates that operate at the sociological level. Lower class and minority communities are more likely than other income or race groups to have elevated probabilities of lead exposure" (Stretesky, 2004). Another study has determined that "[o]ther things held equal, we find a statistically significant association between tonnages of air Pb [lead] released 22 years prior with present period aggravated assault rate; our full statistical model explains 90% of the variation in aggravated assault across US cities examined" (Mielke, 2012). In other words, there is a correlation between the removal of lead pollution due to the introduction of unleaded gasoline, and lowering crime rates.

Environmental issues generally, however, are frequently oversimplified as a choice between good and bad behaviors. This attitude belies the fact that many environmental issues present choices between societal benefits that will impact the human environment in different ways.

Likewise, environmental justice cases are not always obvious; in fact they generally involve a compelling environmental problem that needs to be solved. Solutions to those "straight-forward" problems often have unforeseen consequences.

While many of these problems do not involve an overt racial component which would evoke a narrative of environmental racism, many do. Neither do they all happen in the South. The nature of these problems can be seen in the following examples:

The environmental advocacy group Riverkeeper, Inc. was requested to support the removal of a waste-transfer station from a new park in New York City (Confessore, 2007). Riverkeeper is a not-for-profit group whose mission is to: "To protect the environmental, recreational and commercial integrity of the Hudson River and its tributaries, and safeguard the drinking water of nine million New York City and Hudson Valley residents" (Riverkeeper). While New York City on the surface appears to be and in many ways is among the most progressive in the United States, it has a long history of segregation, and many contemporary issues that are a result of that legacy (Purnell, 2013). Key among those is *de facto* school segregation (Kucsera, 2014), based on the continued existence of sharply segregated community boundaries.

At first blush, it appeared that the decision to protect the Park was a very reasonable request. The park is part of a larger lineal green space and trail around the island of Manhattan. This section of park had been liberated from the threat of development of a $2.1 billion dollar elevated expressway which came to be known as Westway (Buzbee, 2014). The 15 year battle pitted environmentalists (including the Hudson River Fishermen's Association, the predecessor to Riverkeeper, Inc.), against powerful politicians, including Governor Nelson Rockefeller and Mayor Ed Koch. The project was ended in litigation in the case of *Sierra Club v. U.S. Army Corps of Engineers*, 732. F.2d 253 (2nd Cir. 1984), that enjoined the construction due to the fact that the "the interpier area [slated to be part of a massive landfill] houses young striped bass--one of America's good game and commercial fish--and that this area of the Hudson is an important and productive habitat for them" (255). The court found that this action (a landfill in the Hudson River), which required a permit from the Army Corps of Engineers under the federal Clean

Water Act, was based on an inaccurate Environmental Impact Statement (EIS) required by the National Environmental Policy Act. The environmentalists' victory was sweetened by the subsequent agreement to create the Hudson River Park.

Riverkeeper's legal staff began to examine the unintended consequences of relocating the transfer station, especially as murmurs of counter-protest from groups representing underprivileged communities in Harlem and the Bronx (both far from the pier itself) began to resound. The bottom line was that there had to be a transfer-station somewhere, and if it wasn't going to remain in this more affluent neighborhood, it would be sited in a less-affluent one, one less capable of making its case (Confessore, 2007). Without the support of environmental groups like Riverkeeper, the effort to move the transfer station to less-affluent communities stalled.

Another example of *in*justice in the making of an environmental decision threatened to destroy the City Park neighborhood of New Rochelle, NY. Such was the potential when the Swedish furniture retailer IKEA looked to site an enormous box-store in what was describe as a "well-integrated neighborhood, with Latino immigrants, older Italians, African-Americans, and a variety of businesses coexisting side by side" (Columbia, 2001).

The law allows for condemnation of what can be demonstrated to be a blighted community. Such heavy-handed local planning was upheld by the United States Supreme Court in the landmark case of *Kelo v. City of New London*, 545 U.S. 469 (2005). In that case, the Court determined that economic development was indeed a public purpose that justified the taking of private property by the government, and upheld "their determination that the area was sufficiently distressed to justify a program of economic rejuvenation is entitled to our deference" (483). Logic will suffice to demonstrate that "sufficiently distressed" would disqualify affluent neighborhoods, while allowing state and local governments a relatively free hand to undertake "urban renewal" (Hwang, 2014).

The city of New Rochelle designated a community with 33 commercial structures, two churches and 31 residences as "blighted" (Cohen, 2001). The residents in this integrated neighborhood, many of whom were "senior citizens who had lived there all their lives," faced the destruction of their community (Cohen, 2001).

Ultimately, a coalition of social justice organizations including the Pace Law School Social Justice Clinic utilized "a three-part model inspired by Dr. Martin Luther King Jr.'s Letter From a Birmingham Jail – investigate, organize, and then, if negotiation fails, litigate" (Cohen, 2001), and were able to dissuade the city from proceeding.

These cases were resolved with empowerment being achieved through community-organizing combined with legal assistance, to secure the civil rights of members of the affected communities. This has long been the case in the history of the Civil Rights Movement. There is no case challenging Jim Crow laws in the Post-Reconstruction South like *Plessy v. Ferguson*, 163 U.S. 537 (1896), without the Comité des Citoyens in New Orleans and the lawyers who supported their efforts (Medley, 2012); no recourse for Barbara Johns and her schoolmates in Farmville, Virginia, if not for the lawyers who agreed to take her case on school segregation ultimately to the United States Supreme Court (Pratt, 2002); neither is there a successful bus boycott in Montgomery, Alabama by Rosa Parks without the assistance of lawyer Fred Gray (Gray); and the list goes on-and-on. However, those successes were fueled by a movement that congealed in the 1960's only to – arguably - dissolve by that decade's end (Delgado, 2002).

In addition, the synergies that led to the Movement's many successes were fueled by the fact that it was *legal* segregation that was the enemy rather than the *de facto* segregation that plagues us today.

DE JURE DISCRIMINATION

Jim Crow segregation was a system of legal measures designed and applied to prevent racial integration. Following the Civil War and emancipation of the slaves, the period known as Reconstruction, which lasted from 1865 until 1877, was a period of false hope and intense controversy. In the former Confederate states the newly freed slaves, empowered by Union soldiers and Republican influence, saw glimmers of civil rights and their concomitant political power. They were allowed to vote, giving political control of state legislatures to the Republicans. Many African-Americans were elected to state and local offices as well as congressional seats.

In 1875 Congress passed a Civil Rights Act which prohibited discrimination in public accommodations, and allowing redress in federal courts. Fatefully, the Act was based on the Equal Protection Clause of the 14th Amendment, making it vulnerable to a legal challenge that set the stage for over 70 years of legalized racial discrimination.

The first section of the Amendment reads as follows:

> All persons born or naturalized in the United States, and subject to the jurisdiction thereof, are citizens of the United States and of the state wherein they reside. *No state shall* make or enforce any law which shall abridge the privileges or immunities of citizens of the United States; *nor shall any state* deprive any person of life, liberty, or property, without due process of law; nor deny to any person within its jurisdiction the equal protection of the laws (emphasis added).

It was in fact the very language of the 14th Amendment's "Equal Protection Clause" that perpetuated legalized discrimination into the Twentieth

Century. That language limited those acts subject to protection to those per-
petrated by the government by the use of the phrases "[n]o state shall" and
"nor shall any state." The decision of the Supreme Court in the clumsily
styled, *Civil Rights Cases*, 109 U.S. 3 (1883) that held the 1875 Act unconstitutional, stating that:

> And so, in the present case, until some State law has been passed, or some
> State action through its officers or agents has been taken, adverse to the rights
> of citizens sought to be protected by the Fourteenth Amendment, no legislation
> of the United States under said amendment, nor any proceeding under such
> legislation, can be called into activity, for the prohibitions of the amendment
> are against State laws and acts done under State authority (13).

An interesting comparison of judicial interpretation might be drawn between the logic applied in the *Civil Rights Cases* to that used to resolve the
case of *NFIB v. Sebelius*, 567 U.S. __ (2012), 132 S.Ct 2566, which held the
Patient Protection and Affordable Care Act (26 U.S.C. §5000A) to be constitutional. There, the government's argument that the law, commonly known
as "Obamacare" was constitutional was the Constitution's Commerce Clause
(Art. I, §8, cl. 4). The Court, in an opinion by Chief Justice Roberts, after
finding that the Commerce Clause was inapplicable, turned to the Tax Clause
of Article I, holding that "every reasonable construction must be resorted to,
in order to save a statute from unconstitutionality" (2573). Sadly, the Court
in the *Civil Rights Cases* failed to apply that rule of construction, noting,
despite the urging of Associate Justice John M. Harlan's (the elder) dissent-
ing opinion, that it would not decide whether the commerce power would
authorize the regulation of public accommodations.

The Court's decision emboldened states, particularly in the South, to pass
legislation that required and enforced segregation. These laws included Louisiana's Separate Car Act of 1890 (Louisiana Acts of 1890, No. 111, p. 152),
which included in its first section:

> that all railway companies carrying passengers in their coaches in this State
> shall provide equal but separate accommodations for the white and colored
> races by providing two or more passenger coaches for each passenger train, or
> by dividing the passenger coaches by a partition so as to secure separate
> accommodations: Provided, That this section shall not be construed to apply to
> street railroads. No person or persons, shall be admitted to occupy seats in
> coaches other than the ones assigned to them on account of the race they
> belong to (Plessy v. Ferguson, 1896).

In response to this offensive law the New Orleans Comité des Citoyens, a
committed group of activists, many of whom thrived as civic leaders during
the years after the Civil War, plotted a legal challenge to the law based on the
14th Amendment (Medley, 2012). The resulting Supreme Court decision,

Plessy v. Ferguson, would etch the shameful doctrine of "separate but equal" into American law, where it would remain in force for 58 years until discarded by a unanimous Court in the landmark case of *Brown v. Board of Education*, 347 U.S. 483 (1954). It would not be, however, until 1964 that Congress would use commerce as a basis for a Civil Rights Act that would ban discrimination in public accommodations (Civil Rights Act of 1964). The Commerce Clause basis for banning segregation in public accommodations was ultimately upheld by the Supreme Court in the case of *Heart of Atlanta Motel, Inc. v. United States*, 379 U.S. 241 (1964).

While this did not mean that racially-neutral laws could not be applied in a racially discriminatory way, the law as noted in case of *Ricci v. DeStefano*, 557 U.S. 557, (2009), "prohibits both intentional discrimination (known as "disparate treatment") as well as, in some cases, practices that are not intended to discriminate but in fact have a disproportionately adverse effect on minorities (known as "disparate impact")" (577). Thus concluded the long-awaited demise of *de jure* discrimination.

ENVIRONMENTAL *INJUSTICE* AS *DE FACTO* DISCRIMINATION

The 50-years following the demise of legal discrimination has seen undeniable positive changes with regard to discrimination. But while we have elected our first African American president, it appears quite evident that race still matters in America. This continuing legacy of the disadvantages imposed by law has manifested into a continuing set of travails for African Americans who clearly remained burdened by their present circumstances.

Much of that *de facto* discrimination is laid on the doorstep of economic disparity, rather than racial prejudice. The economic argument does not hold water with regard to the mass incarceration of African American men and the high percentage of those who are shot by police, but despite the obvious disparate impacts, economics does play a role in *de facto* school segregation, income disparity and, notably, environmental justice.

As described above with reference to the Hudson River Park and IKEA scenarios, it is always easier for decision makers to take the path of least resistance in resolving choices regarding an environmental problem. The more powerful the "not in my backyard" (hereinafter referred to as "NIMBY") interests are, the more difficult it will be to resist them. While there are pejorative references to the idea of NIMBY, this attitude is a perfectly normal reaction to the threat of environmental harm by a local population. The negative aspects of this attitude arise due to the divergent levels of power that different communities have by virtue of their affluence and political acumen. Protection needs to be afforded to the less powerful, and empowerment comes by definition, through civil rights.

An example of gravity of the path of least resistance is the issue of where to safely dispose of toxic PCB-laden sediments taken from the Hudson River. PCBs are polychlorinated biphenyls, a persistent organic pollutant that is a probable human carcinogen. For decades, the General Electric Company disposed of PCBs into the upper-Hudson River in New York State.

When dealing with the toxic PCBs removed from the Hudson River Superfund site, the priority of environmental advocates was to get it out of the River (DePalma, 2005). There will always be someone affected by the transference of an environmental problem elsewhere. A great deal of attention was paid to the prospect of the contaminated sediments being shipped by rail to Texas where a local company would be well paid to properly dispose of it (McKinley, 2009). In fact, the agreement negotiated with EPA assured the local groups who militated for the PCB removal that it would not be sent to any site within the relatively affluent and politically powerful Hudson River Valley (McKinley, 2009). In essence, dozens of trains filled with toxic waste were transported half-way across the United States to mollify a powerful NIMBY. However, PCBs were regulated as hazardous waste by the federal government, which meant that their transport and ultimate disposal would be managed appropriately (Resource Conservation and Recovery Act (RCRA), 90 Stat. 2795 (1976)).

There is a mechanism at work here that requires explanation. While there is a vast array of federal regulation on pollution, unregulated pollution has created a perverse incentive for states to minimize otherwise prudent regulation to maximize state revenues. This is called the "race to the bottom" (Revesz, 1997). Naturally, states that seek to receive these noxious materials (for money) will agree to locate them in localities that will not have the power to exercise NIMBY influence (McGurty, 1997). Surprisingly, coal ash has not yet been designated a hazardous waste by the federal Environmental Protection Agency (although they are inching in that direction), and thus is still regulated only by states (Foster, 2011).

"States generally exempt coal combustion byproducts, including coal ash, from hazardous waste regulations" (Moon, 2009-2010). The lack of state regulation makes the handling of coal ash ripe for competition in the race to the bottom (Evans2).

In a comprehensive study by the EPA published in 2010, the toxic constituents of coal combustion waste (coal ash) were identified as including arsenic and chromium, both known carcinogens; beryllium and cadmium, probable human carcinogens; and an array of constituents that pose both human and ecological health risks (EPA, OSWER, 2010). Despite the understanding of coal ash and its constituents, the politics behind coal ash regulation is a testament to the power and influence of the mining and energy lobbies in the United States (Moon, 2009-2010). Interestingly, the so-called Bevill Amendment to the federal law on solid waste (RCRA) excepted coal ash from federal regulation, and was named for its sponsor in the House of Representatives Alabama Congressman Tom Bevill, who according to his obituary in the Washington Post, on March 31, 2005, earned the title "King of Pork" (Estrada, 2005). Bevill represented both the 4th and 7th districts of Alabama during his tenure in the House. Uniontown, a place which will be discussed below, is currently situated in Alabama's 7th congressional district.

While this influence prevented designation of coal ash as a hazardous waste under federal law, it affirmatively stymied state regulation as well. In North Carolina, for instance, Duke Energy, the nation's largest utility company actually rolled back their exposure to liability for the cleanup of groundwater contaminated by coal ash in state "regulatory reform" legislation (NC Gen Stat § G.S. 143-215.1(i-k)(as amended 2013)). This was accomplished by aligning a disposal system permit holder's "compliance boundary" with their "property boundary." The process that allowed this legislative fix for a problem that might affect Duke's bottom line is documented in an investigative piece which noted:

> Working closely with lawmakers, the lobbyists [for Duke] helped craft a provision to conform to the way state regulators had been interpreting the law. The change would allow Duke to contaminate groundwater until it crossed onto a neighbor's property.
>
> Duke Energy and its executives have donated millions in recent years to both Republicans and Democrats. Though 2013 was not an election year, records show the company continued to give generously as its lobbyists sought to protect its ash pits (Biesecker, 2014).

Coal industry lobbyists turned the issue of regulating coal ash as a hazardous waste into a debate over the merits of recycling (Quinones, 2011). Ostensibly, if you favor labeling coal ash a hazardous waste, you are opposed to recycling! A cynical argument, but apparently, when backed by millions of dollars in campaign funds, an effective one.

THAT "DRY LANDFILL IN ALABAMA"

So what about that "dry landfill"? Uniontown, Alabama is the place. One can view the *60 Minutes* segment about the spill from the Kingston Fossil Plant in 2008 many times and hardly notice the one-line mention in that piece regarding the final disposition of the coal ash in Alabama. One might take for granted that since the EPA was involved with the cleanup, and because of the publicity that the spill had garnered, the final disposition would be highly scrutinized. However, with little or no fanfare, the problem would be out of sight and out of mind. In fact when the Staff Ride participants were invited by Mitch Reid of the Alabama Rivers Alliance to visit a coal ash site in

Alabama, it was not apparent that there was any connection between Union-town and the notorious Kingston spill.

The coal ash shipped from the Tennessee spill is in an unsightly facility from which, according to the Black Warrior Riverkeeper, a local environmental group, "[r]esidents continually witnessed ash blowing from the landfill to cover their homes, cars, yards, gardens and wash lines in the fin-gray-black powder" (Dillard, 2015). Eve Dillard notes that, "[i]n 2010, John War-than, Hurricane Riverkeeper, filed a complaint with the EPA, outlining the health threats from the landfill, which included test results of runoff flowing into residential ditches and nearby creeks which indicated high levels of arsenic, which is commonly associated with coal ash" (Dillard).

Uniontown is a small town located in Perry County, Alabama. The County has a shrinking population, estimated by the United States Census Bureau to be 10,020 (Census, 2014). The County is 67.6% African-American (Census, 2014). In Perry County, the median household income is $31,008, and 26.9% of persons live below the poverty line (Census, 2014). Census data indicate that it is among the poorest counties in the United States (Census, 2014).

Abject poverty was not always the identity of Perry County. Prior to the Civil War, the area was described as one containing "wealth, culture, and power [that were] unsurpassed throughout the state" (NPS, 1993). This was largely based on its "agricultural potential" (Webster, 1992). Such potential was seen in the "relatively dark soils derived from the Selma chalk (Webster, 1992), which gave rise to the region being identified as the "Black Belt."

> A combination of several factors promoted the aggressive agricultural development of cotton plantations in the Alabama Black Belt. First, a new cotton variety was introduced in 1830 which was suitable for the limy soils found in the Black Belt. Second, although cotton production was already entrenched in the Tennessee Valley of northern Alabama, producers had to ship their product down the Tennessee, Ohio, and Mississippi rivers to New Orleans, a distance of 1,500 miles. In contrast, cotton produced in the Alabama Black Belt could be shipped to the deepwater port of Mobile via the Tombigbee and Alabama Rivers, a distance of only 150 miles (Webster, 1992).

The "Black Belt" was also a term which denoted as an area which "is a black district, the negroes still largely outnumbering the whites" (Webster, 1992).

> A third factor leading to the rapid development of the Black Belt's agricultural potential were the increasingly profitable world prices for cotton. Since cotton production was labor-intensive and cheap labor was in limited supply in the South, slaves were imported to labor on the newly developing cotton fields of the Alabama Black Belt. By 1850, 20 years after the beginning of intensive

plantation development, the proportions of blacks in the counties of this region
were frequently above 50, 60 and even 75% (Webster, 1992).

Within the Black Belt, an area of "roughly 650 square miles," and encom-
passing Perry County and the town of Uniontown, was defined as the "Canebrake" region. (NPS, 1993) "When American planters from Virginia and the
Carolinas bought out the French farms, the Canebrake became the very seat
of Black Belt aristocracy" (NPS, 1993). Inside this region settlers developed
cotton plantations with large slave populations emblematic of antebellum
prosperity which, after the Civil War, transitioned to "tenant farming" and
"sharecropping" only to be done-in by the destructive pestilence of the boll
weevil (NPS, 1993).

> [By 1920] Black Belt farmers reduced their cotton acreage and because of the
> pests, they obtained approximately one-fifth to one half less cotton lint than
> before per acre. Few sharecroppers and black owner-operators could afford
> expensive insecticides or poisons and it was almost impossible to contain the
> spread of the insects. 'Field after field of cotton was eaten away,' . . . . Some
> farms were spontaneously 'abandoned' (Marable, 1979).

Racism accompanied the economic downturns of the early-1900s in the
Black Belt (Marable, 1979). That racism, coupled with Jim Crow segregation
would symbolize life in the Black Belt for most of the Century, scarring
those African American who did not flee to northern urban areas (Falk,
1992).

Perry County would play an outsized role in the Civil Rights Movement
of the 1960s. The birthplace of Coretta Scott King, the County would be the
site of a protest over voting rights that resulted in the shooting of Jimmie Lee
Jackson by Alabama State Troopers in 1965. Jackson died in a Selma hospital a week later, precipitating the Selma-to-Montgomery March that would
punctuate the Civil Rights Movement (Cobb, 2008).

It was the latter events that brought the Civil Rights Staff Ride to Perry
County. There cadets met with Adam Johnston, who works for the Alabama
Rivers Alliance. He is cut from the same mold as the first Riverkeeper on the
Hudson River, John Cronin, whose pioneering patrols on the Hudson River
led to prosecutions and law suits against dozens of polluters. Adam knows
every detail (that is knowable) about Uniontown and the fledgling citizens'
group, the Black Belt Citizens Fighting for Health and Justice, that is attempting to deal with this environmental *in*justice. He showed cadets the
streams that flowed from the facility carrying unmistakable evidence of coal
ash. He noted how a nearby resident could no longer keep his windows open,
and had trouble breathing outside his home. He introduced the Staff Riders to
neighbors of the facility whose laundered clothes were blackened while
hanging out to dry.

Neighbors of the facility are largely black and mostly poor (Foster, 2011). Cadets met with the leaders of the citizens' group, people who were meeting with this injustice head-on. Their local government had let them down. Some alleged that the funds received by the community for allowing the facility to be sited in Uniontown were unaccounted for (Shelby, 2010). All were afraid of the long term impact the coal ash would have on their health and the health of their children (EPA, OSWER, 2010).

These fears are, sadly, very reasonable (Deonarine, 2012). Studies have generally concluded that exposure to the waste of burning coal is a health hazard, whether through the medium of air pollution or by other vectors (Burt, 2013). The health impacts of coal ash are largely a function of their components. (Stant, 2010) These include those known human carcinogens arsenic and chromium (Korb, 2011). Each of the toxic components can travel far from its source, whether volatized from combustion and wind erosion or leached into ground and surface waters. It has been noted that exposure to stored coal ash may also cause "respiratory and emotional and behavioral disorders" (Zierold, 2014).

Alabama happens to be a state that has very limited regulation of coal ash. A 2011 report by the environmental organization Earthjustice noted that, "Alabama represents the worst of the worst when it comes to coal-ash disposal. First, Alabama has no laws or regulations on the books to specifically ensure the safety of the state's coal ash dams. It is the only state in the country without such laws" (Evans2). In fact, the report adds, "[u]ntil 2011, Alabama completely exempted coal ash disposal in landfills.

> In May 2011 Alabama became the last state in the Union to acknowledge coal ash waste as solid waste and permit regulation of it as such; yet, this regulation does not classify coal ash as a hazardous waste and simply grants the Alabama Department of Environmental Management the authority to regulate coal ash as a solid waste, just as it regulates household trash (Overby, 2013).

Alabama's coal ash regulation is a law that is race-neutral on its face, but a certain level of empowerment is necessary to resist decisions that have debilitating localized environmental consequences: *disparate impacts*. Despite having *de jure* civil rights, this level of empowerment requires organization, community action, and the creation of external support, in other words, a civil rights movement.

THE CIVIL RIGHTS MOVEMENT TODAY

Cadets were invited to a meeting in the local firehouse held by the community to elicit support for their cause. After an opening invocation, the community leaders took the stage and passionately spoke about every aspect of the issue. Petitions were signed while children played at the rear of the small meeting room. A potluck supper followed. It's safe to assume that 50 years ago cadets would have been witnessing the same efforts by community leaders in support voter registration, or school desegregation (Chestnut, 1990). Today's leaders learned their tactics from civil rights leaders they knew, and from campaigns they themselves had participated in. They understood that the same type of civic empowerment is necessary to address problems of environmental justice that were needed to confront Jim Crow segregation.

Now, some 50 years after the passage of the Civil Rights Act, segregation and discrimination *under the law* have for the most part been eliminated in the United States. Today, however, the struggle continues with widespread inequality based on economic and social divides that are not easily resolved by law (Wright, 2014). Environmental *in*justice is a manifestation of the denial of civil rights, not by law, but by circumstance. That circumstance however, is neither haphazard nor, as evidenced by its disparate impacts, race-neutral. It had its genesis in a history of discrimination beginning in slavery, continued with Jim Crow segregation, and lives on today despite the end of *de jure* inequality. The battle for *de jure* civil rights required a civil rights movement, so does the battle for *de facto* civil rights.

CONCLUSION

Civil Rights include the right not to bear a disproportionate burden of the consequences of pollution. Those rights encompass the basic human rights to access to clean air, water and food. If any rights are inalienable, it is these.

Pollution, that fouls the water, air, and soil, presents a serious threat to health and the quality of life. Environmental problems created by a system which eschews regulations allows for those problems to be absorbed by those who can least afford to challenge them. Despite the end of legal discrimination, environmental *in*justice continues the travails of those whose inequality that began with slavery. Civil rights require empowerment to effectively protect their holders. In Uniontown, Alabama, the many lessons of the Civil Rights Movement are not lost on the community and its civic leaders: if they can emulate their elders they can indeed overcome this challenge.

As the United States commemorates the 50th anniversaries of the victories of the Civil Rights Movement which ended legalized discrimination, the continuing lack of environmental justice is much more than a loose end. It is part of the lasting legacy of a system that had different rules for people based on race. Despite the fact that legal discrimination has largely ended, to finally erase its legacy, a movement must work to end *de facto* inequality however it manifests itself. There are many Uniontowns.

WORKS CITED

Alexander, Michelle. *The New Jim Crow: Mass Incarceration in the Age of Colorblindness*. The New Press, 2010.

Alkhatib, Ahed J. etal. "Lead Exposure and Possible Association with Violent Crimes." *European Scientific Journal* 10 (2014): 30.

Biesecker, Michael and Weiss, Mitch. "Tweak to NC Law Protected Duke's Coal Ash Pits." *Associated Press* 17 Mar. 2014. Web.

Burt, Erica, Orris, Peter and Buchanan, Susan. "Scientific Evidence of Health Effects from Coal Use in Energy Generation." Apr. 2013. *Healthcare Without Harm*. 20 Nov. 2014.

Buzbee, William W. *Fighting Westway: Environmental Law, Citizen Activism, and the Regulatory War that Transformed New York City*. Cornell Univ. Press, 2014.

Carter, Robert L. "De Facto School Segregation: An Examination of the Legal and Constitutional Questions Presented." *W. Res. L. Rev.* 1964: 502.

CBS 60 Minutes Report. *Coal Ash: 130 Million Tons of Waste*. 15 August 2010. Online Video Clip.

Census. *U.S. Census Bureau State and County QuickFacts: Perry County AL*. 8 Jul. 2014. Web. 20 Nov. 2014.

Chestnut, J.L. *Black in Selma: The Uncommon Life of JL Chestnut, Jr*. Farrar, Straus, and Giroux, 1990.

Civil Rights Act of 1964. "Civil Rights Act of 1964 (Pub.L. 88-352, 78 Stat. 241, enacted July 2, 1964)." n.d. Law.

Clotfelter, Charles T. *After Brown: The Rise and Retreat of School Desegregation*. Princeton Univ. Press, 2001.

Cobb, Charles E. Jr. *On the Road to Freedom*. Chapel Hill, NC: Algonquin, 2008.

Cohen, Debra S. "IKEA Thwarted: Victory for Social Justice and Environmental Law." *Environmentally Friendly: Journal of the Pace Center for Environmental Legal Studies* 4.2 (2001).

Columbia. "A Vision for New Rochelle: Plan for Revitalizing the City Park Neighborhood." May 2001. 24 Nov. 2014.

Confessore, Nicholas. "Trash Station on West Side Creates Split in Assembly." *New York Times* 20 Jun. 2007.

Delgado, Richard. "Exploring the Rise and Fall of African American Fortunes -- Interest Convergence and Civil Rights Gains." *Harvard Civil Rights-Civil Liberties L. Rev.* 37 (2002): 369-387.

Deonarine, Amrika, et al. "Environmental Impacts of the Tennessee Valley Authority Kingston Coal Ash Spill 2. Effect of Coal Ash on Methylmercury in Historically Contaminated River Sediments." *Environ. Sci. Technol.* 18 Dec. 2012, 47 ed.: 2100-2108.

DePalma, Anthony. "G.E. Commits to Dredging 43 Miles of Hudson River." *New York Times* 7 Oct. 2005.

Dewan, Shailia. "Coal Ash Spill Revives Issue of Its Hazards." *New York Times* 2008. Document.

Dierringer, Christopher Michael. "'They'd Better Hope for a Lot of Free Parking': Using Monopoly to Teach about Classical Liberalism, Marginalization, and Restorative Justice." *Communication Teacher* 2013: 27.1: 11-15. Article.

Dillard, Eve. "Dot Earth Blog." 28 Jan. 2015. *The New York Times*. Ed. Andrew Revkin. Internet. 5 Feb. 2015. http://dotearth.blogs.nytimes.com/2015/01/19/in-alabama-west-point-cadets-explore-polluted-civil-rights/?_r=0.

Dumas, Bianca. *Robert Parris Moses*. Heinemann-Raintree Library, 2003. Book.

Earthjustice. *Coal Ash Contaminated Sites*. February 2014. Web. 18 November 2014.

EPA, OSWER. "Human and Ecological Risk Assessment of Coal Combustion Wastes (Draft)." Risk Assessment. 2010. Web. 20 Nov. 2014. http://earthjustice.org/sites/default/files/library/reports/epa-coal-combustion-waste-risk-assessment.pdf.

Estrada, Louis. "Rep. Tom Bevill, 84; Alabama democrat." *Washington Post* 31 Mar. 2005: B07.

Evans, Lisa et al. "Alabama Coal Ash Fact Sheet." Sep. 2011. *Earth Justice.* Web. 19 Nov. 2014.

Evans, Lisa, Becher, Michael, and Lee, Bridget. "State of Failure: How States Fail to Protect Our Health and Drinking Water from Toxic Coal Ash." 5 Apr. 2013. *Earthjustice.* Web. 20 Nov. 2014. http://earthjustice.org/sites/default/files/StateofFailure_2013-04-05.pdf.

Evers-Williams, Myrlie. *For us, the Living.* University Press of Mississippi, 1967. Book.

Falk, William W., Rankin, Bruce H. "Cost of Being Black in the Black Belt, The." *Soc. Probs* 1992: 299.

Foster, Mark Harrison Jr. "Ash Holes: The Failure to Classify Coal Combustion Residuals as a Hazardous Waste Under RCRA and the Burden Bourne by a Minority Community in Alabama." *VT. Journal of Environmental Law* 12 (2011): 735, 756-61.

Gabrielson, Ryan, et al. "Deadly Force, in Black and White." 10 Oct. 2014. *Pro Publica: Journalism in the Public Interest.* Web. 20 Nov. 2014.

Gray, Fred. *Bus Ride to Justice: Changing the Sustem by the System.* Montgomery, Alabama, n.d. Book.

Hwang, Jacklyn and Sampson, Robert J. "Divergent Pathways of Gentrification Racial Inequality and the Social Order of Renewal in Chicago Neighborhoods." *American Sociological Review* 79.4 (2014): 726-751.

Johnson, Teddi Dineley. "EPA Considers Proposals to Regulate Coal Ash: Hundreds of Coal Ash Dumps, Waste Ponds May Threaten Health." *The Nation's Health* Nov. 2010: 1-14.

Korb, Blake. "Holding Our Breath: Waiting for the Federal Government to Recognize Coal Ash as a Hazardous Waste." *J. Marshall L. Rev.* 45 (2011): 1177.

Kucsera, John. "New York State's Extreme School Segregation: Inequality, Inaction and a Damaged Future." 26 Mar. 2014. *UCLA Civil Rights Project.* web. 20 Nov. 2014. http://civilrightsproject.ucla.edu/research/k-12-education/integration-and-diversity/ny-norflet-report-placeholder/Kucsera-New-York-Extreme-Segregation-2014.pdf .

Marable, Manning. "The Politics of Black Land Tenure: 1877-1915." *Agricultural History* Jan. 1979: 142-152.

McGurty, Eileen Maura. "From NIMBY to Civil rights: The Origins of the Environmental Justice Movement." *Environmental History* 2.3 (1997): 301-323.

McKinley, James C. Jr. "Heading to Texas, Hudson's Toxic Mud Stirs Town." *New York Times* 21 May 2009.

Medley, Keith Weldon. *We as Freemen: Plessy v. ferguson.* Pelican, 2012.

Mielke, Howard W. and Zahran, Sammy. "The Urban Rise and Fall of Air Lead (Pb) and the Latent Surge and Retreat of Societal Violence." *Environmental International* 43 (2012): 48-55.

Moon, Steven T. & Turner, Amanda B. "Coal Ash Law and Regulation in the United States: An Overview." *SE Environmental Law Journal* (2009-2010): 173.

NPS. "Plantation Houses of the Alabama Canebrake and their Associated Outbuildings (1818-1942)." 2 Feb. 1993. *National Park Service, National Register of Historic Places.* Web. 20 Nov. 2014.

Overby, Robin. "Sitting on Their Ashes: Why Federal Regulations Should Plug the Gaping Holes in State Coal Ash Disposal Regulatory Regimes." *Geo. Wash. J. Energy & Envtl. L.* 4 (2013): 107.

Plessy v. Ferguson. No. 163 U.S. 537, 539. U.S. Supreme Court. 1896.

Pratt, Robert A. "Brown v. Board of Education Revisited." *Reviews in American History* Mar. 2002: 141-148.

Purnell, Brian. *Fighting Jim Crow in the Coundy of Kings: The Congress of Racial Equality in Brooklyn.* Univ. Press of Kentucky , 2013.

Quinones, Manuel. "Coal Industry Deploys Donations, Lobbying as Its Issues Gain Prominence." *New York Times* 13 Oct. 2011.

Revesz, Richard L. "Race to the Bottom and Federal Environmental Regulation: A Response to Critics." *Minn. Law Review* 1997: 535, 539.

Riverkeeper. *Riverkeeper: About Us.* n.d. Web. 20 Nov. 2014.

SE Coal Ash. *SE Coal Ash Waste Map.* 2014. Web. 18 November 2014.

Shapiro, Thomas, et al. "The Roots of the Widening Racial Wealth Gap: Explaining the Black-White Economic Divide." Feb. 2013. *NAACP Legal Defense Fund IASP Research and Policy Brief.* 20 Nov. 2014.

Shelby, Max. "The Grandiose Ego of Albert Turner, Jr.---Perry County, Alabama's Coal Ash Cad." 21 Nov. 2010. *Alabama confidential.* Web. 17 Nov. 2014.

Sierra Club. "Dangerous Waters: America's Coal Ash Crisis." 15 May 2014. Web. 18 November 2014.

Stant, Jeff. "In Harm's Way: Lack of Federal Coal Ash Regulations Endangers Americans and Their Environment." 26 Aug. 2010. *Environmental Intergrity Project, Earth Justice and Sierra Club.* Web. 19 Nov. 2014.

Stretesky, Paul B. and Lynch, Michael J. "The Relationship Between Lead and Crime." *Journal of Health and Social Behavior* 45.2 (2004): 214-229.

Trip, Gabriel. "Ash Spill Shows How Watchdog Was Defanged." *New York Times* 2014. Document.

U.S. EPA. "Information Update -- Kerr Reservoir, No. 4." 5 May 2014. *United States Environmental Protection Agency.* Web. 18 November 2014.

USEPA EJ. *Environmental Justice.* n.d. Web. 18 November 2014.

Webster, Gerald R. and Samson, Scott A. "On defining the Alabama Black Belt: Historical Changes and Variations." *Southeastern Geographer* Nov. 1992: 163-172, 166.

Wright, Matthew. "Economic Inequality and the Social Capital Gap in the United States across Time and Space." *Political Studies* (2014): 1-21.

Zierold, Kristina M. & Sears, Clara G. "Community Views About the Health and Exposure of Children Living Near a Coal Ash Storage Site." *Journal of Community Health* (2014): 1-7.

NOTE

1. Professor of Law and Director of the West Point Center for the Rule of Law, United States Military Academy at West Point, NY. The views expressed are the views of the author alone, and do not necessarily reflect the views of the United States Military Academy, the Department of the Army, the Department of Defense, or the United States Government.

Cynicism and Perennial Intolerance

Mendelssohn against the Decisionists

Dustin Atlas

Tolerance may well be a virtue—for many it is *the* political virtue—but in the face of claims that intolerance is a political constant, toleration often seems effete, or naïve. If it is the case that intolerance is perennial and accompanies all political ventures—perhaps an ineradicable part of human nature, or a brute sociological fact—any serious call for toleration is bound to look naïve and unrealistic. But, no matter how well made, arguments from political "realism" are often deeply cynical. So it seems that, where toleration is concerned, we are forced to choose between cynicism and naïveté.

When choosing between two deeply undesirable options it is often worthwhile to examine the intellectual, political and theological factors presupposed by the choice, to see wheher—as is often the case—the choice is illusory, and the two 'options' merely different vantage points on the same situation. In such cases we are entitled to ask if another model is called for. I suggest that if we want a theory of tolerance that is neither cynical nor naïve, then both "radical" and "realistic" politics are of little help. Instead, I propose revisiting Moses Mendelssohn's contribution to an 18th century political theological debate to help clarify what is at issue, and from his work, to begin developing a framework for thinking about toleration and intolerance that avoids both cynicism and naïveté. Mendelssohn proposes an alternative decisionism of Jacobi, Carl Schmitt, and Leo Strauss, and his work remains relevant if only because of the enduring popularity of decisionism.

It is in the 18th century that the word 'toleration' ceases to refer to the endurance of pain and stress, and begins to approximate its contemporary meaning, referring to political-religious controversies. Edicts of toleration were issued when a state decided to put up with the presence of a religious minority, hoping this would reduce internal strife and spur economic growth. While the word has expanded its scope to cover other domains, from the sexual to the racial, it is with 18th century controversies concerning the status of religion that the words 'tolerance' and 'intolerance' began referring to political persecution.

There has been a cost to the expansion of the domain covered by the idea of tolerance: tolerance sometimes seems more like an attitude than a principled position, and can be a smug and condescending attitude at that; worse, toleration, once intended to protect minorities, is often flipped, with the weak being expected to tolerate the strong—as when corporations invoke "religious tolerance" to justify the maltreatment of homosexuals. So, while I am not suggesting we restrict the concepts of tolerance and intolerance to their 18th century extension, certain aspects of this problem are more visible when we temporarily do so, because here it is more obvious that toleration implicates both the political and the ethical by way of the theological.

Moses Mendelssohn engaged in several political theological controversies: no mean feat for a man almost universally depicted as gentle even under duress.[1] Mendelssohn should be read against this background: while decidedly exoteric, he was very careful not to cause offense to the larger and more powerful Christian community. As a representative of the Jewish community in 18th century Germany it was of the utmost importance that he not rock the boat. While worthy of emulation, this caution, in combination with his artful simplicity, conceals the force of his positions: his lack of obscurity has obscured his contributions.[2]

THE POLITICAL THEOLOGICAL VANTAGE POINT

The last 15 years have seen a rebirth of political theology in the English-speaking world, a rebirth directly associated with the writings of Carl Schmitt. As is usual with Schmitt, the textual source is gnomic: "All significant concepts of the modern theory of the state are secularized theological concepts not only because of their historical development...but also because of their systematic structure, the recognition of which is necessary for a sociological consideration of these concepts."[3] From this has arisen the widespread belief that political concepts are secularized theological concepts, not just because of their historical origin in theological explanatory systems, but because they are structured so as to generate their own legitimacy. "Systematic structure" refers to two different, but entwined, notions of "system," each of which seeks to legitimate the political: a system of analogies whereby political concepts find counterparts in the theological realm; and, an internal system, where political concepts refer to each other so as to mutually reinforce their legitimacy by creating a stable frame. This notion of the political is *prima facie* biased in favour of conservative "continental" politics, favouring stable systems that map onto older structures, generating legitimacy by establishing a self-consistent "normal situation" sustained by a sovereign will—including the "will of the people"—or strong leader.[4]

This framework is one way of dividing up the problem of cynicism and naïveté: the cynical leader uses political and often intolerant means—determining when to go to war, and what constitutes a state of emergency—in order to establish a "normal" situation, within which we can be ethical. The sovereign looks after the political, and the people have the privilege of being ethical (or, in other words, naïve). This is a solution which Mendelssohn will reject, and for good reasons: it is naïve to presume the political will not infect the ethical, and cynical to base an ethical situation on amoral *Realpolitik*.

The vogue—or onslaught—of political theological writings should give us pause, especially when it is assumed they can either provide something like a solution, or can energize a tired discourse. While its sources are often virulent, and its practical track record poor, it remains a powerful force in political theory. For now it suffices to note that the contemporary political theological framework has a more overtly theological precedent: the work of Jacobi, Mendelssohn's chief disputant. The contemporary political theology maps nicely onto the Weimar period, which itself, in similar fashion, echoes the 18th century pantheism controversy.[5] Thus, by exploring Mendelssohn's response to Jacobi, we can develop a response to contemporary political theology, while, hopefully, sustaining its insights: Mendelssohn was not arguing against the need to account for the theological background for political concepts, but rather, for a more nuanced account of the relationship between the political and the theological. His account does not divorce the political, theological, and the ethical, but unlike Jacobi and Schmitt, favours ambiguity over paradox, insecurity over radicality, and is guided by an aesthetic rationalism that negotiates the competing claims arising from multiple domains. Mendelssohn's work does not "disprove" political theology so much as demonstrate that much of what calls itself such is too narrow. The term "political theology" seems expansive, but in practice really allows only one very specific form of theology: a very specific form of Germanic Protestantism augmented by a few Catholic counter-revolutionary theorists.

There is a more specific reason for examining intolerance and tolerance as being part of a political theological network. When we examine intolerance against a political theological background, we aren't speaking about intolerance of just any difference, but intolerance of an enemy *conceived of in quasi-theological terms*. An edict of toleration is intended to ameliorate religious conflicts, and not, for instance, economic or military competition. Not all enmity or divergence is intolerance.[6] To negotiate this problem without cynicism or naïveté will require we address this theological baggage.

BETWEEN CYNICISM AND NAÏVETÉ

By naïve I do not mean the artistic principle, defined by Mendelssohn in
On the Sublime and Naïve in the Fine Sciences as the "unaffected
[*ungekünstelten*] expression which allows the reader or spectator to think
more than is said to him." Instead, by naïve is meant what Mendelssohn calls
niais: "a thoughtless and listless simplicity or an ignorance of the ordinary
ways of the world".[7] Rather than being opposed to the contrived, in the
political naïveté is opposed to the cynical; in the artistic pairing, it can act as
a tonic to the overdone, whereas it is hard to think of any positive political
employment of the term. Where politics is concerned, the 'naïve' serves only
as an insult: a naïve person may be have a beautiful soul, but, it is assumed,
should not be trusted with any policy decisions.

Cynicism is a more complicated phenomenon than naïveté, and arguably
more symptomatic of the present moment. While both can be viewed as
functions of "modernity," the latter being its explicit rejection and the former
an embrace, cynicism is more pervasive, and often considered efficacious.
One expects, if not insists, that a 'world leader' be cynical, while a naïve
leader would be nothing short of disastrous.

Leaving aside the "popular" view of these twin concepts, analysis of
cynicism has played a minor but consistent role in social and political
thought since the 1983 publication of Sloterdijk's *Critique of Cynical Reason*
(*Kritik der zynischen Vernunft*). Sloterdijk presents cynicism as a chief obstacle to Enlightenment, but also as the standard contemporary form of political
ideology. Where once Enlightenment saw ignorance as its chief obstacle, to
be overcome by liberal education and exposure to difference (tactics still
adhered to with questionable success), Sloterdijk proposes the cynic as the
real opponent of Enlightenment.[8] The cynic "knows better," is aware of what
is right, but continues on a self-seeking path. As cynicism already "knows,"
education can in no way repair it. The cynic is often well educated, and
mobilizes education, or "Enlightenment" in the service of cynical projects. If
we are to take seriously the idea that intolerance is a political constant—and
thus not amenable to being removed through education and exposure to
alterity—then I suggest there is either something cynical about intolerance,
or, at the very least, that cynical political models encourage its growth. If this
is the case, it is not enough to naively "take the side" of toleration, or commit
oneself to some sort of Ideal, but rather, to tackle the problem of cynicism as
a structure.

Žižek nicely summarizes *Critique*'s claim that cynicism is a form of
ideology: "Peter Sloterdijk puts forward the thesis that ideology's dominant
mode of functioning is cynical...The cynical subject *is quite aware of the
distance between the ideological mask and the social reality*, but he nonetheless insists upon the mask."[9] From crude interpretations of Leo Strauss to

uninspired neo-conservative appropriations of religion, this ideological form of cynicism sees itself as fundamentally anti-ideological, insofar as older ideologies are "naïve" (they believe in something) and, it is assumed, if we don't believe in an ideal, we cannot be ideological. "Modern cynicism presents itself as that state of consciousness that follows after naïve ideologies and their enlightenment. In it, the obvious exhaustion of ideology critique has its real ground."[10] Sloterdijk's treatment of cynicism is novel if only for stressing it as a diffuse, or "mass" phenomena. Cynicism "is the universally widespread way in which enlightened people see to it that they are not taken for suckers. There even seems to be something healthy in this attitude, which, after all, the will to self-preservation generally supports. It is the stance of people who realize that the times of naïveté are gone."[11] It is thus capable of serving as an ideology for those who are no longer capable of ideals.

Cynicism is not only unexceptional, it is the means by which the unexceptional, or 'normal', situation is sustained. If we accept the contemporary political theological model, we have a bifurcated world. On the one hand, we have the sovereign. This figure can be a God, a king, a people, a curate, or chief bureaucrat, the 'substance' of the sovereign is irrelevant. What defines this figure—to employ Carl Schmitt's well worn expression—is that it can determine what counts as an 'exception'. Carl Schmitt's cryptic presentation of this "borderline concept" has led to extensive speculation as to its possible meaning and employment, speculation that peaked during the "Bush years" when the "exception" seemed to define (or eliminate) the juridical.[12] What unites the standard interpretations is that the sovereign, like God, employs the exception to create, sustain, and protect a 'normal situation,' be it a state, or a state of affairs.

This has two corollaries relevant for the present discussion of cynicism: firstly, ethics only applies in these normal situations (one cannot be ethical where survival is at stake, that would be naïve); secondly, these normal, or ethical situations, are created and sustained by actions that are not ethical, and do not answer to the situation they create. The sovereign is a "borderline concept" because it protects the border of the normal situation. For all of the mystifying language employed in the presentation of this concept, it is, I suggest, rather commonsensical, if not perhaps the content of contemporary common sense: ethics applies in a state, and this state is created and protected by unethical behaviour. However, if we accept this political theological picture then we are consigned to both cynicism and intolerance. Cynicism because those "in the know" understand the ethical is a partial state of affairs sustained by unethical behaviour: to "believe" in ethics would be naïve, leaving cynicism as the only intellectually honest position. Intolerance because the sovereign, whether it 'believes' or not, functions through violent exclusions that take on a theological tone.

The chief concept underwriting this political theological picture is the decision: the 'substance' or 'subject' of the sovereign is irrelevant, *what matters is not who the sovereign is, but that it decides* (on border, on friends and enemies, on exceptions). [13] Therefore, in my attempt to avoid this entire political theological schema, and the intolerance and cynicism it entails, I propose we look for an alternative to decisionism in the work of Moses Mendelssohn in his dispute with Jacobi: Jacobi being the philosophical theological spring from which all significant political theological theories of decisionism have flown. [14]

THE PANTHEISM CONTROVERSY AND POLITICAL THEOLOGY

The Pantheism controversy, or *Pantheismusstreit*, was a protracted conflict of letters between Moses Mendelssohn and Friedrich Jacobi, largely mediated by Elise Reimarus (the daughter of the radical theologian, Hermann Samuel Reimarus). [15] This controversy, ostensibly about Lessing's legacy, touched on fundamental aspects of philosophy, theology, history, and politics. Almost every significant German intellectual weighed in on the controversy at some point, making it difficult to overstate its importance for the development contemporary theory and philosophy. I wish to touch on just one small component of this controversy—decisionism—which has seriously affected contemporary theology, psychoanalysis, and political thought. Of these, I will only treat the last. The basic contours of political decisionism were sketched above: the normal state and situation are created by radical decisions that do not answer to the thing they create. The decision is "radical" because it goes to the root of the structure, and owes its legitimacy to nothing other than itself. This emphasis on the political theological decision can be easily traced from Jacobi's role in the pantheism controversy, through Kierkegaard, Carl Schmitt, and Leo Strauss. [16]

This trajectory is continued by any political thought, whether right or the left, Žižek or Strauss, that considers the decision, and fidelity to it as a basic action that creates and legitimizes structures. [17] I believe such thinking commits us to either cynicism or naïveté, which has disastrous consequences where the problem of tolerance is concerned. Even if we assume the basic stricture of Schmitt's political theology (political concepts are secularized theological concepts) there is no reason to assume only one specific form of secularized theology should win the day. If only for this reason, Mendelssohn's response to Jacobi, at the onset of this trajectory, is important as it provides a compelling alternative to their vision, a form of liberal Judaism formulated to address the same political theological territory. He does this by grounding the political not in a radical decision that separates and purifies, but in a protracted series of negotiations, assuming that the political is never homogeneous, but rather a composite entity in need of development.[18] This lack of separation is a mainstay of his embodied rationalism, and a function of his belief that most bifurcations of existence into "two worlds" (mind/body, religion/state, time/eternity) are in fact over-simplistic images drawn as a result of our incapacities.[19] Thus, for Mendelssohn, there is no complete separation between church and state, the social and the political, the revealed and the reasoned, and even the temporal and the eternal.[20]

Valourizations of the "mixed" and "negotiated" are common, the beneficence of these concepts assumed as an article of faith (much like tolerance itself), and the difficulties opened up by these concepts ignored. This critique cannot be leveled at Mendelssohn. As a Rationalist, he was aware that "mixture" generated more intellectual difficulties than it ameliorates, and as a politically engaged Jew, one constantly negotiating for better treatment and acceptance of Jews, he was acquainted with the anxiety and trauma negotiation generates. However, as a "good student of Spinoza" he knew that, even should we wish to absolutely separate the political and the theological, such a separation is difficult, if not impossible.[21] As he writes about the church and state: "When they take the field against each other, mankind is the victim of their discord; when they are in agreement, the noblest treasure of human felicity is lost; for they seldom agree but for the purpose of banishing from their realms a third entity, liberty of conscience, *which knows how to derive some advantage from their disunity.*"[22] This distinguishes Mendelssohn's view from both classical liberalism and political theological decisionism (including its postmodern variations): there is no attempt to completely resolve the tension between the church and state, but rather, strategies for dealing with them. In general, any resolution seeking to establish political bounds "once and for all" will be arbitrary, foundational arbitrary decisions lead to the cynical impasse of decisionism, and intolerance will appear as a perennial force, part and parcel of the cynical policing of boundaries.

Further, the specific form of toleration that occurs within a decisionist frame is *both* naïve and "part of the problem" (cynical). Mendelssohn was well aware toleration often serves as camouflage for domination. In his time, toleration was often little more than a screen for the imposition of irenic Christianity. Proponents of toleration took great pains to express that they would not go so far as to include "Pagans, Jews, Mahometans, and Theists."[23] Not only could including these groups be used to argue against latitudinarianism, such inclusion would defeat the entire point of toleration: the development of a more expansive and powerful form of Christianity. Mendelssohn's model of toleration is founded on his critique of the "toleration" found in the liberal religious discourse of his day, where disparate groups were united by their enclosure within a big container, be it a state or religion. This is why his politics resists all calls to unification: "Do not believe this to be a merely imaginary fear, born of hypochondria. At bottom,

a union of faiths, should it ever come about, could have but the most unfortunate consequences for reason and liberty of conscience."[24] As Braiterman
writes, Mendelssohn "understood the trap that proponents of alleged toleration set for minorities whose difference they seek to quash by subsuming it
into a false universal, which turns out to be just another, albeit larger and
dominant, particularity."[25] In the contemporary world, Foucauldian analysts
such as Talal Asad and Wendy Brown have similarly marshalled a compelling case for viewing "tolerance talk" as a cover for the imposition of a
particular set of values.[26] What differentiates these critiques from Mendelssohn's is that where contemporary theorists dismiss tolerance as a Western
imposition, Mendelssohn does not presume all forms of Enlightenment will
crush differences. He did not give up on Enlightenment, but sought to develop a flexible Enlightenment which could help cultivate political and religious
entities, rather than flatten them in the name of toleration and civility. For
Mendelssohn, unlike the Foucauldians, the critique of toleration is made in
the spirit of greater toleration.[27]

WHAT COMES FIRST? NEITHER.

I have been arguing that Mendelssohn presents a means for diagnosing
the decisionist political theological complex which presents intolerance as
needful, if undesirable. Further, I have been insinuating that the decisionist
frame, which is widespread, relies upon a secret collusion between cynicism
and naïveté: the political decision cynically creates and protects a "normal"
space in which ethics occurs. That this ethics is naïve should be obvious: it is
incapable of addressing, let alone legislating, the decision that makes it possible. That it is also cynical might be less obvious: it cannot bear to see, let
alone regulate, the violent exclusions which allow it to exist; if protected
space ever catches sight of the violence, it is suppressed or denied (which
leads back into cynicism). However, this 'normal space' cannot be fully done
away with, as it provides the decionist with legitimacy.[28] This puts the decisionist in a strange position: the only ethical argument in favour of decisionism is that it sustains a "normal" situation; but, the ethics which apply within
this normal situation cannot countenance the decisionist position. This is
why, ultimately, the decisionist cannot appeal to any form of legitimacy
other than its own "self-grounding:" the protected "normal situation" is, at
best, a stop-gap argument.

If the decisionist position, by definition, can appeal to no form of legitimacy other than itself, what is its appeal? Why does a system that requires
intolerance *both* as something the normal situation must be protected from
(the intolerant other) *and* as a force to protect the normal situation (my
intolerance for the enemy, theologically conceived) have so many defenders,

and what are the reasons for the endurance of a political theological model that feeds upon, and engenders, cynicism? Here there are many possible and overlapping answers. As this paper is concerned with Mendelssohn's contribution to this problem of cynicism and intolerance, I will emphasize the aspect I believe he is best suited to respond to, and end with a response based on Mendelssohnian principles.

The decisionist can be seen as responding to a classic question of primacy: what comes first, the object or its relations? To this the decisionist replies: we must first have a state before we can have a good, or ethical state, as *social relations, including ethical relations, presuppose a normal state of affairs.* In other words, we need a defined object before it can enter into relationships. This is the 'commonsensical' basis of decisionism. If we grant this claim, tolerance is, strictly speaking, secondary, a luxury afforded only once the existence of the state is secured; any claim for the primacy of toleration will be rightly dismissed as naïve. Intolerance will be a perennial force, because it both protects the state, and is that from which it must be protected. The simplicity of this position is enough to recommend it, but I would argue the contemporary appeal of the Jacobi/Schmitt/Strauss decisionist model is that it combines conservative and relativist positions, and with this odd pairing of contrary impulses, seems able to energize an enervated academic discourse run aground on social constructivism, identity theory, and neo-liberal economics, which are all united in viewing the political as a function or social and economic relations.[29] That the decisionist "complexio oppositorum" brings together conservative and relativist components, and uses both to elevate the political at the expense of the social, the object at the expense of its relations, is not a "bug" but a "feature," and seems a possible antidote against theories that place the political in a subservient position to cultural, ethical, or economic relations.[30] But this antidote's side effects are worse than the poison: while theories that view the political as little more than an expression of social forces or ethical standards are problematic, the cynical and intolerant structure of decisionism is too steep a price to pay for the establishment of a political field.

To return to the above problem: if the decisionist holds the object (state) is prior, and constructivists hold relations to be prior, Mendelssohn holds that neither are, and any solution that seeks to either eliminate one term, or unify them, is mistaken. In this way his political theology echoes his early take on mind/body dualism, and his late treatment of the separation of church and state. Where his early work employed aesthetics as a mid-point between the cognitive and the embodied, his later work examines contractual obligation as a way of working through the impasse generated by the confrontation between the political and the theological. It would be impossible for one paper to fully articulate the processes Mendelssohn develops in order to negotiate these dualisms, but both of these tactics are united by their concern to avoid arbitrary decisions.

VISIONS OF PERFECTIONS

The key vehicle for Mendelssohn's negotiations is the process of perfect-*ing*: it being assumed that we begin with objects and relations, rather than try to establish either by fiat, there is something of a back and forth, or dialectic, between the two, whereby both are improved (or, in his dated language, perfected) in tandem. For Mendelssohn the state is an integral part of the process by which humans improve their lot, but this does not mean it is dissociated from nature, or created by sovereign fiat. In a polemical state-ment about those who would establish a normal situation, complete with political rights, on the basis of sovereign will, he writes:

> As little as cultivation is able to accomplish a fruit of which nature has not
> provided the germ; as little as art, by practice and perseverance, can bring forth
> a spontaneous motion, where nature has not placed a muscle; just as little can
> all the covenants and agreements of mankind create a right, of which the
> foundation is not to be met with in the state of nature.[31]

For Mendelssohn, the "normal situation" where ethics applies *is not de-cided upon, but rather, cultivated.* This is why an almost painfully long section of his political theological work *Jerusalem* is devoted to contract law. For Mendelssohn we use contracts to perfect our mutual obligations, without necessitating an over-arching sovereign authority to enforce them; they are, instead, a means for articulating and clarifying what is otherwise merely nascent.[32] In so doing he seeks to demonstrate that states don't create obliga-tions "from scratch," but rather, perfect pre-existing obligations.[33] His long excursus on contract law provide a tangible, if dated, example of one way that we can cultivate the state and its relations for our mutual perfection, and a model of political power not dependent upon sovereignty.

This process of perfecting our relations and ourselves allows Mendels-sohn to avoid choosing between the primacy of objects and relations. And this, much like the decisionist position it opposes, is recommended by its simplicity. Objects are improved when their relations are improved, and vice versa. Following Spinoza, Mendelssohn holds that this is especially the case for human beings: "[Man] cannot become perfect except through mutual assistance, through an exchange of service and reciprocal service, through active and passive connections with his fellow man."[34] The mechanism by which this is accomplished is articulated in his early aesthetic work as a "back and forth" between parts and wholes, objects and their relations; in his later work, by his theory of contract law and the state.[35] In both the early and late work, the process is one of cultivation and development, and not radical rupture or decision. The artist is one who cultivates the senses, and cultivates objects for the senses, and not a genius who forms images out of nothing. The politician is a person who cultivates a decent and stable state, and not a sovereign who creates by the force of his will.

If we follow Mendelssohn, and view political states as the result of a process of perfecting (and not a radical decision) we can sustain the idea of a state that needs protection, while avoiding the cynical belief that intolerance must be perennial. If we view the political as a space that is *cultivated*, rather than *decided* upon, than toleration is not some "extra," or addition, to be afforded only within a political space, but becomes part of the process of political construction. Further, this does not mean we need to abandon self-protection: the complete abdication of political violence in the name of toleration would be naïve at best. Such a position—the abandonment of all self-protection—is in fact merely the mirror image of decisionist cynicism, but with the 'protected' space trying to dictate the terms for the whole. What I am suggesting is that we employ a Mendelssohnian model, and view states, and states of affairs, as part of a continual process of creation, rather than a creation *ex nihilo*.

It is true that such a program requires that we be both careful and flexible, attentive to both ethics and self-protection simultaneously: Mendelssohn's rationalist aesthetics provide one such model for this form of constructive compromise, but clearly the work of an 18th century philosopher is hardly adequate to many, if not most, contemporary problems. What he does provide us with is an alternative to a form of political theology that has a great deal of intellectual and cultural currency.[36] Mendelssohn proposes what is perhaps a more boring, but arguably more sophisticated, model, where intolerance may well persist, but is not *necessitated*, and where we have a chance of avoiding both cynicism and naiveté.

WORKS CITED

Altmann, Alexander. (1963). *Moses Mendelssohn*. London: Routledge.

Altmann, Alexander. (1981). *Essays in Jewish Intellectual History*. Hanover: University Press of New England.

Badiou, Alain. (2005). *Being and event*. London ; New York: Continuum.

Beiser, Frederick C. (1987). *The fate of reason : German philosophy from Kant to Fichte*. Cambridge, Mass.: Harvard University Press.

Braiterman, Zachary. (2012). Lessing in Jerusalem: Modern Religion, Medieval Orientalism, and the Idea of Perfection *Encountering the Medieval in Modern Jewish Thought*.

Brown, Wendy. (2006). *Regulating aversion : tolerance in the age of identity and empire*. Princeton, N.J.: Princeton University Press.

Freudenthal, Gideon. (2012). *No religion without idolatry: Mendelssohn's Jewish Enlightenment*. Notre Dame: University of Notre Dame Press.

Goetschel, Willi. (2004). *Spinoza's Modernity: Mendelssohn, Lessing, and Heine*. Madison: University fo Wisconsin Press.

Goetschel, Willi. (2007). Mendelssohn and the State. *MLN*(122), 472-492.

Goetschel, Willi. (2013). *The discipline of philosophy and the invention of modern Jewish thought*. New York: Fordham University Press.

Gottlieb, Michah. (2011). *Faith and freedom : Moses Mendelssohn's theological-political thought*. New York: Oxford University Press.

Jacobi, Friedrich Heinrich, Di Giovanni, George, & Jacobi, Friedrich Heinrich. (1994). *The main philosophical writings and the novel Allwill*. Montréal ; Buffalo: McGill-Queen's University Press.

Janssens, David. (2003). The Problem of Enlightenment: Strauss, Jacobi, and the Pantheism Controversy. *The Review of Metaphysics, 56*(3), 605-632.

Maimon, Salomon. (2001). *Solomon Maimon : an autobiography*. Urbana: University of Illinois Press.

Mendelssohn, Moses. (1838). *Jerusalem [Writings Related to]* (M. Samuels, Trans. Vol. 1). London: Longman.

Mendelssohn, Moses. (1983). *Jerusalem: or on Religious Power and Judaism* (A. Arkush, Trans.). Hanover: Brandeis University Press.

Mendelssohn, Moses. (1997). *Philosophical Writings* (D. O. Dahlstrom, Trans.). Cambridge: Cambridge University Press.

Mendelssohn, Moses. (2011). *Morning Hours : lectures on God's existence* (D. O. Dahlstrom & C. Dyck, Trans.). New York: Springer.

Rosenstock, Bruce. (2010). *Philosophy and the Jewish question : Mendelssohn, Rosenzweig, and beyond* (1st ed.). New York: Fordham University Press.

Schmitt, Carl. (1996). *Roman Catholicism and Political Form* (G. L. Ulmen, Trans.). Westport: Greenwood Press.

Schmitt, Carl. (2004). *Legality and legitimacy* (J. Seitzer, Trans.). Durham: Duke University Press.

Schmitt, Carl. (2005). *Political theology : four chapters on the concept of sovereignty*. Chicago: University of Chicago Press.

Schmitt, Carl. (2008). *The Leviathan in the state theory of Thomas Hobbes : meaning and failure of a political symbol* (University of Chicago Press ed.). Chicago: University of Chicago Press.

Sloterdijk, Peter. (1987). *Critique of cynical reason*. Minneapolis: University of Minnesota Press.

Strauss, Leo. (1997). *Jewish philosophy and the crisis of modernity : essays and lectures in modern Jewish thought*. Albany: State University of New York Press.

Žižek, Slavoj. (1989). *The sublime object of ideology*. London ; New York: Verso.

NOTES

1. For one rather touching example, see: (Maimon, 2001, p. 201)

2. For an excellent discussion of Mendelssohn's obscurity, the fallacious view of him as both a populariser and 'translator' between German and Jewish culture, and the ways in which his positions have been unjustly simplified, see (Goetschel, 2013, p. 190) "To view him as a messenger between two worlds, as is often argued, is to ignore his critical trajectory as a thinker firmly grounded in different intellectual traditions, which he helped to shape in no small measure. Mendelssohn's theoretical grasp reaches well beyond the idea of a separate and distinctly identifiable German and Jewish culture."

3. (Schmitt, 2005, p. 36)

4. (Schmitt, 2004, p. 6) This seeming contradiction between the normal situation and the sovereign who sustains it is itself solved 'theologically': for the young Schmitt the ability to unite opposites in a "complexio oppositorum" is the strength of what he considers to be the Roman Catholic political form, or "Every imperialism that is more than jingoism" (Schmitt, 1996, pp. 6,7)

5. (Gottlieb, 2011, p. 6)

6. I am in no way suggesting that intolerance is *only* theological. It is obvious that there are decisive economic and political factors. Nor am I suggesting that religion or theology are the 'cause' of intolerance and the violence that accompanies it. My claim is, rather, that the form of enmity that tolerance seeks to ameliorate is accompanied by theological or quasi-theological positions.

7. (Mendelssohn, 1997, p. 222)

8. (Sloterdijk, 1987, p. 78)

9. (Žižek, 1989, p. 29) (emphasis added)

10. (Sloterdijk, 1987, p. 3)

11. (Sloterdijk, 1987, p. 5)

12. (Schmitt, 2005, p. 5)

13. When Schmitt and others write that the sovereign 'defines the exception,' or 'decides,' this does not mean that there exists some sovereign who has several characteristics, one of which being the 'superpower' of decision making. The 'decision' is what the sovereign is: if you are the decider, you are the sovereign.

14. For Jacobi, decisionism is first and foremost a theological position with political implications; it is not clear how concerned he was with these. For Schmitt and those who follow him, the political implications are more important than the theology—and it is these that I am most concerned with. Thus, to be fair to Jacobi, it is not clear he really understood, or cared about, the political theological implications of his stance. For an excerpt in English, of Jacobi's letters concerning the need for decision, or "leap of faith", see: Jacobi, "On the Doctrine of Spinoza in Letters to Moses Mendelssohn" in (Jacobi, Di Giovanni, & Jacobi, 1994)

15. I do not cover this controversy in any significant depth. For its political theological implications (Gottlieb, 2011) philosophical analysis (Rosenstock, 2010) (Goetschel, 2004) and its impact on the history of ideas (Altmann, 1963; Beiser, 1987)

16. (Janssens, 2003) Each of these impacts a wide variety of other thinkers in turn, with their own emphases and levels of sophistication; for instance, Kierkegaard, while an important thinker for the development of this notion, was largely apolitical, and employs a style that blocks any easy analysis of what he meant.

17. Badiou even goes so far as to claim that set theory and mathematics is grounded by such a decision (Badiou, 2005, p. 3)

18. No one has been as important as Goetschel in highlighting the composite aspect of Mendelssohn's thought (Goetschel, 2013, p. 192)

19. (Mendelssohn, 1983, p. 39) (Mendelssohn, 1997, p. 143) (Mendelssohn, 2011, pp. 11, 20)

20. This is also what Schmitt and Strauss had such contempt for Mendelssohn. (Goetschel, 2007, p. 476). For Strauss, separation is not only the basis of theology ("The first thing created is, therefore, light. Light is the beginning, the principle of distinction or separation") it is also the fundament of the political order. (Strauss, 1997, p. 364) (Strauss, 1997, p. 315) (Schmitt, 2008, p. 60)

21. (Goetschel, 2013, p. 192)

22. (Mendelssohn, 1983, p. 33)

23. (Mendelssohn, 1838, p. 78)

24. (Mendelssohn, 1983, p. 137)

25. (Braiterman, 2012, p. 78)

26. (Brown, 2006, p. 4)

27. Yitzak Melamed's argument, that Mendelssohn preaches a form of tolerance which absorbs minorities into a majority culture, is problematic on several fronts. Most importantly, he ignores Mendelssohn's insistence that intolerance never be unification, or what Strauss calls "pluralism as a monism". Rather than Mendelssohn's notion of endless negotiation guided by an aesthetic vision and tolerant ideals, Melamed suggests a conservative postmodern form of identity politics: "The alternative to toleration is a celebration of the multiplicity of competing cultures and centers, with no host and no guests, no tolerating nation state and no tolerable minorities". For reasons of space, he does not clarify what this celebration looks like, but it seems Melamed's position assumes either the existence of discrete groups whose boundaries are maintained and clarified by expulsion, or, a universal structure within which these positions

vie for supremacy. It is notable that Melamed uses the apolitical Solomon Maimon as his guide, while ignoring the productive tension that existed between Mendelssohn and Maimon that Freudenthal illustrates in "Mendelssohn, Maimon, and Spinoza on Ex-Communication and Toleration: Dispelling Three Enlightenment Fairytales" in *The Philosophy of Moses Mendelssohn*, eds. Michah Gottlieb and Charles Manekin (College Park: University of Maryland Press, forthcoming) (Strauss, 1997, p. 379) (Freudenthal, 2012, pp. 60, 87)

28. One need only note the shrill urgency with which 'values' are invoked to justify intolerant behavior–often a theologically inflected notion of the family, community, or state—in which a genteel, and decent, form of ethics can occur. In a word, the space in which one can 'afford' to be naïve is supposedly protected by intolerance.

29. It is relativist as it supposes there can be no external standard that grants legitimacy, no 'universal' standards; it is conservative in that it proposes sovereignty as the solution to relativism.

30. (Schmitt, 1996, pp. 6, 7)

31. (Mendelssohn, 1838, p. 106)

32. Goetschel notes that another important aspect of Mendelssohn's use of contracts is the absence of a singular authority, or natural law structure: "[Mendelssohn] defines contracts as the legal instrument that entrusts arbitration to a third party in the case of conflicting claims that are transferable, i.e., that are not derived from natural right, in other words inalienable rights. What is contracted, in other words, is the authority and competence to decide such cases…This approach to sovereignty explains why someone like Carl Schmitt considered Mendelssohn's political thought anathema."(Goetschel, 2013, p. 194) Mendelssohn uses contracts to perfect obligations found in 'nature', and not as an expression of natural law.

33. (Altmann, 1981, p. 157)

34. (Mendelssohn, 1983, p. 47)

35. For instances of this dialectic, see: (Mendelssohn, 1997, pp. 15, 54)

36. There are, of course, other models, but many of them share one of two major defects: in attempting to undercut decisionism, the try to be even more radical, and therefore repeat its absolutist tendencies, as is the case with certain theologically inflected forms of anarchism and communism, or they merely repeat an anti-theological liberal position, and thereby are incapable of addressing the very aspects that make decisionism appealing.

Overcoming Modernity and Violence

Gennady Shkliarevsky

INTRODUCTION

Violence is one of the most pervasive problems in the world today. Despite all efforts to apply the powers of reason in order to contain, if not completely eliminate violence, it proves to be capable of escaping capture and re-emerging in new and unexpected forms. Reason and rationality appear to be powerless against violence. This paper explores some philosophical issues that shed new light on the persistence of violence in the modern world. It argues that the failure of modernity to recognize and come to grips with the process of construction that constitutes the basis of our relationship with reality plays a critical role in the continued survival of violence.

MODERNITY AND VIOLENCE

For more than two centuries, the West has exercised an unprecedented hegemony in the modern world. Its powerful influences are ubiquitous. There is hardly an aspect in the life of the modern global community that does not reveal the effects of Western civilization: from politics to economics, to science and technology, philosophical ideas and the arts, fashion, and many aspects of the private sphere—they all bear the unmistakable mark of the impact of the Western influences.The very notions of modernization and modernity that are integral to the contemporary world are hallmarks of Western culture.

The Enlightenment project has been and remains at the heart of the unprecedented role of the West. This project is ultimately not about a rigid set of goals or policies; more than anything else, it is about a promise and a commitment to human reason. In the minds of those who have shaped this project, the rule of reason will pave the humanity's path toward liberation. They all share one profound conviction: that the rule of reason will help to resolve all problems faced by the humanity and will bring democracy, justice, equality, economic prosperity, and peace to our troubled world. The world renewed by the salutary rule of reason will know no violence, no fanaticism, no tyranny, and no war. There will be no oppressors and oppressed, no victims or victimizers. Under the guidance of reason, we should be able to exercise rational and compassionate control over nature and its resources for the benefit of humanity and the world.

Such is the promise that the West has extended to the rest of the world. There have been moments in history when the fulfillment of this promise seemed close; the most recent moment occurred towards the end of the twentieth century with the collapse of communism and the end of the Cold War, when many believed that we were on the threshold of an era of peace, prosperity, and the dominance of liberal democracy throughout the world. Some even hazarded to proclaim that history had finally reached its end (Fukuyama 1992). This moment did not last very long.

Subsequent developments have proven such predictions to be an illusion, a dream of wishful thinkers that had nothing to do with the real world. The attack on the World Trade Center on September 11, 2001 was a rude awakening from the self-congratulatory complacency into which the West lulled itself. It has revealed how deeply divided the world is and what powerful destructive and violent forces are at work. Ever since the events of 9/11, no one has had any doubts that we continue to live in a dangerous, uncertain, and utterly unpredictable world, and that the fulfillment of the Enlightenment promise remains as distant as it has ever been. In what we hear today from politicians and pundits, religious leaders and public figures, and even from common citizens, one can sense the same unsettling and troubling questions: Will the world survive? Will our children see the future? Will the promise made several centuries ago ever be fulfilled? Will reason, rather than power and violence, prevail in our world?

Western culture has viewed reason as a dynamic property of the human mind that is capable of organizing reality and developing it in ways that are beneficial to the human race and the world in general. Much of the project of modernity is about the affirmation, validation, and realization of what it sees as the infinite potential of human reason. The elimination of violence is one of the most important goals that the rule of reason is supposed to achieve. Many continue to believe, that rational human agents guided by reason should be able to find ways of resolving conflicts without resorting to violent, destructive, and brutal forms of behavior. They cherish the hope that wars can become obsolete and violence will have no place in human interactions.

No one sees the project of modernity as a one-time deal with a clearly identifiable set of goals. Rather, most view it as an on-going process with constantly expanding horizons. But this view does not mean that as the project evolves, its goals and promises will constantly receded into a distant future. On the contrary, the project of modernity is about setting rational goals and achieving them. In contrast with otherworldly promises of religion, much of the appeal of the project of modernity rests on its practicality, realism, and the expectation of success. In fact, the very spirit of rationality and empirical proof—characteristic for the project of modernity—implies that those who embrace this project measure its success by the attainment of its goals.

It has become commonplace to critique the project of modernity. Numerous detractors have disparaged Enlightenment civilization for its insensitivity to the plight of the poor and underprivileged and its unrestrained search for gratification. Still more have criticized the ravages of merciless exploitation of people and nature, its acceptance of the oppression of women and ethnic minorities, its racial inequality, its imperialist expansionism and indignity of colonial domination, its disregard of human rights, and its religious intolerance. Many have expressed doubts about its overall direction and prospects for success. The skepticism of post-modernism regarding the capacity of reason to understand reality has gained substantial support in intellectual circles. Even devoted advocates of modernity have expressed doubts about a possibility of its success. In his contribution "Modernity: An Unfinished Project" Jürgen Habermas, one of the most important modern thinkers in the Enlightenment tradition, concludes that the prospects for the fulfillment of the Enlightenment promise "are not very encouraging" (Habermas 1997, 54-55).

Few concerns about the project of modernity attract more attention than the continued survival of violence. More than two centuries separate us from the time when Immanuel Kant reflected on the capacity of reason to create eternal peace, and these centuries have seen violence on an industrial scale. The French Revolution surrendered the ideals of liberty and inviolability of rights to the violence of the Terror and the Napoleonic wars. The revolutions of the 19th and 20th century, colonialism, and nationalism also claimed their share of brutality and barbarity. The massive slaughter of the two World Wars in the 20th century with the extermination of six million Jews under the Nazis shocked even those who were not oblivious to man's capacity for evil. Even the triumphant moment of liberal democracy that followed the end of the Cold War and the collapse of Soviet Communism was marked by outbursts of savagery and barbarism across Europe and the world.

This is the visible record of the period that has experienced an unprecedented growth of material wealth and technological power. But there have also been insidious forms of violence that went unrecorded and unpublicized—violence that has been difficult to track or document. The violence towards women, domestic violence, child abuse, lynching, gay bashing, and even more subtle and insidious forms of violence—such as psychological, verbal, or symbolic—ruined lives and careers and left indelible scars on individual and collective psyche.

One would certainly be in remiss to see the modern period exclusively in terms of violence and destruction. In his well-publicized book *The Better Angels of Our Nature: Why Violence Has Declined,* which has generated a great deal of controversy, Steven Pinker, a Harvard psychologist, has marshaled a great deal of empirical evidence to prove that despite all the wars and destruction, the current exposure to violence is significantly less severe that it was several hundred years ago, to say nothing about several millennia (Pinker 2011). Pinker has no illusions about the human race. He sees humans as equally predisposed to both conflict and cooperation by the evolutionary hard wiring of our brains. However, he also emphasizes what he sees as an encouraging influence of the "civilizing process"—the term he borrows from Norbert Elias. In Pinker's view, the improved material circumstances of human existence as well as ameliorating cultural attitudes have significantly diminished the level of violence in the modern world by comparison with the preceding periods.

Pinker's statistics and arguments are not universally accepted. Some feel that statistics are misleading in assessing the level of violence in the modern world. The declining percentages conceal much greater absolute numbers. The statistical odds may mean little for those who still lose their life to violence today. There is also no guarantee that the relatively peaceful period that we have experienced since World War II will not end in a new cataclysm. Some of the aspects of the civilizing process cited positively by Pinker may appear to be a dubious blessing; For example, the monopolization of violence by the state may diminish the level of violence among individuals, but it certainly preserves violence as a tool of the state vis-à-vis its citizens. The irony has not escaped Elizabeth Kolbert, who in her review of Pinker's book cited Churchill's remark: "It may well be that we shall by a process of sublime irony have reached a stage in this story where safety will be the sturdy child of terror, and survival the twin brother of annihilation" (Kolbert 2011).

Dan Stone also observes that violence "need not involve the relation of individuals; the state is just as capable of treating the 'object of violence' as one 'potentially worthy of bodily harm, or even annihilation'" (Stone 1999). In his review of Pinker's book in *The Christian Science Monitor,* Jordan Smith argues:

> As a proportion of the world's population, or even just Norway's, the sixty-nine casualties on Utøya hardly register. By Pinker's method of accounting,

they received far too much coverage; in an average year in Norway, some three hundred people die from accidental poisoning. But the shootings illustrate in nightmare fashion what we all know to be the case. Hate and madness and cruelty haven't disappeared, and they aren't going to. Systems break down and, worse still, can be subverted. This is one of the lessons of Auschwitz, and it's why, since 1945, most people have hesitated to argue that modernity and violence are opposed . . . The demons may yet return (Smith 2011).

This article does not intend to enter the fray over Pinker's book. Both Pinker and his critics agree that the level of violence in contemporary society still remains prohibitively high. and that violence and the civilizing process have proven to be compatible if not agreeable companions. The questions are: Why do they coexist? What makes their coexistence possible? Will the civilizing process ever be able to get rid of violence and deliver on the promise of modernity?

CRITIQUE OF THE MODERN CONCEPTION OF REASON

The persistence of violence under modern conditions is an enigma that continues to baffle researchers. Explanations of the persistence vary widely: from the emphasis on biology and evolution, to social conditions, to culture and politics.[1] Despite their differences, all these perspectives agree that in one way or another—by omission or by commission—that reason is implicated in this continued survival of violence. Critics of modernity, such as Hannah Arendt or Zygmunt Bauman, lay violence squarely at the doorstep of reason. They see violence as instrumental to reason and view it as a direct outcome of the project of modernity—an inevitable consequence of its efforts to control and compartmentalize human life in the name of putative progress, technocratic efficiency, and governmental bureaucratic logic (Arendt 1970; Bauman 1989). As Gianni Vattimo summarized:

> The discovery that the rationalization of the world turns against reason and its ends of perfection and emancipation, and does so not by error, accident, or a chance distortion, but precisely to the extent that it is more and more perfectly accomplished (as cited in Stone 1999, 375).

Others try to vindicate reason and modernity from the alleged complicity in violence. Dan Stone, for example, in his article "Modernity and violence: theoretical reflections on the Einsatzgruppen"[2] disputes the argument that violence is a logical consequence of modernization. Although he recognizes that violence and modern civilization can coexist, and that violence can survive within modernity, he does not see them as intimately nor logically connected. In his nuanced reading of the reports by Einsatzgruppen, Stone tries to show "how the conjunction of rationalized society and violent passions—which exist now as they did before 1945—erupts at certain moments into so apocalyptic a force" (Stone 1999, 376). Stone sees Nazi violence as a product of the paradox in their project. According to his interpretation, the Nazis attempted to destroy the foundation of modern society; but this attempt, in his view, "was derived from that society itself"(Stone 1999, 375). It is this contradictory agenda of undermining modernity from within modernity that led to the eruption of violence. Stone summarizes:

> What the Einsatzgruppen reports demonstrate is the existence of violence within modernity, not violence that rejects modernity, but nevertheless a violence which, in its shabby brutality, cannot simply be seen as a logical consequence of modernization (Stone 1999, 376).

Contentions over persistence of violence show how intractable the problem is. Despite concerted efforts to contain it, violence remains ubiquitous. It continues to reappear in places where people least expect it. The ideals of the Enlightenment promised a world of peace, justice, and tolerance. Yet they could not prevent the terror of the French Revolution, colonialism, world wars, and the savagery of genocides. Some argue the Enlightenment actually contributed to these events. In trying to understand wars, crimes, abuse, and torture, we seek to assert the power of word and human reason and their supremacy over violence. Yet reason and word appear to be impotent against violence. Despite these efforts, violence remains immune to our words and deeds; it always manages to escape a capture. It is, as David Bell and Lawrence Schehr put it, "an ineffable of our existence"—uncontainable, unrepresentable, and ultimately uncontrollable (Bell and Schehr 1998, 3).

But why should this be so? Why is violence capable of escaping capture? Why reason is powerless against it? Is it possible that reason itself contains violence? The question is not new. This idea gets explored, for example, in a curious inversion of the Malthusian loop by George Bataille, who has argued in his *The Accursed Share* (*Le part maudite*) that the economic rationality produces excess energy that needs to be destroyed (Bataille 1988). To Adorno and Horkheimer, the *Odyssey* reveals "a terrible vengeance" and mutilation that the birth of reason wreaked on the primordial world of myth (Adorno and Horkheimer 1992, 140). Although the answers provided by those who identified reason with violence may not be ultimately convincing, the possibility of reason's complicity in violence that they raise certainly encourages one to explore the conception of reason that has been and continues to be dominant in Western culture.

"Reason" and "rationality" are very familiar words. We often use them without thinking much about the meaning we attribute to them. We tend to forget that these concepts are not neutral, and that their meaning is a product of a particular time and place. The conception of reality that is relevant to the way we think about reason and rationality has originated and evolved during the modern period in Western culture, and despite its numerous evolutionary permutations and peregrinations, it still retains its original core. When reading Voltaire, Rousseau, Kant, or Hegel, we still feel that, despite many differences among them and between them and us, the core conception of reality that underlies these in many ways very different worldviews remains the same. We accept this core conception as self-evident truth—a sort of Kantian a priori judgment. We consider it universal, that is, valid, in all possible circumstances and under all empirical conditions. We are so sure of this core conception that we have rarely, if ever, submitted it to critical examination. We have never really asked a question if it is really true.

So what is this core conception of reality that shapes the way we think about reason and how it operates? Let's take, for example, the two philosophical perspectives that currently dominate our culture and the ways we view reality—realism and anti-realism.

As John Searle defines it,

> Realism is the view that there is a way that things are that is logically independent of all human representations. Realism does not say how things are but only that there is a way that they are (Searle 1995, 155).

According to Searle, the realist view of the world has the following structural features (Searle 1995, 150-51):[3]

1. World (or alternatively, reality or the universe) exists independently of our representations of it.
2. Human beings have a variety of interconnected ways of having access to and representing features of the world to themselves.
3. Some of these representations . . . purport to be about and to represent how things are in reality. To the extent that they succeed of fail, they are said to be true or false, respectively. They are true if and only if they correspond to the facts in reality.
4. Systems of representation . . . are human creations, and to that extent arbitrary.
5. Complete epistemic objectivity is difficult, sometimes impossible.
6. Having knowledge consists in having true representations for which we can give certain sorts of justification or evidence. Knowledge is thus by definition objective in the epistemic sense, because the criteria for knowledge are not arbitrary, and they are impersonal.

As one can see, the ontological separation of the subject and the object is at the very core of the realist view of the world. In accordance with this view, knowledge of reality is possible. It involves an infinite asymptotic approximation between objects of reality and our representations of these objects.

There are numerous philosophical perspectives that disagree with realism. Despite their differences and even incompatibilities, these schools of thought share some common features that allow grouping them under the general rubric of anti-realism.[4] It is beyond the scope of this paper to go into a detailed examination of these disagreements – suffice it to say that they all boil down to one fundamental disagreement over the issue of validation. In contrast to realists, anti-realists maintain that we can never be sure how things actually are because a fit between a theory and data is insufficient for making truth claims. Paul Horwich, for example, offers the following generalization:

> It [anti-realism] derives from an impression of conflict between the alleged autonomy of the facts (their independence of us) and their accessibility (the possibility of our gaining knowledge of their existence). Consequently, it seems to the anti-realist that something of our naive point of view must be given up; some philosophical move must be made (Horwich 1996, 188).

In support of their argument, anti-realists refer to numerous theories in the past that fitted well with empirical data but have ultimately proven to be false (for example, the theory of flat Earth, the theory that placed Earth in the center of our planetary system, or the ether theory of light). They also point to the phenomenon of underdetermination—that is, the existence of different and often conflicting theories that are supported by the same empirical evidence—to say that a fit is no guarantee of the validity of a theory.[5]

There is a fundamental difference between realism and anti-realism, which is the question of whether reality is knowable. Despite this critical difference, both realists and anti-realists have the same core conception of reality and reason. Both posit a gap between the subject and the object, except that the realists believe that this gap can be mediated by reason, while the anti-realists think that the credibility of such mediation is suspect. The gap between the knower and reality in both perspectives indicates that both accept the traditional dualism as a given.

This dualism goes back to the very early periods in the evolution of human thought. Plato, for example, believed that mind and body were ontologically distinct. The division between thought and reality, mind and matter, body and soul, subject and object, and the knower and the known is characteristic for much of the European intellectual tradition.[6] This ontological dualism powerfully shapes the way we conceptualize reason and the way it operates. However, is the positing of this gap justified? Is it supported by empirical evidence?

ONE-SIDED CONSCIOUSNESS AND ITS PREDISPOSITION
TOWARDS VIOLENCE

In order to answer these questions, I will turn to the work of Swiss psychologist Jean Piaget on the origin of intelligence. In his remarkable study *The Origin of Intelligence in Children* Piaget provides a very detailed empirical account of the development of symbolic thought (Piaget 1998).[END NOTES] The starting point in his account of this development is reflexes, or physiological functions (for example, muscle contractions). These functions require neural circuits that coordinate and regulate them. Nerve signals trigger these functions and thus conserve them. The more often this triggering takes place, the more often physiological functions are exercised, and the more stable they are. Stable recursively operating reflex functions form what Piaget calls circular schemata, or sensory-motor operations.

Sensory-motor operations conserve themselves in two ways. First, they become increasingly oriented toward external reality in search of stimulation. This process evolves from random grabbing to a more directed search for stimuli that leads to a gradual construction of the object on the level of sensory-motor operations (but not yet on the representational level). As the growing number of objects is incorporated into sensory-motor schemata— the process Piaget calls assimilation—the infant becomes increasingly orientated toward the exogenous sphere.

Second, sensory-motor operations conserve themselves through coordination with each other as well as through mutual assimilation (for example, tactile, audio, visual, gustatory, and other functions). One example of such mutual assimilation is the activation of the audio function by the visual one, and vice versa. In other words, infants begin to "see" when they hear and "hear" when they see (at a certain age infants begin to turn their head to catch the sight of the mother when they hear her voice). Mutual assimilations on the sensory-motor level require coordination and mutual assimilation on the level of neural networks.

The increasing interaction on the neural level creates the permanent neural organization that combines neural networks and eventually leads to the construction of permanent mental representations, or images. This process is completed at the beginning of the second year when infants begin to look for objects that are hidden from a direct view. The search for a hidden object indicates that an infant has already constructed a permanent mental image of the object; in other words, for infants the object begins to exist even when they do not see it. Mental representations regulate the functioning of combinations of neural networks (that in turn regulate sensory-motor operations) and act recursively on them.

This example shows that one and the same process constructs, on one hand, objects of reality as they appear to us and, on the other, organizes our mind. In other words, it is this process of construction that constitutes true ontological reality, not the subject or the object that are merely its products. The process plays a vital role in the development of our mind and in the construction of our consciousness, or what we call reason. It is the source of reason. Our representations of reality will change, and our consciousness will change. But the process of construction will remain the same in all of its essential features. Yet despite the importance of the process of construction for understanding human reason and how it operates, we exclude the process of construction from our view of reality and represent its products—the subject and the object—as the true ontological reality. Despite the absolute primacy of the process of construction, the conception of reality prevalent in modern culture focuses either on the subject (anti-realists) or on the object (realists) that are merely its products. Our conception of reality is fundamentally flawed.

It is hard to overestimate the role of mind and consciousness in our individual lives and our civilization as a whole. Operations performed in our consciousness powerfully affect the way we interpret reality, which, in turn, shapes our actions. The exclusion of the process of construction from our view of reality and our conception of reason also has a powerful effect on how we interpret reality and, consequently, how we act. The exclusive focus on the products of construction creates a framework for interpreting reality that leaves out the most important part of reality. It should, therefore, come as no surprise then that when we use this deficient framework, we get a very distorted view of reality. When we apply this framework to interpreting reality, we squeeze reality into the Procrustean bed of our extremely limited vision and thus commit an act of violence.

Our interactions with reality involve two principal operations: assimilation and adaptation. Assimilation is a function that integrates objects of reality into internal functional schemata of the organism. This operation reduces the multiple and diverse world to the internal functions of our organism. It deprives objects of their autonomy and subordinates them to the functions of the organism. By contrast, adaptation involves recognition of the autonomy of reality and its objects. It essentially adjusts the functions of the organism to these autonomous objects. For example, due to adaptation, the child begins to modify the mode of prehension depending on the object's shape and texture. Due to adaptation, the organism can establish a more balanced relationship with reality. It creates a possibility for knowing reality as it is rather than reducing it to the functions of the organism. As an operation, adaptation plays an exceptional role in the origin and evolution of human intelligence and knowledge (Piaget 1978).

In his studies of intelligence, Piaget shows that both operations are closely interrelated and play a very important role in the origin and evolution of human consciousness and symbolic thought. When we use a deficient framework for interpreting reality, and when we reduce reality to our mental functions, we essentially limit ourselves to performing only one operation—assimilation. Unrestrained by adaptation, assimilation severely limits our capacity for understanding the multiple and diverse world; it does not recognize the autonomy of this reality; it subordinates reality to our own internally generated schemes. The result is a one-sided and self-centered representation of reality.

Human reason (consciousness) regulates our interactions with reality. When our consciousness excludes the process of construction from its field of vision, it creates an inadequate and flawed interpretation of reality. This violence is not exclusively symbolic—that is, producing merely an inadequate knowledge of reality. It has real physical effects.

As a product of the evolution, our consciousness has much in common with the rest of nature. One of the most fundamental processes that operate in our consciousness, as it does in the rest of nature, is conservation. When our consciousness excludes the process of construction from its field of vision, it excludes the most important part of reality. With the process of construction out of the frame, our consciousness can only focus on the disconnected products of this process—the subject or the object—rather than the process itself. It tends to conserve the products rather than the process; it fetishizes and absolutizes those products and regards them as the only true reality, thus disrupting the process of construction and limiting its creative capacity. As the process of construction evolves and the old products are subjected to the pressure of change, a one-sided consciousness experiences this process of change as a loss of reality.

There are few traumatic experiences that can compare to loss of reality--situations where people get a feeling that they can no longer understand reality or interpret it correctly. For a consciousness that experiences such a situation, reality becomes a void, an abyss devoid of any meaning, or worse, filled with negative meaning. In words of Shakespeare, time gets "out of joint." This consciousness develops a sense of disorientation, confusion, and fear; and violence is a very common corollary of fear. The capacity of such severely limited consciousness to cope with this condition is reduced to only one cognitive operation—assimilation. Such consciousness is incapable of critically examining itself; it simply cannot see the internal sources of its predicament. Rather than address the real source of its fear within itself, this consciousness tends to look for the cause of the fear outside itself: it develops the need to construct the enemy, to create a scapegoat on whom it can project its fears.[7] Since fear causes violent reactions, the enemy becomes the object of this violence and the destruction of the enemy becomes an obsessive but also elusive goal—elusive because the true cause of fear is never addressed.

Freud clearly understood the internal mechanism of the need to construct the enemy when he made a perceptive remark in reference to the Bolshevik

Revolution: "When Bolsheviks destroy all the capitalists, what are they going to do?" No destruction could possibly assuage the Bolshevik or Nazi anxiety, their fear, and consequently their need to construct and pursue the imaginary "enemy." No matter how many victims they sacrificed to their "jealous god," it continued to demand more sacrifices.

Despite numerous failures and much criticism, there are no signs that we will abandon the project of modernity any time soon. Its fundamental message remains a powerful appeal for many of us. As useful as it may be, criticism does not offer alternatives. There are no alternatives for humans other than relying on reason—our most powerful tool in dealing with reality. What other means do we have? What else is powerful enough to give us a hope for a better future? Our consciousness has an infinite combinatorial capacity for constructing new operations. It is by far the most powerful form of organization of matter. There is nothing in the universe that can even come close to its power. Yet, an indisputable fact remains that, so far, our reason has not been able to cope with violence. Despite all our efforts, violence continues to survive. It hides in numerous interstices of our complex society and rears its ugly head at any opportunity.

CONCLUSION

As this paper has argued, the continued survival of violence is not proof that its power is superior to that of reason. Violence is associated with only one operation in the arsenal of tools available to us for dealing with reality. As important as assimilation is for the functioning of the organism, its power cannot even come close in comparison to the infinitely more powerful combination of assimilation and adaptation.

This paper has argued that the remarkable survival of violence is due primarily to the fact that reason has allowed violence to subsist on the powers of reason. Unwittingly and unintentionally, we limited the power of our consciousness by excluding the process of construction from its frame of vision and thus profoundly disturbing the required delicate balance between assimilation and adaptation. Thus reason yields to violence by failing to embrace its true reality and the source of its enormous power—the process of construction. This process lies at the very core of reality and its evolution. Our consciousness inherited it in the course of the biological evolution. It uses this process to create new forms of organization of reality and propel the evolution. The power of our consciousness in creating new forms is infinite. There is nothing that can prevent it from constructing yet another level of organization (Shkliarevsky 2007). Only when our consciousness fails to embrace its true reality does the power of reason turns into a source of its powerlessness. Its remarkable capacity to create reality turns into destructive violence against reality. Indeed, "the sleep of reason produces monsters."[8]

In order to cope with violence, reason has to renew itself. Our consciousness has to embrace the true source of its power—the process of construction. If we consciously embrace and understand the process of construction and its fundamental relation to our consciousness, we will no longer have to experience uncontrollable fear of losing reality. The confusion and disorientation that accompanies the emergence of new levels of organization of reality will lose much of its traumatic impact if we understand that we are not losing reality in these moments of transition; rather, they bring us into a very close and intimate contact with the process that is the source of our existence—our true reality. We will no longer have to experience fear during such transitions. If we understand the inner source of our discomfort and are capable of using our critical powers for controlling it, we will no longer have a need to resort to violence against imaginary external "enemy" as a way of dealing with our fears; we will no longer have to engage in a ceaseless and totally futile effort of coping with this fear. Violence will no longer run amok in its senseless destruction.

This is not to argue an idealistic and utopian vision. Violence is a natural phenomenon. It is a product of an operation that is very important for the evolution of reality. Without assimilation reality would never be able to evolve. As important as adaptation is, it cannot sustain the evolution by itself. Adaptation has to work in close interrelationship and balance with assimilation. However, the importance of assimilation does not imply that violence cannot be contained. Adaptation is capable of ameliorating the detrimental aspects of assimilation. Working together and in balance assimilation and adaptation are capable of providing constructive channels and productive outlets for our creative energies in our pursuit of new and ever more powerful levels of organization of reality.

We live in an age of disbelief and skepticism, if not cynicism. Some critics may be tempted to see in this essay only an inflated ego and megalomaniac illusions. Skepticism is a safe game in our age. It does not really have to provide solutions. Yet when skillfully performed, the work of a skeptic may place him or her into a hallowed position of truth-maker when in fact no truth is being made.

This essay does not appeal to faith. On the contrary, it calls for serious engagement and intense introspection. Only an inveterate idealist can believe that one can easily get rid of political practices, institutions, and social habits that promote and foster violence. Certainly, the elimination of violence will require concerted, consistent, and well-coordinated efforts by many dedicated individuals—activists, professionals, political and religious leaders, and public figures. Theoretical insight is only a step to a solution. Rather than seeking to recruit followers in a faith effort, this paper tries to encourage a liberating critical re-examination of our most fundamental, most dearly held beliefs about reality in the name and in fulfillment of the promise made several centuries ago at the dawn of the modern age—the promise of the Enlightenment.

REFERENCES

Adorno, Theodor W. and Max Horkheimer. 1992. Odysseus or Myth and Enlightenment. *New German Critique* 56: 109-141.
Appadurai, Arjun. 1998. Dead Certainty: Ethnic Violence in the Era of Globalization. *Development and Change* 29(4): 905-925.
Arendt, Hannah. 1970. *On Violence*. New York: Harcourt, Brace & World.
Bataille, Georges. 1988. *The Accursed Share: An Essay on General Economy* (New York; London: Zone; MIT Press.
Bauman, Zygmunt. 1989. *Modernity and the Holocaust*. Ithaca, N.Y: Cornell University Press.
Bell, David F. and Lawrence R. Schehr. 1998. Reading Violence. *SubStance* 86: 1998: 3-4.
Belousek, Darrin. 2005. Underdetermination, Realism, and Theory Appraisal: An Epistemological Reflection on Quantum Mechanics. *Foundations of Physics* 35(4): 669-695.
Bergström, Lars. 1984. Underdetermination and Realism. *Erkenntnis* 21(3): 349-365.
Birmingham, Peg. 2010. On Violence, Politics, and the Law. *The Journal of Speculative Philosophy* 24(1): 1-20.
Casanova, Jose. 2011. Cosmopolitanism, the clash of civilizations and multiple modernities. *Current Sociology* 59(2): 252-267.
Cordero, Alberto. 2001. Realism and Underdetermination: Some Clues from the Practices-Up. *Philosophy of Science* 68(3): S301-S312.
Dickens, Peter. 2010. Alienation, the cosmos and the self. *The Sociological Review* 57: 47-65.
Ducharme, Lori J. and Gary Alan Fine. 1995. The Construction of Nonpersonhood and Demonization: Commemorating the Traitorous Reputation of Benedict Arnold. *Social Forces* 73(4): 1309-1333.
Enserink, Martin. 2000. Searching for the Mark of Cain. *Science* 289 (5479): 575-580.
Eysenck, H. J. 1979. The Origins of Violence. *Journal of Medical Ethics* 5(3): 105-107.
Ferguson, Christopher J. and Kevin M. Beaver. 2009. Natural born killers: The genetic origins of extreme violence. *Aggression and Violent Behavior* 14(5): 286-294.
Fukuyama, Francis. 1992. *The End of History and the Last Man*. New York: The Free Press.
Girard, René. 1986. *The Scapegoat*. Baltimore: Johns Hopkins University Press.
Habermas, Jürgen. 1997. Modernity: An Unfinished Project. In *Habermas and the Unfinished Project of Modernity*, eds. Maurizio Passerin d'Entrèves and Seyla Benhabib, 38-55. Cambridge, Mass: MIT Press.
Hoefer, Carl and Alexander Rosenberg. 1994. Empirical equivalence, underdetermination, and systems of the world. *Philosophy of Science* 61(4) (December 1994): 592-608.
Horwich, Paul. 1996. Realism and Truth. *Noûs* 30: 187-197.
Kolbert, Elizabeth. 2011. Peace in Our Time. *New Yorker* 87(30): 75-78.
Ladyman, J. 2001. *Understanding Philosophy of Science*. London: Routledge.
Lee, Alexander. 2011. Who Becomes a Terrorist?: Poverty, Education, and the Origins of Political Violence. *World Politics* 63(2): 203-245.
Leplin, Jarrett. 1997. The Underdetermination of Total Theories. *Erkenntnis* 47(2): 203-215.
Maiello, Suzanne. 2000. Broken links: attacks or breakdown? Notes on the origins of violence. *Journal of Child Psychotherapy* 26(1): 5-24.
Moore, Jr. Barrington. 1968. Thoughts on Violence and Democracy. *Proceedings of the Academy of Political Science* 29(1): 1-12.
Piaget, Jean. 1978. *Behavior and Evolution*. New York: Pantheon Books.
Piaget, Jean. 1998. *The Origin of Intelligence in Children*. Madison: International Universities Press, Inc.

Pinker, Steven. 2011. *The Better Angels of Our Nature: Why Violence Has Declined*. New York: Viking.

Psillos, P. 1999. *Scientific Realism: How Science Tracks Truth*. London: Routledge.

Robinson, Howard. 2011. Dualism. *The Stanford Encyclopedia of Philosophy*, ed. Edward N. Zalta, http://plato.stanford.edu/archives/win2011/entries/dualism/ (accessed December 6, 2011).

Searle, John R. 1995. *The Construction of Social Reality*. New York: Free Press.

Shkliarevsky, Gennady. 2007. The Paradox of Observing, Autopoiesis, and the Future of Social Sciences. Systems Research and Behavioral Science 24(3): 323-332.

Smith, Jordan Michael. 2011 (October 20). The Better Angels of Our Nature: Why Violence Has Declined. *Christian Science Monitor*.

Stone, Dan. 1999. Modernity and Violence: theoretical reflections on the Einsatzgruppen. *Journal of Genocide Research*, 1(3): 367-378.

Vattimo, Gianni. 1992. *The Transparent Society*. Baltimore: The Johns Hopkins University Press.

NOTES

1. Here are some references to these different perspectives: Enserink 2000; Eysenck 1979; Maiello 2000; Ferguson and Beaver 2009; Lee 2011; Appadurai 1998; Casanova 2011; Arendt 1970; Moore 1968; Bataille 1988; Birmingham 2010; Bauman 1989; Girard 1986; Stone 1999.

2. Special paramilitary death squads in Nazi Germany that were responsible for most of the mass killings of civilian population during World War II.

3. For reasons of convenience and economy I provide a slightly abridged verbatim version.

4. For a good overview of both realism and its opponents, see Psillos 1999; Ladyman 2000; Searle 1995.

5. On underdetermination see Hoefer and Rosenberg 1994; Leplin 1997; Bergström 1984; Cordero 2001; Belousek 2005.

6. In philosophy of science, dualism often refers to the dichotomy between the "subject" (the observer) and the "object" (the observed). Criticism of Western science may label this kind of dualism as a flaw in the nature of science itself. On dualism see Robinson 2011; Dickens 2010.

7. For an interesting discussion of the phenomenon of demonization and scapegoating see Ducharme and Fine 1995.

8. The phrase is borrowed from the title of one of Francisco Goya's series of etchings Los Caprichos.

Contrariety in Philosophy

R.E. Tully

INTRODUCTION

Philosophers believe they breathe the air of reasoning. Given an argument, they examine its structure, pick out the steps of inference, detect assumptions, weigh the degree of logical support the premises give to the conclusion. Philosophers are attracted to claims of discoveries in their field: new solutions to old problems, and refutations of accepted solutions. They also have their own cases to make. Philosophers are like lawyers, except that there are no plaintiffs, defendants or presiding judges, and they routinely switch roles as prosecutor and defender before a voluntary jury of other philosophers. Despite such notable differences, reason is a kind of court. Philosophical analysis, like the Law, aims at objectivity and at being impersonal. As in any adversarial situation, however, there is rhetoric in the air. My aim is to explore why philosophers, the venerable guild of truth-seekers, so committed to the principle that reason and love of wisdom should be the guide of life, divide into opposing, and not seldom warring, sides.

The rhetoric of opposition is occasionally dignified and uplifting. When Aristotle declared his rejection of one of Plato's core doctrines (his theory of the Forms) he did so with respect. ". . . my inquiry," he wrote,

> is made an uphill one by the fact that the Forms have been introduced by friends of our own. Yet it would perhaps be thought to be better, indeed to be our duty, for the sake of maintaining the truth even to destroy what touches us closely, especially as we are philosophers or lovers of wisdom; for, while both are dear, piety requires us to honor truth above our friends. [1]

Aristotle's differences with Plato were fundamental though not unique. Athens accommodated not only the Academy and the Lyceum, but also the

Stoa and the Garden. Since the time of Descartes, however, philosophical opponents are identified not so much by geographical location as by metaphysical commitment. Among other groups there are monists and dualists, realists and idealists, materialists and immaterialists, positivists and emergentists, along with their distinctive subgroups. Although the lexicon of opposing pairs is rich, there is no accepted set of definitions of exactly what makes these groups opposed.

That philosophers should divide into such groups is understandable. Although the rules of good reasoning are designed to manage what follows from a starting point, reason does not mandate the starting points. In a disturbing number of cases, however, more than mere differences concerning choice of starting point are present. Divisiveness and intolerance are evident. Differences are sometimes compatible, but division usually excludes. Philosophers have been known to turn prosecutorial, condemning fellow philosophers to the nether regions whom reason has guided in a different direction, who have stationed themselves under different banners. In an example I'll take up later, some contemporary philosophers, who unhesitatingly celebrate social diversity, show little inclination to treat a professional colleague's recently published views as anything less than heresy.

I think that philosophical opposition runs as deep as our genes. It is also, I believe, an indication of radically different conceptions of the power and limits of human reason itself. Although philosophers have made distinct contributions to understanding the nature of such limits, the question of whether intransigent opposition is an unavoidable price to pay for their achievements, or merely a sign of what deserves deeper exploration, I'll postpone for the moment. My immediate focus, is not on reason but on a compelling phenomenon which stares us right in the face.

I: TERRITORIALITY

Self-interest, self-centeredness and self-promotion are genetic endowments we share with most living things. We regard such characteristics as instincts, as natural gifts so universal, useful and indispensable that, while their causal functioning demands scientific investigation, their very existence hardly needs proving. Moralists and jurists refer to the preserving of one's life as a *right of nature*, a fundamental moral right which since ancient times has been codified in law or allowed the force of an unwritten law. Whether earthworms, spiders and rats have any legal right to life may be doubted, and whether such creatures constitute persons in any sense or have self-awareness may be challenged. Yet even casual observation makes it undeniable that such creatures, when threatened, seek to preserve their own lives and those of dependents, sometimes by flight and in some circumstances by attacking what they take to be a danger, whatever its size. What Hobbes observed about mankind in the state of nature applies much more obviously to non-human species. Even in herds and flocks, individuals are wary, competitive and opportunistic.[2]

Humans are in principle more accommodating to their own kind. Being social by nature, ("political animals" in Aristotle's formulation[3]) they have to be. The right to life is at the same time a right not to be interfered with by others without cause, which carries an obligation not to interfere with others without cause. The 18th Century philosopher John Locke wrote that the natural state of people is *"perfect freedom"* and he claims that this is a *"state also of equality* wherein all the power and jurisdiction is reciprocal, no one having more than another".[4] Locke's political principles about the human condition, although idealizations, are by no means simplistic. They are analogous to Newton's laws of motion in assuming a frictionless environment in which the nature of social interaction and the mutual demands associated with human rights can be observed and appreciated more clearly. Thanks to these natural forces, however, a great deal of friction prevails in both the physical and social worlds. Even a simple apple falling from a tree may encounter obstacles posed by leaves, branches, the wind, and other apples, which prevent it falling to the ground in a perfect straight line, while the ground itself may cause the apple to wobble away with uncertain momentum.

In the world of political animals described by Locke, perfect freedom differs from what might be called 'reciprocal freedom', or the mutual recognition by people of their private spaces. The two are in constant tension. The adjustments between one's own space and others' spaces are dynamic. Like relative motion in Newton's Physics, social equilibrium is a matter of degree rather than a state of final rest. What a person's "equality" means in the eyes of others continuously changes, and it appears to be an axiom of society that there will always be *others* whom we exclude from ourselves for the sake of *being* ourselves. The word *xenophobia* is familiar enough; *xenophilia* is not.

With humans, the scope of one's self—more precisely the space within which the self is located—is easily extended to include such collections known as *family, team, political party, business, community,* and *nation.* The space of private, individual freedom is reduced in proportion as the responsibilities to these other groups accumulate, each group imposing constraints and, in turn, producing conflicts. Should I put duty to my party before duty to the nation? Duty to my family before duty to my job? To my country before myself? To God before the King? Whatever the context, the moral and legal right of preserving one's life is supplemented by an interest in pursuing shared happiness and cementing a sense of well-being within the group, where the quality of life, sometimes even instead of its continuance, might be the primary concern. The dynamics of social interaction become vastly more complicated compared with what any unsupported apple has to face. One person's exercise of freedom may press against, distort, or even invade another's domain of freedom, another's space. Sometimes the language describing such actions is metaphorical, sometimes literal. Actual motion by a person across a boundary need not occur. Words by themselves (understood as more than mere sounds) are effective tools and weapons. Given that each person's space is private, even if to a minimal degree, the right to respond to a challenge, to defend that space, is never questioned, only its manner. Much depends on whether a person judges a challenge as an obstacle to be circumvented, a threat needing to be repelled, or an opportunity for readjusting the content and limits of one's space. Since interactions are dynamic, there will be a range of possible responses to the challenge. Just as equilibrium is a matter of degree, so is symmetry. For instance, much depends on whether the challenge comes from a parent or younger sibling, a coach or a team mate, a boss or a spouse, another driver or a state trooper. The adjustments themselves may hardly be noticed in the give and take of day-to-day life. In fact, they *are* the give and take of social life.

Nevertheless, a different kind of social interaction is characterized less by continuous symmetrical readjustments than by insistent self-reference. Some people's main or even exclusive concern may only be to advertise the private space they already occupy, to define the ground on which, or the things for which, they stand. This is a familiar form of public self-display, common to both individuals and groups. Imagine for a moment the conduct of fans at a football game, of the aggrieved at a demonstration, or the faithful at a political rally. They celebrate their corporate individuality, perhaps even with defiance. In the state of nature which Hobbes portrays, the quest for one's own glory motivates the effort to subordinate others physically, thereby to gain respect, or *street cred*. In a less turbulent society, the quest for respect and esteem takes milder forms of self-promotion. These include political election platforms, the mission statements of companies and hospitals, pledges of improvement made by public officials, and statements of purpose sent by applicants to a college. More frequently, however, self-display by individuals or groups takes a negative form: we define ourselves by means of what we are not. Political candidates imply their own strengths by identifying their rivals' shortcomings and lack of integrity. Sermons about sinfulness help foster a congregation's feeling of righteousness. Propaganda against an enemy in wartime aims to promote the superiority of a nation's own cause, perhaps even of its morality. The contrast produced by such actions is intended to benefit our own space. The words are not meant to change the political opponent, the sinner or the enemy. With little energy expended against them we bask in our own sunshine.

II. PHILOSOPHICAL MONOLOGUES

I've sketched an admittedly grim picture of human society, although more elevated than the one Hobbes paints of the raw state of nature, where there is "no *mine* and *thine* distinct".[5] My sketch is approximately on the same level as his depiction of a contractual society in which competing self-interests are able to flourish by rational compromise. Where, then, in this civil picture are philosophers to be found? Granted that their basic genetic endowments of self-preservation and self-interest do not differ from those of other humans, wouldn't reason play an offsetting, possibly decisive role in their interactions? Since philosophers are conventionally thought to be committed to the search for truth, shouldn't this serve as their common ground? The differences among them—and we know from the history of Philosophy that their doctrines differ greatly—ought at least to be *rational* differences, traceable to contested facts within a web of argument or to assumptions recognized as uncertain but unable to be made less so. Within such a web, philosophers should aim to locate whatever snags hinder their search, united at least by the standards of reason itself. In the theater of civil society they ought to occupy the box seats.

Apart from finding a job after graduate school, or ascending the tenure ladder when fortunate enough to have landed on the bottom rung, professional philosophers do not face dire challenges—not at least within their own profession. Existential threats come from outside. Socrates was not condemned to death by thinkers from a rival school of thought. Cicero was murdered not for his Stoicism but for political intrigue. It wasn't Abelard's views on logic that caused him to suffer the vengeful slice of a knife, and Moritz Schlick was shot in Vienna for personal reasons unrelated to logical positivism. However, sufficient, non-lethal turbulence is generated within the profession. The acrimony and condemnation that philosophers experience customarily originate from other philosophers, and rightly so. The search for truth is a stumbling effort. Any searcher should anticipate detours, *cul de sacs*, loops, impasses and much guesswork, and when many searchers occupy the same path but some appear to be further along, a lot of second guessing and criticisms are inevitable from both directions. For the sake of progress, however, opposition and correction are desirable even if sometimes uncomfortable features of collaboration. The problem with this picture, however, is that it presumes unity, a unity of purpose, and sufficient agreement among philosophers about what their concepts and principles mean. This holds especially for foundational ones such as *fact*, *knowledge*, *mind*, *self*, the nature of the *good*, *certainty* and, ironically, *truth* itself. On all such topics there have been unresolved philosophical disputes, accompanied by disputes about the purpose of Philosophy and even about what counts as genuine Philosophy in the first place. Forward progress along the path is sometimes halted in order to excavate and examine the common ground on which the philosophers have been standing. Predictably, the things some of them dig up are assayed differently by others, and on occasion what has been claimed as a discovery has been dismissed as merely a new way of talking about old and familiar subjects. The general picture of overarching unity, then, is a misleading one. Philosophers may agree about the objective standards of logic and argument, but such standards do not affect the contents of their disputes.

So, philosophers belong in the public galleries after all. Perhaps only saints (in contrast to theologians) belong in the special seats. The real picture is not inspiring. Instead of collaborating in the search for truth, philosophers often seem inclined to concentrate on attacking each other's spaces and reducing the contents to rubble. The philosophical ground is littered with examples of disparagement familiar in other academic fields, in the professions, in business, and, indeed, in nearly all arenas of life. Such conduct is prompted by personal characteristics like egoism, arrogance, ambitiousness, enlarged self-worth, insecurity, delayed maturity, or tribal loyalty. Dedication to the discipline of Philosophy is sometimes contaminated by pettiness and resentment, of which I'll now give six examples, drawn mainly from the Empiricist tradition. These will also help provide background for later discussion.

> A. "Mr. Hobbes was wont to say that had Des Cartes kept himself wholly to Geometrie . . . he had been the best Geometer in the world but that his head did not lye for Philosophy."[6]

Thomas Hobbes was a contemporary of Descartes, perhaps encountered him in Paris, and certainly was very familiar with his philosophy.[7] Before Descartes published his *Meditations* (1641), a set of scholars was chosen to offer critiques of his arguments, and these were published together with Descartes' text and his own replies. Hobbes was one of the critics. Although better known for the political philosophy set forth in his masterwork, *Leviathan* (1651), Hobbes shared with Descartes an interest in Physics and the conviction that the human body is a highly complicated machine whose operations and interactions with its environment are to be understood in terms of physical laws. The first chapters of the *Leviathan* expound his mechanistic conception of human thought and perception, which Hobbes had developed in Paris. Descartes' adherence to a mechanistic view of nature stopped, however, at the perimeter of the human mind. In Descartes' doctrine, the mind is an immaterial substance whose own actions and whose contents (ideas) are similarly immaterial, and the mind itself accordingly is capable of existence independent of the body. Hobbes advocated a fully materialistic account of the human mind, its nature and its actions. He even classified ideas as physical motions, a pre-echo of later views in neurophysiology and the philosophy of mind. The metaphysical positions of Descartes and Hobbes thus overlapped in one area but occupied starkly different terrains in another. There was no meeting of minds on the question of the mind, as their obdurate exchange in the *Meditations* vividly shows.

> B. "To be ingenuous, I must own it to be my opinion, that Locke was betrayed into this question [whether any ideas are innate] by the schoolmen, who, making use of undefined terms, draw out their disputes to a tedious length, without ever touching the point in question. A like ambiguity and circumlocution seem to run through that philosopher's reasonings on this as well as most other subjects."

David Hume made these comments in a long footnote near the beginning of his first *Enquiry*.[8] The nature of an idea was pivotal in both Locke's and Hume's accounts of human knowledge. Hume considered ideas to be copies of what he called "perceptions" or "impressions" which, roughly, are the contents of anyone's immediate experience, for example an individual color being seen, or a feeling like that of anger. Locke treated ideas as the content of events within the mind produced by the body's interactions with other material objects. In this respect Locke's view about ideas coincided with Descartes', and he was similarly inclined towards the Cartesian view of the mind as an immaterial something. Hume rejected the very concept of substance, both material and immaterial, which had prevailed in many metaphysical systems. His condemnation of Locke was thus double-barreled. Not only was Locke a deficient Empiricist, his doctrine preserved and left unanalyzed central assumptions of traditional metaphysics that have no place in an Empiricism guided exclusively by the contents of experience, which Hume considered his own doctrine to be. Condemnations of scholastic philosophy—"the philosophy of the schools", the metaphysical inheritance from the medieval universities—are frequently encountered not only in Hume's writings but also in those of Descartes, Hobbes, Locke and Berkeley. Whatever their own disagreements with each other on matters of doctrine, the five were of one mind in their disdain for the schoolmen. That Hume should banish Locke himself to that group was a cruel insult.

> C. " . . . these *Prolegommena* may persuade [the reader] that [my own contribution to metaphysics] is a perfectly new science, of which no one has ever even thought, the very idea of which was unknown, and for which nothing hitherto accomplished can be of the smallest use, except it be the suggestion of Hume's doubts [whether metaphysics itself is possible]. Yet even he did not suspect such a formal science, but ran his ship ashore, for safety's sake, landing on skepticism, there to let it lie and rot . . . ."[9]

The plug for his own book, the self-praise, the image of Hume's philosophy as a derelict vessel—all point to Immanuel Kant as the author. Kant himself was not a recovering skeptic. He was, as he characterizes it, a slumbering metaphysician confident in his dogmatism until awakened by Hume's attack on the very possibility of metaphysics. Rehabilitating metaphysics as a genuine science became Kant's central project. Hume regarded metaphysics as no more than a remnant of traditional thought now superseded by modern science. Kant was forced by Hume's analysis of the relation of cause and effect to agree that traditional metaphysics (including the doctrines of Descartes and Locke) had mislocated this relation in a world external to the mind and independent of it, imbuing that relation along and hence also the laws of physics with the force of logical necessity. In Hume's analysis, the *force* of the causal relation is reduced to the status of a feeling, a more or less strong anticipation of regular occurrences directly proportional to the kind and quantity of experience. According to Hume, the mind as traditionally conceived plays only a subsidiary role in the management of experience. It transforms (copies) impressions into ideas that in turn are further organized by the mind's built-in laws of association. Instinct often protects more effectively than reason. One touch of a hot stove is enough for a child to steer clear of it in the future. Nature (embedded in instincts) was for Hume the great guide of life. While Kant had no quarrel with this claim, he was convinced that the mind or reason had far more to offer than Hume had noticed. According to Kant, the mind itself provides the structure of experience, and he held that mathematical truths reveal such a structure and point us to a field of knowledge never before noticed, let alone understood, which constitutes the true metaphysics. Hume had merely "struck a spark from which light might have been obtained", declares Kant.[10] He didn't probe the nature of mathematical knowledge. Instead, Hume had deferred to the deliverances of Nature and preoccupied himself with the results of experience. The discovery of the deeper involvement of the mind in all experience, and the restoration of metaphysics, awaited Kant. He was its savior, the one against the many. Such, in Kant's own eyes, was his extraordinary achievement. If only his contemporaries agreed, he groused.

> D. "It follows, then, that if Mr. Bradley means what he ought mean [*sic*] *both* by "Time is unreal" and by "Time exists," he is contradicting himself when he combines these two propositions. . . . But I feel a good deal of doubt as to whether, all the same, he is contradicting himself, because it does seem to me doubtful whether he means what he ought to mean by ["Time exists"]. The kind of thing which I imagine may be happening to him when he insists so strongly that Time *does* exist, *is a fact*, and *is*, is that, properly speaking, he is not attaching to these phrases any meaning whatever—*not*, therefore, that which they properly bear."[11]

These measured, respectful-seeming remarks come near the end of G. E. Moore's classic essay, "The Conception of Reality" (1917). His target was F. H. Bradley, the doyen of the school of British Idealism whose widely respected two-volume work, *Appearance and Reality*, was first published in 1893.[12] If it is a discomfort for any philosopher to be classified or (worse) treated as passé, it is devastating to be accused of, or (worse) caught in, a logical contradiction. A contradiction is not merely a false statement but *necessarily* false: the conjoined statements cannot *both* be true, and the denial of either statement is logically equivalent to the other. Escape from a contradiction is possible only by rejecting one of the statements and thus accepting the other, but the damage has already been done to a philosopher in the trap, which is what Moore had patiently constructed for Bradley in his essay. What does it mean to claim that time is not real? That's not hard to answer for a British Idealist like Bradley who spells the word "time" "with a capital 'T'".[13] Bradley's goal in metaphysics was to depict the essential properties of reality, what he called the Absolute. Space and time do not qualify the Absolute. Rather, they are features of what Bradley calls appearances, which are relative in nature, transient, and an unreliable source of genuine knowledge. The Absolute is not a super-appearance; it transcends all appearances. But Moore refused to see things the Idealists' way. "Of course," he writes, "Time, with a big T, seems to be a highly abstract kind of entity, and to define *exactly* what can be meant . . . does seem to offer difficulties. But if you try to translate the proposition into the concrete . . . and think what it really comes to, you at once begin thinking of a number of different *kinds* of propositions, all of which plainly must be untrue, if Time is unreal".[14] There would be no past, he says, nor present ror future. Nothing happens before or after anything else. Nothing is happening now. Moore's move against Bradley is captured in the word he uses, "translate". He allows no other sense in which Bradley's claim that time is unreal would be true of the Absolute, though not of appearances. Translated in the way Moore wants, the denial that temporal facts exist is absurd; but to concede—as Bradley concedes—that temporal facts involving appearances do exist is an even greater absurdity because it produces a contradiction. Bradley's capital T is a mere ornament as far as Moore is concerned, and with all respect nevertheless deserves to be mocked. Moore's method includes a *coup de grace*. Professing to doubt whether Bradley has contradicted himself, he offers an alternative, namely, that Bradley attaches no meaning at all to his claim that "Time *does* exist, *is a fact*, and *is*". This alternative indeed removes the pressure of self-contradiction, though at the cost of endorsing nonsense.

E. "Wittgenstein respected Moore's honesty and seriousness, and once he said that Moore was 'deep'. At the same time talks with Moore almost always depressed him, because Moore was so 'child-like'. Wittgenstein once remarked that what Moore primarily did, as a philosopher, was to 'destroy premature solutions' of philosophical problems . . . . But he added that he did not believe that Moore would *recognize* a *correct* solution if he were presented with one." [15]

Moore's determination to defend common sense places him in a tradition of philosophers that includes both skeptics and non-skeptics. Well before Bradley's time, Hume had his own common sense critics. Perhaps surprisingly, Kant defended him against some Scottish champions of common sense, although Kant's purpose was not to support Hume's doctrines but to challenge the critics' credentials: "To appeal to common sense . . . this is one of the subtle discoveries of modern times, by means of which the most superficial ranter can safely enter the lists with the most thorough thinker and hold his own. . . . it is but an appeal to the opinion of the multitude." [16] Ludwig Wittgenstein did not consider Moore to be a ranter, and clearly he had no intention of defending Bradley. Wittgenstein's remarks make Moore a target not of rebuttal but of condescension. Despite admiring Moore for defending common sense, Wittgenstein regarded him as an under-laborer in the whole enterprise. This was an unfair judgment. For several decades Moore had undertaken a quite different strategy, which was to confront the British Idealist establishment, as his treatment of Bradley shows. [17] Moore defended common sense against Idealism by seeking to expose the weakness and confusion in its arguments and its air of metaphysical pretension. Wittgenstein's own defense of common sense had a different origin. Starting in the mid-1930s, he attacked the formal analysis of language and the systematic revision of common sense beliefs which had originated in the work of Frege and Russell and indeed was further developed in his own previous writings. [18] Ironically, Wittgenstein criticized Frege and Russell too in his earlier work, not in defense of common sense, but on account of their alleged errors of procedure and failure to recognize the depths which a rigorous logical analysis of language must reach. The earlier Wittgenstein believed he had reached those depths in his work, known as the *Tractatus*, which aspired to portray the essence of language from the standpoint of formal logic. [19] The later Wittgenstein believed that the earlier Wittgenstein was mistaken in that belief for the simple reason that there are no depths to plumb. The very attempt to purify language, he came to believe, destroys what language is supposed to be. It leaves the two most important things, how words mean and how language works, outside the picture. Wittgenstein thus presents an interesting specimen of contrariety in philosophy. He opposed himself. His later writings take the form of imagined conversations with anyone still captively committed to the systematic analysis of language, and if Wittgenstein himself was no longer a captive he knew perhaps more than any of his contemporaries what it is to be held fast by that commitment. Wittgenstein was never free of the need to be free of it, and I think he believed that Moore had never even struggled to be free. Wittgenstein was partly right. Moore's own essay, "A Defense of Common Sense", pulls in two different directions.[20] After confirming a long list of incontestable common sense truths, Moore then turned to another set of 'truths' about the so-called sense-data which various philosophers (including Frege and Russell) had identified in ordinary perception. He wanted to know how the sense-data one experiences of one's own hand are related to that hand. Are the sense-data identical to it? Are they part of the hand's surface? Are they related to it in some other way? It was typical of Moore to pursue these questions patiently, often ponderously, but it was not a child-like method. For the later Wittgenstein, however, such questions are an unwelcome intrusion on the self-governing territory of common sense.

> F. "[Thomas]Nagel's academic golden years are less peaceful than he might have wished. His latest book, *Mind and Cosmos* (Oxford University Press, 2012), has been greeted by a storm of rebuttals, ripostes, and pure snark. 'The shoddy reasoning of a once-great thinker,' Steven Pinker tweeted. The Weekly Standard quoted the philosopher Daniel Dennett calling Nagel a member of a 'retrograde gang' whose work 'isn't worth anything—it's cute and it's clever and it's not worth a damn.'"[21]

Scorn of this sort has a pedigree. During Hume's lifetime, the retrograde gang were leaders of the religious establishment who denounced his work, whom he called zealots. Against them Hume proposed a simple test for making space on library shelves. Books of "divinity or school metaphysics", he declared, make no contribution to areas of formal investigation such as mathematics; nor do they contain information of value to empirical science. Such books, then, should be consigned to the flames, for they contain "nothing but sophistry and illusion".[22] Hume was not the first to recommend book burning, and notorious groups since his time have practiced it. He was a liberal thinker rather than a political activist, however, who meant his words to have symbolic force, to make an ideological statement. The gauntlet he threw down, however, had the weight of an axe. The proper application of reason in Hume's eyes was to "matters of common life". Accordingly, natural science, which for him encompassed chemistry, physics, medicine, psychology, political theory—in short, knowledge "methodized and corrected" according to scientific standards—pass the test. Theology and traditional metaphysics with their interminable controversies fail the test; they are cut away and left to drift into the past as artifacts of superstitious belief. Philosophy thus becomes the handmaid of science. The problems deserving philosophical investigation are based on the phenomena and facts of empirical research. What Hume envisioned has come to be known as naturalized philosophy. Daniel Dennett is a prominent and creative advocate of this view who has reshaped our understanding of philosophical problems from a scientific standpoint.[23] In Dennett's hands, the aims and results of science regarding especially the workings of the brain, viewed as an instrument for gathering and processing data, have been methodized and corrected in a way that Hume would likely have commended, though far beyond any conception he likely ever had about how science would develop. Naturalized philosophy engenders confidence about making progress in comprehending the nature of mind and the physical realm it inhabits. The image of Philosophy's new direction is that of a line of accumulating solutions instead of an expanding circle of controversies of the kind that both Hume and Kant disdained, except that now even Kant's doctrines have been relegated to that circle.

Since consciousness is a critical aspect of the brain's responses, naturalized philosophy's stance is predictable: consciousness can be satisfactorily explained. Can it? Assume for a moment that the brain's activity can be completely mapped when someone sees a blue triangle on a pale green background. During the same moments when the person is concentrating on the triangle, events are occurring somewhere in the subject's neurophysical field that are pertinently involved in this state of awareness. However, a gadfly asks whether the mapping captures the whole phenomenon of consciousness in its net, since nothing resembling colors, triangular images or awareness is evident in the brain's physical field. There seems to be as much difference as between pain and a pulled tendon. Does the residue of difference cash out in appropriately scientific terms? If not, can the residue be safely ignored? From the standpoint of naturalized philosophy, the gadfly's challenges seem no more than remnant worries betraying a reluctance to accept natural science as the measure of all things. If they are mere worries, then that is a psychological condition easy enough to manage; and if superstitions about the mind influence the gadfly's questions, then that is a cultural phenomenon that will eventually disappear, like primitive medical beliefs concerning evil spirits in an aching toe. But such a response has a suggestion of the *ad hominem* to it, not to mention a touch of the fallacy of begging the question, if the supremacy of naturalized philosophy is assumed.

Thomas Nagel has been such a gadfly. His challenge is that science and naturalized philosophy cannot furnish a satisfactory description of consciousness. If Nagel is a skeptic on this subject then his skepticism differs greatly from Hume's. Nagel doubts where Hume did not. His doubt concerns the putative completeness of naturalized philosophy, not the authenticity of the data it associates with consciousness. Ironically, the zealots in this case are Hume's followers.

The ostracism of Nagel, though an extreme case of philosophical contrariety, illustrates a recurrent pattern in the history of Philosophy. In all the cases I've described, the accused is a very good philosopher. So also is his accuser. The dissent is palpable, whatever its form, as shown by Hobbes for Descartes, Hume for Locke, Kant for Hume, Moore for Bradley, Wittgenstein for Moore, or indeed the later Wittgenstein for the early Wittgenstein. Even Aristotle's nobly expressed opposition to Plato reveals what seems to be an irreconcilable difference. But my concern is not with the psychology of philosophers, their twitterings, or their pathology. It is with the nature of this difference. I believe that the difference originates not in the depths of metaphysics but at the familiar surface of natural language. I will sketch my defense of this claim.

III. RADICAL DUALISM

G. E. Moore, defender of common sense, once declared: "It seems to me very curious that language . . . should have grown up just as if it were expressly designed to mislead philosophers; and I do not know why it should have. Yet, it seems to me there is no doubt that in ever so many instances it has."[24]

I think that Moore has spoken a significant truth, even though he had only Idealists like Bradley in mind. Before language ever misleads philosophers, it leads *all* of us. Not only have we grown up with language, it permeates us. Language is the ancestor of text-based social media. Pointing to objects may come first in our lives but soon takes a back seat to naming. Nearly everything gets a word or phrase by which to pick it out, enabling us to connect with it: the people we see or hear and the opinions they express; tastes, headaches and emotions, past events and plans for the future; and when there isn't a name we invent one or pull in stock-words like "this" or "that thing" to do the job. Names point outwards from us. The items we experience become objects because language has provided us a means of reaching out and seemingly grasping them. "I", "mine", "you", "yours" have a privileged role. We couldn't do without such words in order to advance our interests, and to mark off our space from the spaces of others, by pointing to ourselves.

These facts are obvious enough, as is the fact that philosophers have been fascinated by the nature of names since Greek times. What's to mislead in all this? The innate human tendency to point-and-name has encouraged philosophers to identify new objects not previously revealed to the world, such as *form, substance, self, power, primary quality, idea, mind, animal spirits, corpuscles, consciousness*. It's no accident that some of these words belong exclusively to the vocabulary of early science. Metaphysics and science were joined at the hip in the 17th Century. Well before Hume placed the natural sciences on a pedestal, philosophers had modeled their work on science and mathematics, whether in terms of method, or content, or both method and content. Locke, for instance, adapted Robert Boyle's analysis of perception to emphasize a difference between the basic properties of matter (primary qualities) and their mental effects (so-called ideas of secondary qualities). But he made the word "consciousness" serve a special purpose. Since Locke was comfortable with the Cartesian distinction between mind and matter, he needed to identify a person with something other than the living physical body which others take to be that person. Yet he was prevented from classifying persons as *substances*, since he considered a substance of any sort—whether material or immaterial—to be a "something we know not what". So his undeveloped conclusion was to have consciousness depend on substance (or whichever sort) and let *consciousness* do the lifting when it comes to identifying persons.

Locke thereby gave a name to a cognitive detail which was implicit in traditional metaphysics. In the long tradition of European philosophy that preceded Hume, ideas were cognate with the process of thinking and the mind that thinks. The mind was present by virtue of the ideas that bring us objects, that is, the objects which are the very content of these ideas. If *self* and *substance* are less accessible than these contents, philosophers from Descartes through Berkeley never questioned whether such objects exist in some form and provide the basis of things more directly known. Berkeley compensated for the elimination of material substance by assigning to immaterial substance (individual minds and the mind of God) all the ideas associated with a world of supposedly material things commonly believed to exist independently. Rather, he argued, they all depend for their existence on minds. Hume adapted Berkeley's analysis by eliminating even immaterial substance. Since we have *no impression* of either kind of substance, Hume reasoned, we can have literally *no idea* of them, and since we have no impression of self or person, it follows that we have no such idea.

Nevertheless, a distinct metaphysical tradition after Hume's day held steadfast to the tenet that ideas and minds comprise the template of reality. The tradition includes Bradley's Idealism (which Moore accused of harboring contradictions), but its genetic line extends through Kant (the dogmatic slumberer roused by Hume) to Berkeley, both of whose doctrines sought to accommodate the impersonal objectivity demanded by a scientific perspective. These two philosophers stationed the observer and observation—the world from the viewpoint of the individual—at the center of their accounts of knowledge, including scientific knowledge. I group this tradition's various doctrines under the ontologically neutral heading, endocentric. The contrasting approach places itself beyond individual observers, that is, outside the standpoint of any observer other than an omniscient eye, which is the preferred standpoint of science in general and of naturalized philosophy in particular, whose focus is on objects and processes. I will refer to this standpoint as exocentric.[25] That was certainly Hume's chosen position. It seems also to have been where Hobbes located himself. If one looks for consciousness in the exocentric framework, its provisional location is the brain and the various connections whereby the brain influences the body, and its provisional content consists of complex circuits in the brain, neural pathways and sensory input-output functions. The final form of this account, or at least one far more complete than those at present, will have explained the nature of consciousness in such terms. Naturalized philosophy considers this a principal goal.

For all the impressive results of collaborative research supporting this goal, I regard the goal itself as an illusion resting on the mistaken assumption that the word "consciousness" stands for a hidden object or complex process. However elusive, like the Higgs boson, consciousness is considered within the exocentric framework to be a searchable entity, far more complicated than heat lightening, but similarly a complex, observable and quantifiable natural phenomenon. But I contend that consciousness is indeed elusive exactly because it is *not* an observable object. The exocentric framework removes from the objects it observes the fundamental characteristic that makes them contents of knowledge: specifically, of being observed. Objects without implicit reference to experience are objects detached from knowledge. When observation is rendered transparent and the contents of knowledge are converted into objects, the very possibility of understanding consciousness as other than an object has been lost. The concept of consciousness within the exocentric framework is conceptually anemic compared with what long prevailed in the endocentric tradition. In the systems of Descartes, Locke and Berkeley, consciousness of content was built into the very meaning of the word "idea". It was also part of what they meant by specific mental acts like perceiving, imagining and remembering. Kant and some of his Continental predecessors called such contents "phenomena", Bradley's choice was "appearances", while several generations of British philosophers beginning with Mill preferred words like "sensibilia", "sense-data" and "percepts". My wish is not to venerate this tradition but merely to emphasize its acceptance that consciousness of content—whatever the preferred words—is the unavoidable starting point for understanding the nature of knowledge from elementary sensations to scientific constructs.

The difficulty common to both frameworks, however, is that we are constrained by the inexorable tendency of language to point and name. Endocentric philosophers are no less guilty than exocentric ones. Ideas have been treated ambiguously as *both* contents of experience *and* independent constituents of the world. Descartes did so, Locke even more so. Berkeley avoided that particular difficulty by making all such objects immaterial, just as Kant did by treating the world we experience as phenomenal. Yet, by yielding to the unwritten convention of naming, and thus of converting the phenomenon of awareness into an object, or the property of some object, all of these philosophers drew our attention away from the presence of consciousness, even when discussing mental acts such as doubting, willing, imagining, etc., which naturally involve consciousness.[26] For they treated mental acts and cognitive relations as objects. How ironic, then, that exocentric philosophers should now redirect our attention to the complex and pervasive role of consciousness, only to reclassify it as an object capable of being observed and measured. On both sides, however, consciousness is a pseudo-object. There is no object to refer to and describe—which is not to deny its existence, except as an object. Any mystery of consciousness is of our own making. And therefore nothing is hidden, needing to be dislodged. Perhaps the philosophical discovery is that the pursuit of consciousness brings us close to the limits of language itself.

What can be said, then, of a something which, so far as names go, is more like a nothing? And what can be said about the roots of philosophical contrariety when the thickets and brambles have been cleared away or simply ignored? I think that the opposition between exocentrists and endocentrists cannot be construed as a matter of ultimate metaphysical commitment comparable to decisions regarding religion, where one responds to an inner compulsion to believe or disbelieve, whether in God or Nature, and looks upon anyone taking the opposite view with some degree of incomprehension, pity, or contempt. For in the case of commitment to either religion or science, both accounts in the eyes of their believers are complete, each side convinced, though on different grounds, of its efficacy to include, explain or explain away, what the other side professes. There is symmetry. However, exocentrism and endocentrism in philosophy differ in regard to completeness itself, which entails asymmetry. Endocentrists welcome every advance of scientific understanding but find scientific philosophy lacking in its willingness to allow for the presence of consciousness in the very concept of human knowledge. In their eyes, naturalized philosophy has exchanged metaphysics for science. These opponents—and there will always be opposition as long as there are human genes, and as long as there are philosophers—prefer instead a metaphysics of science.

NOTES

1. Aristotle, *Nicomachean Ethics* (*trans*. Ross), Book I, Chapter 6.

2. Thomas Hobbes, *Leviathan*, Chapter XIII. Hobbes' identifies "competition, diffidence and glory" as the principal sources of quarrel among men in the state of nature. Physical display found in some non-human species (though not in others) appears to match glory but opportunism seems to pervade all such species.

3. Aristotle, *Politics*, Bk. I, Chapter 2. "... it is evident that the state is a creation of nature, and that man is by nature a political animal."

4. *Second Treatise of Government*, Chapter 2.

5. *Leviathan*, Chapter XIII.

6. John Aubrey, "*Aubrey's Brief Lives*, pp. 94-95. Aubrey reports this remark in his "brief life" of Descartes. Of Descartes himself Aubrey writes: "The Societie of Jesus glorie in that theyr order had the educating of him." (p. 94)

7. Hobbes was six years older than Descartes and outlived him by more than a quarter-century. Their dates: 1588-1679; 1596-1651. He is the author of the third set of objections published in Descartes' *Meditations*.

8. David Hume, *An Enquiry Concerning Human Understanding*, II, fn. 10. Locke's dates: 1634-1701; Hume's: 1711-1776.

9. Immanuel Kant, *Prolegommena to any Future Metaphysics* (*tr.* James W. Ellington), Preface.

10. *ibid.*

11. G. E. Moore, "The Conception of Reality", *Philosophical Studies*, p. 218.

12. Bradley's dates: 1846-1924; Moore's: 1873-1958.

13. "The Conception of Reality", pp. 209, 211.

14. *ibid.*, p. 209.

15. Norman Malcolm, *Ludwig Wittgenstein – a Memoir*, p. 66.

16. Kant, *Prolegommena*, Preface.

17. Two well-known examples: "The Refutation of Idealism" (*Philosophical Studies*) and "A Defense of Common Sense" (*Philosophical Papers*).

18. Wittgenstein's dates: 1889-1951.

19. Ludwig Wittgenstein, *Tractatus Logico-Philosophicus*, first published in English in 1921.

20. "Proof of an External World" (*Philosophical Papers*) provides a further example.

21. Michael Chorost, "Where Nagel Went Wrong", *The Chronicle of Higher Education*, The Chronicle Review, 13 May 2013.

22. *Enquiry Concerning Human Understanding*, XII:iii.

23. In books such as *Brainstorms*, *The Intentional Stance*, and *Consciousness Explained*.

24. "The Conception of Reality", p. 217.

25. The contrastive words "endocentric" and "exocentric" are adapted from linguistics but given here a new and distinctly different use emphasizing *viewpoint* rather than *object*. The advantage of this use is that it avoids the ontological bifurcations associated with categories of objects: dualism vs. monism, and materialism vs. some version of phenomenalism. Berkeley's Idealism was not ontologically neutral. Neither was Kant's, who (for a time) preferred the term "Transcendental Idealism". Describing their metaphysics as endocentric is therefore not an endorsement of Idealism.

26. The word "presence" helps to deflect focus on "consciousness" as a name.

Who Takes Whom to Tango

UN Neoliberal Peacebuilding in Sierra Leone

Darya Pushkina and Philippe Ch.-A. Guillot
with Susanna An

ABSTRACT

This paper aims to engender a re-imagination of international relationships, particularly those created and sustained by United Nations peacekeeping missions. By investigating the dominant methods of neoliberal peacebuilding and how these govern international relationships, this paper hopes to bolster honest and comprehensive evaluation of the methods by which the international community pursues sustainable global peace. Our main policy suggestion is for the UN to avoid becoming a prey to the local elites and to include not only the local elite, but also "regular local people" and experts of the country and the larger region, in every step of the peace building process: from theory to execution.

INTRODUCTION

In recent decades, there has been a global decline in the number and magnitude of major interstate wars, however, intra-state wars remain a pressing issue. In an increasingly interdependent world, they pose a threat to international security and stability. Civil wars also threaten the most basic human rights. The decades following the end of the Cold War have witnessed the expansion of peacekeeping operations in intra-state wars: the previously simple monitored cease-fires that served as "buffer zones" have become multi-dimensional initiatives. Contemporary peacekeeping operations aid the transition from conflict to a sustainable peace, taking part in processes including, but not limited to political procedure; protection of civilians; assistance in the disarmament, demobilization and reintegration (DDR) of combatants; protection and promotion of human rights; and assistance in restoring the rule of law often in conjunction with economic reconstruction[1].

The broad scope and thus, broad impact, of UN peacekeeping missions make it all the more imperative that they be based upon discourse that provides an avenue of honest introspection. However, it can be argued that the concept of peacebuilding is built upon and sustained by a cycle of identity construction that Anthony Anghie terms "the discourse of difference" which sustains difference vis-a-vis language that distinguishes between the "superior" and the "inferior," between those giving aid and the ones receiving it. Such conceptualizations of identity were heavily influenced by the colonial encounter[2], transforming with the creation of each new benchmark, against which the "inferior" were measured. Following the end of the Cold War, this understanding of international relationships has partially manifested in what has been termed the neoliberal approach to peace albeit with positive intentions.

This paper will examine several dilemmas of neoliberal peacebuilding through an examination of UN efforts in Sierra Leone. In particular, it looks at how the United Nations Observer Mission in Sierra Leone (UNOMSIL) and the United Nations Assistance Mission in Sierra Leone (UNAMSIL) acted to help Sierra Leone in the face of a decade-long internationalized civil war, which resulted in 70,000 deaths, 20,000 wounded, 2,500,000 refugees or internally displaced persons, and 27,000 child soldiers.[3] This paper utilizes Sierra Leone as its case study because the missions there represented one of the UN's largest commitments to peacekeeping, peace enforcement and peacebuilding; they marked a turning point in the approach, scope, and influence of UN peacekeeping missions worldwide.

While the initial UN peacekeeping fiascos in Sierra Leone were to some extent, remedied, they reflect a discrepancy between the solutions prescribed by the international community (heavily influenced by the West) and the social, political, and economic realities in Sierra Leone and West Africa at that time. Although the dichotomous underpinnings of the neoliberal paradigm of peacekeeping efforts has regulated international relations since the end of the Cold War, peacebuilding in Sierra Leone granted the international community an opportunity to reflect on existing international relationships. The relative success of the UN peace operations in Sierra Leone after the establishment of UNAMSIL may be attributed to the international community's willingness to learn from the country and local inhabitants. Furthermore, UNAMSIL indicated a critical change in its ideological foundation – that is, the understanding that there is no universal solution to sustainable peace. Given the military, financial and organizational strength of UN operations in Sierra Leone, these later evoked a reconceptualization of international relationships.

Investigating the connection between neoliberalism and the international pursuit of sustainable global peace, this paper first takes a brief look at the development of international system, closing with an overview of the neoliberal paradigm that currently governs UN peacekeeping missions. This is followed by an examination of the origins of the conflict in Sierra Leone, paying close attention to the warring parties and ECOWAS. The paper then analyzes UN peacekeeping-peacebuilding efforts —UNOMSIL and UNAMSIL— in the country. The final two peacekeeping missions UNIOSIL and UNIPSIL are briefly described, though critical analysis is difficult to provide given their very recent nature. Lastly, the paper evaluates the outcomes of the peacebuilding efforts in Sierra Leone, arguing that UN efforts in Sierra Leone may be classified as a partial success. At the same time, it acknowledges that the UN misconception of Sierra Leone has contributed to the growth of the shadow-state and to a revival of paramount chiefs' power. Thus, we believe that it is the main shortcoming of the UN in Sierra Leone or, in other words, the UN became the prey of SL political animals.

THEORETICAL REMARKS

International law and emerging sovereignty doctrines have, from their inception, been influenced by the colonial encounter. They have also come to dictate international relationships, creating a gap between the West and the rest of the world. This gap was rationalized utilizing ideas of universalism, which took different forms: first emerging as naturalism in the sixteenth century, then positivism in the nineteenth century, and most recently, as pragmatism in the twentieth century. It created a universal standard, a Western standard, to which colonies were held. Based on this standard, differences between the colonizers and colonized were identified and systems were implemented to bridge the gap.[4] However, progressively sophisticated techniques identified further deficiencies, thus requiring continued assistance and oversight by the West. Anthony Anghie terms this endless and self-sustaining process, the dynamic of difference.

These "universal benchmarks" derived from changing definitions of sovereignty. Naturalism created a distinction based on cultural differences; Indians were non-sovereigns, while Europeans were sovereigns.[5] This provided just cause for colonialism, characterized by a civilizing mission. However, in the twentieth century, colonialism was increasingly condemned and eventually abolished. The colonies were designated semi-sovereign status by Western powers and in the process, a new goal was established: the achievement of sovereignty. At present neoliberalism contends that liberally constituted states (democracies with market economies) will be more peaceful in both domestic and international affairs than illiberal ones and thus, post-conflict peacebuilding efforts should incorporate liberal political and economic structures. Against these measurements, former colonies, the "semi-sovereigns," remain in pursuit of fully sovereign status. However, liberal peacebuilding in post-conflict societies does not always result in the democratic peace envisioned, thereby, debunking the legitimacy of the designation of colonies as "semi-sovereigns." They instead produce hybrid governing structures that fall short of both local and international expectations.[6] Unsurprisingly, the neoliberal paradigm has recently been criticized by a number of scholars and practitioners.[7]

According to the most critical perspective, current peacebuilding practices entrench its recipients in a system for which they are ill suited. This entrapment often results from peacebuilding advocates' lack of attention to the historical roots of the conflicts within which interventions occur. Still further, scholars point to the deeply ingrained understanding of international relationships as ones defined by opposition. Far from transcending the dialogue of difference, neoliberal peacebuilding efforts are founded on reincarnations of earlier theories of international law, thereby upholding the "dynamic of difference." Critical theorists contend that the system governing liberal peacekeeping projects was shaped by and grew out of the colonial encounter between European and non-European states, creating international institutions, particularly economic international institutions, that delay reversal of the effects of colonialism.

In response, advocates maintain that liberal peacebuilding, while not without faults, has ultimately contributed more positively than negatively to societies' post-conflict reconstruction. Recognizing that current liberal peacebuilding is in need of reform, it has been argued that its problems do not doom the project itself to failure.[8] In order to reform itself, neoliberal peacebuilding must make room for increased engagement with its recipients, or 'locals.'[9] This paper largely agrees with the latter position, that of the critical advocates of neo-liberal peacebuilding.

I. THE CONFLICT IN SIERRA LEONE

"La Sierra Leone, c'est le bordel, oui, le bordel au carré. On dit qu'un pays est le bordel au simple quand les bandits de grand chemin se partagent le pays comme au Liberia; mais quand, en plus des bandits des associations et des démocrates s'en mêlent, ça devient plus qu'au simple."[10]

Created as a British colony in 1785, Sierra Leone has been a haven for former African-American slaves now known as "creoles," a Western-educated elite, as well as the British naval base. Sierra Leone's hinterland consisted of several independent kingdoms (from which originate today's 149 paramount chiefs of the country); these passed under British indirect rule in 1896.

The British government in 1924 divided the country into Colony (Freetown and surrounding areas) and Protectorate (mostly inland territories), thus leading to increasing tension between these two areas in the country. Sierra Leone gained independence in 1961 as the result of the conference held with Britain in 1960. Several years of democratic government were followed by increasing authoritarian tendencies, three military coup d'etats and resulting one-party rule between 1968 and 1991.

In March 1991, Sierra Leone was invaded by members of the Revolutionary United Front (RUF) who were backed by Liberian warlord, Charles Taylor's National Patriotic Liberation Front. This was in response to the Freetown government's support of the Economic Community of West African States Cease-Fire Monitoring Group (ECOMOG) intervention in Liberia.[11] Violent conflict ensued for four years, until the Sierra Leone government and the rebels agreed to a peace plan. Another ECOMOG was established to facilitate its implementation. The UN intervened with peacekeeping missions from 1998 to 2005.

A 'Shadow State': Economic and Social Causes of the Civil War

The civil war was largely fomented by economic and social factors that stemmed from the neopatrimonial character of Sierra Leonean political culture. Neopatrimonial regimes exhibit four primary characteristics: i) clientelism based on privileged access to state resources, rationed by leaders following a strict political logic to gain and maintain political support, ii) blurring the distinction between public and private; iii) centralization of power; and iv) a hybrid structure within which informal mechanisms of political authority coexist with characteristics of a modern state[12] . Thus, those who are excluded from the governing regime and therefore, state resources, develop antagonism toward the political system. Attempts to bind society around issues beyond economic-corporate interests fail. Consequently, the ruling elite resorts to domination or annihilation of opponents in order to maintain power. Such a political system is characterized by high instability, with detrimental consequences for long-term development. Instead of relying on a set of rules to regulate the allocation of resources and conduct a peaceful settlement of grievances, Sierra Leoneans have a long history of employing violence and fear. The state historically has been viewed as a means to patronage, power, and personal wealth rather an entity with which a citizen may establish a viable social contract. A leader's personal agenda has often taken precedence over national development. It is within this context that attempts at economic liberalization took place.

Another influential aspect of the Sierra Leonean context is its diamond mines. As the country's primary source of income, this particular industry constitutes nearly seventy percent of exports. Given both the high value per unit of the gems and the relative ease with which they may be smuggled, controlling this resource has proven difficult for the state. During the colonial era, a monopoly was granted to the Sierra Leone Selection Trust (SLST). However, numerous clandestine prospectors, brokers and merchants created an illicit diamond market, resulting in corruption and revenue losses for the state. The Licensed Diamond Miners Scheme was set up, but illicit mining continued, making it almost impossible to ascertain diamonds' origins. Moreover, smuggling operations between Sierra Leone and Liberia increased, and the chiefs[13] of diamantiferous regions amassed greater wealth, simultaneously gaining influence with prominent politicians. Combined, these factors culminated in the emergence of a "shadow state", a fig-leaf government concealing a kleptocracy, under Siaka Stevens' rule[14]. Stevens nationalized SLST and reoriented diamond production toward his clientele, and ensured that local opponents involved in mining were either marginalized or joined the All People's Congress.[15]

During the 1970s and 1980s, faced with a declining economy and rapid population growth, Sierra Leone applied for aid from international financial institutions (IFIs). As was characteristic of the structural adjustment plans (SAPs) of the time, the accompanying policy provisions sought to instill macroeconomic stability and establish the foundations of a market economy, demanding free trade, deregulation, decreases to the state's role and size, and cuts to the welfare system. The result was currency speculation, inflation, and an economically wounded middle class. Privatization led to the emergence of monopolistic and oligopolistic markets, and increased the average cost of living. There was no "trickle-down" effect. Given the neopatrimonial characteristics of the regime, economic liberalization and privatization benefitted the elite and strengthened already-established systems of patronage. The late 1970s and 1980s witnessed a sharp fall in state revenue from diamonds and other exports, while many government officials and private companies benefitted from the informal economy. By 1985-86, domestic revenue collection had sunk to 18 percent of 1977-78 levels.[16]

The privatization of agricultural markets in the 1980s backfired, as they became increasingly inaccessible to government taxation, further limiting the already paltry taxable economy. Further exacerbating the situation, privileged private companies manipulated their political allies to avoid taxation. Smuggling rates also increased. Credit continued to flow into the country through the mid-1980s, but with little oversight from IFIs, the ruling elite remained effectively responsible for the distribution of funds. The structural adjustment did little to turn the economy around and instead reinforced the importance of clientelist networks. As the diamond industry fell further into private hands, again, only those with political allies reaped the benefits.[17]

While in part, the "greed factor" drove the conflict,[18] the grievance aspect must also be considered. According to UNDP and several authors, the marginalization of the country's youth is directly linked with the onset of conflict. The socioeconomic ramifications of neoliberal reforms coupled with the severe reduction in public spending stipulated by SAPs sharply slashed employment opportunities. Furthermore, fiscal austerity significantly reduced the availability of social welfare. Individuals are statistically more likely to join a rebellion if they are economically deprived, marginalized from decision-making, and alienated from mainstream political processes[19]. Sierra Leonean youth faced all three at the outbreak of the conflict. These negative socioeconomic consequences of neoliberal reforms for the youth population contributed significantly to the outbreak of violence.

Overall, the conflict in Sierra Leone may be attributed to a multiplicity of factors. Ethnic and religious diversity and regional political divisions do not seem to have played a causal role. Instead, it was instigated and perpetuated by the (mis)management of the diamond sector, neopatrimonial political culture and "shadow state," troubled economy, alienation of youth, and personal interests of the warring parties.

The Warring Parties

There were several parties to the conflict, each with its own social, economic and political motives. Oftentimes, the state was indistinguishable from or collaborated with the rebels.[20]

The RUF was the main oppositional force. It was created by a former British Army corporal, Foday Sankoh. Despite its name, the RUF was far from being a unitary actor[21], but was rather a conglomerate of 'maverick groups of jobless youth, criminals, [and] defected soldiers like the so-called West Side Boys and illegal diamond diggers like the so-called San San Boys'[22]. The RUF received training in Liberia and Libya and material support from Charles Taylor and Burkina Faso. Upon invading Sierra Leone, the RUF seized the most lucrative diamond fields, thus controlling $250 million in annual trade.

To counter the rebel threat, President Joseph Momoh more than quadrupled the army's strength, but was unable to finance this expansion. In May 1992, a group of junior Sierra Leone Army (SLA) officers who called themselves the National Provisional Ruling Council, conducted a coup d'état, and Captain Valentine Strasser assumed the presidency. Instead of centralizing military power, Strasser counted on local militias. Strasser also equipped his military front with private companies[23]. After former British Army Gurkhas proved ineffective, the South African company Executive Outcomes (EO) was brought in.[24] In return, the "contractors" were guaranteed $1.5 million a month in profits from diamond mines.[25] One scholar argues that "EO ran a substantially more cost-effective operation than the UN is able to do."[26] Though EO succeeded in stabilizing the situation, it simultaneously created a system of dependency, in which a continued state of war proved favorable to certain army contingents and foreign firms.[27]

In January 1996, the Chief of Defense Staff Brigadier-General Julius Maada Bio pushed Strasser out of power. Elections took place as planned in February 1996, and Ahmad Tejan Kabbah (SLPP) was elected President. However, in RUF-controlled areas, not a single ballot was cast. On 25 May 1997, disaffected members of the military[28] – later known as the Armed Forces Revolutionary Council (AFRC) – overthrew President Kabbah, who subsequently fled into exile in Guinea. Major Johnny Paul Koroma became the new head of state and invited the RUF to join its administration, cementing a relationship of convenience between soldiers and rebels. In response to the rise of the RUF/AFRC, citizens in various regions formed militias known as Civil Defence Forces (CDF) or *Kamajors,* organized loosely along tribal or ethnic lines, that backed President Kabbah. After the deposed President requested Nigerian military assistance, Nigerian troops intervened, but failed to oust the AFRC and the RUF.

The Economic Community of West African States (ECOWAS) and the Conflict

In February 1995, the UNSG appointed the Ethiopian diplomat Berhanu Dinka as special envoy to work in collaboration with ECOWAS and the Organization of African Unity (OAU; now known as the African Union) to negotiate a settlement to the conflict. ECOWAS had already sent ECOMOG to Liberia, even though ECOWAS had at that time neither the institutional structures nor the legal framework to do so[29], encroaching on the role of the Security Council by intervening in a domestic crisis[30] . At the request of the OAU, ECOWAS agreed to contribute 9,000 troops to reinstall the democratically elected Kabbah government. Within ten months, ECOMOG had succeeded in forcing the AFRC/RUF government from power and committed the belligerents to a six-month transition period for Kabbah's restoration[31].

ECOMOG intervention was only a partial success, since it departed from the basic tenets of peacekeeping: the behavior of its members to a certain extent fuelled the war (corruption, poor discipline, lack of *esprit de corps* and significant numbers of the officer corps were reportedly in Sierra Leone for personal profit[32]), and 'ECOMOG displayed a complete disregard for the principle of impartiality'[33]. Moreover, troops lacked appropriate equipment to undertake counterinsurgency operations, and there was no real coordination between national contingents. As a result, Nigerian troops often had to deploy alongside SLA units that included rebel elements or sympathizers who sabotaged operations.[34] However, given the Sierra Leonean government's instability and inability to contain or ameliorate the situation, ECOMOG's intervention might have been the only option at the time.

II. UNOMSIL AND UNAMSIL

UNSG Special Envoy Dinka assisted in negotiating the Abidjan peace agreement, which was eventually signed in November 1996. The UN was thus a moral guarantor of the treaty alongside the government of Côte d'Ivoire, the OAU and the Commonwealth[35]. Consequently, when President Kabbah was toppled, an arms and oil embargo was imposed by Security Council resolution 1132 (1997).

In July 1998, the Security Council established UNOMSIL, an observer mission intended to support the peace process and to supervise the DDR of the rebel fighters. UNOMSIL was to include 60 military observers, who in turn, were to be backed by 720 troops, but as the RUF refused such a deployment, only 40 unarmed observers were deployed[36]. Consequently, these blue berets had to be protected by ECOMOG soldiers.

UNOMSIL's mandate and capabilities were based on the assumption that local actors would observe the Abidjan peace process. However, this was not the case, and despite its efforts, UNOMSIL was unable to prevent the recurrence of fighting. In January 1999, UN personnel were evacuated from Freetown to Conakry, as rebel forces had captured the capital city. After ECOMOG recaptured Freetown, Special Representative Oleko launched a series of negotiations that ended with the Lomé Accord, an agreed ceasefire and a liberal power-sharing arrangement. At the request of the parties, the Security Council expanded UNOMSIL to 210 military observers, and, upon President Olusegun Obasanjo's announcement that Nigeria would be withdrawing its troops from ECOMOG, replaced UNOMSIL two months later with the more ambitious UNAMSIL operation.

UNAMSIL was required to actively provide security at all DDR sites, facilitate the free flow of people, goods, and humanitarian assistance along specific thoroughfares, and assist and coordinate the Sierra Leonean law enforcement agencies in security sector reforms.[37] Protection of civilians "under imminent threat of physical violence" was included in UNAMSIL's mandate by Resolution 1270.

The Lomé Accord deferred to the Abidjan agreement, because in 1996 the government had the upper hand and so was able to force the RUF to sign. However, in 1999, the government had to accept power-sharing with the rebels and the status of vice president for Sankoh[38], who was additionally appointed as the head of a commission to manage diamond resources, 'a position he used for continued arms acquisitions,'[39] and AFRC leader Koroma was appointed as chairman for the Commission for the Consolidation of Peace[40] . As a result, the Lomé Accord has been described as "'an appeasement of the RUF,'"[41] a "monumental fiasco," and "'one of the most absurd peace accords ever negotiated."[42] Peace was disconnected from justice: Sierra Leone offered RUF members an amnesty for all crimes, though the UN entered a reservation in cases of crimes against humanity, acts of genocide, war crimes and other grave violations of human rights[43] . Still, this deal did not bring peace to the country.

In order to avoid a security vacuum during the UNAMSIL build-up, four ECOMOG battalions from Ghana, Guinea and Nigeria were "re-hatted" as blue helmets[44] . President Obasanjo eventually allowed 3,500 soldiers to stay in Sierra Leone. The slow deployment of UN troops was exploited by the RUF. UNAMSIL peacekeepers were seen by rebel forces as a hostile presence jeopardizing their livelihood (pillage and illicit diamond mining). In April and May 2000, the RUF was detaining as hostages nearly 500 peacekeepers. Eventually, a British intervention ended this crisis.[45] It should be noted that UNAMSIL experienced internal problems at the time as UN assessment mission in June 2000 found out, including serious management problems, a lack of common understanding of the mandate and the rules of engagement, tensions between its military and political leadership.[46] In a leaked confidential report by the UNAMSIL Force commander General Vijay Jetley, he accused senior Nigerian military and political officials of sabotaging the UN operation by colluding with the RUF in order to benefit from the illicit diamond trade, causing a diplomatic crisis[47] . Nigerians refused to be placed under Jetley's command, which resulted in withdrawal of the 3,000 Indian contingent. The Jordanian contingent followed citing the refusal of the UK forces to be placed under UN command as the reason for their departure.[48] The UK forces were allowed albeit with the agreement of the UNSC to be on its own. This last event illustrates rather well how unequal standards when applied to the so-called developed and so-called developing world can result in the lack of cooperation and eventually detriment of the UN operations. To avoid mission's failure, ECOWAS leaders agreed to deploy a 3,000-strong U.S.-trained rapid reaction force composed of Nigerian, Ghanian, and Senegalese troops to UNAMSIL.[49]

In November, the Abuja ceasefire agreement was signed, demanding that the RUF return all weapons and equipment taken from UNAMSIL. In May 2001, the Abuja Ceasefire Review agreement was adopted, leading to the implementation of DDR by the RUF and the CDF. In a significant step towards international regulation of so called 'blood diamonds', Security Council resolution 1306 (2000) prohibited the global importation of rough diamonds from Sierra Leone until a certification scheme was put in place, while resolution 1343 (2001) imposed sanctions on Liberia's diamond exports[50].

III. UNAMSIL AT EXIT: FINAL SUCCESS?

UNAMSIL was the first UN operation to explicitly include the term "peacebuilding" in its mandate[51]. UNAMSIL had to provide an 'enhanced management role'[52] in support of the government of Sierra Leone, while the latter and the UN agreed to establish a special court alongside the Truth and Reconciliation Commission which started functioning in 2002.[53] This same year, UNAMSIL worked in close cooperation with the UN Country Team in the preparation of the UN Development Assistance Framework for Sierra Leone.[54]

Under the command of Kenyan Lieutenant General Daniel Opande, UNAM-SIL turned into a robust peacekeeping operation. It followed a carrot-and-stick approach, confronting potential military spoilers whilst also engaging them in political negotiations[55]. By January 2001, UNAMSIL had disarmed all the warring factions. For a year and a half, the blue helmets provided a secure environment, allowing elections to be held in May 2002, but also permitting the international presence to become "the principal source of patronage."[56]

Several key strengths of UNAMSIL have been identified. Ambassador John Hirsch stresses SRSG Oluyemi Adeniji's contributions after the hostage crisis, including a two-track strategy linking the RUF's participation in a DDR process with an opportunity for them to take part in the upcoming election, strong leadership from the permanent members and the role of British and U.S. forces in disarmament[57]. Adebajo and Keen highlight the role of Guinean armed forces in fighting the RUF, international efforts to regulate the diamond trade and to obstruct Liberian President Taylor's attempts to support the RUF, greater levels of funding and troops given to UNAMSIL after its various crises, as well as the adoption of a clearer enforcement mandate, and Sankoh's replacement by Isa Sesay as the RUF leader.[58]

A *Refugees International* survey emphasizes the alignment of military force with stability programmes that helped foster positive alternatives to conflict, such as DDR, and long-term commitment to peacebuilding that allowed elements of good governance, such as democratic elections, a legal system, and credible police and military forces to be put into place[59]. Jean Krasno points out that UNAMSIL's community development work[60] and infrastructural work[61] enabled Sierra Leoneans to be productive and return to normal lives.[62] The DDR programme was bolstered by the presence of UN forces, which created a sense of security, thus increasing combatants' willingness to turn in their weapons. The reorientation and overhauling of the DDR programme in 2001 played a large role in its progress. At the same time, some scholars question its administrative efficiency. They point out the "unpredictable delays in the payment of cash allowances or delivery of toolboxes, short training period and little or no support provided for finding or creating employment."[63] The disarmament and demobilization goals of the programme were largely achieved with the help of the National Committee for DDR, which placed consistent pressure on RUF and AFRC leadership.

Reintegration was also hampered by poor coordination, inefficient planning, and lack of interministerial cooperation and public outreach as well as by an incomplete understanding of the needs of Sierra Leonean communities.

This is perhaps at least partially due to the application of the general neo-liberal peacebuilding approach rather than engaging serious teams to investigate the deep conflict causes. The number of ex-combatants awaiting placement in reintegration programmes was reduced slowly. When the reintegration programme was officially closed on 31 March 2004, approximately 2,800 eligible ex-combatants still awaited placement and were instead given one-time assistance packages the following June. Furthermore, assistance programmes lacked a broad outlook, generally focusing on male ex-combatants and material needs. There were limited measures for female ex-combatants and former war brides and few community sensitization programmes and psychological counseling centers[64]. The international community disproportionately focused on Freetown[65], neglecting the countryside where the conflict started, and international assistance could be criticized to have promoted somewhat "'illiberal version of civil society bearing questionable democratic credentials.'"[66] Moreover, the reconciliation process is not limited to elections or justice, and must engage all social strata. Neither the government nor the UN had sufficient financial or human resources to conduct widespread national dialogue.[67]

Existing analyses of UN efforts in Sierra Leone reach different conclusions. Page Fortna states that "'... many people, including government leaders, ex-RUF leaders, UNAMSIL staff, and members of civil society, emphasized that peace would not have been possible without the UN mission...'"[68] Berman and Labonte go further, pointing out that 'Sierra Leone...demonstrate[ed] not only what can go wrong but also what can go right in [UN] endeavors.'[69] UN Secretary General Ban Ki Moon has even stated that it was 'one of the world's most successful cases of post conflict recovery...in peacebuilding.[70] In contrast, Morjé-Howard cautions that 'mandate fulfillment does not necessarily equate with long-term, successful state building'[71]. Salih speaks critically of the international community's efforts: "'...the emphasis on democracy and civil liberties alone, while ignoring the social conditions, will continue to fuel the tension between the liberal peace and the socioeconomic conditions of the poor.'"[72]

Generally, UNAMSIL can be considered at least, a partial success[73]. However, success depends on how and by whom it is defined, and is further complicated by the multidimensional nature of peacekeeping missions.[74] Using criteria developed in previous studies of United Nations multidimensional peacekeeping operations,[75] UNAMSIL could be said to have been relatively successful in security sector reforms and elections monitoring as part of state rebuilding efforts despite a lack of interagency coordination, institutional rivalries with the European Union, and poor communication with non-governmental organizations that have harmed the civilian aspect of international aid.[76]

After UNAMSIL's mandate expired in 2005, the first Integrated Office (UNIOSIL) was established to address the roots of conflict, signaling the emergence of a new criterion for an appropriate mission exit. The essential objective of integrated missions became linking peacekeeping with peace-building structures to avoid a relapse into conflict.[77]

IV. UNIOSIL AND UNIPSIL

The establishment of the United Nations Integrated Office in Sierra Leone (UNIOSIL) in January 2006 marked the transition from peacekeeping to peacebuilding. While UNAMSIL operated with the longer-term goal of peace building in mind, its greatest concern had been that of halting conflict and between the warring parties and establishing the basic tools (i.e. security sector reforms, DDR, reintegration programs, support schema for elections) with which to maintain peace. UNIOSIL was tasked with assisting the Sierra Leonean government with addressing the root causes of conflict in greater depth and conjointly emphasized the strengthening of human rights and the rule of law in the country. UNIOSIL simultaneously signaled a broadening in scope: it was responsible for addressing regional issues that influenced the domestic happenings in Sierra Leone. These included "cross-border challenges such as the illicit movement of small arms, human trafficking and smuggling and illegal trade in natural resources, as well as coordinating with the Special Court for Sierra Leone"[78] and required greater cooperation with state institutions.UNIPSIL continued the work set out by UNIOSIL, combining both political and development activities. These included providing political support to national and local efforts for identifying and resolving tension and threats of potential conflict; monitoring and promoting human rights, democratic institutions and the rule of law; consolidating good governance reforms; supporting decentralization; closely coordinating with and supporting the work of the Peacebuilding Commission[79] and other project supported through the Peacebuilding fund; and emphasizing the important role of women in the prevention and resolution of conflicts and in peacebuilding.[80] While UNAMSIL's mandate certainly stated the need to cooperate with and assist the Government of Sierra Leone, UNIPSIL reflected an expanded understanding of the holistic nature of a successful peace building mission.[81] The mandate emphasizes the "need for closer cooperation" between a multiplicity of organizations including, but not limited to, "UNIPSIL, ECOWAS, the Mano River Union, International Partners and other United Nations missions in the region...local authorities and the population outside of Freetown...[and] local development initiatives with local authorities."[82] Further underlining this nuanced mindset, words such as "joint," "cohesion," "support," and "harmonization" may be found throughout the mandate. It also establishes joint regional field offices, joint outreach initiatives, and joint medical and security services. On March 5, 2014, UNIPSIL officially closed and transferred its duties to the UN Country Team. This final mission truly does seem to have been a culmination of lessons learned from earlier fumbles but the overall effectiveness of international efforts directed towards Sierra Leone's longer-term economic and social stability remains questionable.

V. LESSONS AND PROSPECTS

Security in the region remains challenging. The Sierra Leonean government is experiencing a financial crisis, which affects the capacity and the morale of the police and the army[83]. Additionally, British military trainers have stated that their efforts to professionalize the renovated army were not very effective[84] . Consequently, the army remains a potential threat, and a coup d'état cannot be ruled out, especially in the case of downsizing the personnel.[85]

UN state-building efforts in Sierra Leone may be considered a success from a neoliberal perspective if we focus mostly on elections as a sign of state-rebuilding. Following the SLPP victory in the UNAMSIL-assisted presidential and parliamentary elections of 2002, the APC won the UNIOSIL-supervised election in 2007, leading to "the country's first peaceful transfer of power from the ruling party to the opposition."[86] This was confirmed by the 2012 elections, in which President Ernst Bai Koroma was reelected. The electoral process was peaceful overall and was considered roughly free and fair by international observers. However, there were some indicators of political instability leading up to the 2012 election. In September of 2011, the Minister of Internal Affairs was attacked in the district of Kono, after which security and police fired weapons. That same month, yet another bout of political violence ensued with the attack of the SLPP presidential candidate, Julius Maada Bio and burnings of APC party buildings in response.[87] State-building measures that worked elsewhere would be difficult to fully utilize in Sierra Leone, as "behind the rational-legal façade of statehood, informal decision-making processes that are strongly determined by personal relations dominate national politics." Thus, "the centralizing desire to reconstruct the formal state may neglect or even undermine the local institutional initiatives,"[88] raising the question of whether informal institutions can be influenced by external actors[89]. One scholar argues "the model applied for reconstruction was not viable because it was premised on crucial misconceptions about the nature of the Sierra Leonean state and its ability to change and adapt to a Western model of statecraft."[90] This comment illustrates our original point that the current model of peacebuilding might not be fitting for all post-conflict situations, warranting a close examination of each situation for successful UN peacebuilding undertaking.

The *Paramount Chiefs Restoration Programme* was intended to decentralize administrative and fiscal policy to the district and local levels as a way to increase accountability of local elites. However, decentralization does not seem to be the best remedy, as chiefs at the local level have power over distribution of resources.[91] Moreover, rights-based and participatory approaches by NGOs neglected to account for the chiefs' influence. Customary land tenure issues ('a primary contribution' to war) were not properly addressed, leading to a kind of legal pluralism in which the fast development of informal 'legal fields' contrasted to the slow internationally sponsored law reform, to a forum shopping in dispute settlements (including humanitarian donors and NGOs)[92], and finally to an inequitable system which does not attract investment.[93] Drawbacks in anti-corruption policy and in diamond sector reform[94] tend also to attenuate the international efforts in peacebuilding.

The UN agenda for peacebuilding and state-building in Sierra Leone included economic development, whose debatable success has heavily influenced longer-term economic and social stability in the region. Up until 2002, the international community's principal focus was consolidating peace and security, and only afterwards the focus began to shift to addressing socioeconomic causes.

An emphasis on socioeconomic factors may be observed in some UN and IFI reports. The Secretary General's reports on Sierra Leone, published regularly from 2001 on, discuss economic developments, but focus on macroeconomic stability and growth while saying little regarding actual plans to tackle socioeconomic issues. The 2005-2007 *Poverty Reduction Strategy Paper's* (PRSP) two 'pillars' included promoting good governance, peace, security, and pro-poor sustainable growth, but more than half of the PRSP was left unfunded.[95] The 2008-2012 PRSP II also shows a move away from security consolidation towards socioeconomic issues, as seen through its two pillars, promoting inclusive growth and providing basic services for all.

The major role that the marginalization of Sierra Leone's youth played in igniting conflict has been recognized by both the country's government as well as by a number of UN and World Bank studies.[96] Both recognize the importance of youth employment in maintaining peace and promoting pro-poor growth. Several presently active World Bank loans such as the 2010 *Youth Employment Support* and 2007 *Vocational Training for Youths with Disabilities in Western Area and Kono Districts* specifically target youth. Even with these initiatives, not enough is being done to tackle youth unemployment. Macroeconomic imperatives appear to be overtaking social programs.[97] Under the IMF's PRGF program, macroeconomic stability is once again the main priority.[98] Job opportunities remain scarce, while spending on education has suffered and poverty and inequality remain high. As made apparent by the Ebola crisis, the downsized healthcare budget has also proven insufficient and fatal.

Furthermore, IMF reviews revealed "the government lacked sufficient fiscal space for its development and poverty reduction programs."[99] Budget cuts and reduced government spending limit the expansion of social services into war-affected areas. Primary school participation (net attendance ratio) from 2005-2010 for males was 62 percent, dropping to 31 for secondary school. Adult literacy rates in 2009 stood at 27 percent and at 40.9 percent in 2011[100] . Additionally, the 2004 *Human Rights Watch* report revealed that children exploitation continues and that former RUF child soldiers are wandering with neither home nor job.[101]

In February 2013, the Extractive Industries Transparency Initiative (EITI) decided to suspend Sierra Leone's bid for EITI membership due to discrepancies in the recording of revenue or payments by mining companies.[102] In order to increase transparency, Sierra Leone passed the freedom of information law in October 2013, which should bolster the country's recovering economy by inviting foreign capital and improving foreign relations.

According to the World Bank and Africa Development Bank, Sierra Leone's economy has grown by 21 percent in 2014 (the fastest growth in Sub-Saharan Africa) albeit it is important to recognize that the starting point was very low. The Sierra Leonean economy was expected to experience sustained growth, falling inflation, and improved fiscal and external positions. Unfortunately, the Ebola outbreak has put a strain on Sierra Leone's overall socio-political economy, resulting in 9,700 deaths, food shortages, and a depreciating currency despite increases in cost of living. Withdrawals of foreign investment and foreign human capital, mostly by mining companies further exacerbated the Sierra Leone economy. Moreover, the "iron ore price decline affected macro-financial stability and reversed the country's remarkable positivegrowth trajectory as economic growth declined from a buoyant 20.1% in 2013 to 4.6% in 2014 and thereafter contracted by 21.5% in 2015".[103]

The epidemic is now over, but conversation on reconstruction has begun and the breakout revealed holes in the country's economic and social systems that the Sierra Leonean and international community can address. Lessons from the Ebola outbreak may force the country to diversify away from ore mining, while increasing accessibility to credit for small and medium sized business[104], and push corporations to place a greater emphasis on supporting health care system.[105] At this time, no significant institutional efforts have been made to reconcile these gaps.

As of July 2014, Sierra Leone's Human Development Index ranks 183 out of 187 countries.[106] Every indicator places Sierra Leone in either the 'lowest development' category or marginally above it.[107] According to the *International Crisis Group*, a large part of the population continues to live in abject poverty.[108] While patronage networks seem to be diminishing, they continue to restrain government performance. Identity politics are experiencing resurgence as people struggle for access to resources. The UN SRSG to Sierra Leone stresses that politics follows a North-South divide.[109] Thus, despite some achievements, economic and social development in Sierra Leone still faces many challenges – but a return to civil war remains unlikely.[110]

While a specific suggestions for reform lies outside the scope of this paper, the case of Sierra Leone provides a segue into a growing discussion on how to do better, to improve current peacekeeping methodologies, and to learn from our past. UN Peacekeeping missions in Sierra Leone were not as abysmal failures as those prior (i.e. Rwanda, Bosnia Herzegovina), but it would also be misleading to say they were successes. The peacekeeping missions in Sierra Leone were indeed a step in the right direction—with UNAMSIL the international community began to focus more on country specific needs. Being the first peacebuilding missions in the UN, the missions in Sierra Leone both were groundbreaking in expanding the scope of the UN involvement but also demonstrated the difficulties of building peace in war-torn societies with international involvement. Unsurprisingly, Western states are the largest financial contributors to the peacekeeping budget and also dominate units in charge of policy development the DPKO. On the other hand, the bulk of manpower is provided for by oftentimes, less financially robust nations.[111]

With the promulgation of several policy documents by units of the UN DPKO, a renewed discussion of robust peacekeeping emerged. Interestingly, "For European states, robustness has been a response to a lack of effectiveness of peace operations, and is aimed at enabling peacekeepers to properly protect themselves and to have the freedom of maneuver to implement a mandate...By contrast, robustness is perceived by many [Non-Aligned] countries as deviating from the key principles of peacekeeping and as a potential threat to the sovereignty of host countries."[112]

With Western states creating UN peacekeeping mission directives and developing countries providing manpower, the result is a disconnect between the conceptual and functional. Developed countries may support and impose concepts that developing countries will implement. This division of labor still further invokes the dynamic of difference, reinforcing a dichotomized international order.

This relationship of difference can also be seen on a slightly less macro scale in the privatized sectors of crisis-ridden countries. As mentioned earlier, many root causes of conflict are linked to the global economy as demand and supply chains. In Sierra Leone, the diamond mining industry and consequent systems of patronage and corruption are the most glaring examples. The central issue with the large presence of foreign ownership in developing countries is this: the leadership focuses too much on bending its politics and economies in favor of these foreign interests, while placing the interests of its citizens at risk. The two main reasons this seems to happen is because either 1. the leadership is protecting only its own—often, personal—interests; and/

or 2. the leadership has no leverage when negotiating with foreign investors. Even within the privatized spheres that neoliberally designed peacekeeping missions created as a step to sustainable peace, it is difficult to escape the original superior-inferior relationship.

CONCLUSION

UN efforts in Sierra Leone reflect developments in ongoing debates about the most effective path to sustainable global peace. While UNOMSIL and UNAMSIL at its onset failed to fulfill their mandates, the latter largely completed its security sector reform and state rebuilding agendas. This may be attributed to the renewed support from the Security Council support and clearer and stronger mandates. UNAMSIL eventually succeeded in halting and preventing the reoccurrence of combat, whilst also creating a favorable climate for free and fair elections. The changes in UNAMSIL's mandate also indicate the organization willingness to revise current neoliberal understanding of the relationships between "developed" countries and their "developing" counterparts. The last two missions UNIOSIL and UNIPSIL were a step in the right direction, with their greater focus on working with locals. The approach was much more holistic and multifaceted. However, it is unclear whether these logistical successes and intellectual reconceptualization bode well for Sierra Leone's longer-term stability. Corruption and patronage survive in the new state structure, economic development continues to maintain a macro focus, and opportunities for youth and reintegration of the population remain insufficient.

At the same time, honest appraisal of UN peacekeeping missions in Sierra Leone serves to encourage, rather than discourage the international community's continued commitment to achieving global peace. In fact, within the overhaul of the failing UN efforts in Sierra Leone and consequent at least partial successes lies a potential path to UN peacebuilding success. This paper suggests a two-pronged approach: first, continued monetary and logistical support of basic human rights and needs in Sierra Leone; second, committed and pro-active introspection with regards to the neoliberal framework underpinning the schema of international relationships.

A peacekeeping mission is not simply a plan for sustainable peace, it reflects the current international order. As international relationships are understood as two-way streets based on cooperation and contingent on difference, this shifting paradigm may be applied to the design and implementation of future UN peacekeeping efforts throughout the world. For UN peacekeeping missions specifically, this might mean a design that defines successful achievement of peace as the development of political systems and economics that are taking into account country or region specifics. Furthermore, as

UNAMSIL confirmed, understanding a host country and being receptive to input by its citizens are critical to building sustainable peace. This comprehensive, collaborative, and communicatory technique may manifest in the establishment of teams that are tasked with a thorough assessment of the main contributing factors to the crises. Analytical efforts should continue throughout the lifespan of a peacekeeping mission, taking care to examine elements that persist in derailing peace. Equally critical is the composition of these teams. Each should be a mixed body of local experts, local non-experts ("regular people"), as well as historical, political, and economic specialists from the international community.

As an international organization whose concepts trickle-down into societies' political, economic, and civil institutions, the United Nations is the most appropriate entity to spearhead a re-imagination of present-day international relationship. Change may be achieved incrementally, but only with the active participation of the international community at every level of society. It always takes two to tango.

NOTES

1. See UN DPKO, *United Nations Peacekeeping Operations: Principles and Guidelines*, 2008, p. 6 (at: http://pbpu.unlb.org/pbps/library/capstone_doctrine_eNg.pdf).

2. See Antony Anghie, *Imperialism, Sovereignty, and the Making of International Law*, Cambridge: Cambridge University Press, 2005; and Phillip Darby, 'Rolling Back the Frontiers of Empire', *International Peacekeeping*, Vol. 16, No. 5, p. 701; *contra*: Vivienne Jabri, 'Peacebuilding, the Local and the International', *Peacebuilding*, Vol. 1, No. 1, 2013, pp. 3-16.

3. See Mark Malan et al., *Peacekeeping in Sierra Leone*, Institute for Security Studies Monograph, No. 68, 2002, p.1. www.issafrica.org/uploads/Mono68Full.pdf.

4. See for example, Anghie, *op. cit.*, p. 11; Martii Koskenniemi, *The Gentle Civilizers of Nations. The Rise and Fall of International Law, 1870-1960*, Cambridge: Cambridge University Press, 2001, p. 176.

5. See Michel Morin, *L'usurpation de la souveraineté autochtone. Le cas des peuples de la Nouvelle-France et des colonies anglaises d'Amérique du Nord*, Québec : Boréal, 1997, pp. 32-40; see also John R. Morss, 'Riddles of the Sands.Time, Power and Legitimacy in International Law', in Prabhakar Singh & Benoît Mayer (eds.), *Critical International Law*, Oxford: OUP, 2014, pp. 55-63.

6. Edward Newman et al., *New Perspectives on Liberal Peacebuilding*, Tokyo: United Nations Publications, 2009, p. 15.

7. See for example, Oliver P. Richmond, *The Transformation of Peace*, Palgrave, 2005; Michael Pugh, 'The Political Economy of Peacebuilding: A Critical Theory Perspective', *International Journal of Peace Studies*, Vol.10, No.2, 2005, pp.23-42; Oliver P. Richmond, 'Resistance and the Post-Liberal Peace', *Millennium*, Vol. 38, No. 3, 2010, pp. 665-692; Charles Thiessen, 'Emancipatory Peacebuilding. Critical Responses to (Neo)Liberal Trends' in Thomas Matyok et al., *Critical Issues in Peace and Conflict Studies*, Plymouth: Lexington Books, 2011, pp. 115-140; David Roberts, 'Saving Liberal Peacebuilding From Itself', *Peace Review*, Vol. 24, No. 3, 2012, pp. 366-373; Nicolas Lemay-Hebert, 'Critical Debates on Liberal Peacebuilding', *Civil Wars*, Vol. 15, No. 2, 2013, pp. 242-252; Jan Selby, 'The Myth of Liberal Peace-Building', *Conflict, Security & Development*, Vol. 13, No. 1, 2013, pp. 57-86; John Heathershaw, 'Towards Better Theories of Peacebuilding', *Peacebuilding*, Vol. 1, No. 2, 2013, pp. 275-282.

8. For details see Roland Paris's chapter 'Does liberal peacekeeping have a future?', pp. 97-111 in Newman et al.(See n. 6 above); see also Madhav Joshi et al., 'Just How Liberal is the Liberal Peace', *International Peacekeeping*, Vol. 21, No 3, 2014, pp. 364-389.

9. Darya Pushkina & Philip Maier,'UN Peacekeeping in Timor-Leste', *Civil Wars*, Vol. 14, No. 3, 2012, pp. 324-343; see also Antonia Does, 'Inclusivity and Local Perspectives in Peacebuilding', *Geneva Peacebuilding Platform Papers*, No. 8, 2013, pp. 3-13; Claudia Simons & Franziska Zanker, 'Questioning the Local in Peacebuilding', *Working Papers of the Priority Programme 1448 of the German Research Foundation*, No. 10, 2014, pp. 6-14; Thania Paffenholz, 'International Peacebuilding Goes Local', *Peacebuilding*, Vol. 2, No. 1, 2014, pp.11-27.

10. Ahmadou Kourouma, *Allah n'est pas obligé*, Paris: Seuil, 2000, p. 161; in his multi-prized novel, the Ivorian writer Kourouma (1927-2003) describes, *inter alia*, the conflict in Sierra Leone through the eyes of an Ivorian child soldier who fought in Liberia and Sierra Leone.Tentative translation : 'Sierra Leone is a mess ! Yes, a complete mess. People say that a country is a simple mess when brigands in the woods are sharing the country like in Liberia ; but, if, you don't have just brigands, if N.G.Os and democratic entrepreneurs are jumping in the bandwagon, then it's more than a simple mess.'

11. See I.S. Ogundiya, 'Domestic Rebellion in Africa', *International Journal of Peace and Development Studies*, Vol. 1, No 2, 2010, p. 28.

12. See Newman et al. (see n. 6above), pp. 161-2; Michael Bratton & Nicholas Van de Walle, 'Neopatrimonial Régimes and Political Transitions in Africa', *World Politics*, Vol. 46, 1994, No 4, pp. 58-9.

13. Paramount chiefs are traditional landlords in 'feudal' rural Sierra Leone; their autonomy is due to the fact that these areas were colonized later than the coast, and that they are indigenous nobles, contrary to Creoles of Freetown, who are descendants of freed African-American slaves.

14. See Alfred Zack-Williams, 'Sierra Leone: The Political Economy of Civil War', *Third World Quarterly*, Vol. 20, No. 1, 1999, pp.143-162; Christopher Clapham, 'L'Etat en Afrique'. Trans. François Gaulme. *Afrique contemporaine*, No. 199, 2001, pp. 177-191; Jimmy D. Kandeh, 'Subaltern Terror in Sierra Leone', in Diane Frost et al. *Africa in Crisis*, London: Pluto Press, 2002, pp. 180-3.

15. Philippe Le Billon, 'Diamond Wars? Conflict Diamonds and Geographies of Resource War', *Annals of the Association of American Geographers*, Vol. 98, No. 2, 2008, p. 357.

16. See David Keen, 'Liberalization and Conflict', *International Political Science Review*, Vol. 26, 2005, No. 1, p. 76.

17. Ibid, p. 74-76.

18. See Global Witness, *Lessons UNlearned. How the UN and Member States must do more to end natural resource-fuelled conflicts*, 2010 (at: www.globalwitness.org/sites/default/files/pdfs/lessonsunlearned_online_low.pdf).

19. See Macartan Humphreys & Jeremy Weinstein, 'Who Fights? The Determinants of Participation in Civil War', *American Journal of Political Science*, Vol. 62, No. 2, 2008, p. 440.

20. See Adekeye Adebajo, *UN Peacekeeping in Africa*, Boulder: Lynne Rienner, 2011, p. 141.

21. See Ibrahim Abdullah, 'Bush Path to Destruction: the origin and character of the Revolutionary United Front/ Sierra Leone', *Journal of Modern African Studies*, Vol. 32, No. 2, 1998, pp. 220-1.

22. Monika Heupel & Bernhard Zangl,'On the Transformation of Warfare', *Journal of International Relations and Development*, Vol. 13, 2010, p. 46.

23. See Eric G. Berman & Melissa T. Labonte, Melissa, 'Sierra Leone', in William J. Durch (ed.) *Twenty-first-century Peace Operations*, Washington, D.C.: United States Institute of Peace, 2006, p. 145.

24. Strasser employed this private military partially because he was unable to divert all state resources to the war effort, given the slew of debt repayments his government was committed to, see Paul Williams, 'Peace Operations And The International Financial Institutions', *International Peacekeeping*, Vol. 11, No. 1, 2004, p. 114.

25. See Clifford Bernath & Sayre Nyce, 'Sierra Leone – A Peacekeeping Success: Lessons Learned From UNAMSIL', *ReliefWeb Report*, 2002 (at: http://reliefweb.int/node/111652).

26. Doug Brooks, "Messiahs or Mercenaries?"*International Peacekeeping*, Vol. 7, No. 4, 2000, p. 142.

27. See Christopher Clapham, 'African Security Systems', in Greg Mills & John Stremlau (eds.) *The Privatization of Security in Africa*, Johannesburg: South African Institute of International Affairs, 1999, p. 43.

28. 'One of the immediate causes of the 1997 coup (..) was an IMF-imposed reduction in a rice subsidy that benefited the military', Neil Cooper & Michael Pugh, 'Security Sector Transformation in Post-Conflict Societies', *The Conflict, Security & Development Group Working Paper*, No 5, February 2002, p. 39.

29. See Isaac T. Sampson, "The Responsibility to Protect and ECOWAS Mechanisms on Peace and Security," *Journal of Conflict & Security Law*, Vol. 16, No. 3, 2011, p. 514; Papa Samba Ndiaye, *Les organisations internationales africaines et le maintien de la paix: l'exemple de la CEDEAO*, Paris: L'Harmattan, 2014, pp. 92-93.

30. See Andrew McGregor, 'Quagmire in West Africa: Nigerian Peacekeeping in Sierra Leone', *International Journal*, Vol. 44, No. 3, 1999, pp. 483.

31. See Sarah-Myriam Martin-Brûlé, 'Assessing Peace Operations' Mitigated Outcomes', *International Peacekeeping*, Vol. 19, No. 2, 2012, p. 243.

32. See Eric G. Berman & Katie Sams, *Peacekeeping in Africa*, Geneva: UNIDIR, 2000, p. 120.

33. Peter Arthur, 'ECOWAS and Regional Peacekeeping Integration in West Africa', *Africa Today*, Vol. 42, No. 2, 2010, p. 17.

34. See Berman & Labonte (see n. 24 above), p. 155.

35. See Funmi Olonisakin, *Peacekeeping in Sierra Leone. The Story of UNAMSIL*, Boulder: Lynne Rienner, 2008, pp. 20-1.

36. See Adekeye Adebajo & David Keen, 'Sierra Leone', in Mats Berdal and Spyros Economides (Eds.) *United Nations Interventionism, 1991-2004*, Cambridge: Cambridge University Press, 2007, p. 251.

37. A Commonwealth Police Development Task Force assisted UNAMSIL in reforming the Police Force; see Joseph P.C. Charley & Freida Ividuni McCormak, *Becoming and Remaining a 'Force for Good' – Reforming the Police in Post-conflict Sierra Leone*, Brighton: Institute of Development Studies, 2011.

38. Helga M. Binningsbø & Kendra Dupuy, 'Using Power-Sharing to Win a War', *Africa Spectrum*, Vol. 44, No. 3, 2009, p. 94.

39. Cooper & Pugh (see n. 29 above), p. 36.

40. See Binningsbø & Dupuy (see n. 39 above), p. 96.

41. Adebajo & Keen (see n. 37 above), p. 257.

42. Frederick H. Fleitz, *Peacekeeping Fiascoes of the 1990s*, Westpoint: Praeger, 2002, pp. 165-6.

43. See Adebajo (see n. 21 above), p. 149.

44. See Olonisakin (see n. 36 above), pp. 81-82.

45. See Simon Chesterman, *You, The People. The United Nations, Transitional Administration, and State-Building*, Oxford: Oxford University Press, 2004, pp. 100-111.

46. Adekeye Adebayo, *UN Peacekeeping in Africa*, Boulder, Colorado: Lynne Rienner Publishers, 2011, p. 151.

47. Ibid,p. 151.

48. Ibid, p. 151.

49. See Adebajo & Keen (see n. 37 above), p. 264.

50. See Laurence Boisson de Chazournes & Théo Boutruche, 'Sécurité collective et droit de l'OMC', *Annuaire français de relations internationales*, Vol. 8, 2007, pp. 867-868 ; on the Kimberley Process, see Abiodun Alao, 'Natural Resource Management and Human Security in Africa', in Ademola Abass (Ed.), *Protecting Human Security in Africa*, Oxford: Oxford University Press, 2010, pp. 113-115; Shawn MacDonald, 'Peacebuilding and the Private Sector', in Craig Zelizer (Ed.), *Integrated Peacebuilding. Innovative Approaches to Transforming Conflict*, Boulder: Westview Press, 2013, pp.134-137.

51. See UNSC Resolution 1270 (1999) § 21.

52. See UNSC Resolution 1346 (2001) § 12.

53. The roles of the TRC and of the Special Court for Sierra Leone exceed the scope of this article, see Edward Newman, "'Transitional Justice": The Impact of Transnational Norms and the UN', *International Peacekeeping*, Vol. 9, No. 2, 2002, pp. 42-5; Gill Wigglesworth, 'The End of Impunity?', *International Affairs*, Vol. 84, No. 4, 2008, pp. 809-827; Wendy Lambourne, 'Towards Sustainable Peace and Development in Sierra Leone', *Journal of Peacebuilding & Development*, Vol. 4, No. 2, 2008, pp. 34-6, Ozonnia Ojiello, 'Breaking with the Past: Transitional Justice in Sierra Leone', in Hany Besada (Ed.), *From Civil Strife to Peace Building*, Waterloo: Wilfried Laurier University Press / CIGI, 2009, pp. 97-127; Proscovia Svärd, 'The International Community and post-war reconciliation in Africa', *African Journal on Conflict Resolution*, Vol. 10, No. 1, 2010, pp. 35-61; and M.C. Nmaju, 'The Role of Judicial Institutions in the Restoration of Post-Conflict Societies', *Journal of Conflict & Security Law*, Vol. 16, No. 2, 2011, pp. 357-384.

54. See Olonisakin (see n. 36 above), p. 116.

55. See Malan et al. (see n. 3 above), p. 7.

56. Alex de Waal, "Mission without an End?" *International Affairs*, Vol. 85, No. 1, 2009, p. 107.

57. See John Hirsch, 'Sierra Leone', in David Malone (ed.), *The UN Security Council*, Boulder: Lynne Rienner, 2004, pp. 521-36.

58. See Adebayo & Keen (see n. 37 above), pp. 256-7.

59. See Bernath & Nyce (see n. 26 above), p. 2.

60. Community development work included operating health centres, radio stations, schools; rehabilitation of churches/mosques and market structures; and raising awareness of human rights.

61. Infrastructural work included, but was not limited to building roads and bridges, quality water wells, and shelters, as well as the rehabilitation of prisons.

62. See Jean Krasno, *Public Opinion Survey of UNAMSIL's Work in Sierra Leone*, New York: UN DPKO, 2005, p. 29.

63. Christiana Solomon & Jeremy Ginifer, *Disarmament, Demobilisation and Reintegration in Sierra Leone*, Bradford: Centre for International Cooperation and Security, 2008, p. 5.

64. See Berman & Labonte (see n. 24 above), pp. 190-1.

65. See V. Kanyako, 'Think Global, Transfer Local: The Perils and Opportunities of a Locally Owned Peace Process in Post-War Sierra Leone', *Accord Conference Paper*, No. 2, 2012, pp. 28-30.

66. Christine Cubitt, 'Building an Illiberal Peace', *Africa Peace and Conflict Journal*, Vol. 4, No 11, 2011, p. 13.

67. See Anne M. Street et al., 'Experiences of the United Nations Peacebuilding Commission in Sierra Leone and Burundi', *Journal of Peacebuilding & Development*, Vol. 4, No. 2, 2008, p. 42.

68. Virginia P. Fortna, *Does Peacekeeping Work?*, Princeton: Princeton University Press, 2008, p. 124.

69. Berman & Labonte (see n. 24 above), p. 206.

70. UN News Centre, *Secretary-General Ban Ki-moon: Toast at state dinner in Freetown Sierra Leone*, 2010 (at: www.un.org/apps/news/infocus/sgspeeches/statments_full.asp?statID=857#.ULkUIqXue-9).

71. Lisa Morjé Howard, *UN Peacekeeping in Civil Wars*, Cambridge: Cambridge University Press, 2008, p. 303.

72. Newman et al. (see n. 6 above), p. 155.

73. See Alhaji Sarjoh Bah, "Sierra Leone", in Richard Caplan (ed.), *Exit Strategies and State Building*, Oxford: Oxford University Press, 2012, pp. 109-112.

74. Several scholars elaborate on the difficulties of evaluating such multifaceted missions, noting, for example, that rebuilding state structures does not automatically ensures their 'effective service delivery'. See Paul Diehl & Daniel Druckman, *Evaluating Peace Operations*, Boulder: Lynne Rienner, 2010, pp. 114-5; Jevgenia Victoria Milne,*Returning Culture to*

Peacebuilding: Contesting the Liberal Peace in Sierra Leone, Ph. D. thesis, University of St. Andrews, 2009, pp. 134-137 https://research-repository.st-andrews.ac.uk/ .

75. See Darya Pushkina, 'A Recipe for Success? Ingredients of a Successful Peacekeeping Mission', *International Peacekeeping*, Vol. 13, No. 2, 2006, pp. 133-149.

76. See John Hirsch, *Sierra Leone: Diamonds and the Struggle for Democracy*, Boulder: Lynne Rienner, 2001, pp. 100-1..

77. See Gisela Hirschmann, 'Peacebuilding in UN Peacekeeping Exit Strategies', *International Peacekeeping*, Vol. 19, No. 2, 2012, p. 176; on UNIOSIL, see: Sunday Abogonye Ochoche, 'Post-Conflict Peacebuilding', in Besada (see n. 54 above), pp.129-143.

78. UN Security Council. "Security Council Establishes UN Integrated Office in Sierra Leone to Further Address Root Causes of Conflict." *United Nations: Meetings Coverage and Press Releases*. United Nations. 31 August 2005. Web. 10 June 2015. http://www.un.org/press/en/2005/sc8487.doc.htm

79. On the Peacebuilding Commission and Sierra Leone, see Rob Jenkins, *Peacebuilding. From Concept to Commission*, London: Routledge, 2013, pp. 83-88 & 113-115; Anne M. Street et al., 'Experiences of the United Nations Peace-building Commission in Sierra Leone and Burundi', *Journal of Peacebuilding & Development*, Vol. 4, No. 2, 2008, pp. 33-46.

80. "OHCHR in Sierra Leone." *Office of the High Commissioner for Human Rights*. OHCHR. Web. 10 June 2015. http://www.ohchr.org/EN/Countries/AfricaRegion/Pages/SLSummary.aspx

81. See Fairlie Chappuis & Heiner Hänggi, 'Statebuilding through Security Sector Reform', in David Chandler & Timothy D. Sisk (eds.), *Routledge Handbook of International Statebuilding*, London : Routledge, 2013, p. 179.

82. "Mandate and Approach." *UNIPSIL United Nations Integrated Peacebuilding Office in Sierra Leone*. United Nations. Web. 11 Jun. 2015. http://unipsil.unmissions.org/Default.aspx?tabid=9613.

83. See *Fifth Report of the Secretary-General on the United Nations Integrated Office in Sierra Leone*, UN doc. S/2007/204, § 4.

84. See William Reno, 'Understanding Criminality in West African Conflicts', *International Peacekeeping*, Vol. 16, No. 1, 2009, p. 52.

85. See Desirée Nilsson & Mimi Söderberg Kovacs, 'Different Paths of Reconstruction', *International Peacekeeping*, Vol. 20, No 1, 2013, pp. 10-1.

86. Arthur (see n. 33 above), p. 13.

87. "Freedom in the World 2012." *Freedom House*. Web. 30 Mar. 2015. https://freedomhouse.org/report/freedom-world/2012/sierra-leone#.VR0uFROUdew.

88. Pierre Englebert & Denis M. Tull, 'Postconflict Reconstruction in Africa', *International Security*, Vol. 32, No 4, 2008, pp. 112, 116 & 125; see also Lisa Denney 'Overcoming the State/Non-State Divide', *International Peacekeeping*, Vol. 21, No. 2, 2014, pp. 257-263.

89. See Christof P. Kurz, 'The Limitations of International Analyses of the State and Post-Conflict Statebuilding in Sierra Leone', in Berit Bliesemann de Guevara (ed.), *Statebuilding and State-Formation*, New York: Routledge, 2012, p. 127; see also Eldridge Vigil Adolfo, 'An Appraisal of the Liberal Peacebuilding Exercise in Sierra Leone', in Mikael Eriksson & Roland Kostić (Eds.), *Mediation and Liberal Peacebuilding*, New York: Routledge, 2013, pp. 147-151.

90. Christine Cubitt, *Local and Global Dynamics of Peacebuilding. Post-Conflict Reconstruction in Sierra Leone*, New York: Routledge, 2012, p. 164.

91. See Melissa Labonte, 'Same Car, Different Driver? The Impact of Peacebuilding Partnerships and the Chiefdom System in Sierra Leone', *Journal of Peacebuilding & Development*, Vol. 4, No. 1, 2008, p. 6.

92. This forum shopping is generally not understood correctly by non-elite people, thus it generates frustration, see Gearoid Millar, 'Expectations and Experiences of Peacebuilding in Sierra Leone', *International Peacekeeping*, Vol. 20, N0 2, 2013, pp. 189-203.

93. See Jon Unruh, 'Land Rights and Peacebuilding', *International Journal of Peace Studies*, Vol. 15, No 2, 2010, pp. 95-96, 110-112 & 121.

94. See Kurz (see n. 89 above), pp. 125-6.

95. See Samuel G. Doe, 'Poverty Reduction Strategy in Collapsed States', *Journal of Peacebuilding & Development*, Vol. 5, No. 2, 2010, p. 50.

96. See James Ahearne, 'Neoliberal Economic Policies and Post-Conflict Peacebuilding', *POLIS Journal*, Vol. 2, 2009, p. 31.

97. See Pusha Iyer, 'Development versus Peacebuilding', *Africa Peace and Conflict Journal*, Vol. 4, No. 1, 2011, pp. 20-1.

98. See Ahearne (see n. 96 above), p. 32.

99. UN News Centre, *Head of UN Sierra Leone Office Calls for Full Support for Unified Strategy, Praises Political Leadership for Communique Signed in Wake of March Violence*, UN doc. SC/9673, 2009.

100. "At a Glance: Sierra Leone." *UNICEF*. Web. 01 Apr. 2015. www.unicef.org/infoby-country/sierraleone_statistics.html#90.

101. Berman & Labonte (see n. 24 above), p. 190.

102. Human Rights Watch, *Whose Development ? Human Rights Abuses in Sierra Leone's Mining Boom*, 19 Feb. 2014. https://www.hrw.org/report/2014/02/19/whose-development/human-rights-abuses-sierra-leones-mining-boom.

103. African Development Bank/OECD/UNDP, *African Economic Outlook*, 2016, p. 314; see also Ighobor, Kingsley. "Ebola Threatens Economic Gains in Affected Countries." *Africa Renewal*. Web. 30 Mar. 2015. http://www.un.org/africarenewal/magazine/december-2014/ebola-threatens-economic-gains-affected-countries.

104. See Emmanuel Nnadozie & Shiham Abdulmelik, 'The Role of the Private Sector in Sierra Leone's Post-Conflict Reconstruction Efforts' in Besada (see n. 54 above), pp. 159-160

105. Chonghaile, Clar Ni. "Ebola Crisis Could Force Sierra Leone to Diversify Away from Mining." *The Guardian*. Web. 30 Mar 2015. http://www.theguardian.com/global-development/2015/mar/10/ebola-crisis-sierra-leone-diversify-mining-economy .

106. Sierra Leone Moves One Place Up the Human Development Index but inequality and multidimensional poverty Still Very High." *UNDP*. Web. 01 Apr. 2015.

107. UNDP, *Sierra Leone HDI Values and Rank Changes in the 2014 Human Development Report.*

108. See International Crisis Group, 'Sierra Leone: A New Era of Reform?' *Africa Report.* No. 143, 2008. http://www.crisisgroup.org/en/regions/africa/west-africa/sierra-leone/143-sierra-leone-a-new-era-of-reform.aspx.

109. Michael von der Schulenburg, *Sierra Leone: Statement to the UN Security Council*, 2012. http://unipsil.unmissions.org/LinkClick.aspx?fileticket=ssPP0CjE0Y0%3D&tabid=9634&language=en-US. The SRSG was removed from his post because he was accused by President Bai Koroma of favoring the opposition, see: Lauren Hutton, 'Internal and external dilemmas of peacebuilding in Africa', *Institute for Security Studies Paper*, No 250, 2014, p. 6.

110. See Kieran Mitton, 'Where is the War ? Explaining Peace in Sierra Leone', *International Peacekeeping*, Vol. 20, No. 3, 2013, pp. 326-334.

111. Thierry, Tardy. "A Critique of Robust Peacekeeping in Contemporary Peace Operations," *International Peacekeeping*, Vol. 18, No. 2, 2011, p. 158.

112. Ibid.; on Brazil, Russia, India, China and South-Africa, see : Oliver P. Richmond & Ioannis Tellidis, 'Emerging Actors in International Peacebuilding and Statebuilding', *Global Governance*, Vol. 20, No. 4, 2014, pp. 563-584.

Epilogue

A Taxonomy of Intolerance

R. E. Tully

With this epilogue, the Bard-West Point *project* on intolerance comes to an end, although the *problem* of intolerance almost certainly never will. The stark reason for its endurance was expressed in the joint proposal for this project:

> Individuals acquire layers of group identity anchored to race, gender, geography, language. This complex social phenomenon transcends the existence of mere opposition and difference. Differences can be accepted, compromise might reconcile opposed views, but intolerance is pernicious and pervasive. The inevitability of divisions, leavened by a marked tendency to reinforce self-identity by means of difference-with-others, runs so deep in human nature that holding up a mirror to ourselves seems inevitably to reveal a double image: of the people we want to see and the people we're glad we're not.

The preceding papers in this volume hold up a succession of mirrors. They give us glimpses of intolerance that is sometimes covert, sometimes overt but tolerated, sometimes reigning openly and championed. But who are the "we", and who are those "we're glad we're not"? Gazing back into a sample of those mirrors will help provide at least partial answers.

1. Robert Goldstein's essay exposes a contemporary instance of pernicious intolerance ("Residue of Intolerance: Polluting Civil Rights"). He describes the plight of a small black community in Alabama whose town has acquired an unscenic mountain of industrial coal waste, along with the hazards of pollution to its residents, thanks to a combination of a lax environmental laws, the pressing need of a large corporation to dump the waste somewhere, and the comfortable complicity of business leaders, bureaucrats

and state legislators who ensured that the waste, wherever it ended up, would be "not in my back yard" (NIMBY). They agreed it should be in the community's back yard. Decades of Civil Rights legislation have freed the members of that community from legal (*de jure*) discrimination. But this is only half of the story, as Goldstein makes clear. They now live under the shadow of both coal ash and *de facto* discrimination.

2. Bruce Chilton reveals how deeply embedded in human culture has been the acceptance of an intolerable act, the sacrificing of someone most dear to us—our child—to propitiate the gods or to fulfill their wishes ("Poisoned Virtue: Child Sacrifice in Abrahamic Scriptures and Interpretation"). The essay in itself is a mirror with many facets. Child sacrifice was not unfamiliar in Middle East and Mediterranean life. The story of Abraham and Isaac belongs to a pattern: the gods and the purpose may differ but not the practice. Infanticide itself was held to possess such significance that some commentators, without denying that Isaac survived when an angel intervened, suggested that Abraham's knife did indeed draw blood from his son's neck. Over many centuries within both the Hebraic and Christian traditions, Abraham's willingness to sacrifice his son was inoculated with a variety of interpretations. Modern tradition has isolated the story of Abraham and Isaac as a unique example of the testing of faith, even as marking the end of human sacrifice. Yet Christians celebrate rather than lament that God sent his only son into the world who was obedient even unto death on the cross. The Chilton essay also recounts the atrocities committed by Pope Urban II's holy Crusaders against both Jews and Muslims under an assurance of eternal salvation. Confronted with religious intolerance, some of their Jewish victims, as parents, were willing to raise the knife against their own children. Osama bin Laden's condemnation of enemy Crusaders strikes many Westerners today as quaint and archaic; they fail to realize that the barbarism of beheading, burning and mutilation carried out against innocent Muslim families in the Eleventh Century is a nightmare remembered and, among Wahhabis, nurtured.

3. The intolerance that Maritza Ryan documents is deplorable and unnerving ("All *Men* Are Created Equal: Misogyny under Law"). We look to the law for authority and to judges for their wisdom and discretion. Ryan forces us to recognize that, from ancient times forward, the objectivity and majesty of the Law belonged to those who had the authority to make and enforce the rules, namely men, and that the legal protections they decreed for women were adverse to their freedom and interests as citizens. Misogyny has never been virtuous. Compassion, however, is respectable. The British and American Jurists whom Ryan mentions might well have thought that laws which presume proper places for women (the home, the pedestal) were both natural and right, even deferential. They had legal tradition on their side, the uniformity of ethnic customs, the Bible, and possibly also their own mothers.

Fortunately, the law is correctable for the common good by the agreement of the governed. America was founded on the principle of equality of citizenship, except that custom had preordained the stratification of the rights of citizens according to gender, and women were not consulted on the merits of this anti-democratic presumption. No wonder that, in the course of time, women should regard the spirit of the laws which confined them to their places as misogynistic. The Ryan essay raises a thorny issue worth reflection: does the legitimacy of the law necessarily lie with the lawmakers or are there independent standards by which to judge both laws and lawmakers? If the latter, who will articulate those standards, and with what authority?

4. Andrew Forney examines phenomena less memorialized than terrorist attacks on office towers and government buildings ("Plagues and Politics: Epidemics and 'Re-Framing' in Modern American History"). Speaking to the nation shortly after 9/11 President Bush said that those assaults brought out the best of human nature (the heroism of Americans coming to aid strangers) as well as the worst that human nature is capable of inflicting on the innocent. Indeed, attacks by foreigners and natural disasters like tornadoes, earthquakes, floods and fires seem often to bring out the best from people. For a while such events unite citizens. Epidemics, however, push them away from each other. Apart from rescue workers and medical personnel, compassion tends to be reserved for the victims among one's own kin. The walls close around the family for protection; the unseen enemy is contagion, to be kept outside. Forney examines two such epidemics in American history, the outbreak of influenza during World War I and the appearance of AIDS during the early 1980s. The former led to extravagant measures to overcome the fear of infection. The latter fostered in some citizens an attitude of moral censure towards the victims. More recently, Ebola caused feelings of panic among Americans when that disease was feared to have breached the nation's walls. But the walls held, and the media's sense of crisis subsided and rapidly disappeared, which leads Forney to observe that epidemics do not enjoy "a long shelf life in the American mind". Perhaps the reason lies not with the media but in ourselves. Unlike enemy attacks, floods and earthquakes, epidemics are subversive social upheavals. They seem to arouse an instinctual sense of self-preservation and a reaction of xenophobia to possible bearers of harm to ourselves and our families, even when those others are fellow citizens. If this is a latent human trait, it is not a noble one. Perhaps this is why we don't like to remember rampant epidemics (such as influenza) but prefer to put our faith in the walls of medicine. That faith allows us even now to keep the memory of plagues like syphilis in South America and the Black Death in Europe at a safe psychological distance.

5. If the emergence of religious belief and ritual was a major step for mankind, then the expression of intolerance in matters of religion was a short and easy one to take. Religious intolerance seems cursed by long memory.

The rampant and dedicated intolerance shown towards Jews and Muslims by Urban II's Crusaders (described in Bruce Chilton's essay) continues to have convulsive consequences in the Middle East, but so also does the reciprocal intolerance between Christian and Christian since the time of the Reformation and never far below the surface today in Northern Ireland. Muslims remain bitterly divided on the proper successor of the Prophet and, as we know, are willing to kill in the name of correctness. In Myanmar, Buddhist thugs have found their targets among Muslim Rohingyas; and Muslim factions in India and Pakistan assault both Hindus and Christians and destroy their places of worship. A Boston Irish candidate for office once declared that "all politics is local". Perhaps something similar holds in the case of religion, that it cannot be divorced from political issues (local or regional) related to legal authority, self-determination, class differences, tradition, and the ownership of land or claimed entitlement to it. But such grounds for intolerance suggest that religion itself can often be used to mask political agendas. In that case, politics might better be considered a concomitant of religion, though also a contaminant, but not one of its essential properties. The challenge, then, is to isolate whatever properties in religion are incompatible with intolerance.

6. Ellen Charry strives to meet this challenge directly in her essay, and so too Dustin Atlas and Nelly Lahoud in theirs, indirectly. Charry limits her focus to the relationship of Judaism and Christianity ("Theological Complicity in Religious Violence"). She speaks "from but not for" these two traditions (leaving Islam to speak "from and for itself"), and she identifies the fundamental theological task as "the work of sustained reflection on God and the things of God", which would take the form of a "theological partnership" between them. The goal for each partner is to recognize that the goodness and sovereignty of God connects both of their traditions in a widening rather than broken circle of one chosen people. The implicit moral imperative is that religious people, and particularly theologians, must not be intolerant, since God's own goodness is not. What Charry calls "theological contempt" is merely intolerance under a different name, perhaps invested with political righteousness, but is not God's way. Charry is concerned not to promote toleration from a distance, or some passive and polite form of ecumenism. She holds that the connection between both traditions should take the form of a committed embrace of spiritual identity.

In contrast, the perspective adopted by Dustin Atlas is notably world-centered ("Cynicism and Perennial Intolerance: Mendelssohn Against the Decisionists"). Although the topic is historically remote (18th Century Germany), its theme is politically universal: the limits of toleration by any social group whose identity is threatened by assimilation, and whose resistance is therefore deemed intolerant. The challenge here is to distinguish between toleration which non-aggressively marginalizes a minority and toleration which encourages its proportional contribution to the whole in the interest of creating greater social cohesion. It is no small challenge, since an aura of fairness and generosity seem to permeate both kinds of toleration, and since the distinction itself may fail to be clearly understood by the promoters of either kind. This was the challenge that Moses Mendelssohn faced at different times, both in his controversy with Friedrich Jacobi over Spinoza's metaphysics and in his resistance to political movements which he foresaw as a threat to the soul of Judaism in Germany. But Mendelssohn was also a child of the Enlightenment and thus willingly navigated in two worlds. Instead of surrendering his deeply religious sense of identity, however, he sought to enlist reason in its service. Atlas introduces us to a world of tangled loyalties where toleration is both praised and blamed, preferred and feared.

The modern Western world may suffer from a presumptively clear understanding of what toleration ought to mean to those who are tolerated. The secular trickle-down concept of toleration is assumed to extend properly to religious denominations and to distinct religious traditions: they should tolerate each other, indeed should promote an ecumenical understanding of each other, given that the overarching state tolerates them. Nelly Lahoud takes us into these lesser worlds ("On Religious (in)Tolerance"). She reminds us that *doctrinal differences*—these she stresses, not animosities—are foundation stones in the adjacent buildings of the three major Western religions. Lahoud identifies several of the most important firmly held beliefs that hold them apart. There is, she contends, a legitimate form of intolerance which the three religions allow. The acceptance of exclusiveness is thus natural to those who cherish their own tradition and practices, and who believe that the values these express fulfill the word and will of God. However, although such circumstances are the very tinder of a hostile intolerance conflicting with their values, it is not religion itself which ignites it. More likely it is the unstable social impulse of self-protection created by fear or suspicion of injury. In the spirit of John Locke, Lahoud advocates the existence of a state acknowledged for its authority and intelligent enough to enable religious adherents to be fully themselves, a state which avoids creating an atmosphere in which the three religious traditions are encouraged to be ever more tolerant of each other, in conformity with the example set by a tolerant state. Instead, the three traditions would be free to cultivate their different religious identities. The question not asked by Lahoud is whether there might nevertheless exist some underlying set of common, ecumenically accepted beliefs among the three Western religions that could balance their differences, if not neutralize them. Perhaps theologians will articulate that set (in the way Charry suggests). But any answer which draws mainly upon human experience will likely be negative. The God-as-understood in any one of the three religions is less remote than the God who is. The beliefs of any ecumenical proto-religion would be necessary but never sufficient to encourage people to believe that they remain faithful, living and acting in the way their God wants.

7. Social changes are also social forces. Forces in physical nature have been classified and captured numerically since the 18th Century, but social changes still lack an international system of units by which to be measured. There is no algorithm for converting personal resentment into joules of energy expended by whatever causes it. The impacts of social change are nevertheless palpable and observable, but where direct observation is no longer possible, we must rely on a verified and responsible historical record. This is what Ty Seidule gives us in his revealing account of intolerance at West Point over a span of some 150 years, first towards African American cadets, later towards female cadets ("From Slavery to Black Power: Racial Intolerance at West Point, 1778-2015"). Who were the intolerant "we" at West Point? In a systemic sense, *everyone*, both officers and cadets. Given the hierarchical system of the Academy, itself a microcosm of the U. S. Army, orders are transmitted downwards; so also are attitudes. It isn't necessary to establish that literally everyone at West Point acted with intolerance towards these two groups. The despicable acts directed at black cadets did not cause protests or result in the punishment of offenders. Racism, in the sense we now understand it, was condoned. African American cadets were tolerated, Seidule writes, "only when they accepted 'their place'." Seidule reports the following incident: In the Spring of 1880, Henry Whittaker, the sole black cadet at the time, was found in his room gagged, trussed and slashed. By reasoning difficult to comprehend, Whittaker's injuries were deemed to be self-inflicted and the Superintendent ordered him to be court-martialed.

8. Racial intolerance was prevalent in the United States during the post-Civil War decades. It was not of course germinated at West Point; it migrated there from many regions of the country and flourished in a controlled environment. The Academy, both then and in many ways now, was a seminary with a mission to create leaders of honor and character, comfortable with giving and taking orders, and also constitutionally subject to civil authority (the President). The Corps of Cadets at any given time was merely the most recent in a long line of former cadets, some of whom had returned to West Point as officers charged with developing them for their future responsibilities in the Army, and the discipline they exerted was in turn mirrored in the authority that the senior cadets had over their juniors. The Academy in those decades remained a chivalric world of unquestioned authority and respect for tradition, an all-male environment of pride as well as arrogance, and also of resistance to social changes. Like much of the country from which they hailed and most of the world itself at that time, these officers and cadets suffered from moral blindness. This comment, however, is not intended as censorious. Blindness can be a condition suffered from birth.

West Point's reaction to female cadets was therefore easy to predict. The decision to admit women to the Corps was made democratically, by Congress. It was neither invited by the senior leadership at West Point nor welcomed by the Corps of Cadets in 1976, when the first women arrived. That the Academy, dedicated to honor, trust and respect, should have been required from beyond its walls to do the morally right thing was a humiliating irony. The new cadets nevertheless were subject to insults, taunts and other types of abuse comparable to those hurled at black Americans on a broader scale during Civil Rights protests. Yet, in the forty years since, the excellence and example of so many black and female cadets have created a sea change of attitude and have become a new source of pride that would have appalled, and now shames, the distant parts of the long gray line. West Point has at last exploited the advantage of its enclosed, seminary world to inculcate in cadets a sense of the moral foundation on which their responsibilities to each other rest, as well as their duties to those whom they will lead.

In these eight different mirrors it's not difficult to spot "the people we're glad we're not". They are the socially, if not legally, disenfranchised Alabama citizens whose community ended up with coal waste produced in another state; the innocent young whose elders make sacrificial offerings of them; the generations of women whom the laws, made by men, denied many of the rights of citizenship; the victims of plagues and epidemics; religious believers deemed to be practicing the wrong religion; fellow humans judged by their peers to be of the wrong race or gender.

It is more difficult, however, to characterize the "we" who are responsible for these results. They are people who presume their superiority in religion, in gender, or in political entitlement, and who are willing to assert it by force if necessary. But the "we" also includes people wanting to protect their own lives and their loved ones, which has been long regarded a natural right. Should self-protection that requires walling out others be classified as intolerance? What greater right do the walled-out possess? And in the case of sacrificial infanticide, if the victim is a child valued as part of oneself, the parent's action might be counted a profound example of self-sacrifice, which in many circumstances is held in esteem. The expired victim no longer feels anything; but the person who performed the sacrifice must live with the deed and the loss, however much compensated by the conviction of having dedicated the victim to a higher power. Similarly, religious faith excluding all compromise might form part of a person's innermost identity. Is this intolerance? If so, holy martyrs are guilty of it.

The principle that all human beings are created equal must cohabit with the persistent, conflicting evidence of inequality. Responsibilities, power, talents, material possessions; age, experience, health; intelligence, education, opportunities—such factors affect people in whatever social group they find themselves, starting with families, and perhaps inevitably may also divide them. Tensions within and between human social groups are unavoidable. History demonstrates it, as does the nightly news. Considered from this angle, intolerance is a release of pressure. At one extreme it involves a temporary adjustment towards a balance, a rumbling; at the other extreme, more like an earthquake, genocide; and in the vast middle are the resentments we are willing to live with most of the time, except when stored pressure leads to protest. As a nation, we frame laws to protect the rights of individuals and groups. Court decisions have ensured an ever widening circle of recognized rights and responsibilities. Correlatively, there are increased opportunities for new sources of tension to arise which are voiced by trial lawyers in court and by aggrieved groups in the media. This species of resentment might be called self-righteous intolerance. The standard remedies for intolerance through legislation and litigation might also be recipes for creating it.

Who, then, are the *we* that we *want* to be? The principle of human equality by itself will not instruct us. Taken as a political first truth, this principle must be interpreted, and the legal history of our country is a continuing process of attempts to understand and apply it, made by jurists who (whichever their gender) do not descend from on high. Taken as a moral injunction to humanity, the principle of equality in Western culture has been even more slowly appreciated for the hard demands it makes of us in our dealings with other people. But looking into mirrors can helps us, if it helps us also to look into ourselves.

* * * * * * *

Please note: *The essays by West Point faculty in this volume represent their own scholarly views and are not intended to express those of either the United States Military Academy or the U. S. Government.*

Index

Aaron, 126, 151
Abba. See father; source
Abbasids, 114–115, 153
Abelard, Peter, 114, 245
Abidjan peace agreement, 267
abolitionists, 72–73
abortion, 100–101
Abraham, x, 110–111, 112, 120, 152, 169n1; idolatry of, 171n19; Mesha compared with, 155. *See also* Genesis; sacrifice
Abrahamic religions, x, 110–116, 120, 147–169
Abu Ghraib prisoner abuse scandal, 13
Abuja Ceasefire Review agreement, 268
abuse, 72–73, 74–76, 77–78, 78, 84–85
Abzug, Robert, 132, 132–133
accountability, theological, 122–124
The Accursed Share (Bataille), 230
acquired immunodeficiency syndrome (AIDS). *See* human immunodeficiency virus/acquired immunodeficiency syndrome
Adams, Abigail, 91
Adams, John, 91
ad-Din, Imad, 154
Additional Protocol I to Geneva Conventions, 17n47, 52, 53–59, 63n20; Article 48 of, 63n22; Article 52 (2) of, 63n24, 64n34
Adebajo, Adekeye, 269

Adeniji, Oluyemi, 269
Adler, Harry, 131, 133–134
Adorno, Theodor, 230
Aelred of Rievaulx, 122–123
AFRC. *See* Armed Forces Revolutionary Council
Africa, 184, 184–185, 185–186. *See also* Sierra Leone
African Americans, viii, 69–85, 196, 201
aggression, theory of (*jus ad bellum*), 21–26, 31, 51
AIDS. *See* Gay-Related Immunodeficiency Disease/acquired immunodeficiency syndrome; human immunodeficiency virus/acquired immunodeficiency syndrome
Alabama, 79, 194, 203, 203–206, 207
Albert of Aachen, 151
Alcibiades, 37–38, 39–41
Allah, 154, 163, 167–169
Allah n'est pas obligé (Kourouma), 278n10
Allies, 131–142, 144n6
All People's Congress (APC), 264, 272
Ambrose, Stephen, 74
American Civil War, vii, 51, 72–74, 77
Americans United for Life, 100
anarchy, 34, 36–47
Anderson, Joseph, 79
Andrew, George, 74
Anghie, Anthony, 260, 261

291

List of Contributors

Susanna An majored in Russian and Political Science at Amherst College. She spent 2011-12 in the Bard-Smolny Study Abroad Program in St. Petersburg, where she enrolled in Prof. Pushkina's "The 3 C's of War: Causes, Cures, and Consequences", a course that would inform her career path. She returned to Russia on a Fulbright Grant from 2014-2015. Currently, Susanna is a Corporate Paralegal in New York City at Wachtell, Lipton, Rosen & Katz. She plans to attend law school in the United States, eventually pursuing a career in International Criminal Law.

Dustin Noah Atlas, Assistant Professor of Religion at the University of Dayton, wrote his dissertation on several approaches taken by German Jewish philosophers to the problem of uniqueness. He is currently working on Moses Mendelssohn's theory of imperfection.

Stephen F. Barker, Major in the U.S. Army major and Instructor in the Department of History at United States Military Academy at West Point, focuses on modern European history. He discovered the intersected, personal histories of the Holocaust and U.S. military personnel while completing a master's degree at Brown University. In the area of Holocaust studies, Major Barker continues to investigate the role and reactions of historical figures as liberators, and he intends to incorporate this research in his doctoral studies.

Mirjam de Bruin is legal advisor on International Humanitarian Law at The Netherlands Red Cross. She publishes in a personal capacity, and the views expressed in her contribution do not bind her employer. De Bruin has a background in Military Law as well as in Public International Law and International Relations. Her work involves analyzing contemporary armed conflicts and advising on matters related to the Fundamental Principles of the Red Cross, such as impartiality and neutrality. Previously she worked in academia, teaching courses on public international law, intelligence studies, moot court skills, and the functioning of IOs/NGOs.

Ellen T. Charry is the Margaret W. Harmon Professor of Theology at Princeton Theological Seminary. She joined the faculty in 1997, having previously served on the faculty of the Perkins School of Theology at Southern Methodist University (1992-1997) and as a Post-Doctoral Fellow at Yale Divinity School under a grant from the Henry Luce Foundation (1989–91). She designed and administered programs in interfaith understanding for theology students at the National Conference of Christians and Jews under grants sponsored by the Pew Charitable Trusts (1985–91). She holds degrees from Barnard College (BA), Yeshiva University (MSW) and Temple University (MA and PhD).

She has served on the editorial boards of *The Christian Century, The Scottish Journal of Theology,* and *Pro Ecclesia.* She edited *Theology Today* from 1997 to 2004. Her current research undertakes a thorough reconstruction of the theological relationship between Judaism and Christianity, currently entitled *For God's Sake: The Wall of Hostility has come down.*

Bruce Chilton, Bernard Iddings Professor of Religion at Bard College, wrote the first critical commentary on the Aramaic version of Isaiah (*The Isaiah Targum*). His interest in the Targum came out of his analysis of Jesus' identity as a rabbi of the first century. His most popular work, the best-selling *Rabbi Jesus,* correlates with academic monographs, including *A Galilean Rabbi and His Bible, The Temple of Jesus, Pure Kingdom* and *Visions of the Apocalypse.*

Andrew Forney, Major in the U.S. Army, is an Assistant Professor of History at the United States Military Academy at West Point. He is currently completing his Ph.D. in American Political History at Texas Christian University. He has book chapters published or pending publication in *The Companion to the Little Bighorn Battle* and *Proceedings of the 2013 McMullen Naval History Symposium.* He has also published reviews and articles in several different journals, including *The Register of the Kentucky Historical Society, Essays in History, New York History,* and *Hudson River Valley Review.*

Robert J. Goldstein, S.J.D., is professor of law and Director of the Center for the Rule of Law at West Point, where he teaches Constitutional Law, Civil Rights Law, and Environmental Law. He created and leads the West Point Civil Rights Staff Ride. As general counsel for Riverkeeper, Inc., he managed many high-profile environmental cases, including: the Hudson River

PCB Superfund site, and power plant pollution cases that culminated in Entergy v. Riverkeeper, decided by the U.S. Supreme Court. Prior to joining Riverkeeper, Dr. Goldstein served as director of environmental programs at Pace Law School where he taught courses including Environmental Justice.

Philippe Ch.-A. Guillot holds an M.A. in International Conflict Analysis (University of Kent at Canterbury), a Ph.D. in Public Law, and an *habilitation à diriger les recherches* (both from the University of Rouen). From 1995 to 2010, he was senior lecturer in public law at the University of Rouen and taught International Relations and International Law. Since 2010, he has been Professor of International Relations at the French Air Force Academy in Salon-de-Provence. His main field of research is international security.

Nelly Lahoud is Senior Fellow for Political Islamism at the International Institute for Strategic Studies – Middle East, in Bahrain. Prior to her current position, Lahoud was Associate Professor in the Department of Social Sciences at the U.S. Military Academy at West Point and Senior Associate in the Combating Terrorism Center (CTC) at West Point (2010-2015); and an Assistant Professor of political theory at Goucher College (2004-2010). She was a postdoctoral scholar at St John's College, University of Cambridge (2003); a Rockefeller Fellow in Islamic studies at the Library of Congress (2005), and a Research Fellow at the Belfer Center for Science and International Affairs, Harvard University (2008-2009). Her publications include: "The Evolution of Modern Jihadism" (*Oxford Research Encyclopedia of Religion*, 2016); the lead author of *Letters from Abbottabad* (CTC: May 2012), the report that analyzed de-classified documents captured in Usama bin Ladin's compound; "The Neglected Sex: The Jihadis' Exclusion of Women From Jihad", *Terrorism and Political Violence* (2014); and *The Jihadis' Path to Self-Destruction* (Columbia University Press/Hurst, 2010).

Cynthia Marshall holds the rank of Captain in the U.S. Army and is an Assistant Professor and Executive Officer in the Department of Law, United States Military Academy at West Point. She received her A.B. from Dartmouth College, her M.A. from Johns Hopkins School of Advanced International Studies, and her J.D. from Cardozo School of Law. Her previous assignments as an Army Judge Advocate include being a defense attorney in Kandahar, Afghanistan, in Camp Arifjan, Kuwait, and in Baumholder, Germany. Previously she served as the chief of client services for Camp Casey, Korea, and as an administrative law attorney, at Camp Red Cloud, Korea.

Graham Parsons is Assistant Professor in the Department of English and Philosophy at the United States Military Academy at West Point. He regularly teaches the core ethics course as well as electives in ethics and political theory. He also teaches in the Bard Prison Initiative. His research focuses on the philosophy of war and peace, especially its history. He has recently become extremely interested in the role of gender in the ethics of war. His most recent article is "What is the Classical Theory of Just Cause?" in the *Journal of Military Ethics*.

Darya Pushkina (B.A., Reed College, 1995; Ph.D. University of Maryland, 2001) is an Associate Professor at the Faculty of Liberal Arts and Sciences at St. Petersburg State University. She is a specialist in international relations and comparative politics and examines the issues of war and peace from both perspectives, specifically concentrating on the United Nations peace missions. She teaches a variety of courses in both Russian and English, including "The 3 C's of War: Causes, Cures and Consequences;" "International Security," and "International Humanitarian and Criminal Law."

Maritza S. Ryan, Brigadier General (Ret.), U.S. Army, served as the Professor and Head of the Department of Law, United States Military Academy at West Point until her retirement from the military in December, 2015. She has taught courses in Constitutional and Military Law, Advanced Constitutional Law, Military Justice, and Jurisprudence and Legal Theory, and has published and presented in the areas of Law and Leadership, the Law of Armed Conflict, and Military Justice. She is a fellow with the Helen Gurley Brown Foundation.

Ty Seidule, Colonel in the U.S. Army, is Professor and Head of the Department of History at the United States Military Academy at West Point. He writes on race and the memory of the Civil War at West Point. Additionally, Colonel Seidule is a leader in digital history. He is the senior editor of the award-winning The West Point History of Warfare , a seventy-one chapter military history enhanced digital text. He is an editor of The West Point History of the Civil War and of The *West Point History of World War II*, Vols. I and II, published by Simon and Schuster (and also by Rowan Technology as an enhanced eBook). He is the creator and senior editor of the *West Point Guide to the Civil Rights Movement*, a digital primary source reader used by all cadets at West Point. Online courses and videos created by Colonel Seidule and the Department of History have garnered millions of views through Facebook, YouTube and iTunes U.

Scott Silverstone is a Professor of International Relations at the United States Military Academy at West Point and a Future of War Fellow at New America, a think-tank in Washington, D.C. His most recent books include *Preventive War and American Democracy*, and *Stopping Hitler: the Enduring False Promise of Preventive War*, forthcoming in 2017.

Gennady Shkliarevsky, Emeritus Professor of History at Bard College, is author of *Labor in the Russian Revolution: Factory Committees and Trade Unions, 1917-1921*. His interests in systems theory, constructivism, complexity theory, and theory of self-organization have resulted in a number of articles on subjects ranging from sustainability to protest movements, to the problems of science, religion, and violence.

Robert Edmund Tully is Professor of Philosophy at the United States Military Academy at West Point and Professor Emeritus at the University of Toronto. He is the co-author (with Frederic Portoraro) of a textbook on symbolic logic and co-editor (with Bruce Chilton and Jacob Neusner) of *Just War in Religion and Politics*, to which he also contributed an essay. He is the author of many articles on Russell, Moore and Wittgenstein, and of five short articles on a variety of topics in the fourth edition of the *Cambridge Dictionary of Philosophy*. At West Point he teaches courses on Ancient Philosophy, Logic, 17th and 18th Century Philosophy, and Just War Theory. His research interests include Natural Logic (the embeddedness of logical concepts in natural language); the doctrine of Neutral Monism; the foundational period of analytic philosophy (Frege, Russell, Wittgenstein); and the evolution of George Berkeley's Idealistic metaphysics. His current project is a book on Berkeley's neglected philosophical work, *Alciphron*, written during the philosopher's three-year stay in Newport, RI, starting in 1729.

David Wallace, Colonel in the U. S. Army, is Professor and Head, Department of Law, United States Military Academy at West Point, where he has served for 15 years on the faculty. He has also served as a Deputy Staff Judge Advocate; Assistant, then Associate Professor at the Judge Advocate General's School of the Army; Trial Attorney, Contract Appeals Division, United States Army Legal Service Agency; Trial Counsel and Legal Assistance Attorney, 3rd Infantry Division; and Public/Civil Affairs Officer, 81st Infantry Brigade. Colonel Wallace deployed to Afghanistan in 2004 and 2010 in support of Operation Enduring Freedom. In 2004, he served as a member of an implementation team working to establish the National Military Academy of Afghanistan (NMAA). He is a professor of discipline with expertise in International Humanitarian Law.

Made in United States
Troutdale, OR
10/07/2023